HEALTH CARE POLICY
IN AN AGE OF
NEW TECHNOLOGIES

HEALTH CARE POLICY
IN AN AGE OF
NEW TECHNOLOGIES

Kant Patel and Mark E. Rushefsky

M.E. Sharpe
Armonk, New York
London, England

Library of Congress Cataloging-in-Publication Data

Patel, Kant, 1946–
    Health care policy in an age of new technologies / by Kant Patel and Mark E. Rushefsky.
      p. cm.
    Includes bibliographical references and index.
    ISBN 0-7656-0645-3 (alk. paper)
    1. Medical technology. 2. Medical innovations. 3. Medical instruments and apparatus
industry. 4. Social medicine. I. Rushefsky, Mark E., 1945– II. Title.

R855.3.P384 2002
362.1—dc21
                                            2001058178

Printed in the United States of America

The paper used in this publication meets the minimum requirements of
American National Standard for Information Sciences
Permanence of Paper for Printed Library Materials,
ANSI Z 39.48-1984.

BM (c)   10   9   8   7   6   5   4   3   2   1

Contents

x

List of Tables

Foreword

**Brave New World: Biomedical Research and Health Care
Delivery in Modern America**

The United States of America, the sole remaining superpower, is the marvel of the world and is its prime example of a successful industrial democracy. As a continental state and beyond, its geographic scope is huge. Its people are vigorous and thriving. Their heritage is varied—multiethnic and multicultural elements are prominent—but they share a national commitment and strong elements of a national character. They are inventive and energetic, working far more than is customary around the world, and have been blessed with a favored location, enormous natural resources, and a superior political system. They have created the strongest economic power in history.

American influence is pervasive—many would argue even that it is too pervasive—and to a large extent it has shaped global expectations and practices. This often is for the better. Other countries, for instance, have looked to the United States as an example as they have democratized their political systems. Sometimes it is for the worse, as when the American-dominated World Bank pressures other countries to revise their public income-support systems to reflect the principles of private enterprise—that ideologically driven obsession so common in the United States—thus, changing their functions and damaging them immeasurably.

America's power and privilege make it difficult for its citizens to evaluate their own social institutions. Such preeminence makes it understandable why Americans frequently fail to recognize instances in which their own systems are lacking; instances in which other countries have developed systems that perform better. Nowhere is this so obvious as in health care.

Along with its other successes, the United States is notable for its medical advances. The state of its technological development and the quality of its facilities and health care professionals are the envy of much of the world. Along with such outstanding quality, however, has come one of the least rational—or at any rate one of the least satisfactory—health care delivery systems among advanced industrial countries.

The American system is cumbersome and complicated. It generates huge profits for insurance companies, administrators, investors, and others who have no direct role in providing care, but it leaves millions of U.S. citizens without adequate access to health care. Even without comprehensive coverage, however, it spends far more than any other nation.

This situation belatedly emerged as a major political issue in the early 1990s. Nevertheless, despite the issue's potential potency, the catastrophic failure of the Clinton health care plan quickly consigned it back to political oblivion. This was shrewdly planned, and was the result of many factors.

The president was inexperienced. Political partisanship was so venomous that a small group of opponents in key positions refused under any circumstances to accept the president's legitimacy. Lobbying from insurance and small business associations intensified the confusion with multimillion-dollar propaganda campaigns. The nonsensical assertion that the plan would have been a "government grab" of America's heath care system and if adopted would result in the "socialization of one-seventh of the country's economy" became a mantra from the opponents. Although initially even most of those opponents assumed that some sort of reform would result, the plan ultimately died without even a congressional vote. Regardless of the merits of the Clinton plan—and it had both merits and major weaknesses—the United States had a rare opportunity to reform its health care system and it did nothing.

At the same time, other troublesome issues were bubbling below the surface. Today, they cause major concern. These are issues that medical advances—and even more broadly, scientific advances—are creating. As Patel and Rushefsky point out, modern medicine has produced enormous benefits and has the potential for future advances that dwarf those of the past. At the same time, they pose "threats to freedom of choice, self-determination, and human dignity."

Although many observers eagerly anticipate technological restructuring of the world and welcome its benefits, some are only cautiously optimistic, and many others are nervous at the prospects or even frightened. Those who fear the future cover the spectrum of concern. Some are sensitive to the philosophical issues that are implicit, and are thoughtful observers who recognize the possibilities of great harm. Others exhibit the same level of perception as the opponents of flouridated drinking water who charged officials with "dumping rat poison in the reservoirs."

New technological capabilities and the promise of new developments unquestionably raise moral and ethical questions, but they go well beyond. They create new economic problems, new political considerations, and new administrative challenges as well. Moreover, they generate legal issues that previously could hardly have been conceived.

Modern society is faced with unprecedented challenges resulting from biological issues. American policy formulation, for all its strengths, has never found it easy to anticipate challenges and to plan for them in advance. Policy makers in the past have been anything but systematic in dealing with major issues—as is demonstrated by the chaotic health care delivery system that has evolved in the United States. In view of the immensity of the issues that now face society, and of others that soon will face it, they must be more sensitive to the need for truly rational systems and regulations than they have appeared to be in the past. A comprehensive study of the issues is the first prerequisite for such rational planning.

Patel and Rushefsky have provided just such a study. In a single volume they have succeeded in providing an encyclopedic overview of the relevant issues. They describe the health care system as it exists, and analyze its history and development. They examine systems in other countries to use as comparisons. They consider various approaches to health care delivery both here and abroad, and provide insights not only into new developments in health care, but also into the more exotic possibilities emerging from biological research, possibilities that have major implications for society. They view ethical and religious positions and implications, they raise the key legal issues some of which already are finding their way into the judiciary, and they examine various administrative arrangements and the effects that they are likely to have on society at large, and on the individual.

Patel and Rushefsky recognize that there are many valid differences of opinion on such complex issues. Still, there would appear to be certain core values that most observers could accept as vital parts of any coherent policy. The authors provide just such a group of values as guidelines. They are so well-crafted that many observers should be able accept them as part of the core. At the very least they establish a solid basis for rational discussion.

Patel and Rushefsky consistently place the emphasis where it should be, on the promotion of human dignity as the prime value whenever politicians formulate policy. Close behind human dignity as a second value they rate access to good health care. This means that expensive techniques should not be limited to the wealthy, and that there must be fairness in the allocation of resources. Public policy similarly must encourage healthy lifestyles as a part of a "civic ethos of duties and responsibilities on the part of citizens," a third value. Fourth should be treatment of health care as a social or public good, rather than as a private matter. A fifth value would be creating a healthy society by adequate implementation of preventive care. This would also involve general changes in mindset, and in the training of physicians and health care workers. Such an emphasis is important even from a strictly economic point of view, because prevention tends to be vastly cheaper than therapy.

Patel and Rushefsky incorporate as a sixth value a holistic approach to health care that moves away from a model that views patients merely as "organic systems to be manipulated and corrected." A holistic approach, as they define it, would involve consideration of the patient's "cultural values, spiritual needs," and "psychological well-being." Their final value deals with revision of medical education to produce physicians devoted to these values, and to "restore a sense of public service" among them. They also must assert professional independence on behalf of their "patients' health and well-being."

This is a tall order, admittedly, but it would seem to be essential as a basis for a sound democratic public policy that preserves human rights. Patel and Rushefsky have produced an impressive and comprehensive study. It, too, is essential—for the informed public, and especially for those who make that policy.

Max J. Skidmore
University of Missouri
Curators' Professor of Political Science
University of Missouri–Kansas City

Preface

The origin of this book stems from the two previous books we wrote for M.E. Sharpe. The first book, *Health Care Politics and Policy in America*, is in its second edition and is doing very well. It is a fairly comprehensive book, covering many, though not all areas of health care policy. The second book, *Politics, Power and Policy Making: The Case of Health Care Reform in the 1990s*, honed in on the health care policy debates at the federal level during the middle part of the 1990s. More specifically, it examined health care policy making from 1993 and 1994, dominated by President Clinton's failed attempt at obtaining the passage of national health insurance, and from 1994 through 1996 (with some of 1997 included), when the Republican-controlled Congress dominated the health care policy agenda. Cutbacks in some of the major health programs were attempted, but not entirely successfully. Some health legislation was passed in 1996 and 1997. These events were explored from the political perspectives of Congress, the presidency, interest groups, public opinion, and the media.

The present book is much different, though like the previous two its focus is health care. One important difference is that this book is very future oriented. It was written at the beginning of the new millennium, the twenty-first century, about policy issues we thought might be important now and in the future. The main focus of the book is on challenges facing health care policy makers in a new technological age and values or principles that should guide policy making in such areas as organ transplants, the right to die, genetic research and privacy, and confidentiality of medical records. Some of these are issues that we discussed in the first book. Rationing will become more important in the future as will applications from research in genetic medicine. Education of physicians and organization of health care policies will need to reflect changes that came into focus at the end of the twentieth century.

Health Care Policy in an Age of New Technologies looks at how other countries confront issues raised in each of the health care policy areas. It quickly becomes clear that other countries have thought about many of these issues and often arrived at plans different from the ones the United States chose. For example, where rationing of health care is a subtheme in debates over health care in the United States, with the exception of organ transplantation, many other countries have explicitly considered rationing. While the United States places limits on stem cell research, it goes on with little restraint in England. Cloning is prohibited in most countries that have considered it, but some issues that we deal with here are not problems overseas. For example, discrimination and possible loss of health insurance because of genetic defects is a nonissue in countries that have universal coverage (national health insurance).

We also are explicit about values that underlie debates in all these areas. We take a quasi communtarian view on these issues, suggesting that individuals, the larger society (and even corporations) have both rights and responsibilities. Our goal is to see how we can promote a healthy republic at a time when technological development is fostering considerable change in the practice of medicine and our understanding of what health is.

This is the third book (and fifth project) that we have undertaken together. It has been a very fruitful partnership, though we do not claim to be anywhere in the league with, say, Gilbert and Sullivan or Rodgers and Hammerstein. Our friendship has remained strong through the past seventeen years and our interests remain pretty much the same. We both are avid sports fans (and not particularly good athletes) which, as we have noted in our previous books, has created friendly rivalries. Patel is from Houston, Rushefsky from New York City. We both place basketball on the highest step, we enjoy ribbing each other about other professional sports. As we finish this manuscript, baseball is entering its World Series phase. Sure enough, Rushefsky's team from youth, the Yankees, are there again. Patel's team, the Houston Astros, do well during the regular season but badly falter during the playoffs. Then again, our basketball teams, the Houston Rockets and the New York Knicks, are not likely to make waves for a while.

We must take note of the terrorist attacks of September 11, 2001. Rushefsky is a native New Yorker and though he has not lived there since 1967, he is still a New Yorker (he certainly talks like one). His older daughter Rachel works in Manhattan, and her office had a view of the World Trade Center. She saw the second, north tower collapse. Like many New Yorkers, she was depressed for some time. She has somewhat recovered as will the city and the rest of the country.

But like those old enough to remember John F. Kennedy's assassination in 1963 or the Challenger tragedy in 1986, we will remember where we were when we heard about or saw these events. While reading about the baseball playoffs, we read columnists who grew up hating the Yankees who now wanted them to win the World Series. Certainly New Yorkers want it. In 1961, President Kennedy went to West Berlin at the height of the cold war and declared that the whole world were Berliners, indicating his support for the partitioned city in the heart of East Germany. In the same way, perhaps, the country could say we are all New Yorkers. This is not to slight the attack on the Pentagon or, at this point, the undecipherable incidents of anthrax being sent through the mail. The new threat of bioterrorism has elevated the role of public health in addressing the country's preparedness for dealing with such threats. Public health in the twenty-first century will be a major player in ways that it has never been before.

Acknowledgments

As we have said in our previous books, this one is not the product of only its authors. Mark Rushefsky would like to thank the Faculty Leave Committee at Southwest Missouri State University for the fall 2000 sabbatical that helped provide him time to complete this project. We would also like to thank Patricia Kolb, editorial director at M.E. Sharpe, for her continued support of our work, as well as her assistant, Irina Belenky. Thanks are also due to Henrietta Toth, project editor, and to her staff for the copyediting. Of course, any remaining errors are ours.

Kant Patel
Mark E. Rushefsky

HEALTH CARE
POLICY
IN AN AGE OF
NEW
TECHNOLOGIES

CHAPTER 1

Technology, Values, and Health Care Policy in the New Millennium

> The single most frequent failure in the history of forecasting has been grossly underestimating the impact of technologies. (Schwartz 1996, 166)

Yogi Berra once said, "the future ain't what it used to be" (Berra 1998, 118). Perhaps in no other field is this statement more prophetic today than in health care. Revolutionary changes that once were unimaginable are now taking place in health care as a result of rapid and dramatic advances in biomedical technology. In fact, what we might have envisioned about the future of health care only ten years ago is probably already outdated today. As we proceed into the new millennium, changes of such scope and magnitude are about to take place that twenty years from now, when we look back, late twentieth century medical practices in the United States, although some of the best in the world, will appear antiquated and rudimentary. Technological advances taking place in the health care field today will impact every aspect of health care, from simple actions such as patient record keeping and making an appointment with a doctor, to more complex tasks of diagnosis, surgical procedures, and the treatment regimen. These changes will affect all health care practitioners, from nurses to physicians to administrators.

Medicine in the Twentieth Century

Twentieth century medicine helped eliminate once terrifying diseases such as smallpox, polio, and tuberculosis. The twenty-first century promises to be even bolder (Strohl 1999). Not only did twentieth century medicine help to virtually eliminate certain diseases, it also gave us penicillin in 1928. The birth of antibiotics influenced not only the face of bedside practice but also the course of medical research. In 1953, James Watson and Francis Crick demonstrated DNA's double-helix structure. This allowed medical scientists to focus their attention on the internal functioning of the cell and the chemical interactions that are at the heart of activities of all living things. The first human heart transplant was performed by Dr. Christian Barnard in 1967, and in 1972 British engineers invented the computed axial tomography (CAT) scanner. The year 1978 witnessed the birth of the first test-tube baby in England. In 1982, the U.S. Food and Drug Administration (FDA) approved the first drug developed with recombinant-DNA technology. In 1995, surgeons at Duke University successfully transplanted hearts from genetically altered pigs into baboons, demonstrating the possibilities of cross species operations and transplants (Nuland 1996). The medical advances of the final third of the twentieth century were quite impressive with respect to surgery and drug therapy. This included arthroscopic and laparoscopic surgery, effective chemotherapy, and new reproductive technologies. CAT and positron emission tomography (PET) scans, magnetic resonance imaging (MRI), and radioisotope methods helped improve diagnosis and treatment (Nuland 1996). A technique such as an MRI is less risky than exploratory surgery because it allows a physician to peer beneath a patient's skin to see what might be wrong without using surgery (Kevles 1997–1998).

Health Care in the New Millennium

As we enter the new millennium, three forces are dramatically transforming the American health care system: One force is the managed care revolution that began in the 1980s. Managed care has revolutionized not only the financing but also the delivery of health care services. The second force is the changes in the information technology that has produced more powerful computer chips and digitized imaging among others. The third and perhaps the most important force is the rapid advances in biomedical technology. The blending of information and biomedical technology is about to transforms the U.S. health care systems in ways we could not have imagined only thirty years ago.

Despite all the impressive advances in twentieth century medicine, they did little to increase the natural life span of healthy humans. The twenty-first century, best described as the century of biotechnology, is poised to change this. The new medical revolution in genetic engineering has the potential to conquer cancer, grow new blood vessels in the heart, create new organs from stem cells, and potentially even reset the genetic coding that causes cells to age (Isaacson 1999). The twenty-first century promises to open bold new frontiers in the field of medicine. Medical science is accelerating at such a rapid pace that medical knowledge is said to double every five years (Trafford 1985). Just as the twentieth century brought more powerful treatments, the twenty-first century promises to bring even more powerful, yet gentler, treatments. Surgeons are learning to work on the human body through incisions the size of keyholes rather than manholes. Instead of slicing their patients from hip to hip, surgeons will pierce the abdomen with slender probes that house miniaturized lights, cameras, and surgical tools (Cowley and Underwood 1997–1998). Currently, the biomedical community is utilizing the new technologies in four major ways: (1) to see parts of the body more accurately to make a better diagnosis and to plan surgery; (2) to obtain more accurate pictures of a procedure during surgery; (3) to perform a variety of noninvasive surgeries; and (4) to model interactions among molecules at a molecular level (Stevens 1995).

Virtual Medicine

The best example of the multiple uses of the new biomedical technologies is in the world of virtual reality in medicine. Virtual reality is transforming the way surgery is performed, making it look more and more like playing a videogame. Today, a surgeon is able to perform heart surgery sitting in front of a console, peering into a binocular-like viewer, adjusting with a foot pedal a 3-D picture of the patient's chest, and using joysticks by inserting his thumb and index fingers through their Velcro straps. The patient can be lying on a table in a room twenty feet away. Robotic arms replicate the surgeon's motions. Milestones are being set in the field of heart surgery using a combination of robotics and virtual reality (Moukheiber 2000). Open-heart surgery requires six weeks for a patient to recover, while a robotic procedure has the patient back at work in about ten days (2000). This virtual world of medicine is nothing like television's *ER*. Surgery is no longer about feeling one's way through diseased tissues. Rather, surgeons are able to use robotic arms that snake into a patient's body cavities through an opening as small as a fountain pen. Minimally invasive, or "keyhole" surgery, in which surgeons cut, reattach, and extract through tiny holes in the skin by manipulating computer controlled robotic arms with powerful miniature cameras, will become more common (Sheppard 2000). Furthermore, high-powered magnetic and ultrasound imaging software allows the surgeon to see the flow of blood through the smallest of blood vessels without having to inject dyes or radioactive probes into the bloodstream (Sheppard 2000). The "virtual human," a three-dimensional model of the human body, was developed by Johns Hopkins University from magnetic resonance, computed tomography, and anatomical sectioning of male and female bodies. The basic data was messaged from Silicon Graphics technology so that any part of the body can be viewed and the viewer can fly through blood vessels, watch joints move, and see the heart beat. A pair of 3-D glasses can be used to simulate three-dimensional viewing (Stevens 1999).

Virtual reality can also play a role in the training of health care practitioners by providing a way for future physicians to practice surgical techniques. For example, the Medical Readiness Trainer—a virtual emergency room—at the University of Michigan enables doctors, nurses, and students to get hands-on medical training under a simulated real world condition. The facility features a life-size robotic patient that responds to treatment as a real patient would. The facility also contains a virtual room that consists of large screens on three walls and the floor that reflect 3-D images when viewed through computer-controlled goggles. This virtual room can be programmed to simulate a variety of conditions—an emergency room patient bay, an operating room, or a sick bay aboard a ship or helicopter. What is even more amazing is that trainees in remote locations can operate the simulator over the Internet (Menduno 2000).

Telemedicine

Today, video conferencing is allowing surgeons to "participate" in complex operations from thousands of miles away, making it possible for doctors and patients who are miles apart to face each other through a computer screen. Ultrasounds, X rays, and other records are transferred instantly. According to some, distance medicine is the precursor to delivering electronic diagnosis to the patient directly to the home or workplace (Sheppard 2000). The Department of Defense anticipates the use of virtual reality technology in the battlefield by putting a virtual surgeon in every foxhole—computerized mobile surgical units would be standing by to pick up wounded soldiers behind the lines, and transmit their images to surgeons hundreds to thousands of miles away (Stevens 1995).

E-Health and E-Commerce

The brave new world of Internet communication allows free online visits to the doctor. There are about a hundred medical professionals who have contracted with AmericasDoctor.com, a World Wide Web company headquartered in Owings Mills, Maryland, to provide online medical advice. The Web site attracts more than 3,000 persons per day to its around-the-clock "Ask-the-Doc" feature. Dozens of sites on the Web let computer users anonymously pose questions to physicians and get answers (Brown 1999).

We are witnessing an explosion in the use of the Internet in the health care sector as an outlet for providing information and services and for connecting patients and health care providers. Electronic health, or "e-health," is the online connecting of patients, providers, payers, and vendors. "E-health" commerce is growing at a rapid pace, and e-health systems are in the process of being designed to provide consumers and providers with significantly expanded connectivity and access to information (Marx 1999). The interface of computer, information, and medical technology is revolutionizing the health care sector in many ways. In 1997, Biomoda, Inc. of Albuquerque, New Mexico, showcased its revolutionary lung cancer diagnostic technology to the general consumer for the first time on the company's Web site at http://www.biomoda.com (Key and Marble 1997).

In June of 1997, at the meeting of the American Association of Health Plans Institute in Seattle, Brian Welcker of Microsoft demonstrated the application of the Internet to provide a seamless flow of information, from the patient's attempt to make an appointment to the health plan's analysis of claims data. According to this program, a patient can log onto the Web site of a doctor's practice, look at the schedule of available appointments, and make an appointment. The patient's health plan immediately confirms insurance availability. At the doctor's office, the doctor can look at a list of appointments and click on any name to call up a profile for that patient and see the reason for the new appointment. The doctor enters the exam room with a pocket computer containing the patient's electronic chart. After the exam, the doctor can type in the diagnosis and choose a prescription from a list of drugs. The system checks the patient's profile to make sure there are no allergies to the drug that the doctor selected. The doctor can also choose the level of dosage. When the patient checks out, the necessary information flows into the billing program which calculates the charges and transmits an electronic claim to the payer's system. The claim is checked against a rules database to make sure it meets the health plan's criteria. The system is capable of handling 25,000 transactions per hour (Tracking patients in cyberspace 1997).

Electronic Information

With the power of the computer, information technology in the health care field is used to connect components of the health care system that have traditionally been separate in the hope of creating an integrated system-wide approach (Tobias 1996). In the United States, Lilly's pharmaceutical card services (PCS) health systems subsidiary provides a range of services that connect 54,000 pharmacists and 1,300 health plans to the prescription information of 56 million Americans who are members of the health care plans the company serves (1996).

Similarly, the French company Schlumberger has developed a smart card with a computer chip that links a health care provider with a patient's electronic health record. The provider inserts a card into the smart card "reader," the patient keys in a personal identification number, and the provider is connected to the patient's health record. USSI Health, an Austin, Texas, based provider of an online health data management system and a Schlumberger partner, is the link to and keeper of these cyber records (Mellen 1999). HMOs are particularly hungry for such data. Needless to say, electronic medical records keeping raises all kinds of concerns with respect to protecting patient privacy and preventing the potential misuse of these records in the hands of the wrong people (Goldstein 1999; Wiese 1999). Others have argued that such electronic medical record keeping can serve the common good without violating a patient's privacy (Etzioni 1999).

Organ Transplants

Major advances are also being made in the field of organ transplants. Heart and liver transplants were already common in the latter part of the twentieth century. However, a major paradigm shift is about to occur in transplant thinking. Dr. Thomas Starzl, who performed the first successful liver transplant in 1967 in Denver (the same year that Dr. Christiaan Barnard performed the first successful heart transplant in South Africa), argues that rather than beating the patient's immune system into submission with drugs until it accepts the donor organ, the new trick is to convince both the body's defense mechanism and the new organ that the intruder is really "self," a recognized member of the host body. Thus, scientists hope to lull the body's immune system into accepting selected foreigners into the neighborhood and thus minimizing the use of drugs (Colen 1996). The difficulty with human-to-human organ transplants is that the demand for organs is much higher than the supply available, often requiring a long waiting period while a donor organ becomes available.

When Dr. Robert Jarvik's artificial heart extended the life of Barney Clark for 112 days in the winter of 1982–1983, it appeared that the artificial heart might be the answer to the shortage of hearts. However, after Clark's death and other less than successful attempts, the interest in artificial devices such as mechanical pumps waned. However, a major dramatic step forward was taken on July 2, 2001, when heart surgeons from the University of Louisville in a seven-hour surgery implanted the first self-contained artificial heart into Robert Tool, a seriously ill patient in his 50s who was suffering from diabetes and had a history of heart and liver problems. The device known as AbioCor weighs only two pounds, has a small battery-driven pump about the size of a grapefruit, and is made of plastic and titanium. Mr. Tool died on November 30, 2001. His death followed severe abdominal bleeding and was not due to malfunction of the AbioCor. He had lived for 151 days, much longer than expected. The FDA has approved implanting of this device into a small number of patients in clinical trials (Cowley and Underwood 2001; The quest for an artificial heart 2001). A total of six patients have been implanted with AbioCor hearts, one of whom did not survive the surgery. Four AbioCor patients have attained a sixty-day survival milestone, while one patient (the second recipient) has reached a six-month (181 days) milestone.

However, since this is still in an experimental stage, partial or total artificial hearts are used not as permanent organ replacements but as bridges that help keep patients alive until donor hearts can be found (Colen 1996). Most in the field of organ transplants seem to agree that greater use of animal-to-human organ transplants (i.e., xenografts, enhanced through genetic engineering), will help meet demands for healthy hearts. The most promising research is being done with pigs. To help the recipient's defense mechanism accept a pig's liver or heart, scientists are prepping their donor pigs genetically by introducing human genes designed to make pig organs less foreign. Not in the same class as solid organs, cells may be the ultimate unit of transplantation. Cells taken from human fetuses have been used with varying levels of success to treat Parkinson's disease and certain types of diabetes (Colen 1996). The use of human and animal organ transplants, as well as the use of cells taken from fetuses for transplants, raises a host of difficult and ethical concerns.

In the not too distant future, surgeons will be able to implant a computer chip in the brain or spinal cord to give artificial vision to the blind, hearing to the deaf, and speech to the victims of strokes. Other laboratories and companies are developing products that will restore movement to the paralyzed and regulate bladder function for the incontinent. Artificial kidneys and blood vessels are also being tested in several laboratories (Artificial eyes, turbine hearts 2000).

Genetic Research

Along with America's revolution in medical machine technology, another major and even more important revolution is beginning in the area of treating diseases. This is due to advancements in the area of genetics. Even though at present the science of genes is in the infancy stage, the cracking of the human genetic code that controls the functions of the body has the potential to unravel the origins of disease (Trafford 1985). The federally funded Human Genome Project is working toward the major goal of mapping the genome and identifying all of the genes (Jaroff 1996). In fact, a working draft of the entire human genome sequence was completed by June 2000. Genome, in fact, is a blueprint of the human body. Genome researchers are making steady and significant progress toward their goals. By 1996, scientists had already discovered and identified more than 6,000 human genes (1996). Developing successful drug treatments for many disorders and diseases depends on discovering and identifying disease genes as well as on identifying the protein they control. The new technologies and gene discoveries are helping to develop an army of new drugs (Gorman 1999). If a gene defect results in a protein that does not function, the defective gene can be replaced by introducing a correct version of protein into the body (Jaroff 1996). There are also companies such as Palo Alto based Alza Corp. that specialize in drug delivery systems—therapeutic systems that administer drugs at a steady, controlled rate in a predetermined pattern over an extended period of time. There are several advantages to such a system. These include enhanced safety, efficacy, and compliance; reduced adverse effects; and less frequent administration of medicine (Narain 1997).

Despite the emphasis on the development of new drugs, many medical researchers believe that the ultimate solution to gene based research lies in gene therapy—replacing a bad gene with a good, healthy one. By introducing the new gene and consequently the protein it produces it can eliminate or ameliorate the defect, or at least slow down the progression of the disease (Jaroff 1999). After several initial failures, research into gene therapy is progressing steadily. By 1996, over 1,500 patients were injected with some form of altered genes as part of more than 200 gene therapy trials taking place throughout the world (Jaroff 1996). If gene therapy lives up to its promise, parents may someday be able to not only weed out undesirable traits but also actually start inserting genes they want in their children. The biotechnology critic, Jeremy Rifkin, calls it "the ultimate shopping experience—designing your baby" and is appalled by such a prospect. He warns that in a society such as ours that is used to cosmetic surgery and psychopharmacology, this will not be a big step (Lemonick 1999).

Cloning

The announcement in February 1997 of the birth of a sheep named Dolly, an exact genetic replica of its mother, sparked an intense debate over the issue of cloning and harvesting of human organs. The prospect of human cloning has raised serious concerns, and many state governments in the United States and several European countries have placed a ban on the cloning of human beings. However, there is no guarantee that all scientists in all countries of the world will exercise self-restraint and respect for such a ban. In fact, some South Korean scientists have already claimed that they have taken the first steps in human cloning (Wilmut 1999). Similarly, in the United States, an eccentric scientist named Richard Seed has announced his plan to clone humans. Most scientists have dismissed his plan as "kooky" (Cole 1999). In August of 2001, three scientists, Dr. Brigitte Boisselier, chemist, Dr. Panayiotis Michael Zavos, scientist-entrepreneur, and fertility specialist Dr. Severino Antinori announced their intentions to clone a human being despite warning from leading experts about the dangers of experiments in human cloning (Stolberg 2001). The National Advisory Council for Human Genome Research has called for the creation of a committee that will contribute to the formulation of the government's genetics policy by examining the ethical, legal, and social implications of genome research (Wadman 1997).

The Value of Biomedical Technology in Health Care

Biomedical technology is advancing so rapidly that it can recreate the origins of life by in vitro fertilization in which conception occurs in a petri dish. In the near future, coronary bypass surgery will be viewed as obsolete and antiquated as doctors learn to treat clogged arteries with drugs and lasers. One day, a doctor may be able to treat a patient by administering a normal, healthy gene to overcome a defective one. Gene therapy may become tomorrow's penicillin. However, progress has its price. Dr. Arno Motulsky, director of the Center for Inherited Diseases at the University of Washington, Seattle, warns us that,

> It's important for people to realize that, although we have learned a great deal in medicine in a very short period of time, we are only just beginning to understand the basic human biology. Disease has been around for millions of years—science has existed for only a fraction of that time." (Trafford 1985, 46–47)

The same biomedical technology that promises so much also raises many difficult and troublesome issues. One such question has to do with the cost of such technologies. The debate over health care cost inflation often centers on the role of medical technology. One argument is that medical technologies contribute to significant increases in overall health care costs (Nitzkin 1996; Schwartz 1987; Newhouse, 1993). Others have argued that the problem is not the cost but the overuse of new technologies (McClellan 1996). Still others have argued that pressure for cost controls is having a negative influence on the development and diffusion of medical technology (Spencer 1995). There is an increasing emphasis on the development of cost-effective technologies that will result in lower medical costs without sacrificing the quality of health care (Fletcher 1997).

Aside from the issue of new medical technologies and costs, another challenge is determining the effectiveness of many of the new technologies. It is not clear which patients will benefit the most from certain technologies and what the balance is between the positive and the negative impacts of such technologies. Some have argued it is important to manage the four stages involved in identifying and evaluating new technologies: (1) identifying new and emerging technologies, (2) selecting the most important topics for assessment, (3) using appropriate research methods for assessment, and (4) operating a system for knowledge dissemination and implementation (Stevens et al. 1999).

In addition to the issue of cost, new medical technologies are raising a host of other complex issues about ethics, values, and laws in the field of health care. The biomedical revolution is mired in scientific politics. For example, the FDA, which plays a key role in deciding which drugs and devices will be allowed in the marketplace, has been criticized as being too bureaucratic, requiring too many years of testing, and as a barrier to innovation. On the other hand, others have criticized the FDA for being too lax and for allowing patients to serve as guinea pigs for questionable therapies (Trafford 1985).

Many wonder treatments are raising difficult ethical questions about how lifesaving tools should be used, whose life should be saved, who decides, and who should pay. Are there limits to how many resources we devote to health care? Issues of managed care, cloning, organ transplants, right to die, and protection of the privacy of a patient's medical records, raise a host of troubling questions. As we enter the new millennium, what values should guide public policy making in the field of health care, especially as it relates to issues raised by biomedical technologies? Is there a basic right to health care? If so, should protection and promotion of the value of individual rights be the dominant guiding principle of public policy making in the field of health care? Is the value of individual rights an absolute value? Do community values matter in formulating public health policies? How do we determine what community values are? Should individual rights be sacrificed if doing so promotes the common good? Is it possible to achieve a balance between individual rights and community values or interests?

These are indeed very difficult questions. As Daniel Callahan, director of the Hastings Center on Medical Ethics, puts it, "medicine now has the genuine power, and that always produces moral dilemmas" (Trafford 1985, 47). As we enter the new century, how we learn to resolve these dilemmas will be a crucial factor in shaping the future of health care policy in the United States.

Health Care and Values

Public policy in the United States has always been influenced, explicitly or implicitly, by certain underlying values. Health care policy is no exception.

Health care policy in the United States reflects the dominant value paradigm at a given point in time. The language of both the common good and community good and individual rights has dominated the political discourse.

Professional Domination and the Value of Paternalism

For the first half of the twentieth century, professional authority dominated much of the health care decision making. Medical ethics was considered the province of practicing clinicians. Professional codes of ethics were developed to guide the behavior of health care professionals and those codes were enforced through professional boards and institutions. These codes were designed to serve two purposes: One purpose was to maintain order among members within the profession, and the other was to foster public respect for professional authority (Malinowski 1996). Paul Starr (1982) has provided an excellent detailed account of how the medical profession consolidated its professional authority during the period of 1850 to 1930. Attempts at consolidation of professional authority were designed to reduce the amount of competition that existed in medical practice. During the mid-nineteenth century, homeopathy was one of the leading forms of treatment in the United States. The homeopaths had three central doctrines: disease could be cured by drugs which produced the same symptoms when given to a healthy person (i.e., the "law of similars"); administering drugs in minute dosages could heighten the effects of drugs; and nearly all diseases were the result of a suppressed itch or "psora." The homeopathic treatment was based on the notion that a patient's natural disease could be replaced after taking homeopathic medicine for a weaker, but similar, artificial disease that the body could more easily overcome (Starr 1982). The homeopaths were a major challenge to the "regular" doctors. As the medical profession succeeded in professional consolidation of its powers, homeopathy fell out of favor in the early part of the twentieth century. In 1900, there were about twenty-two schools of homeopathy. By 1940, all the homeopathic medical colleges had closed (Henig 1997).

It is not too surprising that prior to the 1960s, health care decision-making practices in the United States were very paternalistic and authoritarian. Paternalism refers to a system in which treatment decisions are made without taking into consideration a patient's preferences or even without a patient's knowledge and consent (McCormick 1993). It can best be summarized as the notion of "doctor knows best." It was very common for patients to simply defer to the doctor regarding treatment decisions. Doctors were often reluctant to tell patients about serious illnesses, especially if the prognoses were terminal (McLaughlin and Braun 1998).

Today, the main debate over values in the field of health care has centered on the values of individual rights, and values of community or common good (communitarianism).

The Individual Rights Perspective

Personal autonomy or individual rights is a key liberal concern. Liberal commitment to autonomy involves individuals being free to make their own informed decisions, to form, revise, and rationally pursue their own conceptions of the good. Liberals' strong belief in individual autonomy leads them to view communities negatively if they deny their members the right to decide for themselves what is a good life. Thus, liberals defend the rights of individuals and are willing to challenge the appropriateness of groups as right-bearing entities, that is, the communitarian perspective (Burtonwood 1998). Liberals assign higher priority to personal autonomy over group survival. Liberals place a strong emphasis on rationalism and rest on the belief that the individual is largely responsible, being the main active agent, for constructing meaning. The liberal rationalist model of morality is grounded in western conceptions of selfhood and the Enlightenment belief in objectivity and value-neutrality. The liberal rationalist values of personal autonomy and individual rights arose from the ideas of John Locke, John Stuart Mill, and Emanuel Kant (Haste 1996; Aday 1993). John Rawls reinforces the Kantian dimension of impartiality and respect for people (Rawls 1971).

Many different theories of distributive justice emphasize different criteria for a fair and reasonable distribution of benefits and burdens as a way of defining the nature and limits of a right to health care (Dougherty 1988). Robert Nozick's (1974) *entitlement theory* argues that fairness is rooted in the freedom to possess and use one's property and resources as one chooses. Under this perspective, public policy designed to maximize consumer choice and satisfaction facilitates the right to health care. Robert Veatch's (1981) *egalitarian theory* argues that each individual should be treated as being of equal worth. From this standpoint, health policies should focus on narrowing or eliminating subgroup disparities in health care. John Rawls's *contractarian theory* (1971) argues that if reasonable people were asked to come up with a set of fair principles for distributing societal good, they would endorse principles of maximizing everyone's rights and liberties, equality of opportunity, and making sure that those who are worse off receive some benefits. In Norman Daniels's (1985) *needs based theory* of justice, the right to health care is justified as a way of assuring a fair equality of opportunity for living a normal life. This requires that health care policies help those who are least able to buy health care to meet minimum human needs. The *utilitar-*

ian theory found in the writings of David Hume, Jeremy Bentham, and John Stuart Mill is based on the concept of maximizing utility, or, promoting the greatest happiness of the greatest number (Dougherty 1988).

In the United States, policy debates about how to improve access to health care have traditionally focused on the principle of distributive justice (or equity) that justifies societal assurances of a right to medical care. While it is important to remember that at present no such assurances of a legal right to health care exist in the United States, the debate about expanding health insurance coverage to the uninsured can be viewed as debate about whether a right to health care should be broadly extended and assured (Aday 1993). It is fair to say that some people do not believe there is a universal right to health care. According to this view we have a right to what we pay for. Anything else is charity (Shafer-Landau 1994).

During the 1960s and 1970s, the individual rights revolution that swept through the country had a significant influence on the health care field in the United States. The emphasis in the health care field shifted from provider-centered health care to a patient-centered framework. It defined medical ethics in terms of individual rights. The guiding principle became patient autonomy (Malinowski 1996). Advances in medical technology created increased treatment options and provided patients with more choices. Patients often sued their physicians for withholding information and demanded more information about treatment options and the consequences of each option (McLaughlin and Braun 1998). The elderly and poor achieved statutory rights to access publicly funded health care and the courts added many procedural protections. Critically ill patients and their families won the right to refuse aggressive, life-sustaining treatments (Bloche 1998). No longer was the paternalism or a "doctor knows best" attitude acceptable in the health care field (Dossetor 1997).

Individualist health care decision making and the right to self-determination have become strongly implanted in American health care policy through the law. The 1973 Patients' Bill of Rights elevated patient self-determination from an ethical concern to a legal obligation on the part of physicians. The Patient Self-Determination Act of 1990 required health care institutions to follow patient preferences for medical treatment as outlined in advance directives. This emphasis on individual right, autonomy, and self-determination is clearly reflected in two of the most important health care concepts, informed consent and advance directives.

The medical informed consent process requires physicians to communicate to patients their diagnoses, prognoses, and alternative treatment options. Furthermore, information must be communicated in a way that the patient understands. Patients make the decision about how to proceed with treatment. In a sense, the requirement of informed consent shifts some authority from the physician to the patient. Advance directives are designed for people who are no longer capable of making decisions for themselves to exercise self-determination. Advance directives allow patients to determine their course of treatment when they are incapacitated and unable to express their wishes clearly. Advance directives generally take two forms: (1) a living will, which is a written document that outlines the kind of medical treatment an individual wants to receive or not receive in case they become incapacitated and unable to express their wishes about treatment; and (2) a living power of attorney, a written document in which an individual designates another person to make health care decisions in the event of incapacitation.

The Communitarian Perspective: Community/Common Good

The communitarian (community oriented) sentiments are based on the values of reciprocity, interdependence, and public responsibilities as necessary ingredients for commitment to the common good (Aday 1993). A journal, *The Responsive Community: Rights and Responsibilities,* devoted to espousing the communitarian philosophy, was created in early 1991. Writers such as Michael Sandel (1996), Amitai Etzioni (1996; 1995), and Michael Walzer (1997) have articulated these communitarian values. Etzioni, in 1993, founded the Communitarian Network to support a grassroots movement of concerned individuals and groups who believe that individual rights presume strong responsibilities. The network has produced several lengthy position papers laying out the communitarian position on a variety of subjects (Coughlin 1996). Etzioni (1993) argues that social responsibilities go hand in hand with individual rights. He provides a sharp criticism of radical individualists such as libertarians and liberals. He blames them for fostering lopsided concerns with individual rights that undermine the capacity for communities to provide for the collective well-being of their members. At the same time, Etzioni also criticizes the "religious right" as a moral authoritarianism philosophy that wants to impose its own narrow vision of moral order on the rest of society. Etzioni further argues that the quest for ever greater liberties does not make for a good society. The new golden rule requires a profound commitment to a moral order that is voluntary and to a social order that is well balanced with autonomy (Etzioni 1996).

Communitarians argue that too much emphasis on individual rights by liberals has led to fragmented experiences and weakened solidarity on the part of citizens. Individuals are not abstract and detached persons. Rather, they ought to be seen as socially embedded persons. They further argue that diversity, which the liberals cherish, is not an absolute good. In fact, it leads to division, limited horizons, and social fragmentation. What is required is a collective responsibility for the common good that includes social integration and a moral environment. True community depends on personal virtues of commitment, caring, and enhancement of individual responsibility (Selznick 1995). Thus, the liberal values of freedom and autonomy are in sharp contrast to a communitarian emphasis on duty and responsibility. According to communitarians, what is needed is reestablishment of communities that act as guardians of social order and as sources of individual identity (Haste 1996). Technology needs to be reconceptualized as serving human and benevolent goals rather than seeing it as an icon of the success of instrumental rationalism as the liberals do.

The communitarian paradigm has characterized traditional public health and practice by focusing on community welfare through the use of public health regulations, inspections, and quarantines to protect the public health (Aday 1993). However, beginning in the 1970s, public health policy has placed more emphasis on individual lifestyle oriented interventions rather than community ones to promote and protect public health (Tesh 1988). Dan Beauchamp (1988) applies communitarian principles to translate the public health perspective into principles of social justice and equality. He argues that public health policy not medical care should be at the center of a theory of equality to serve the common good.

Communitarians have criticized the "individual rights" approach to health care and argue that the pluralistic, private, business-dominated health policy alternatives in the name of market competition represent the unchecked self-interest harmful to community or common good (Bellah et al. 1985; 1991; Mulhall and Swift 1992). Some have argued that the individual rights approach that came about as a reaction to paternalism was dominant in health care during the first half of the twentieth century, and has led to the extreme notion of individual rights or individual autonomy as absolute. This has led to an exclusion of the consideration of community values or common good from debate over health care policies and reform (McCormick 1999). Similarly, a great deal of Daniel Callahan's writings criticize our health care policy as being dominated by an emphasis on individual rights and self-interest and for ignoring the value of common good and community values (1998; 1990).

The Communitarian Network has published several position papers on a variety of topics, including one on health care reform that provides a communitarian perspective. A communitarian approach to health care reform calls for placing emphases on prevention, health promotion, cutting administrative waste, defensive medicine, and reducing profiteering by the health care industry, and warns against excessive commercialism and the managerial imperative, among others. In addition, it argues that the U.S.

health care system must make serving children its top priority since children are the most vulnerable group in our society. It calls for sustaining the balance between individual rights and a social responsibility. When all else fails, it should be the responsibility of the government to provide health care for people who cannot take care of themselves. Finally, it argues that health care professionals have a special social responsibility not to simply minister to their patients as individuals but also to the societal conditions that affect their patients (Cassel et al. 1993).

The communitarian philosophy has resulted in a community health decisions movement. The focus of this movement is on grassroots activities that create community health decisions projects dealing with public policy issues of access, resource allocation, health care priorities, cost containment, and rationing. Such grassroots organizations deal with national policy issues as well as state experiences and policies. In fact, a national organization, American Health Decisions, has been launched to coordinate various activities and help facilitate formation of new groups (Jenner 1990). For example, the state of Vermont has established a statewide public education and discussion project to explore the public's priorities regarding health care (Wallace-Brodeur 1990). The state of Oregon has created a prioritized list of Medicaid services to be funded by public funds. The list of priorities was established through citizen involvement.

In recent years, attempts have been made to reconcile the concept of individual autonomy with that of group identity, that is, liberalism and communitarianism (Burtonwood 1998). Etzioni, for example, has argued for instilling more personal autonomy in countries such as Japan that have strong social order, and demanding more social order in countries such as the United States that have a strong tradition of individualism (Schilcher 1999). However, others have argued that the rhetoric in Etzioni's books has been terribly overblown and that there is a banality about many of his statements, even though the core of his work is difficult to dismiss (Lloyd 1997). Finding a balance between values of freedom on one hand, and community on the other, is very difficult at best. According to some, the communitarian movement has lost considerable momentum since its initial success (Newman and De Zoysa 1997).

Health Care, Values, and Public Policy in the New Millennium

The United States is undergoing a revolution in the field of biomedicine. On one hand, biomedical technology holds a great deal of promise in the areas of diagnosis and treatment of diseases. On the other hand, it also raises a variety of concerns and ethical issues about health care rationing, managed care and patients' rights, euthanasia and right to die, privacy of medical information, genetic research, organ transplants, and the medical training and education of future physicians. What values should guide us in formulating public policy in these and other areas, or what criteria should we use in making and evaluating public policies? Is it possible to arrive at a synthesis between the communitarian and individual rights perspectives in health care? How can we create a healthier society that provides for the good life?

There is a noticeable difference between how we as a nation view our economic well-being and how we assess our social health and well-being. We pay a great deal of attention to the nation's economic performance by constantly examining a host of economic barometers, such as the Dow Jones average, the consumer price index, the gross domestic product picture, the index of leading economic indicators, and the index of consumer confidence. There is widespread coverage of these indicators in the mass media. In sharp contrast, the social well-being of the nation is reported much less frequently, and often only in anecdotal fashion. The social well-being of individuals is reported in an isolated fashion and without an overall view of the nation's social health or well-being. The economic side of our nation is very visible, but the social side is largely hidden.

The Fordham Institute for Innovation in Social Policy developed the Index of Social Health. It combines one measure from sixteen different indicators that include five major categories: children (infant mortality, child abuse, children in poverty); youth (teen suicide, drug abuse, high school dropouts); adults (unemployment, average weekly earning, health insurance coverage); aging (poverty and out of pocket health care costs for 65 and over); and all ages (homicides, alcohol-related highway deaths, food stamp coverage, access to affordable housing, the gap between the rich and the poor). The index of social health in America declined from 74 out of a possible 100 in 1970 to 41 in 1992. Yet, the 1993–1994 health care reform proposals, and the health care debates that centered around them rarely focused on many of these indicators, with only a few exceptions (Miringoff and Miringoff 1995). In 1996, the index stood at 43, down from its peak of 76.9 in 1973 (Miringoff and Miringoff 1999). The main focus of the health care reform proposals was on extending health insurance coverage to the uninsured, while it indirectly touched on poverty and unemployment as contributing factors to the lack of health insurance.

As a nation, we need to pay more attention to our overall health and to promoting the good life or enhancing the quality of life. We can think of the good life in a broad, classical sense of social and civic well-being. A healthy republic is one that provides its citizens with the opportunities to live a good life. Needless to say, the term "the good life" carries many connotations, and no definition will satisfy everyone. But, what is the alternative? Should we as a society not care about what would make people strive to do well and to enhance their quality of life (Ruark 1999)?

According to Clement Bezold, there are four scenarios about what the future may hold in the field of health care. One possible scenario is that of "business as usual," letting state governments continue to deal with the problems of the U.S. health care system. Another possible scenario is that we will undergo difficult economic times in the form of a recession or a depression, and let the federal government set prices. Some discretion will be left to the states to determine what types of care are eligible for payment, and to establish some priorities among health services, as is done by the state of Oregon. The third possible scenario is that health care will truly become a buyer's market, and the market will determine the health services and prices. Under the fourth scenario, healing the body, mind, and the spirit of individuals and communities will become the main focus of health care because healthy individuals make for healthy communities and vice versa (Bezold 1996).

We have a good handle on what the future holds with respect to biomedical technologies and medical breakthroughs. However, future changes in individual behavior, societal values, and public policy are more uncertain. Yet these changes may be more important to the future of health care than the medical breakthroughs themselves (1996). Thus, it is all the more important that we as a society begin to consider and deliberate on what values should guide future health care policy making in light of not just the promise of biomedical technology but also the ethical dilemmas it presents with respect to privacy, confidentiality, genetic engineering, rationing, and organ transplants, among others.

We must learn to separate and understand the difference between the quality of a nation's health care system and the quality of its medicine. Victor Fuchs (1995; 1993; 1986) has suggested three yardsticks by which we can judge the quality of a health care system: (1) the quality of its physicians, hospitals, and medical technology; (2) access to health care; and (3) health care outcomes. He correctly points out that the United States leads the world with respect to the first yardstick. However, we fall far short with respect to access and outcomes, compared to health care systems of the other countries. We still have close to 40 million people who do not have health insurance coverage, and we do not rank at the top with respect to health outcomes when we look at indicators such as infant mortality and average life span in the United States. This is in spite of the fact that we spend more money on health care and a much larger percentage of our gross domestic product (GDP) goes to health care than most other industrialized nations of the world. It is clear that if we are to maximize the health of a nation, our public policies must take into consideration all aspects of the nation's health and not just the individual patient or the quality of its medicine.

As former governor of Colorado Richard Lamm points out (1999a), we need to keep in mind that medicine is a profession, while health care policy is a matter of public policy choice and debate. Both are important but different. For example, physicians are concerned with questions of how to keep a patient healthy, what is good medicine, and how to maximize the health of the patient, while health care policy is concerned with questions that are more broad, such as how do we keep a society healthy, what is the best way to deliver health care to the society, and how to maximize the health of the society. The macroallocation of health care by public policy is significantly different from the microallocation of medicine. He further argues that medicine is a key part of the health care system but not the only part, and public policy that affects the health of a nation cannot and should not be judged only by the quality of its medicine. According to Lamm, we need to change our value that places too much pride in the technological capabilities of our health care system and overemphasizes meeting the demands of the providers instead of those of the patients (Lamm 1993). He further asserts that public policy needs to do more to emphasize the broader public interest and not assume that health and health care are the same and that an ethical health care system is synonymous with medical ethics (Lamm 1999a). If one were to base a health care system solely on today's medical ethics of unlimited care, our health care system would fall under its own weight and bankrupt the nation. The medical profession operates on the Hippocratic oath of "do no harm." No public policy maker can operate on the principle of "do no harm" because public policy's role is to maximize good for the broader public with limited taxpayer resources, and in the process of making choices among various competing societal needs, public policy makers cannot help but inadvertently do some harm (1999b).

According to Lamm, significant parts of medical ethics are inconsistent with the way we finance our health care system. We have shifted much of health care funding to the public sector. If we are to follow the goal of creating a healthy society by reducing human suffering and enhancing human well-being, public policy must devise some method for maximizing health with limited resources. Thus, it may involve some limits. As he puts it, "If public policy allows health care ethics to trump all other considerations, we risk having a medical Taj Mahal amidst massive social squalor" (1999a).

What values should guide health care policy making in the twenty-first century? Both the individual rights perspective (rights, autonomy, self-determination) and the communitarian perspective (community values, responsibility, common good) have something meaningful to say. What is clear is that each approach is untenable if taken to the extreme and in isolation. For example, even if one accepts the position that each person has a right to health care, does this mean that it is an unlimited right and every individual can have all the health care they want? Similarly, if a community believes that smoking and alcohol consumption lead to health and other social problems, should a community be able to ban smoking and alcohol consumption because it will be in the best interest of the community? Furthermore, when we talk about community values, whose values are we talking about and how do we determine those values? Do we stand in danger of a too powerful community imposing its dictates on citizens?

It is clear that the current revolution in biomedical technology is going to shape almost every aspect of health care in the next century in the United States. Since such technology poses many potential dangers as well as many positive benefits, we suggest that in order to create a healthy republic that provides its citizens with an opportunity to live a good life or enhance the quality of their lives, health care policy making in the new millennium should be informed and guided by the following principles or values. While these principles and values are not necessarily strongly embedded in a solid ethical and/or theoretical framework, they nonetheless provide a useful, if only a limited, framework for generating questions that lead to informed debate and discussion about future health care policy making and also provide a useful criteria for assessing health care policy.

1. Health care policy must be guided by the principle of protecting and promoting human dignity whenever and wherever possible. The dignity of the individual must be seen as the driving force in designing health care policies in the twenty-first century. Both the dominant Judeo-Christian and secular Enlightenment traditions that shape American experiences focus on the human being as a central intrinsic value. The idea of a person's intrinsic value is captured by the concept of human dignity (Dougherty 1992). Being human, quite apart from rationality, moral competence, and so forth, is at the center of our determination of what matters most. Our health matters, because we matter (Cherry 1997). Admittedly, the definition of human "dignity" itself is complex and often illusive and unsatisfactory. We have not yet fully developed a vocabulary that allows us to discuss violations of human dignity. Yet, we all know when our dignity is violated, that is, when we experience or are subjected to actions that give us a powerful feeling of shame, powerlessness, and despair (e.g., rape, physical abuse, mental abuse, and so on). We feel our humanity violated in a profound way. It is also clear that such dignity-violating experiences and feelings, if evoked repeatedly, tend to have negative effects on our physical, mental, and social well-being. By the same token, a dignity-affirming environment can help promote health.

Rapid advancement in biomedical technology presents potential for creating a dignity-impugning environment in several aspects of health care. It is clear that we need guard to against such a possibility.

2. Health care policy must be guided by the belief that every person has a right to adequate health care. The assumption that every individual life has dignity or incalculable worth is one of the foundations of individual moral rights. One of the important issues at stake in the current health care field is the issue of right of access to health care. The intrinsic value of the person supports the claim of a positive right of access to some level of health care (Dougherty 1992). Health care is an essential safeguard of human life and dignity.

Today, every major industrialized country in the world except the United States provides its citizens with health insurance coverage. More than 40 million individuals, including children, in our country lack basic health insurance coverage. The United Nations' Universal Declaration of Human Rights, adopted on December 10, 1948, declares that everyone has the right to a standard of living adequate for health and well-being (Universal Declaration of Human Rights 1997–1998). If we are to live up to the UN's declaration and the American dream of life, liberty, and pursuit of happiness, we must provide health insurance coverage to everyone. For without right of access to adequate health care, an opportunity to live a good life or enhance one's quality of life becomes highly problematic. However, it is also important to emphasize that the right of access to health care is not an unlimited or unrestricted right. The fact that human beings have intrinsic worth does not mean necessarily that everyone or anyone should be kept alive at any cost (Cherry 1997).

3. If the dignity of the individual is to be the driving force in designing future health care policies, it is also important that health care policy be guided by the principle of dual obligation. On one hand, society has an obligation to provide access to good health care to those who need it. On the other hand, individual citizens have an obligation to attempt to live healthier lives thus requiring less health care overall. We as individuals must accept responsibility to learn to adopt and live healthier lifestyles.

4. Health care policy must operate on the assumption that health care is a social or public good and not a private good. If health care is to be treated as a social or public good, then health care has to be seen as a common responsibility to be shared by all of society (Bouchard 1995). Health care should be viewed more as a service provided, similar to education or police protection, rather than as a commodity such as a car or clothes (Lamm 1993). Thus, every person should have access to health care but not necessarily unlimited access. The positive right of access to health care must be a limited right

(Dougherty 1992). It cannot translate to mean that every person is entitled to whatever they want with respect to health care. Society should be obliged to provide access to basic care but not unlimited care. We often want everyone to have health care, but we are unwilling to pay for it through higher taxes or other cost-shifting mechanisms. We as a society need to come to terms with this issue, and there are no magic bullets. Some restrictions and limitations on access to health care are inevitable. However, such restrictions must be reasonable and well thought out.

5. Future health care policies must focus not only on providing care but also on creating and maintaining a healthy society. Our perception of health care must be broadened to include the social health of the society. While the care of the individual patient should remain at the center of our health care system, it must be balanced against the collective health of groups and populations (Kavanaugh 1998). Creating and maintaining a healthy society requires a much greater emphasis on preventive care. This in turn requires a major focus on education and promotion of a healthy life style among its citizens. Despite some recent changes, our overall health care system still puts too much emphasis on cure and less on prevention and health promotion.

6. Future health care policies also must take a more holistic approach to health care, from treatment to designing health care facilities (Dix 1994). This means that at a minimum health care systems must treat a patient as a whole person taking into consideration cultural values, spiritual needs, and psychological well-being and not as a biological system to be manipulated and corrected when certain parts break down. Health care systems must take a more comprehensive and integrative approach in patient care. It is interesting to note that the revolution in biomedical technology has paralleled an unprecedented increase in interest among American consumers in alternative medicines. Thousands of Americans are increasingly exploring and subjecting themselves to alternative treatments. A third of adult Americans, most of whom consult medical doctors as well, spend an estimated $13.7 billion a year out of their own pockets for a variety of treatments including meditation, homeopathy, hypnotherapy, and acupuncture. More than 1,000 homeopathic medicines are sold over the counter along with an amazing variety of vitamins, herbal remedies, and minerals (Langone 1996).

The alternative medicines movement has progressed from offbeat practitioners and is entering the mainstream medical establishment. Harvard Medical School, the bastion of high tech biomedical research, offers a course on alternative medicines' effect on clinical practice and research. In addition, it has endowed the Mind/Body Medical Institute. Similarly, Boston's Beth Israel Hospital has a Center for Alternative Medicine Research. Stanford University offers a course on alternative medicines to its students and has a

Center for Research in Disease Prevention that participates in a federally funded project to evaluate promising nonorthodox treatments (Langone 1996). The National Institutes of Health (NIH), the nation's mecca of biomedical research, houses an Office of Alternative Medicine established under a congressional mandate. This office encourages practitioners of "alternative" or "complementary" medicine to submit their approaches to first class scientific scrutiny (Henig 1997).

7. Finally, if we as a society are to succeed in creating a healthy republic that provides for the good life or at least provides an opportunity for the enhancement of the quality of life, it is essential that health care policies in the future address the question of educational training of physicians. Physicians will have a crucial role in any significant transformation of health care policy based on the above-outlined principles. The training must be able to bring physicians up to date in the twenty-first century, requiring them to understand both the curing and the caring aspects of health care. At present, most physicians are not very well trained and thus are ill equipped to deal with end of life care in terminal cases. Physicians will need to become teachers, informing and educating their patients about diagnoses and treatment alternatives, making them partners in health care decision making, and being sensitive to the cultural values of an increasingly diverse population and a pluralistic society.

Organization of the Book

The remainder of this book examines seven major policy areas in the health care field that we believe will be shaped by and influenced significantly by the advances in biomedical technology. We plan to use the major values that we have outlined in this chapter to examine how future health care policies that support these values can be shaped. Existing policies can also be examined from the perspective of whether these policies support and promote these values. We also plan to examine different policy alternatives and how they strengthen or weaken these values.

Chapter 2 examines the right to die movement. It discusses the complex ethical and legal issues involved in passive and active euthanasia. Is there a right to die with dignity? What are the potential dangers? How can one prevent potential abuse and/or misuse of euthanasia? How have such policies worked in countries that have established a legal right to die with dignity? What are the national and state governments doing in this area? What have the courts said?

Chapter 3 examines the issue of organ transplants. It discusses issues such as organ donation, criteria for deciding who receives the organ, human to human and animal to human organ transplants, cloning and harvesting of human organs, and the ethical, legal, social, and political concerns involved.

Chapter 4 analyzes the whole field of genetics research and its implications. Should an insurance company be able to deny access to health insurance once it is established that an individual, in the future, is likely to suffer from a certain illness or disease because he/she has inherited a defective gene? Should future parents be able to select the physical traits they want in their children? Should every person be subjected to genetic testing? Should cloning of humans be permitted? What are the potential benefits and costs involved?

The potential dangers created by the computerization of medical records are discussed in Chapter 5. How can society protect the privacy and confidentiality of medical records? What kinds of safeguards are needed to make sure that only those who have a legitimate reason to access these records are able to do so? What about the potential misuse of such records by the government? Is it possible to establish a balance between an individual's right to privacy and confidentiality and the public's right to know in case of major public health danger?

The sixth chapter deals with the question of health care rationing. It asks questions such as whether we as a society can afford to provide unlimited care to everyone. If so, how? If not, is rationing health care inevitable? How do other countries ration health care and how has it worked? The chapter examines some of the attempts by the national and state governments at rationing and its consequences.

Chapter 7 provides an analysis of the issue of a patients' bill of rights. It examines the managed care movement in the health care field. It explores some recent trends in managed care and health maintenance organizations (HMOs) in the public and private sectors. Some of the controversies generated by managed care also are discussed. The national and state governments' public policies related to a patients' bill of rights and the controversies surrounding it are analyzed.

In Chapter 8 the topics of medical education and the training of future physicians are addressed. What kind of education and training do medical students receive today? What changes have been going on in medical school curriculum? What additional changes will be required to prepare physicians to practice their craft in the twenty-first century?

Chapter 9 provides a summary and conclusion. In this chapter we examine the lessons of the past and prospects for the future in creating and maintaining a healthy republic.

Each chapter includes study questions. In Appendices A and B, we have provided a list of relevant Web sites and videos (documentaries and films) dealing with a host of ethical, legal, and political issues raised by biomedical technologies in the areas of right to die, organ transplants, genetic research, confidentiality and privacy of medical records, health care rationing, and patients' bill of rights. We encourage teachers to give students assignments based on these Web sites and videos. For example, students can be asked to write a paper that requires them to make use of these Web sites or students can be asked to watch a video and to write a paper analyzing the ethical, legal, and political issues raised in the documentary and/or film. Assignments should encourage students to reflect on such issues and to express their own views.

Study Questions

1. Discuss the impact of information technology on the practice of medicine in the twenty-first century. How does the practice of medicine of today differ from that of the nineteenth and twentieth centuries?
2. Discuss the impact of advances in biomedical technologies on fields of organ transplants, genetics, and cloning.
3. Advances in biomedical technologies are raising some troublesome ethical, legal, and political questions. Write an essay in which you discuss these questions.
4. According to the authors, what values should guide future policy making in the health care field? Do you agree or disagree and why?
5. Discuss the different perspective of paternalism, individual rights and the communitarian in the field of health care. What are the underlying assumptions of each perspective?
6. Should health care be treated as a private good or a public good? Why?
7. As you look to the future, what do you think the practice of medicine will look like fifty years from now?

CHAPTER 2

The Right to Die

Death is not the ultimate tragedy of life. The ultimate tragedy is deperson-
alization—dying in an alien and sterile area, separated from the spiritual
nourishment that comes from being able to reach out to a loving hand,
separated from a desire to experience the things that make life worth living, separated from hope. (Norman Cousins 1979, 133)

Socrates argued that "man was a prisoner who had no right to open the
door of his prison and run away. . . . A man should wait, and not take his
own life until God summons him" (Potter 1999, 103). Ironically, after he
was accused of corrupting the youth of Athens and condemned to death
by poison, Socrates took his own life by drinking a cup of hemlock. He
was reported to have said, "When man has reached my age, he ought not
to be repining at the approach of death" (Veatch 1989, 297). He chose to
commit suicide to maintain his personhood to the end. The concept of
dying with one's personhood intact is often referred to as "Socratic death."
In today's parlance it is often referred to it as "dying with dignity" (Dying with dignity 1996; Solovy 1999). The term euthanasia is a Greek
word that literally means good (*eu*) death (*thanatos*). The Greeks saw
sickness as a curse and viewed suicide as a worthy, noble, and humane
choice (Jasper 1996). The right to die movement in the United States has
advocated that a person has a right to die with dignity and that a terminally ill patient should have the right to commit suicide, including
physician-assisted suicide.

   Prior to the 1950s, the right to die was not a great concern simply because medical science was not capable of extending the life of terminally ill
patients considerably. Before the use of antibiotics and the control of communicable diseases, people died quickly when they contracted common illnesses such as pneumonia, tuberculosis, and influenza that were prevalent

in the early 1890s. Patients suffering from cancer and heart disease or victims of debilitating accidents often contracted pneumonia and died before their otherwise terminal illness took its toll. Furthermore, until the early 1950s most people died at home without extraordinary medical equipment or treatment (Glick 1992). In 1949, 50 percent of the U.S. population died in institutions such as hospitals, nursing homes, or medical centers. In 1958, the figure had jumped to 58 percent. By 1978, the number of people who died in institutions had increased to 71 percent. Today, over 80 percent of people who die in the United States die in medical institutions (Humphry and Clement 1998).

Today, a great majority of Americans die in medical institutions with very little choice about how they spend the last moments of their lives. Modern medical technology allows even incurable or terminally ill patients to remain alive almost indefinitely because mechanical life-support systems can perform vital bodily functions even in a person who is unconscious (Burnell 1993). The way in which we perceive death and the circumstances in which we die have changed dramatically in the past thirty to forty years.

Advances in biomedical technology have produced some wonderful results. It has extended life for many who a few years ago would have died much sooner. It has produced cures for certain diseases, and has significantly improved diagnoses and treatment alternatives. Mechanical ventilators can sustain the breathing process for a long period of time, while techniques for artificial nutrition and hydration can keep a patient alive whose ingestion-digestion system has failed. Resuscitation techniques can revive a person who has stopped breathing, and immunosuppressive drugs make organ transplants a viable option (Cantor 1993).

In the past thirty to forty years, two revolutions have taken place in American medical technology. First, there has been a tremendous increase in the sophistication and accuracy of diagnostic technology that make it possible for medical personnel to foresee with a great deal of accuracy the development of a threatening medical condition. Early detection allows physicians to pursue remedial strategies before a patient's life is threatened. The second revolution has occurred in rescue medicine. Even when diagnostic procedures fail or medical personnel do not accurately anticipate future life-threatening medical conditions, advances in biomedical technologies have made it possible to "rescue" patients, literally pulling them back from the brink of death. In the past, primary organ failure would have led to the death of a patient, but such is not the case today. Many people have rebounded from heart, kidney, and lung failures and have gone on to live for many years (Hoefler 1994). There is no end to medical innovation or the power of doctors and new machines to prolong life. The explosion in medical technology perpetuated the myth that medical technology can cure all diseases that confront us and perhaps can even eliminate death (Humphry and Clement 1998). As a result, our culture has come to view death not as a natural end process of life but as something to be avoided at any cost and for as long as possible.

However, advances in medical technology and practice, combined with the fear of liability for discontinuing treatment and traditional medical training, and ethics that view death as the enemy and prolonging life as the ultimate goal of medicine, have created the specter of a lingering death for many terminally ill, comatose, and elderly patients (Glick 1992). A degenerative dying process has come to be viewed by many as a fate worse than the death itself. Many people dread a difficult and protracted dying process in some medical institution, with the ultimate specter of prolonged suspension in a helpless state sustained by a variety of tubes and machines (Cantor 1993). Such concerns have led to the rise of the right to die movement that has increased public awareness and created a national debate on the issue. Public opinion polls show a strong support for the right to die among Americans. According to a survey conducted by RxRemedy Inc., a health information company in Westport, Connecticut, 65 percent of 30,000 mature Americans (age 55 or over, median age 71) surveyed agreed that terminally ill patients should have a legal right to commit suicide with a doctor's assistance, and 64 percent favor legislation to give people this right. Fifty-three percent of the respondents in the survey agreed that physicians should be allowed to give people instructions on how to end their own lives, while 33 percent disagreed (Americans report strong support 1997). A recent Gallup poll conducted during the weekend of March 12–14, 1999 found that 61 percent of Americans believe doctors should be allowed to assist a terminally ill patient who is living in severe pain to commit suicide. The results were consistent with trends over the past two years in which about six out of ten Americans approve of the concept of physician-assisted suicide (Gillespie 1999). However, when the question becomes a personal matter Americans are far more reluctant to consider the idea of suicide as a way to end the pain from a terminal illness. Forty percent reported that they would consider committing suicide in that case and 51 percent said that they would not (1999).

Interest in improving care of the dying patient has increased significantly in the past thirty years and has spread from being a concern of a few health care professionals to being a widespread social concern. A considerable discussion has generated about the quality of a patient's death, a patient's end of life experiences and the promise of a "good death" (Emanuel and Emanuel 1998). An increasingly aware public is asking many questions: Can we retain control and make our own decisions about life and death situations? Do we have a choice about withholding or withdrawing treatment in certain circumstances? What are those circumstances? Do we have a right to expect a good death? Can we expect a painless death? Can we avoid unwanted intrusion of medicine into our body and avoid humiliation that comes with the total deterioration of our bodies? Who will make decisions for us if we lose control? Do we have a right to die with dignity (Burnell 1993)? Do terminally ill patients have a right to take their own lives? If unable to do so, do terminally ill patients have a right to physician-assisted suicide?

In the United States, a patient's right of self-determination, advanced directives, and durable power of attorney (health care surrogate or health care agent) have been well established under the law. The courts in the United States also have explicitly recognized the right of a competent patient to refuse life-supporting treatment (mechanical ventilator, tube feeding, etc) or to request withdrawal of such treatments. However, the right to physician-assisted suicide remains a very controversial issue and courts have thus far failed to recognize such a right.

This chapter addresses many of the questions related to the issue of the right to die. First we examine the issue of the right to die from an international perspective by looking at what policies some other countries have pursued. Next, we examine the historical developments in the United States with respect to right to die issues. Following this, we examine the policy developments in the state governments and the role played by the state courts, the U.S. Supreme Court and the Congress of the United States. We then analyze some of the major arguments advanced by the proponents and opponents in the right to die debate. Finally, we examine current public policies within the context of the framework of major principles that should guide health care policy that were discussed in the first chapter.

Right to Die: International Perspective

It is fair to state that throughout much of Western civilization, suicide has been considered a criminal act with some exceptions (Minois 1999). Most of the established religions in the West also oppose suicide (Urofsky 1993). For example Orthodox Judaism disapproves of any act or decision that ends life. Dating back to the seventh century, canon law in Catholicism has declared suicide to be a mortal sin (Cohen 1998).

In the Western culture, attitude about death seems to range from sublime denial of death as in the United States to an open acceptance of euthanasia as in the Netherlands. Attitudes about death in most other countries fall somewhere between these two extremes (Hoefler 1994). The Dutch position is certainly outside the mainstream of Western political and legal thought. Since the Netherlands is the only country in the world today that allows euthanasia it is worth examining in greater detail.

In April of 2001, the Netherlands became the first country in the world to pass a law legalizing physician-assisted suicide for terminally ill patients. The law went into effect in 2002. Under the law, a patient can ask a physician's assistance in ending his life if the patient is undergoing irremediable and unbearable suffering, is aware of all other options, and has sought a second professional opinion. The patient's request has to be voluntary, persistent, and independent while the patient is of sound mind. However, doctors are prohibited from suggesting physician-assisted suicide as an option to their patients. The law also allows patients to submit a written request for euthanasia giving doctors the discretion when patients become too physically or mentally ill to decide for themselves. An independent commission is authorized to review such cases to make sure that the guidelines were followed (Deutsch 2001).

The law simply formalized a practice that has been used discretely in the country for many decades. Even prior to the passage of the law, the Netherlands had openly allowed and accepted euthanasia, including physician-assisted suicide. In cases of mercy killing, a doctor is protected from prosecution if she follows established guidelines in the carrying out of assisted suicide (A Request for medication 1997). These official guidelines were established in 1986 by the Dutch Medical Association in collaboration with the nurses association and approved or sanctioned by the courts and the government. The five criteria that the physician must meet before he engages in assisted suicide or euthanasia include the following: (1) the patient must voluntarily request the physician's assistance, (2) the request must have been well considered by the patient, (3) the patient must have exhibited a persistent desire for death, (4) the suffering of the patient must be unacceptable, and (5) the physician must consult with another colleague (Physician-assisted suicide 1998).

Ironically, since 1886, Articles 293 and 294 of the Dutch Penal Code have prohibited euthanasia by request, and made assisted suicide an action punishable by law. These articles have remained unchanged, and thus the statutory prohibition against assisted suicide and euthanasia have never been abolished or amended. The current Dutch position on euthanasia and assisted suicide has evolved over a period of time through criminal codes, legislative proposals, and court decisions (Griffiths, Bood, and Weyers 1998).

Beginning in the 1970s, the Dutch courts began to tolerate physician-assisted suicide and euthanasia for terminally ill, competent patients. In 1981, the court at Rotterdam listed nine criteria that if met, would justify not only assisted suicide but also the performance of active euthanasia: (1) the patient must be suffering unbearable pain, (2) the patient must be conscious when he expresses the desire to die, (3) the patient voluntarily makes the request for euthanasia, (4) the patient was given alternatives and time to consider these alternatives, (5) it must be a viable solution for a patient, (6) the death does not cause unnecessary suffering on others, (7) more than one person is involved in the decision, (8) only a physician must perform euthanasia, and (9) the physician must use great care in making a decision (Griffiths, Bood, and Weyers 1998).

In 1985, the State Commission on Euthanasia released a report that argued that there were circumstances under which euthanasia was justifiable. In 1986, the Dutch Medical Association, in collaboration with the National Nurses Association, established the "Guidelines for Euthanasia" incorporating the five criteria discussed earlier. In January of 1990, the Attorney General of the Supreme Court of the Netherlands, Professor J. Remmelink, appointed and chaired the commission to study the practice of physician-assisted suicide in the Netherlands. The commission conducted a survey of Dutch physicians about their practices. The Remmelink Report found that in 1990 there were 2,300 cases of euthanasia (defined as deliberate termination of another's life at their request), 400 cases of assisted suicide, and more than 1,000 cases of life termination without an explicit request from the patient. Based on the report, the government established new reporting procedures that apply to euthanasia on request, assisted suicide, and euthanasia without the request of the patient. When physicians engage in one of these acts, they are required to notify the coroner. Thus, Dutch society moved from voluntary euthanasia to nonvoluntary euthanasia. In 1994, the Dutch Supreme Court ruled that euthanasia might be justified even in cases where the patient is not suffering unbearable physical pain but is afflicted with unbearable psychological pain (Shapiro 1997). The incidence of non-treatment decisions increased between 1990 and 1995 (Groenewoud et al. 2000). In 1999, the Dutch government proposed comprehensive euthanasia and physician-assisted suicide legislation. Under this proposed legislation, active euthanasia will still remain punishable by law unless the physician has followed certain procedures. Under this procedure it must be clear that the patient freely asked for euthanasia, a second independent physician must be consulted, and a written report of the process must be kept. Every case has to be reported to one of the five regional committees who will judge whether the legal requirements were fulfilled. The Dutch parliament passed the proposed legislation in 2001 and it went into effect in April 2002.

In 1995, there were 3,200 reported cases of euthanasia (by lethal injection from a doctor) and 400 assisted suicides (by pills that the patients took themselves). In 19,000 additional cases (19 percent of all deaths that year), doctors ended treatment or administered potentially life-shortening dosages of pain control medicine (Weber 2000). How are such liberal attitudes toward euthanasia and physician-assisted suicide justified in the Netherlands? What factors explain this?

The conditions that make the practice of euthanasia acceptable in the Netherlands are deeply rooted in culture, politics, and the provisions of the country's health care. One of these conditions is the doctor-patient relationship. The bond between doctor and patient makes it easier for doctors to talk to their patients about death. In the Dutch health care system, patients do not switch their doctors often, and thus a long relationship is established between the doctor and patients. Another favorable condition is the national health insurance system. Dutch family doctors are considered public servants and they do not compete for the highest paying patients. Thus, the rich and the poor get comparable medical care. A third condition is that it is easier to achieve consensus in a small country with a relatively homogeneous population of only 15 million. Fourth, in the Dutch political culture, individual choice is highly valued and it is reflected in a very tolerant culture that accepts liberal attitudes about things such as prostitution and drug use. Fifth, the influence of religion is limited in Dutch politics. Thirty-seven percent of Dutch citizens claim Roman Catholicism as their religion. However, they are renowned for their liberal, progressive, and antiestablishment attitudes. Nearly two thirds of the rest of the population claim no religious denomination at all. Sixth, the Dutch courts have a strong liberal tradition, and finally, the Dutch claim that their acceptance of euthanasia reflects respect for individual autonomy (Hoefler 1994; Shapiro 1997).

The opponents of euthanasia and assisted suicide have criticized the Dutch policies on several grounds. One of the major criticisms is that the official guidelines are vague. For example, one of the criteria is that the patient must be experiencing "unacceptable suffering." However, the concept of unacceptable suffering is imprecise and not conducive to objective verification. Similarly, the guidelines stress that the patient must be well informed and able to weigh alternatives and that the request for euthanasia must not be the result of a temporary depression. However, a survey taken in 1990 found that in 13 percent of cases, the interval between the first request for euthanasia and the performance of euthanasia was one day or less, while in 35 percent of cases the interval was one week or less. In 22 percent of cases the patient had made only one request. Also, the guidelines require that the physician must at least consult one colleague about the request of the patient. However, the guidelines do not require that the colleague personally speak to or examine the patient. There is not even a requirement that the colleague agree with a physician's assessment of the situation or the decision to perform euthanasia (Physician-assisted suicide 1998). A second criticism leveled against the Dutch system is based on the concept of "slippery slope." Critics charge that once the Dutch accepted the concept of euthanasia and assisted suicide for terminally ill patients, it was very easy to slide down that path further by accepting euthanasia and assisted suicide without a patient's consent, or for incompetent, disabled, and elderly patients who are not terminally ill. In fact, critics argue that statistics and analysis of the Dutch experience clearly show the slide down the slippery slope in the Netherlands. A 1987 study of the attitudes of the elderly found that 60 percent of the elderly were afraid that their lives could be ended against their will and that an overwhelming majority of elderly living in senior citizen's homes were opposed to euthanasia (1987). However, more recent analysis has tended to dispute the often repeated claim that the legalization of euthanasia would lead down a slippery slope. The results of a study completed in 1996 that partly replicated the 1990 Remmelink Report indicate that the rate of voluntary euthanasia has increased from 1.8 percent of all deaths in 1990 to 2.4 percent in 1995, while the number of involuntary cases of euthanasia actually seems to have declined slightly from 1990 and 1995 (Thomasma et al. 1998).

Following the example of the Netherlands, Australia's Northern Territories in 1995 passed (by a margin of 15 to 10) the Rights of the Terminally Ill (ROTI) Act. It became law on July 1, 1996, and the Northern Territories of Australia became the first place in the world to have officially legalized euthanasia. The law permitted physicians to prescribe lethal medication to terminally ill patients who requested help in dying (Kissane, Street, and Nitschke 1998). Under the law, a terminally ill patient experiencing pain, suffering, and distress that is considered unacceptable can request a medical practitioner for help to end her life. The medical practitioner must be reasonably satisfied that the illness was terminal and would result in the patient's death in the normal course without application of extraordinary means. The medical examiner also needed to certify that the patient was competent (of sound mind) and his decision was made voluntarily and after due consideration. Furthermore, the law required a second medical practitioner, with specialty in the field of the patient's illness, to examine the patient to confirm the existence of terminal illness and to give a recorded opinion on the prognosis. However, the law provided no remedy in case of disagreement between the two medical examiners. Also, a psychiatrist was required to examine the patient and confirm that the patient was not suffering from a treatable clinical depression derived from the illness. A waiting period of seven days was required between the initial request from the patient for assistance in suicide and the signing of the consent form that was to be witnessed by two medical examiners. Assistance could be provided after another 48 hours had passed. A copy of the death certificate along with the patient's medical record had to be submitted to the coroner (1998).

The law was challenged in the Australian Supreme Court and was ruled valid. The parliament of Australia passed the Euthanasia Laws Bill of 1996 that repealed the ROTI Act. The repeal went into effect on March 25, 1997.

In Australia, parliament has the authority to repeal laws of its territories but not the states. Thus, the law was in effect for a nine-month period from July 1996 to March 1997, during which time seven patients made use of the law. Four patients died under the law. Two patients sought euthanasia but died before the act became law and one died after the law was repealed. All seven patients had cancer (Kissane, Street, and Nitschke 1998).

Recent surveys have shown that the public is in favor of voluntary euthanasia though the level of support varies depending upon the type of euthanasia being discussed. The highest support is found for voluntary and passive euthanasia and the least support for involuntary and active euthanasia (Ho 1999). Even though it is a criminal offense for a doctor to administer drugs with the intention of hastening death, in a recent poll hundreds of Australian surgeons admitted to having given drugs in doses greater than those required to relieve symptoms with the intention of hastening death. Of these, more than half indicated that they had done this without an explicit request from the patient (McGovern 2000). The right to die activists are currently looking for trial drugs that can be used in the future as the basis for a suicide pill (McGovern 1999).

The passage of the ROTI Act in 1995 in the Northern Territories of Australia attracted a great deal of attention in New Zealand. The mass media commented on the desirability of such a law in New Zealand, and this, in turn, created a groundswell of public support. Consequently, a legislation labeled the Death with Dignity Bill was proposed in 1995, which would have authorized voluntary active euthanasia under certain strict conditions. The bill would not have gone into force until a majority of those voting in the next general election, in 1996, would have voted yes to the proposal. The bill provided for a five step process: (1) a written request from a patient to the attending physicians, (2) a second medical opinion from a "consulting doctor" regarding the patient's diagnosis and prognosis, (3) a psychiatrist's examination to assure that the patient was mentally fit, (4) a trained counselor to counsel the patient about the implications of his decision, and (5) a statutory "cooling off" period of at least forty-eight hours to allow the patient to reflect on her request and rescind it if so desired. The bill was defeated in the early stages of the legislative process by a decisive margin (Ahdar 1996).

The opposition to the bill was based on the arguments of sanctity of life, the "slippery slope" concept, potential pressure on the elderly, opposition of the New Zealand medical profession, the difficult role of the doctor under the bill, and rejection of the argument that voluntary euthanasia was solely a private, individual right. Furthermore, voting on the proposal was by a free or "conscience" vote. Members in this situation are freed from their usual dictates of tight party discipline. Such nonpartisan "safety-valve" voting in the New Zealand parliament has been traditionally reserved for issues such as liquor sale, abortion, homosexual law reform, gambling, and such. In addition, the Catholic Church's *Tablet,* a de facto church publication, also had launched an attack against the bill, even though the Church itself did not overtly involve itself in the debate (Ahdar 1996).

Despite the fact that active euthanasia is illegal, Switzerland is the only country that allows nonphysicians to help the terminally ill commit suicide. The Swiss law provides for prosecution of those who help in suicide for a "selfish motive." However, the law does not detail any penalty. About 70,000 people out of a population of 7 million are members of the Swiss-French Exist organization. This organization is able to obtain pentobarbitone from sympathetic doctors for a terminally ill member who had repeatedly asked to die. Its volunteers can pass the drug to someone but may not help with its administration. A government appointed commission had proposed decriminalization of euthanasia in extreme cases. However, the government has not taken any action thus far (Kaap 1999).

Like everywhere in the world, the French law does not allow for euthanasia. However, in practice people brought to court for helping others commit suicide have generally been given suspended sentences and have invariably been treated leniently (A French debate about death 1998). In Great Britain, the British Suicide Act of 1961 decriminalized suicide but the criminal prohibition against aiding and abetting were retained. Court rulings have also established that living wills are legally enforceable under the common law. However, many think that this is not enough. They would like to a see a law passed by parliament that would make living wills (advance directives) binding on doctors. According to a poll of 1,960 adults, 65 percent favor such legislation, while only 21 percent oppose it. At present, a living will could not authorize a doctor to do anything unlawful such as practicing euthanasia or force doctors to carry out treatment against their clinical judgment (Dyer 1999; 1998). The British Medical Association's debate on the guidelines for the care of the terminally ill provoked a debate among Council of Europe (COE) parliamentarians in June of 1999. COE's Parliamentary Assembly passed a resolution emphasizing the fundamental right to life and stating that a terminally ill person's wish to die never constitutes any legal claim to die at the hand of another person (Rogers 1999). A conference of the British Medical Association in March of 2000 firmly rejected any attempt to change laws that would allow physician-assisted suicide (Ramsay 2000).

The Supreme Court of Ireland in 1995 ruled that a life-supporting feeding system could be removed from a 45-year-old brain-damaged woman. The court ruled that the woman, who had been in a near-permanent vegetative state for twenty-three years, should be allowed to die. The Chief Justice wrote that the treatment of the woman involving feeding through a gastrostomy tube was intrusive and constituted an interference with the integrity of her body. The Chief Justice further stated that the process of dying is part of and the ultimate consequence of life. The right to life necessarily implies the right to have nature take its course and to die a natural death (Wall 1995). However, the organization representing palliative care professionals—the Irish Association for Palliative Care (IAPC)—has recently released a position paper outlining its opposition to euthanasia in response to attempts at euthanasia legislation in the country. The organization endorsed the right of competent informed patients to refuse medical treatment (Birchard 2000).

A Scottish court in 1996 granted permission to remove the feeding tube of a woman who has been in a persistent vegetative state for four years. Her family issued a statement in which they stated, "We know that she has no awareness of being alive, and we are therefore convinced it is better that she be given the *right* after four years to die peacefully and with dignity" (Dyer 1996) (emphasis in original).

In Germany, euthanasia is banned and assisting people to die can carry a prison sentence of up to five years. Numerous studies have demonstrated that many Germans fear a painful and undignified death (German euthanasia guidelines 2000). According to a poll conducted by the German Society for a Humane Death, more than 80 percent of Germans are in favor of assisted suicide, and one out of every two indicated that they would choose to put an end to their own life rather than endure an incurable and painful disease. Seventy-one percent of those surveyed favored new euthanasia legislation (Glass 2000).

Most Western cultures tend to be very individualistic and thus place considerable emphasis on individual rights. As a result, debate over euthanasia in Western societies has tended to focus on individual rights, personal autonomy, and state or public interest. Non-Western cultures tend to be more communalistic and place more emphasis on social bonds. For example, the

LoDagga people of Northern Ghana do not fear death and confront it openly in long and elaborate funeral ceremonies—a communal act (DeSpelder and Strickland 1992). Even though Islamic teaching prohibits outright suicide, it does teach that natural death or death for a good cause is not to be feared. Islamic courts have tended to take a "benefits-burdens" approach in considering the preferences of the medical community, family, and the good of society in general in dealing with end of life decisions for terminally ill patients (Aseer 1990). Japan tends to go farther along the right to die path than any other non-Western society. Under certain conditions, an act of suicide is glorified as exemplified in acts of *hara-kiri* (ultimate act of chivalry) and *kamikaze* (ultimate sacrifice for the love of the country) (Hoefler 1994). The influence of Buddhist tradition helps explain the Japanese approach to death. One of the central tenets of Buddhism is centered on the word *"mujo"* which mean impermanence, and as such death is simply one of many endings in the cosmic scheme of things. Thus, the Japanese attitude elevates *sonshi* or beautiful death with dignity. Equivalent to this in the West is the saying "all good things must come to an end" (1994).

The Jain sect in India is known for its moral stance of not injuring, harming, or killing any living creatures—the virtue of *ahimsa,* that is, a "reverence for all life." Yet the Jain community continues to watch its members starve themselves to death under certain conditions, and these deaths by fasting are celebrated by the community. Similarly, Gandhi elevated the virtue of *ahimsa* to the principle of nonviolence with a positivist-idealistic slant, although he himself on many occasions engaged in fasting as a means of political protest. Under the Indian Penal Code (Section 309) adopted during the British rule, suicide of any kind is deemed a criminal act punishable by law. Similarly, those helping another person to commit suicide are also punishable by law. The traditional Hindu *dharma* codes had pronounced attempts at suicide as immoral even though Hinduism, like Buddhism and Jainism, approves of certain kinds of voluntary deaths. For example, Hinduism fails to condemn suicide for religious purposes such as the practice of suttee—the immolation of a widow (Urofsky 1993). In 1987, the state of Maharastra's Bombay High Court argued that there was recognition in the law of the right of the individual to deal with her body as she chooses. The court ruled that the guarantee of right to life and liberty in Article 21 of the Constitution assures not only protection against an arbitrary deprivation of life and personal liberty, but also a positive right to enable a person to live life with human dignity. The court further argued that the Indian Penal Code adopted in 1860 had failed to keep pace with the changing context and attitudes in society. The court further stated that the right to die or end one's life was not new to civilization. It cited examples of Hindu and Jain traditions that under certain conditions accepted suicide. The court did make a sharp distinction between terminating one's own life by one's own act and an act that involved or implied the intervention of another person to terminate life (Bilimoria 1995). The Supreme Court of India in April of 1994 basically upheld the conclusion of the Bombay High Court that Section 309 of the Indian Penal Code was contrary to Article 21 of the Constitution (which confers a fundamental right to life and personal liberty—including a positive right to enable an individual to live life with human dignity). This in fact had the effect of declaring section 309 unconstitutional (1995).

Overall, it is fair to state that in both Western and non-Western countries religion and law have not consistently forbidden suicide. There have been times in history when altruistic suicides have been considered worthy of praise under certain circumstances. Many major religions including Judaism, Islam, Buddhism, Jainaism, and Hinduism, among others, have accepted and celebrated an individual taking his own life for the sake of religion, higher cause, or out of obedience to a political entity. Often preemptive suicides are condoned in which a person commits suicide as a means of avoiding inevitable pain, suffering, and human indignity. Examples include Jews imprisoned within the Nazi concentration camps who sometimes ended their own life by preemptive suicide rather than suffer the indignity of having their humanity stripped by the Nazis. Clinical suicides in which persons end their lives due to some mental disorder have been the major focus of psychiatry (Cohen 1998).

Altruistic suicides rarely occur within a medical context. Preemptive suicides can occur in the context of physical illness. Preemptive suicide in this case involves behavior or actions that hasten death. The current debate and controversy over the right to die, euthanasia, and physician-assisted suicide is centered on the notion of preemptive suicide, whether the terminally ill patients have a right to end their own lives (by themselves or with the assistance of a physician) or to end physical and/or mental pain and suffering (Cohen 1998).

Right to Die in the United States

Many scholars trace the origins of the current debate over the right to die to Great Britain in the 1870s when several intellectuals proposed voluntary active euthanasia for the terminally ill. In 1935, a group of intellectuals, teachers, protestant theologians, and others formed the Voluntary Euthanasia Legislation Society to propose legislation allowing voluntary euthanasia for terminally ill patients over the age of 21. However, the bill was easily defeated and subsequent attempts in the 1950s following World War II were also defeated (Glick 1992).

Following the establishment of the Voluntary Euthanasia Legislation Society in Great Britain, a similar group of Americans formed the American Euthanasia Society in 1938 in New York. This group proposed voluntary active euthanasia legislation (no distinction was made between withdrawal of treatment and active euthanasia) to the New York state legislature. The opposition was so strong that not a single legislator was willing to sponsor the bill. The society offered another bill dealing with voluntary active euthanasia in 1941 in New York which met the same fate. A similar attempt in New Hampshire in 1950 also failed. The society dropped its effort to win active support for voluntary active euthanasia in 1952. The public support for such legislation was weak. Polls in the 1930s showed that only between 37 to 46 percent of Americans favored voluntary euthanasia for the hopelessly ill. Following World War II, national and state public health officials, state medical societies and Catholic clergy denounced euthanasia legislation. A Gallup poll in 1947 showed that only 37 percent answered in the affirmative when asked whether a doctor should be allowed to end a patient's life through some painless means if the patient suffered from disease that could not be cured and if the patient and her family requested it (Glick 1992).

Despite such early efforts, euthanasia and the right to die were not major burning issues during much of the 1950s and 1960s. New books on the subjects written in the late 1960s and early 1970s helped revive public awareness of the issue (Ramsey, 1970; Kubler-Ross 1969). The establishment of the Hastings Center in 1969 and the Kennedy Institute of Ethics at Georgetown University in 1971 exemplified the increased scholarly interests in bioethics and public policy. The emphasis on individual rights and autonomy (women's rights, civil rights for African Americans) during the 1960s and early 1970s also helped change the U.S. health care system from doctor-centered to patient-centered and emphasized patients' rights in the field of health care with patient autonomy as its guiding principle. Rights of patients in making health care decisions and the right to self-determination began to be implanted in the U.S. health care system. For example, the 1973 Patients' Bill of Rights elevated patient self-determination from an ethical concern to a legal obligation on the part of doctors. In 1974, the Euthanasia Society changed its name to the Society for the Right to Die, and in 1975 it proposed a model living will bill.

Life-Sustaining Treatments and the Courts: 1970–1980s

Karen Ann Quinlan Case (New Jersey)

A major turning point in the debate over the right to die came with the Karen Ann Quinlan case in New Jersey in 1976. This case highlighted the legal and ethical dilemmas involved in keeping an individual alive in a vegetative state with the help of feeding tubes and a respirator. At the young age of 21, Karen Quinlan had slipped into a deep coma and was hooked up to a respirator in a hospital. The doctor informed her parents that Karen's brain was severely damaged and she would never come out of the coma. Kept on a life-support system, she might live this way for many years. When her parents asked the doctor to turn off the respirator the doctor refused and they went to the courts. The judge in the lower court refused to order the doctor to remove the respirator and argued that there was no constitutional right to die that can be asserted by a parent for her incompetent adult child (Urofsky 1993). Her parents appealed the decision to the New Jersey Supreme Court. The Supreme Court, relying on an expansive interpretation of the constitutional right to privacy and the rights of the parents to act as guardians, ordered the respirator removed. The court reasoned that the constitutionally protected right to die could be exercised by a family on behalf of an incompetent patient as long as the family could establish that its decision was consistent with the decision the incompetent person would have made if able to do so. This reasoning by the court would come to be known as the "substituted-judgment" standard. It holds that a third party's best guess about the wishes of the incompetent patient could be substituted when the expressed wishes of the patient is impossible to obtain (Hoefler 1994). Karen Quinlan's respirator was removed and she was moved to a nursing home. She was able to breath on her own. Karen Quinlan was fed artificially and she lived for another ten years.

The Quinlan case generated a tremendous amount of publicity in the mass media and raised a national debate. In 1976, California became the first state to pass a living will law and seven other states did so in 1977. In fact, by 1977 nearly all states were considering living will legislation (Glick 1992).

Elizabeth Bouvia Case (California)

In 1983, Elizabeth Bouvia, a quadriplegic suffering from cerebral palsy, sued a California hospital to let her die of self-starvation while receiving comfort care at the hospital. The hospital had refused such a request. She lost the case and filed an appeal. In 1986, the California Court of Appeals ruled in her favor and granted her the right to refuse life-sustaining medical treatment (forced feeding in her case). After her victory, Bouvia changed her mind about killing herself. The court ruled that the right of the competent adult patient to refuse treatment is a constitutionally guaranteed right. What was unique about this case was the fact that Bouvia was not terminally ill.

Nancy Cruzan Case (Missouri)

Another major landmark case was the case of Nancy Cruzan. On January 11, 1983, 26-year-old Nancy Cruzan was involved in a car accident. Paramedics on the scene resuscitated her. Prior to that she had not been breathing for twelve to fourteen minutes causing permanent brain damage. When she arrived at the hospital, she was unconscious, had a lacerated liver, and a contusion of the brain. She was subsequently diagnosed as in a persistent vegetative state. She was being fed and received water through a gastrostomy feeding tube that was surgically implanted. Cruzan remained unconscious and unable to respond to anyone around her. She was transferred to the Missouri Rehabilitation Center, a health care facility operated by the state (Burnell 1993).

After four years, Cruzan's parents were appointed coguardians. After considerable deliberation, they requested that the feeding tube be removed, which the health center refused, and the parents sought a court order. The trial court found that Nancy was not terminally ill and could live for another thirty years in her condition. The court also found that Nancy had made prior expressions that she would not want to be maintained on such a life support system and ordered the Missouri Rehabilitation Health Center to follow the instruction of her legal guardians and remove the feeding tube. The Center appealed the trial court's ruling to the Missouri Supreme Court. The Missouri Supreme Court disagreed with the trial court and ruled by a 4 to 3 majority that keeping Nancy Cruzan alive was better than allowing her to die because Nancy's prior statements were not clear and convincing. The court ruled that while a guardian may consent to treatment for the ward, it does not include the power to terminate life-sustaining treatment. The court argued that the state has interest in preserving and protecting life without regard to assessing the quality of that life (Glick 1992; Burnell 1993).

The Cruzan case was the first right to die case to reach the U.S. Supreme Court. However, the question before the U.S. Supreme Court was a narrow one. Did the state have a right to require clear and convincing evidence? The U.S. Supreme Court, in 1990, ruled that the U.S. Constitution did not forbid Missouri from requiring clear and convincing evidence and concluded that the Missouri Supreme Court in insisting on clear and convincing evidence had not made an error. Ironically, on December 14, 1990, the probate judge of Jasper County in Missouri, after hearing testimony of two of Nancy Cruzan's former coworkers who testified that Nancy would have never wanted to live in such a condition, ruled that the testimony provided clear and convincing evidence of Nancy's wishes and ordered the removal of her feeding tube. The feeding tube was removed and Nancy Cruzan passed away on December 26, 1990 (Burnell 1993).

In 1990, the Congress of the United States passed the Patient Self-Determination Act that went into effect on December 1, 1991. The law requires all health care facilities, such as nursing homes, hospitals, hospices, HMOs, and other health agencies that receive federal Medicare or Medicaid funds, to inform patients (inpatient population) in writing about their rights with reference to advanced directives, that is, patients' wishes about their medical care when they are seriously ill or near death, and not able to communicate their preferences (Kuritzky 2000). The law requires health care facilities to ask patients if they have signed an advance directive. It was hoped that the law would increase citizen awareness and educate health care practitioners about advance directives (Doukas and Reichel 1993).

Physician-Assisted Suicide: 1990s

The origins of physician-assisted suicide can be traced to 1978 when Derek Humphry published the book, *Jean's Way*, in which he described how he obtained pills to help his wife die after she pleaded with him for a lethal overdose to relieve her of the pain and anguish of advanced breast cancer. The book was subsequently published in the United States. After moving to the United States in 1978, Humphry became one of the most well-known leaders in the right to die movement in the United States. He has also become a leading proponent of legalizing physician-assisted suicide. In 1980, he founded the Hemlock Society to promote a climate of public opinion that is tolerant of the right of terminally ill patients to end their own lives in a planned manner. In 1981, the Society published a book by Humphry titled *Let Me Die Before I Wake*. The book detailed stories of people who had successfully committed suicide and outlined the precise drug dosages for readers' information (Nuland 1998).

As we discussed in the previous section, by the end of the1980s many issues related to living wills, health care surrogacy, and life-sustaining issues had been somewhat resolved through the courts, even though courts in different states often took varying positions. Much of the focus in the 1990s on the right to die movement in the United States had shifted to physician-assisted suicide.

A number of important and significant developments occurred in 1991 regarding the right to die movement, specifically regarding the issue of physician-assisted suicide: (1) Two organizations, Concern for Dying and the Society for the Right to Die, merged into a new organization called Choice in Dying with a mission of defending patients rights and promoting advance directives; (2) Dr. Jack Kevorkian gained notoriety when he helped two patients end their lives; (3) Dr. Kevorkian published a book advocating physician-assisted suicide (1991); (4) Derek Humphry published a book on self-deliverance that in a very short period of time hit the *New York Times* bestseller list (1991); (5) Dr. Timothy Quill published an article in the *New England Journal of Medicine* in which he admitted to helping a leukemia patient kill herself with lethal drugs. A grand jury decided not to indict him; (6) The voters in the state of Washington, by a margin of 54 to 46 percent, defeated Ballot Initiative 119, which would have legalized physician-assisted suicide in the state. The initiative failed by fewer than 100,000 votes out of 1.3 million votes cast; (7) The Oregon chapter of the Hemlock Society succeeded in introducing the Death with Dignity Act in the state legislature. However, the bill failed to get out of the committee.

In 1992, the voters in the state of California, by a margin of 54 to 46 percent defeated proposition 161. The proposition would have allowed physicians to hasten the death of terminally ill patients by either actively administering or prescribing medication for self-administration. The year 1992–1993 was dominated by the national debate on health care reform that ultimately failed. After the death of First Lady Hillary Clinton's father, both President Clinton and Hillary Clinton publicly supported advance directives, and they signed living wills for themselves.

Physician-Assisted Suicide and the Courts

Two significant and controversial U.S. Court of Appeals decisions were handed down in 1996. The Ninth Circuit Court of Appeals in the state of Washington, in the case of *Washington v. Glucksberg*, ruled that a dignified death included the right to have oneself killed based on the "due process clause" of the Fourteenth Amendment to the U.S. Constitution. The court held that the liberty interest exists (protect personal liberty and privacy) in the choice of when and how one dies. Therefore, the court overturned Washington state's ban on assisted suicide as applied to competent terminally ill adults who chose to hasten their death by obtaining medication prescribed by their doctor (Kavanaugh 1997). In the case of *Quill v. Vacco*, the Second Circuit Court of Appeals in the state of New York ruled that New York's law criminalizing assisted suicide violated the equal protection clause of the Fourteenth Amendment to the U.S. Constitution because there is no difference between the refusal or withdrawal of medical treatment and intentional killing. The right to suicide must be treated like the right to refuse treatment (1997).

The U.S. Supreme court agreed to hear both appeals court's rulings. In

June of 1997, a unanimous Supreme Court reversed the decisions of both courts of appeals and upheld laws banning assisted suicide as constitutional in both states. The Court ruled that there is no constitutional right to use a physician to assist in a suicide under any circumstances (Marquand 1997). One of the reasons cited by the Court for its decision was the risk that a dying patient's request for assistance in ending his life might not be truly voluntary ("No" to euthanasia 1997). The Court further stated that the concept of assisted suicide was in conflict with the country's history, legal tradition, and practices (Moore 1997). The Court further suggested that the issue should be left to the state legislatures to decide whether they want to legalize assisted suicide or to ban it. The Court stated that its ruling allows the debate on the issue to continue, as it should in a democratic society (Reibstein 1997).

Oregon's Physician-Assisted Suicide Law

The states' battles for the right to assisted suicide had already begun in Oregon in 1994. On November 8 of that year, voters in Oregon, by a margin of 51 to 49 percent, approved a ballot initiative known as Measure 16, Death with Dignity Act. The law allows terminally ill patients to obtain a physician's prescription to end life in a humane and dignified way under proper safeguards. However, on November 23, the National Right to Life Committee filed a motion for injunction against Measure 16 in the federal district court. On December 7, Judge Michael Hogan placed a temporary restraining order on Measure 16 and later extended the temporary restraining order. After another hearing on December 27, Judge Hogan placed a preliminary injunction on Measure 16 until a later hearing. Finally, on August 3, 1995, Judge Hogan ruled Measure 16 unconstitutional. The Oregon Death with Dignity organization appealed the decision to the Ninth Circuit Court of Appeals, and on February 27, 1997, the Ninth Circuit Court of Appeals ordered Judge Hogan to lift the injunction in twenty-one days. The Court stated that the enforcement of the law did not pose any immediate threat to the rights of the women who sued to block the law or the doctors who objected to the measure. Furthermore, it argued that the specter of involuntary suicide raised by the opponents was merely speculative. The Court also rejected the argument that depressed, terminally ill adults would be prevented under the law from making informed decisions (Associated Press 1997; Biskupic 1997). Opponents of the measure appealed to the U.S. Supreme Court, but the Court refused to hear a challenge to Oregon's physician-assisted suicide law.

The Oregon state legislature decided to put Measure 16 on the state ballot again in the November 1997 elections for the purpose of its repeal. Oregon voters defeated the attempted repeal by a margin of 60 to 40 percent (Hill

1997). The Oregon Death with Dignity Act went into effect and Oregon became the first state to implement such a law in the United States.

Physician-Assisted Suicide and Congress

After the U.S. Supreme Court refused to hear an appeal to Oregon's law, efforts have been initiated in Congress to try to overturn it. On November 5, 1997, Thomas Constantine, administrator of the Drug Enforcement Agency (DEA), wrote in a letter to Senator Orrin Hatch (R-UT) and Representative Henry Hyde (R-IL) that doctors who participate under the Oregon Death with Dignity Act will be violating the federal controlled substance act which could lead to revocation of their licenses. In June of 1998, Attorney General Janet Reno released a Justice Department ruling that the DEA does not have the authority to revoke the prescribing licenses of doctors who participated under the law. Representative Hyde and Senator Don Nickles (R-OK) introduced an almost identical bill—Lethal Drug Abuse Prevention Act of 1998—to amend the Controlled Substance Act to give DEA the authority to revoke prescribing licenses of doctors. However, the bill did not make it to a vote either in the House or the Senate. In August of 1999, the House Judiciary Committee approved the Pain Relief Promotion Act of 1999. The main intent of the bill is to overturn Oregon's Death with Dignity Act. The bill advocates aggressive pain care for terminally ill patients, and it would make it illegal for doctors to prescribe federally controlled drugs with the intent of hastening death. Under the bill doctors can be sent to jail for prescribing such drugs. The bill is backed by the National Right to Life Committee and the Roman Catholic Church (Cloud and Donnelly 1999; Knockerbocker 1998). In October, the House of Representatives voted in favor of the bill by a margin of 271 to 156 (Grunwald 1999). However, the Senate has failed to pass the bill. On November 6, 2001, Attorney General John Ashcroft, reversing the policy of the Clinton administration, authorized the Drug Enforcement Administration agents to take action against doctors who prescribe lethal drugs for terminally ill patients. Under the Ashcroft directive, the penalty could include revocation of license to prescribe any drugs. Ashcroft argued that assisted suicide was not a legitimate medical purpose for prescribing lethal drugs to terminally ill patients (Verhovek 2001). Oregon public officials have already filed a lawsuit challenging the Attorney General's action. The issue is ultimately likely to end up in the U.S. Supreme Court for resolution. A national poll conducted by the same group that wrote and promoted Oregon's Measure 16 showed that 69 percent favor Oregon's approach, while 75 percent oppose Congressional efforts to overturn Oregon's law. Other national polls have found similar results (Knockerbocker 1998).

State Governments, Right to Die, and Public Policy

State governments have been the most active in setting public policy in the area of right to die. While the federal courts have played an important role in this area, Congress and the U.S. Supreme Court thus far have played a limited role. The U.S. Supreme Court, as we discussed earlier, has preferred to leave the matter up to the states.

Advance Directives

When Congress passed the Patient Self-Determination Act in 1990, it acted out of the belief that people want control over their health care treatment when they are no longer capable of making decisions or expressing their wishes. It was hoped that having written advance directives of a person's wishes would resolve conflicts and avoid litigation like the Nancy Cruzan case (Michel 1997). Furthermore, advance directives are grounded in the concept of patient autonomy. Advance directives extend the patient's autonomy to a future state of incompetence by allowing patients to participate in their decision making regarding the end of life care they receive (Ikonomidis and Singer 1999). While prospective autonomy is not the same as contemporaneous autonomy it shares a common foundation in the concept of self-determination. Many courts have sided with a patient's prerogative to reject life-sustaining care or treatment by arguing that a patient's control of medical intervention is anchored in the U.S. Constitution and in state constitutions' protection of liberty. However, the courts also have stated that an individual's right to refuse life-sustaining care is not an absolute right. Individual liberty interest must be weighed against the government's interest or public interest in limiting a patient's decision to reject life-sustaining care. Thus, state statutes dealing with advance directives must also respect constitutional constraints (Cantor 1993). Advance directives generally involve a written document by a competent person that outlines a person's preferences in medical care in case the person is unable to express her wishes and preferences. In some situations (the Nancy Cruzan case) a court may honor previous statements about treatment preferences if no written document by a patient is available. The advantage of having a written advance directive is to avoid potential uncertainties, confusion, and misinterpretation (Doukas and Reichel 1993).

Today, all states have laws on the books that deal with health care advance directives. Advance directives can be classified into two types—living wills and durable power of attorney or health care surrogacy.

Living Wills

A living will is a statement or a declaration allowing a person to direct the type of life-sustaining care he does not want to receive in the future if the person becomes terminally ill, permanently unconscious, or is conscious but suffers from irreparable brain damage and is no longer able to make a decision. A living will allows a person to describe the kind of treatment she wants to receive in certain situations. Often it is common to expressly allow a doctor to terminate extraordinary life-sustaining care, including withdrawal of artificial nutrition and hydration. However, a living will does not allow the selection of someone else to make decisions on behalf of the infirm (Hanson and Morris 1997). In a sense, a living will is a person's declaration of his desire for a natural death. However, state legislatures are very careful under living will provisions in separating what limited types of actions they allow as part of a "natural death" from other types of "arranged death," that is, assisted suicide or active euthanasia (Hoefler 1994).

Living wills are recognized in almost all states; however, requirements often vary from state to state. For example, until recently, "do not resuscitate" orders were not honored for people dying at home or in other nonhospital settings. Many states have changed their laws in the past ten years or so in this area and allow refusal of emergency resuscitation in nonhospital settings. People often are confused or do not fully understand the use of paramedic services. Paramedics are trained to do everything possible to keep trauma victims alive to get them to the emergency room. Paramedics' services are not intended for dying patients. Due to this misunderstanding, people often call 911 because they want oxygen or comfort care for the dying person. However, they do not realize that paramedics will not honor advance directives in an emergency (Advance directives: an update 1995). States also vary with respect to how they define "terminal" illness. Some states require that death be imminent regardless of whether the life-sustaining treatment is continued, while other states consider individuals to be terminal if death would be imminent without the use of life-sustaining treatment. Similarly, in many states, pregnancy automatically voids the validity of an advance directive (Hoefler 1994).

Despite the variations in state requirements with respect to living wills, there also are some common elements. All states require that the person preparing the living will be of majority age (18 in most states, 21 in others). The document must be witnessed generally by two individuals, neither of whom have a financial stake in the disposition of the estate of the person making the living will. Typically, all prohibit and impose criminal penalties for falsification, destruction, purposefully withholding of living wills, or coercion associated with execution of it (Hoefler 1994).

Having a valid living will does not guarantee that a person's wishes would be honored automatically by health care practitioners, health care facilities, or others. A persons' living will may not be executed due to a variety of reasons. One of the most common reasons is the problem of interpreting vague terms and phrases often included in the language of a living will. Second, it is very difficult to spell out precisely the kind of treatment one does not want to receive in the future because it is impossible for a person to anticipate any and every conceivable future condition and possible treatment alternatives. Medical conditions and treatment alternatives change over a period of time. Thus, there is always a possibility of positive or negative unforeseen developments. On the positive side, for example, a new drug or treatment may be discovered that was not available at the time of the writing of the living will. On the negative side, a drug or treatment that was administered for its potential therapeutic benefits may be discovered later on to be ineffectual or actually harmful to the patient. Third, a temptation to ignore or deviate from the patient's wishes arises when those wishes or preferences may be viewed to be in conflict with what is in the best current interest of the patient. In other words, what was in the best interest of the patient in the past when he wrote the living will may not be viewed as in the best interest of the patient at some future date. Fourth, since an advance directive represents an autonomous expression of a competent person, it is sometimes difficult to reconcile what the person may have expressed in a living will when he was competent compared to the patient's expressed wishes when he is incompetent. Also, state laws governing living wills often fail to make appropriate differentiation among incompetent patients. For example, state statutes typically provide that a patient may revoke a directive. Thus, any statement a patient makes in a considerably deteriorated mental state contradicting the instructions in the living will has the effect of revoking those instructions. Fifth, the provisions of the living will may not be honored because of opposition from a family member or members, physician, or health care institution. Often, such entities have successfully challenged living wills in the courts (Glick 1992; Cantor 1993). We already have mentioned the potential conflict between what is in the patient's best interest as expressed in a living will and the state's interest in protecting or preserving life. For example, a state may claim an interest in preserving life by ignoring a pregnant patient's expressed desire not to be hooked up to life-sustaining treatment in her living will.

Living wills have often been criticized because as many studies have demonstrated, they have very little impact on end of life care because such documents are often ambiguous and completed by people without any discussion with health care professionals and/or family members. Thus, physicians are often left to interpret ambiguous living wills even though they may have very little knowledge about the patient (Tonelli 1997).

Durable Power of Attorney (Health Care Agent or Surrogate)

Another type of advance directive is what is often called the durable power of attorney or health care surrogacy. Such a document allows an individual to appoint another person (health care surrogate or agent) to make health care decisions on his behalf if the individual becomes unable to make those decisions. Such a person then is authorized to consent to or refuse medical procedures, treatment, or medication on the patient's behalf. Most states do not allow an individual to name a health care provider or nursing home employee to be named as a person's health care agent (Hanson and Morris 1997). A durable power of attorney in health care is different from other durable powers of attorney in the sense that health care power of attorney's decision making is strictly limited to health care and not business or financial decision making on behalf of the patient. A proxy, also known as an agent, is the person appointed to serve as health care surrogate under the durable power of attorney. Such a person is expected to make decisions based on her understanding of the patient's values and preferences, previous conversations, and written advance directives, if any (Doukas and Reichel 1993).

Over the years, courts have recognized three possible substantive standards for surrogate decision making concerning end of life care. The "best interest standard" calls for the surrogate to make decisions based on factors such as the relief of suffering, the restoration of functioning, the quality of life, and the extent of life to be sustained. The "pure subjective" standard calls for the surrogate to rely solely on the prior expressed wishes of the patient. In case of insufficient evidence, the surrogate is not permitted to withdraw a life-support system under any circumstances. The "substituted judgment" standard takes a middle ground between the first two, allowing the surrogate to form his own conclusion about what the patient would have wanted from prior statements, patient's values, beliefs, personality, and prior lifestyle (Mello 1999; Hoefler 1994).

The health care agent or "proxy" faces an awesome responsibility often alone and unprepared. Such a person often has informational and emotional needs that should be met by the health care provider team. A health care agent's task can be made easier by establishing a close working relationship early on between the patient, health care provider, and the proxy (Lane and Dubler 1997).

Criticisms of the Health Care Advance Directives

One criticism centers on the notion that advance directives help promote and protect individual autonomy. The argument favoring advance directives is based on the assumption that autonomy over one's future as an incompetent patient is a very valuable freedom that law and public policy should go to great lengths to protect. When patients cannot tell us how they would exercise their autonomy, we should look to their past experiences of autonomy, that is, precedent autonomy, to guide us. Such is the position often taken by many philosophers who favor advance directives. However, critics argue that empirical findings suggest that subjects in many studies have demonstrated a lack of understanding about what an advance directive is and that, despite public opinion polls that show a strong majority of the public in favor of advance directives, not many people have taken the trouble to write advance directives for themselves. This suggests that the exercise of autonomy might not be as important to the public as it is to many philosophers (Dresser 1994).

Others also have challenged the necessity and sufficiency of individual autonomy. First of all, they argue that the liberal concept of autonomy implies a misconception of the individual self because it conceives of self as a rational, independent agent who is totally detached from other social beings. Such is not the case in reality. Second, it ignores the value of social justice. The liberal concept of autonomy cannot account for advance care planning when the interests of the society outweigh those of the individual. Third, the liberal conception of autonomy does not account for justifiable acts of paternalism as is the case of justifiable paternalistic acts in relation to children. Finally, critics charge that the liberal conception of autonomy ignores the importance of personal relationships in the advance care planning process. Patients interviewed in empirical studies have indicated that their reasons for writing advance directives is often to prepare not for incapacity but for death, relieving the burden on loved ones, among others. Thus, advance directives are rarely, if ever, solely based on a person's desire to exercise control and autonomy. Others disagree with such criticisms and insist that liberalism is a necessary component of a theoretical framework for advance care planning (Ikonomidis and Singer 1999).

A second criticism leveled by critics of advance directives is that those who favor it assume a single meaning of autonomy, generally one common to the traditional, white, middle class. However, there are many subtle nuances and variations about the concept of autonomy and end of life care that are based on cultural differences among various ethnic groups. A study of four ethnic groups (200 each of European Americans, African Americans,

Mexican Americans, and Korean Americans) in 1997 found that African Americans tended to have a more positive attitude about advance planning for end of life care than Mexican Americans or Korean Americans. However, despite this positive attitude, African Americans had significantly less knowledge about advance directives than Mexican Americans or European Americans. Furthermore, only 2 percent of African Americans and no Korean American had advance directives (Michel 1997).

A third major criticism of advance directives centers on the fact that studies that have measured patients' reactions to the process of advance care planning, that is, discussion about advance care planning and completing forms of written advance directives, suggest that many find the process depressing and uncomfortable, and it creates a great deal of anxiety (Dresser 1994). Finally, a fourth argument leveled again advance directives is that it is based on the false premise that the individual is able to accurately determine the type of treatment he would have adopted had he been competent. People are often ill informed or at least not as well informed as they should be about the consequences of choices they make about some future state. Furthermore, many are likely to greatly underestimate their desire to have medical intervention should they become ill (Ryan 1996).

Euthanasia and Physician-Assisted Suicide

As we mentioned earlier, the most controversial debate over the right to die in the United States in the 1990s focused on the notion of euthanasia, and specifically physician-assisted suicide. Euthanasia is classified as either passive or active. Passive euthanasia involves letting a patient die a natural death by not using or by withdrawing life-sustaining means or withholding treatment such as respirators, tube feeding, and the like that allow a patient to live but in a vegetative state. Passive euthanasia can be considered voluntary if it happens at the request of the competent patient. Involuntary passive euthanasia involves a situation in which life-sustaining treatment is refused or withdrawn not at the request of the patient but rather at the request of a family member. This can happen when the patient is incapable of expressing her preferences. Within certain constraints, courts in the United States have recognized a terminally ill person's right to refuse or request withdrawal of life-sustaining treatment and the right of family members to exercise that right if the patient is incompetent and unable to express a preference (Ho 1999).

Active euthanasia involves administration of a lethal drug to terminate the life of a patient who has requested it. There are two possibilities here. The physician may simply supply drug/medication to the patient and the patient takes the drug on his own. Or, a physician actually administers the drug to the patient to hasten the death of the patient. Voluntary active euthanasia occurs at the patient's request, while involuntary euthanasia occurs when a health care provider, generally a physician, hastens a patient's death or terminates a patient's life by administering a drug to the patient without such a request from the patient (Ho 1999). Active involuntary euthanasia has been universally condemned by most. Active voluntary euthanasia, or, physician-assisted suicide, has generated the most intense debate in the United States with many groups supporting legalization of physician-assisted suicide, while other groups strongly oppose such legislation. As we discussed, the U.S. Supreme Court in its rulings has indicated a preference for letting the states establish their own policies on physician-assisted suicide. More than thirty-five states have passed laws that prohibit physician-assisted suicide, while some states are considering legislation that would legalize physician-assisted suicide. Currently, Oregon is the only state that has legalized physician-assisted suicide.

State of Oregon and Physician-Assisted Suicide

In November of 1997, Oregon became the only state in the United States to legalize physician-assisted suicide (White 1998). Pursuant to the law, a task force to improve the care of terminally ill Oregonians sponsored by the Greenwall Foundation has issued a guidebook to promote excellent care for the dying and to develop standards for clinical practice under the law (Haley and Lee 1998). The task force emphasizes the legal and moral freedom of an individual clinician to refuse to assist in a suicide to which he conscientiously objects (1998).

The law gives a competent terminally ill adult the right to request and receive physician aid in dying under carefully defined circumstances. Adult is defined to mean a person who is 18 years of age or older. The law defines a terminal disease as an incurable and irreversible disease that has been medically confirmed and according to reasonable medical judgment will produce death within six months. The patient must voluntarily request suicide assistance of the attending physician by requesting medication for the purpose of ending her life. The patient must make two oral and one written request for assistance in suicide. Fifteen days after the first oral request, the patient must repeat the oral request a second time to the attending physician. An additional forty-eight hours must pass before the patient can make a written request. At this point, the patient must sign and date the written request. The patient can revoke the request anytime by any means. Two persons, one of who must not be a relative of the patient by blood, marriage, or adoption, an heir, or an owner, operator, or employee of a health care facility at which the patient is receiving care, must witness the directive. At the time of the request, the patient's attending physician also may not be a witness. The attending physician must request that the patient notify his next of kin. However, such a notification is not a prerequisite for assistance (Humphry and Clement 1998).

A consulting physician (qualified by specialty or experience to make a diagnosis and a prognosis of a patient's illness) must verify the attending physician's diagnosis and prognosis and determine whether the patient is capable of making her own health care decision and is acting voluntarily. The attending physician is authorized to order a psychiatric consultation with the patient's consent if there is any question about the patient's competence to make a request for help in dying. At least fifteen days must pass after the second oral request and forty-eight hours after the written request before the patient can receive a prescription for medication to end his life. Once the prescription is filled by the pharmacy, the patient decides when, where, in what manner, and with whom present to self-administer the medication. Neither the attending physician nor anyone else can administer the medication. ·The law requires that a record be kept of all the oral and written requests of the patient; the attending physician's diagnosis and prognosis; the outcome and determination made during counseling; and the physician's determination that the patient is competent, acting voluntarily, had made an informed decision, and so forth. The Health Division of the state of Oregon is required to review annually a sample of such records and make public an annual statistical report. Physicians who comply in good faith with the provision of the law are immune from criminal or civil liability or professional disciplinary action (Humphry and Clement 1998).

Since the law has been in effect for over two years now, what do early results indicate? During 1999, twenty-seven terminally ill patients committed suicide with the help of lethal prescription from their physician. There were 29, 281 deaths in the state or Oregon during 1999. In 1998, sixteen terminally ill patients had made use of the law. Thus, during the two-year period, forty-three terminally ill patients made use of the law (McMahon and Koch 2000). About 15 percent changed their mind and revoked their request after counseling or better pain management. Thus, at least initially, it appears that the opponents' fears that such a law would be abused and a large number of terminally ill patients would rush to commit suicide has not materialized. The number of patients who have taken advantage of the law has remained small (Schiff 2000; Miller 2000). A study based on interviews of doctors and surviving relatives of the twenty-seven people who died from assisted suicide in 1999, conducted by the Oregon State Health Department, indicated that there was no evidence to suggest that the poor, uneducated, mentally ill, or socially isolated are disproportionately seeking or getting assistance under the law as the opponents had feared. In general, people opting for assisted suicide are well educated, well insured, and often in hospice care. Of the twenty-seven patients, half were college graduates and none were without insurance. Family members also went out of their way to state that the dying relative was worried about future pain and suffering (Brown 2000).

Another study was based on a survey of 4,000 Oregon doctors who were eligible to consider suicide requests because of their specialty. Of those 4,000 doctors 65 percent responded to the survey. They provided details about 165 patient requests for assisted suicide that ultimately led to seventeen assisted suicides. About half of the persons who requested assistance in suicide were men and married. Only 5 percent were not high school graduates, and only 2 percent had no health insurance. Two-thirds had terminal cancer and the mean age of the requesters was 68. The main reasons cited by the patients for their request was pain, fatigue, and breathlessness as symptoms they either had or feared developing. Over half the patients mentioned loss of independence, poor quality of health, desire to control circumstances of their death, and readiness to die as reason for their requests (Ganzini et al. 2000). Again, the fear expressed by the opponents of the law that it would lead to a disproportionately higher number of uneducated, poor, uninsured, and women seeking assisted suicide has not materialized.

Physician-Assisted Suicide in Other States

During the debate over Oregon's Death with Dignity Act, opponents warned of a "slippery slope" in which other states would follow Oregon and pass similar laws that could pressure vulnerable people into feeling that it was their duty to die. Thus far, such fears have not been realized. In fact, the trend seems to be in the opposing direction. More than thirty-five states have passed laws that explicitly ban physician-assisted or any assisted suicide. There has been no copycat rush by other states (McMahon and Koch 1999). In fact, ballot initiatives designed to legalize physician-assisted suicide have suffered defeat in several states recently.

Such an initiative was placed on the ballot in the state of Michigan—the home of Dr. Jack Kevorkian and politically powerful and sophisticated right to life organizations (Gianelli 1998). Voters soundly defeated it. Kevorkian, who claims to have assisted more than a hundred people to commit suicide during the 1990s, was convicted by a court and sentenced to ten to twenty-five years in prison for injecting a lethal drug into a patient with Lou Gehrig's disease. Previous attempts at convictions had resulted in acquittal or hung juries because of lack of clear evidence that he actually administered the lethal dosage. However, in this case, Kevorkian had made a videotape of the suicide and sent it to *60 Minutes* for nationwide broadcast. The videotape provided clear evidence of Kevorkian actually administering the lethal drug to the patient. The case is under appeal (Kozloski 2000).

Similar ballot initiatives have been rejected by voters in states such as California and Washington (Lewis 2000). About twenty states have either rejected or blocked laws that would have legalized assisted suicide (Beeder 1999).

The battle for physician-assisted suicide has shifted to the state of Maine. A citizen-initiated proposal to legalize physician-assisted suicide went to the state legislature (Maine logs support 2000). The legislature sent the proposal to the voters rather than acting on it themselves. Polls in the state indicated that 62 percent supported the bill while 26 percent were against the bill (Moore 2000). However, the proposal to legalize physician-assisted suicide was defeated in the November election (Adams 2001).

Arguments For and Against Physician-Assisted Suicide

In this section we examine some of the major arguments made by proponents and opponents of physician-assisted suicide. First, we examine the arguments in favor of physician-assisted suicide.

Arguments in Favor of Physician-Assisted Suicide

1. One of the major arguments in favor of physician-assisted suicide is based on the notion of individual autonomy and self-determination. Immanuel Kant defined autonomy as moral freedom, a crucial element of one's moral identity. He argued that the nature of rational beings and the moral law requires that the autonomy of everyone be respected. Kant occasionally referred to suicide as an expression of the individual's desire for greater autonomy or self-control over his own death. However, he showed some ambiguity in his own thinking by also arguing that there is an intrinsic value in preserving life and it may be so great that it prohibits intentionally destroying oneself. John Stuart Mill defined personal autonomy more as a political and social condition than a moral one (Norden 1995). Accordingly, proponents of physician-assisted suicide argue that just as a person has the right to determine as much as possible the course of her own life, a person also has a right to determine the course of her own dying. As long as a person freely and rationally chooses to seek assistance in ending his life, such assistance should be available from a person (physician) who is willing to provide it. Proponents argue that autonomy is a very fundamental American

value and should not be dismissed (Emanuel 1999). The famous "philoso-phers' brief" written by six distinguished philosophers was submitted to the U.S. Supreme Court in support of physician-assisted suicide when the Su-preme Court was considering the cases of *State of Washington v. Glucksberg* and *Vacco v. Quill*. The brief argued that the Court should uphold the deci-sions of the Second and Ninth Circuits affirming that patients have a consti-tutionally protected right to secure the help of willing physicians in terminating their own life, at least in a limited number of cases. The brief was based on a general moral and constitutional principle that every competent person has the right to make major personal decisions based on one's fundamental reli-gious or philosophical convictions about life's value to himself or to herself. Liberal democratic governments cannot legitimately prevent citizens from acting on their most fundamental liberty interests (Weithman 1999).

The critics counter by arguing that true autonomy is rarely if ever pos-sible, especially for a person who is dying, not only because most of our choices are socially formed but also because in terminal illness depression and other forms of psychological disorders are likely to be present. Propo-nents' counter argument is that even if our choices may be socially shaped, they must be respected as autonomous choices, and it is possible for a rational person to choose death without suffering from depression and other psycho-logical problems. Furthermore, legislation legalizing physician-assisted sui-cide provides sufficient safeguards such as the voluntary and repeated nature of the request for assistance by the patient, requirement of consultation with a second physician, and counseling, among others (Emanuel 1999).

2. A second major argument of the proponents of physician-assisted sui-cide is that the courts have already recognized the right of a competent per-son to refuse or request withdrawal of life-sustaining treatment, allowing one to die a natural death. The courts also have recognized the right of a health care surrogate or family member to make such a request in case of incompetence on the part of the patient. The philosophers' brief argued that there was no distinction between the right to refuse or remove life-sustaining treatment and the right to physician-assisted suicide because the common sense distinction to be made is not between acts and omissions, but between acts or omissions that are designed to cause death and those that are not. According to the philosophers' brief, both actions—withdrawal of life-sustaining treatment and physician-assisted suicide—are designed to pro-duce the same result—the death of a patient—and thus, there is no ground to make a constitutional distinction between assisted suicide and the removal of life support (Weithman 1999).

The counterargument presented by the opponents of physician-assisted suicide is that there is a fundamental moral difference between removal of life support and physician-assisted suicide. The distinction is between allowing patients to die a natural death and killing patients. Killing is active, while allowing one to die is passive. There is a distinction between allowing a patient to die and causing the death of a patient. The U.S. Supreme Court, in rejecting challenges to the constitutionality of laws prohibiting physician-assisted suicide, explicitly invoked this distinction (Sulmasy 1998). Furthermore, it is not a certainty that withdrawing life-sustaining treatment such as a ventilator would lead to certain death (Weithman 1999). However, the counterargument is that the distinction between passive and active is partly misleading. A doctor who does not connect a patient to life support decides to merely let the patient die normally. However, when a doctor withdraws life support, he is not just standing by, doing nothing, but the doctor is actively intervening by removing or shutting off medical equipment that is keeping the patient alive. This intervention does not involve just letting a patient die, it denotes assistance (Thomson 1999).

The opponents of physician-assisted suicide further argue that contrary to the notion that voluntary euthanasia and physician-assisted suicide will demedicalize death and provide an ultimate break on the unrestrained use of medical technology at the end of life, the fact of the matter is that physician-assisted suicide will actually medicalize suicide by taking a private act (suicide) and turning it into a medical event. Physician-assisted suicide, in fact, extends, not constrains, medical power over life and death (Salem 1999).

3. The third major argument in favor of physician-assisted suicide is based on the notion that no person should have to bear pointless terminal suffering. If the physician is not able to reduce a patient's suffering in other ways, and the only way to avoid such physical pain and suffering is by death, then it is acceptable to bring about death with the help of a physician, especially when a mentally competent person is suffering from terminal illness and makes an informed decision and requests such help. Such cases are likely to amount to less than 1 percent of all deaths that occur in the United States annually (Emanuel 1999).

Opponents counter by arguing that due to pain management techniques developed by hospices and others, it is possible to treat pain to relieve virtually all suffering. Today, palliative care has improved tremendously. Appropriate, sound, and acceptable palliative care practices, such as withdrawal of life-sustaining treatments, terminal sedation, voluntary cessation of eating and drinking, and providing opioids, are very distinct from actively aiding someone in dying (Norris 1997). Proponents counter by arguing that virtually all pain cannot be treated and controlled and thus there will always be a few patients who would benefit by physician-assisted suicide.

4. Proponents also argue that having the option or alternative of physician-

assisted suicide might be reassuring to many terminally ill patients. According to a study, 41.6 percent of cancer patients (not all terminally ill), and 44.4 percent of the general public thought that a discussion with their physician(s) about end-of-life care, including discussion of euthanasia and physician-assisted suicide, would increase their trust in their physicians (Emanuel et al. 1996). Opponents argue that, in fact, legalization of physician-assisted suicide might generate fear among the elderly and mentally incompetent that they might be put to death without their consent.

Arguments Against Physician-Assisted Suicide

1. Opponents argue that there is no such thing as complete autonomy. It is impossible to know for certain whether a patient who chooses to end her life is truly doing it of her own free will, fully understands the consequences of her decision, is well-informed, and thus truly exercising her autonomy. Furthermore, a person's right to autonomy and self-determination is a limited right and must be judged against overall social values and societal interests such as sanctity of life and protection of those who are vulnerable to medical or family abuse (Salem 1999).

2. One of the major arguments made against physician-assisted suicide is that such a policy would undermine the medical profession and will place unnecessary emotional burdens on physicians. It may make them change their practice or leave the profession altogether (Emanuel 1999). However, a counterargument is that legislation such as the Oregon law does not force all physicians to engage in the practice, and physicians who object to such a practice are allowed to not provide assistance in dying. Opponents of physician-assisted suicide also argue that such a policy will destroy trust in patient-physician relationships and also may harm public trust in the medical profession. Furthermore, it will generate unnecessary anxiety on the part of the patient. The survey which showed that 41.6 percent of the patients thought it would increase their trust in their doctor if they were able to discuss end of life care, including euthanasia and physician-assisted suicide, showed the same number of patients stating that such a discussion would decrease trust in their physicians. Also, patients may chose to end their own lives because they believe their doctor wants them to do so rather than acting out of a genuine desire of their own because of the power differential between a patient and a doctor (Weithman 1999). Physician-assisted suicide will also undermine the integrity of the medical profession because it goes against the Hippocratic Oath.

3. Another major argument against physician-assisted suicide is that terminally ill patients may be coerced into opting for physician-assisted suicide

by family members because of financial or care-giving burdens. While some anecdotes about such coercive pressures have come to light, no solid empirical data are available. Opponents argue that such a policy also will create the possibility of premature euthanasia and produce a great deal of suffering on family members (Emanuel 1999).

4. A fourth argument against physician-assisted suicide is that it will undermine the fine work of organizations such as hospice and the tremendous progress that has been made in end of life care and palliative measures.

5. A fifth argument against physician-assisted suicide is based on the notion that the taking of a human life is simply wrong. Killing is intrinsically wrong and it is evident in the commandment "thou shall not kill." Such an argument essentially comes from religious groups, particularly conservative groups such as conservative Catholic groups and right to life groups.

6. Finally, the argument against physician-assisted suicide is based on the notion of the "slippery slope" concept. A belief that once physician-assisted suicide is legalized for terminally ill patients, it would open doors for and lead to legalizing physician-assisted suicide for patients who are not terminally ill and for children, and might even lead to the elimination of voluntary euthanasia with some patients being killed against their will, that is, without their consent.

Right to Die, Values, and Public Policy

The second half of the twentieth century witnessed a major revolution in the field of biomedical technology that had many impacts, one of which was the increased capacity to prolong and sustain the life of terminally ill patients indefinitely through medical intervention. This, in turn, raised concerns about patients' rights that led to the transformation of the U.S. health care system from doctor-centered in the first half of the century to a patient-centered health care system in the second half that placed greater emphasis on patients' rights to self-determination and autonomy. As a result, the second half of the twentieth century also generated intense debate about what often is referred to as the right to die. Do competent, terminally ill patients have a right to refuse extraordinary life-supporting treatment? Do they have a right to end their own life and thus determine the manner and the timing of their death? Do they have a right to seek the assistance of a physician in ending their own life?

Formulation of public policy in this area has been very difficult and very problematic for many reasons. However, two reasons, ironically contradictory ones, stand out. One of the reasons is that in a large, pluralistic society such as ours consensus building is always problematic due to the significant amount of cultural, religious, ethnic, economic, and political diversity. Ironically, the second reason is the fact that our culture is preoccupied with an emphasis on youth and a fear of aging, and avoiding honest, open discussions of aging and death. The debate about euthanasia and physician-assisted suicide has thus far been largely confined to the ivory towers of academia, mainly among philosophers, centered around ethical, moral, and legal or constitutional arguments. During the 1990s, the right to die movement has forced this debate onto the public square of the United States.

In the United States, the Supreme Court has largely left public policies regarding the right to die and how one chooses to die up to the states. While it has set a few parameters, the state courts have established public policies through interpretations of state constitutions in individual cases that have been brought before them. State legislatures have often reacted by clarifying their intentions through laws, often reluctantly. Thus, policy innovations are diffused among state courts and legislatures in a very inconsistent manner. The result often is disjointed and has produced diverse policies among different states (Keigher 1994).

How do the values that we enunciated as a guide to health care policy making in the new millennium apply with respect to the right to die issue?

One of the arguments we have made is that future public health care policy must focus on not only providing care but also on creating and maintaining a healthy society by requiring an emphasis on preventive care, education, and promotion of a healthy lifestyle. This requires that as a society we must confront and engage in a healthy discussion of issues such as aging, end of life care, and the process of dying. This means that we must view death not as something unnatural to be avoided at any cost but rather as a natural end process of life. Open and honest discussion of such issues must take place between patients and their doctors as well as among and between family members.

All states today have public policies that deal with advance directives. This is a step in the right direction. However, for advance directives to work well, a thoughtful discussion with family members and one's physician is an absolute necessity. This could avoid potential problems of doctor or family members left with a lot of uncertainty and trying to interpret patients' preferences. Public opinion polls also indicate that while a strong majority of the public favor and support public policy advance directives, less than a majority of the general public has actually written advance directives. A major public educational effort is needed to inform and encourage more people to create advance directives for themselves.

The holistic approach to health care means that public policies in the area of the right to die focus more on a broad perspective that takes into consideration social, psychological, and religious/cultural aspects related to death and dying and less on legal/constitutional or moral/ethical aspects. In a highly pluralistic society such as ours it is imperative that public policy deal with advance directives, refusal or withdrawal of life-sustaining medical interventions, euthanasia, and/or physician-assisted suicide from a pluralist viewpoint rather than impose one particular perspective. Future policy makers must respect and honor the legitimate differences and values of disparate groups and individuals.

The educational training of future physicians must change to equip them with the skills and training to better deal with caring for terminally ill patients. The educational training of future physicians must inculcate in them the notion that there is a limit to medicine, and they must learn to accept that at some point patient care must shift from cure to humane and dignified caring for the dying patient.

Public policy in the area of the right to die must respect patients' rights to self-determination and autonomy and protect and promote human dignity. However, public policy also must recognize health care as both a public or social good and a private or individual good. Along with the notion of dual or mutual obligation, public policy must balance individual interests and societal interests. Thus the individual's right to self-determination is not an absolute right but one with reasonable restrictions or restraints that may be imposed by public policy. Similarly, the right to die, if such a right becomes established public policy, must not be based on the economic status of a patient.

In the most controversial area of the right to die debate, physician assisted-suicide, like the controversial area of abortion, the debate has been structured totally in terms of a for/against or either/or format. Unfortunately, such structure invites arguments and counterarguments that produce polarization, which does not help in achieving a consensus in the formulation of public policy (Battin 2000). While a for and against format often helps illuminate strengths and weaknesses of specific policy alternatives, it does not help policy formulation. At some point, as the debate matures, the structure of the debate must change from a for/against, either/or format to finding common ground that can help illuminate the formation of a public policy. That is exactly what is needed with respect to the current controversy over physician-assisted suicide.

Part of the answer may be found in the palliative care movement in the United States. It has made progress in the recognition, assessment, and treatment of pain and suffering. The end of life care controversy has improved over the past years and promises to improve further with newer drugs that allow for better management of pain and suffering. Hospice care provides a good example but it still has a long way to go. The palliative care movement has come to recognize that in some cases and under certain circumstances, pain management may not be possible. In such cases, the palliative care movement has come to accept the use of terminal sedation, that is, sedating the terminally ill patient into unconsciousness and then withholding or withdrawing artificial nutrition and hydration required for keeping an unconscious patient alive. Terminal sedation generally occurs when pain is unmanageable and the patient is expected to live only a few days. Many people do not view terminal sedation as significantly different from assisted suicide.

While the palliative care movement has made some progress in addressing the problems of pain and suffering, a lack of high quality end of life care for dying patients still remains a major concern. Furthermore, the palliative care movement has failed to address the question of patient self-determination and autonomy. We must recognize that in those extreme cases where it is not possible to manage pain and suffering, patients may prefer physician-assisted suicide. Also, even if immensely significant progress was made in improving the care of dying patients, some patients will still prefer physician-assisted suicide because it best fits their view of a humane and dignified death (Brock 1999). This is reflected in the fact that over the years public opinion has steadily moved in its favor, allowing doctors to end a terminally ill patient's life through painless means if the patient and his family request it.

The principles we have outlined can provide a middle ground for formulating a public policy with respect to euthanasia and physician-assisted suicide. We suggest that a middle ground between the proponents and opponents of physician-assisted suicide could be based on the following propositions:

1. Adult, competent individuals should have a right to self-determination and autonomy to make health care decisions for themselves if the decisions they make are well informed, voluntary, and made after serious deliberation and not the result of temporary circumstances.

2. The principle of dual/mutual obligation means that a patient should exercise her right of self-determination and autonomy in a responsible manner and not without regard to the pain and suffering her decision may cause to others.

3. Since health care is a public/social good and not a private good, it should also be recognized that a patient's right to self-determination is not an absolute right, and public interest may require reasonable limits to be placed on exercise of this right.

4. Patients should be treated in a humane and dignified manner that protects and promotes their dignity. We need to recognize that patients may have a somewhat different view of what is a humane and dignified death. However, we suspect that patients' views of what constitutes a "good death"

may not be significantly different. The aspects of death that most people fear are physical pain, needless and useless prolongation of the dying process, alienation and isolation, diminishment of faculties, dependency on others, and becoming an undue burden on others in dying (Callahan 1997; McCormick 1997; Flemister 1997; Alexander 1997; Pickard 1997).

5. Euthanasia and physician-assisted suicide should be the last resort after all other alternatives have been fully explored and when everything else has failed.

6. Physician participation in assisted suicide should be voluntary.

7. Extreme care should be taken to make sure that vulnerable members of the society such as children and others who are unable to speak for themselves are protected from potential misuse and abuse.

8. Physicians should be better trained for providing end of life care.

We suggest that a public policy dealing with physician-assisted suicide that is based on the propositions discussed above can be justified in extremely limited circumstances. While a public policy cannot guarantee us a "good death," it can at least provide us an opportunity that allows us to die with dignity.

Study Questions

1. Write an essay in which you discuss the experience of the Netherlands in the development of public policy regarding euthanasia and how the policy has worked thus far. What are some of the criticisms of the current Dutch policy?

2. Discuss the right to die from an international perspective. How do different religions and cultures deal with the issue of right to die and euthanasia?

3. Write an essay in which you trace the development of the right to die movement in the United States.

4. What role have the courts played regarding issues of life-sustaining technologies, right to die, euthanasia, and physician-assisted suicide? Be sure to discuss some of the major court cases.

5. Write an essay in which you discuss Oregon's physician-assisted suicide law. What are some of its major provisions? How has the law worked thus far?

6. Explain advance directives, living wills, and durable power of attorney. What are the advantages and disadvantages of each?

7. What are the arguments for and against physician-assisted suicide?

CHAPTER 3

Organ Transplants

Where once only angels would tread, now goes man. With embryo-cloning, DNA mapping, genetic cleansing and organ transplants the technological system has invaded a realm held sacred by all previous civilizations. . . . What then will become of angels? And what will become of man? Will he find himself so close to the secrets of life, yet, as T.S. Elliot darkly foresaw, "further from God and nearer to the dust?" (Gardles 1994, 2–3)

Advances in biomedical technology have begun to blur the traditional boundaries between life and death. As biomedical science has begun to unravel the mysteries of life, it has raised questions about when life begins, when life should end, who has the right to decide, and whether we should draw the line between human and divine and, if so, where and how do we draw such a line?

Progress in biotechnology and genetic research generates hope among some and fear among others. Biotechnology is unfortunately often seen by many as either Promethean, engaged in saving human kind, or Faustian, dabbling with dark forces beyond our comprehension. The truth of the matter is that biotechnology has elements of both (Long 1998). On one hand, biotechnology is giving us the potential to treat previously incurable diseases and develop faster and more efficient diagnoses and treatments for diseases such as cystic fibrosis, sickle cell anemia, and diabetes. On the other hand, it also raises concerns about ethical treatment of animals and humans, the risk of environmental and biological contamination, loss of individual rights and privacy, and the loss of human dignity, among others. We as a society need to deal with both the Promethean and the Faustian aspects of biotechnology (1998).

As a result of advances in biotechnology, not only has the average life span increased over the years, but also we have developed the technological tools to keep terminally ill patients alive for an indefinite period of time through the use of feeding tubes and artificial ventilators. As we discussed in Chapter 2, this has given rise to the issue of the right to die. In the past thirty years, major advances have been made in the field of human organ transplants. A variety of factors such as improved surgical techniques, better understanding of immunology and drug therapy, and development of new antirejection drugs have significantly improved the survival rates of transplant recipients (Gorsline and Johnson 1994). Furthermore, improvement in organ preservation techniques has made it possible to transport donor organs for longer distances. This has given hopes to thousands of people suffering from diseases of the heart, lung, kidney, liver, or other organs, who would die without a transplant.

Today, organ transplants have become a commonplace occurrence. In fact, multiple organ transplants are also becoming a reality. In 1998, a 13–year-old boy, Daniel Canal, made medical history in the United States when he became the first patient to receive three multiple organ transplants. Surgeons in Miami worked for nineteen hours on Daniel's new stomach, liver, pancreas, and small intestine. Over a period of time the boy had received a total of twelve organs. This in turn also raised questions and concerns about equity in organ distribution (Daniel Canal 1998).

It was not so long ago that people joked that the market value of a dead human body's constituent chemicals was worth about $2. The revolution in organ transplant technology has turned human bodies into mines of valuable human body parts (DeLong 1998). For example, the *Chicago Tribune* estimated that all the usable tissue in a human body has a market value of over $230,000 (Body Shop 2000). However, the persistent shortage of donor organs for transplants has also generated long waiting lists in most countries. The shortages of donor organs and the long waiting period, combined with the fact that almost all countries in the world ban the sale of human organs, has given rise to a black market in human body parts. In March of 1998 Cheng Yong and Xingqui Fu, residents of New York, were charged with attempting to sell human corneas to an undercover FBI agent. According to the U.S. Attorney's office, these two individuals were peddlers of body parts taken from executed Chinese prisoners. Many human rights groups have alleged that China illegally markets human organs (Murray 1998). In October of 1999, bids for a human kidney hit $5.7 million on the Internet auction site eBay, before the company closed the auction and informed the FBI (Henderson 1999a). Tales of "kidney heist" and "organ napping" have become urban legends (Loerner 1997). In 1999, the University of California in Berkeley opened an Organ Watch Center to watch for and investigate illegal trafficking in human organs around the world (Henderson 1999b).

A swap meet in human organs is also taking hold. Scientific obstacles and difficult legal and ethical concerns deterred swapping kidneys and other organs in the past. However, today some doctors are beginning to challenge the prevailing view. More doctors are growing comfortable with the notion of live donor organ swaps and argue that such swapping of organs between live donors does not violate the 1998 law prohibiting the sale of organs because no money changes hands. They further argue that the practice is also ethically acceptable as long as the donor understands what she is agreeing to, the donors give informed consent, and donation is not likely to produce a significant risk of shortening life (McMenamin 2000).

Advances in the field of genetics have the potential to advance the field of organ transplants much further than ever before. Cross-species organ transplants have the potential to save thousands of lives. Scientists are working to eliminate the shortages of organs for transplants by developing genetically engineered pigs whose organs can be transplanted into humans.

However, advances in the transplantation field is also raising a host of social, ethical, economic, and political issues that are complex, troublesome, and daunting for policy makers to address. Some of the questions are as follows: What are and what should be the sources of organs used in transplants? How can we increase the number of available organs for transplants to meet the increased demand and reduce the current shortages? How can we make sure that organs are allocated to those in need in a fair and equitable manner? What criteria do we use to establish need? Should we legalize the sale of organs and create a futures market in organs? Should someone who has received one transplant be allowed to get a second transplant? Should an alcoholic be given a liver transplant? Are all transplants worth the economic costs involved? Should laws in cadaveric donation require consent of the donor and/or family member? Should a family member be able to override an organ donor's wishes? Should animals be bred and cloned for the manufacture of organs? Should human beings be cloned for harvesting organs (Caplan and Coelho, 1999; Gardels 1994)? These are very difficult questions. However, as we move into the new millennium, these issues will have to be addressed in the political arena and current public policies will need to be changed to keep up with medical advances, and new public policies will have to be devised.

Organ Donations and Transplants: International Perspective

According to a reference guide for clergy published by the United Network for Organ Sharing (UNOS) and the South-Eastern Organ Procurement Foundation (SEOPF), with few exceptions religions of the world see organ donation as an act of charity (Henderson 1998b). All Protestant denominations share the belief in a person's right to make decisions regarding his own body. Catholics view donation as an act of charity. In Judaism, organ donation is seen as *mitzvot*, or good deeds that individuals can perform after death (Religious views 2000). Many of the major Eastern religions, such as Hinduism and Buddhism, also view donation as an act of compassion designed to save life and see it as an individual decision (2000). However, given the fact that different religions have varying views about death and rituals associated with funeral and memorial services, there are some variations and exceptions regarding organ donation and transplant. For example, the Chinese tend to express considerable resistance to organ donation. According to Confucian belief, since our hair and flesh are gifts from our parents, to give them away or destroy them shows disrespect. There is also a concern that people who receive organ donations may be reborn with the donor's face (Braun 1997). Since 1984, Chinese law has permitted organ harvesting from executed prisoners (Jensen 2000). The Chinese government has been accused by many human rights organizations of allowing organ removal from executed prisoners for sale and transplants without the consent of the relatives, even though Chinese law requires such consent. The Chinese government has repeatedly denied allegations that such sales are widespread (Chelala 1997).

Similarly, opposition among Japanese to organ donation also stems from hesitation to deface one's body, which is considered a sacred gift from ancestors. People do not like the thought of going to the next life with some organs missing in their body (Chelala 1997). However, the situation in Japan is even more complicated. The major religions of Japan are Shinto, Taoism, Confucianism, and Buddhism. A typical Japanese household adopts a combination of these different traditions. However, majorities of Japanese practice Shinto, which is indigenous to Japan. According to the Shinto faith, extraction of organs from a donor's body is acceptable for saving or bettering human life. Otherwise, organ removal is viewed as sacrilegious. However, Shinto followers also oppose the notion of "brain death," (widely accepted in Western societies) and believe that to declare death while the heart is still beating is premature (McConnell 1999). According to Shinto religious tradition, the spirit exists not only in the mind but in body matter as well. The Cartesian notion upon which brain death is predicated in Western societies, "I think, therefore I am," is very different from the Japanese belief that "We are, therefore I think" (Gardels 1994, 2–3).

Taoism's views about the afterlife also affects many Japanese attitudes about organ donations. Taoism teaches that since the human body is a microcosm of the universe, the body must be preserved to provide the soul with a resting place upon death (Gardels 1994). In addition, the metaphor of organ donation as "the gift of life" widely accepted in Western countries does not carry any meaning or significance since the Japanese culture is founded on the notion of a traditional exchange system or reciprocal obligations (Clark and Boyles 1997).

As a result of these religious influences, the Japanese public policy, for a long time, did not allow a patient to be pronounced dead until her heart stopped beating. By this time, it is too late to donate any of the major organs because organs are not healthy enough to use in transplants. Thus, Japan did not permit legalized organ transplants but many Japanese traveled abroad to receive them. When a government advisory panel in 1992 recommended recognizing brain death, it generated considerable debate in Japan. As a result, no action was taken for several years (Heartless Japan 1996). Finally, in October of 1997, Japan legalized organ transplants from brain-dead donors (Clark and Boyles 1997). The passage of the law was made possible by a compromise between the two houses of the Japanese parliament that created a dual definition of death in Japan. Japan legalized brain death when the deceased is an organ donor. However, when the deceased is not an organ donor, the time of the death is recorded when the heart stops beating. To the dismay of the Japanese medical establishment, the law created a dual standard on the determination of death (McConnell 1999).

As far as laws and public policies of different countries with respect to organ donations and transplants are concerned, it is impossible to deal with or examine the policies of many individual countries. Kennedy and Sells (1998) have tried to classify policies of different countries into five broad categories. According to them, in the absence of a wish expressed by the donor during life, organs may be removed in the following circumstances: (1) with the consent of the person who is in legal possession of the body and subject to objections expressed by the deceased or the nearest relatives (e.g., Great Britain); (2) after relatives have been informed of the intention to remove organs irrespective of the relatives' objections, except the nearest relative (e.g., Norway); (3) once it has been ascertained that the relatives do not object (e.g., Italy); (4) when the dead person had not expressed an objection and this is confirmed by the relatives, and consent is presumed (e.g., Italy); and (5) irrespective of relatives' wishes (e.g., Austria).

As organ transplants have become more common, the demand for organs has increased worldwide. Many countries have followed a variety of strategies to increase the rates of organ donations. It is impossible to discuss policies regarding organ donations and transplants of so many different countries. Thus, we discuss a few examples to illustrate strategies that different countries have followed. The shortage of donors has led many liver transplant centers in Europe to widen their definition of liver donor suitability, accepting marginal quality livers from donors (Mirza and Gunson 1994).

During the early 1990s, many European countries adopted a policy of "contracting out" or an "opt out" system, also referred to as a presumed consent as a way to increase the supply of organs available for transplants. Under such a system, organs may be removed after death unless individuals have positively indicated during their lifetime that they did not wish this to be done. In the absence of an expressed statement of objection, it is presumed that the individual has consented to organ donation. Some countries have adopted a strong presumed consent model under which the only criteria used in the decision to harvest organs from the body of a dead person is whether or not the deceased had clearly expressed objection to organ removal. Countries such as Austria, Poland, and Switzerland follow such a model. Countries that have adopted a weak presumed consent model include Finland, Greece, Norway, Italy, Spain, and Sweden. In these countries the next of kin of the deceased person may object to organ removal (Gorsline and Johnson 1994). The laws of France and Belgium are based on the concept of presumed consent. However, they allow a great deal of flexibility in how the wishes of the deceased person may be expressed. Written evidence of a deceased person's objection is required, but physicians are bound by any objection to organ removal through a third party. While the physicians, by law, are not required to inform the next of kin before organ removal, physicians prefer to discuss the matter with family members (Gorsline and Johnson 1994).

Has the adoption of presumed consent laws in many European countries led to an increase in the availability of organs for transplants? The results have been mixed. Some have argued that the presumed consent system in combination with other factors did result in an increase in organ supply in countries such as Spain, Austria, and Belgium (Kennedy and Sells 1998). Spain has become the world leader in organ donation and has a rate of more than thirty donors per million people (Bosch 1998; 1999a; 1999b; 2000). France also increased organ donation through the presumed consent law (Dorozynski 1998). However, others have argued that presumed consent laws do not necessarily result in larger organ supplies (Jensen 2000).

Some countries have tried other methods to increase the availability of organs for transplants. For example, Sweden in 1996 adopted a new transplantation law that allows physicians and hospitals to harvest organs from the deceased as long as they indicate that they were willing donors. Under the law relatives and parents no longer have the final say in the matter (Awuonda 1996a; 1996b).

Despite the various efforts made by different countries shortages of available organs for transplants are a reality in many countries. For example, Canada has experienced a severe organ shortage (Baer 1997; Nichols 1999; Martin 2000; Henderson 1999c). Great Britain has not only experienced a shortage of donor organs but also of transplant surgeons (Carnall 2000; Kmietowicz 1999; Henderson 2000a). In addition, issues of racial discrimination in organ allocation also have been raised (UK analysis of racism 2000).

In recent years, the trend in Europe has been away from the presumed consent laws and a return to a voluntary system of organ donation. For example, to increase organ donations, Brazil, in 1997, enacted a law that declared all adults potential organ donors unless they filed for an exemption. However, given the intense criticism from the professional medical organizations in Brazil and strong public opposition, the law was abolished in 1998 (Csillag 1997; 1998).

Enforcement of presumed consent laws has also been more flexible in practice. For example, even when the law allows doctors to harvest organs without the consent of family members, most doctors choose to follow the wishes of the family members. In fact, in 1997 several European countries signed a treaty, which provides that the express and specific consent of a donor must be given before an organ is removed, and the treaty prohibits removal of organs from those who are unable to give consent (Jensen 2000).

In recognition of the potential of human rights abuses, the treaty also declared financial gain in organ marketing highly unethical. Today, almost every country prohibits sales of organs and considers such practices unethical. The World Health Organization (WHO) also has condemned the trade of human organs (Jensen 2000).

Brief History of Organ Transplants

The first human-to-human kidney transplant was attempted in 1933. However, the transplanted kidney did not function. In 1954, Dr. Joseph Murray of Brigham and Women's Hospital in Boston performed the first successful kidney transplant from one twin to another. No antirejection drugs were necessary. Most kidney transplants performed immediately following this were between identical twins. During 1963 and 1964, Dr. Thomas Starzl grafted baboon kidneys into six patients in Denver. The patients survived between nineteen and ninety-eight days. During the same period, chimpanzee kidneys were transplanted into twelve patients in New Orleans. Most failed within two months, but one recipient survived for nine months (BBC News 1999). Doctors Richard Lillechei and William Kelly of the University of Minnesota performed the first successful simultaneous pancreas and kidney transplant in 1966. Dr. Lillechei, in 1968, also performed the first isolated pancreas transplant.

Dr. Thomas Starzl of the University of Colorado Health Sciences Center also performed the first successful liver transplant in 1967. Between 1969 and 1974, three children received chimpanzee livers, but they survived between one to fourteen days.

Dr. Christiaan Barnard of South Africa, in 1967, performed the world's first human-to-human heart transplant. In 1968, Dr. Denton Cooley performed the first successful human-to-human heart transplant in the United States at Houston's St. Luke's Episcopal Hospital. Prior to this, there were attempts made to transplant animal-to-human heart organs. For example, in 1964, a 68-year-old man received a chimpanzee heart in the United States, but the recipient survived for only two hours. In 1977, in Capetown, South Africa, a baboon heart was transplanted into a 25-year-old woman and a moderate level of blood circulation was maintained for six hours, after which acute rejection took place. In 1984, a newborn baby (known as Baby Fae) received a baboon heart and lived for twenty days. Dr. Leonard Bailey, a pediatric heart surgeon, and his associates performed the operation at the Loma Linda University Medical Center in California. The heart of a 7-month-old baboon was used in the transplant. This case received a tremendous amount of media publicity. It also created a great deal of furor in the medical community and the general public (Fox and Swazey 1992).

During the 1980s, several experiments were also conducted in implanting an artificial, mechanical heart. On December 2, 1982, Dr. William C. DeVries and his colleague Dr. Lyle Joyce removed the heart of a patient, Barney B. Clark, who was facing imminent death due to chronic congestive heart failure and implanted an experimental device called the Jarvik-7, a totally artificial heart. This artificial heart beat steadily for 112 days—Barney Clark died on March 23, 1983 (Fox and Swazey 1992). The media heralded Dr. DeVries as a hero, a pioneer, and a superstar young surgeon. But some medical peers criticized him, and he also received death threats from people who considered implantation of an artificial heart as unnatural and an evil act (1992). The Jarvik-7 heart was used in several other implant experiments. In 1985, Dr. Jack Copeland at the University Medical Center in Tucson, Arizona, implanted another totally artificial heart called the "Phoenix heart" into a patient whose body was rejecting his newly transplanted heart. Dr. Copeland indicated that he used the artificial device to sustain the patient until a second donor heart could be obtained. Thus, an artificial heart came to be viewed as a bridge to transplants. More than 300 such implants had been performed in the United States and other countries by the end of the 1980s (1992). However, on January 11, 1990, the Food and Drug Administration (FDA), citing deficiencies in conduct of clinical trials, manufacturing quality controls, and servicing and training of personnel, withdrew its approval of the Jarvik-7 in clinical use, either as a permanent device or as a temporary bridge in patients awaiting transplants (1992).

A major breakthrough in artificial heart transplants occurred in July 2001, when surgeons at the University of Louisville implanted a self-contained artificial heart made of plastic and titanium and weighing only two pounds into a patient in his 50s who was suffering from diabetes and had a history of heart and liver problems. The device, called AbioCor, produced by AboMed Company, is operated by a small battery pack. The FDA has authorized implanting of this device into four other patients on clinical trial bases. The patient who received the first totally self-contained artificial heart was expected to live an extra month with the help of this device. However, he lived for 151 days (Cowley and Underwood 2001; Milestone for heart recipient 2001; Quest for an artificial heart 2001).

Dr. Joel Cooper of Toronto General Hospital in Canada performed the first successful single lung transplant in 1983. In 1986, he also performed the first successful double-lung transplant.

One of the most important developments in the history of organ transplants took place in 1983 when cyclosporine, a revolutionary antirejection drug, was approved for commercial use. The drug was actually discovered in the mid-1970s. The commercial use of the drug sparked a major increase in organ transplants worldwide. In recent years, the clinical use of FK 506 (tacrolimus), a new immunosuppressive drug, has generated a great deal of excitement and hope in the transplant community. However, it should be pointed out that in November of 1993, the FDA advisory committee agreed unanimously that the clinical trials had not shown that tacrolimus was safer or more effective than cyclosporine-based treatment. The committee recommended approval of tacrolimus to provide another alternative for preventing rejection of transplanted livers. The FDA in April of 1994 approved the drug FK 506 (tacrolimus) for preventing graft rejection in liver transplant patients.

Today, organ transplants are no longer viewed as experiments, and have become commonplace. They have moved from the experimental stage to the therapy stage. As organ transplants have become more successful the survival rate, as well as survival time, has also improved considerably. However, rejection of new organs by the body of a transplant recipient still remains a major medical challenge.

The 1980s also witnessed a series of groundbreaking clinical trials of tissue transplants into the brain for different disorders involving damage to the central nervous system. Despite some of the setbacks, such as the Jarvik-7, the field of organ transplants grew tremendously in the 1980s and 1990s.

Organ Transplants and Organ Donations in the United States

The number of organ transplants performed in the United States increased steadily in the 1990s. In 1999, there were a total of 21,990 organ transplants performed in the United States with kidney transplants representing the largest number. Table 3.1 demonstrates the numbers and types of organ transplants performed in the United States between 1988 and 1999.

Table 3.1

Numbers and Types of Organ Transplants Performed in the United States, 1988–1999

	1988	1989	1990	1991	1992	1993	1994	1995	1996	1997	1998	1999	Total
Kidney[a]	8,873	8,657	9,416	9,676	9,739	10,359	10,644	11,045	11,317	11,626	12,251	12,529	126,132
Kidney/ Pancreas[a]	170	334	459	452	493	661	748	918	859	853	974	1,188	8,109
Pancreas[a]	79	83	69	78	64	113	94	107	165	207	245	368	1,672
Liver	1,713	2,201	2,690	2,953	3,064	3,441	3,649	3,924	4,063	4,169	4,463	4,700	41,030
Intestine[b]			5	12	22	34	23	45	45	67	68	71	392
Heart	1,676	1,705	2,107	2,126	2,171	2,297	2,340	2,361	2,345	2,294	2,345	2,185	25,952
Lung	33	93	203	405	535	668	723	871	810	929	862	901	7,033
Heart/Lung	74	67	52	51	48	60	71	69	39	61	47	48	687
Total[a]	12,618	13,140	15,001	15,753	16,136	17,633	18,292	19,340	19,643	20,206	21,255	21,990	211,007

Source: United Network for Organ Sharing Web Site, October 2000 [http://www.unos.org].

Note: Double kidney, double lung, and heart/lung transplants are counted as one transplant. All other multi-organ transplants are being included in the total for each individual.

[a]In this table, simultaneous kidney/pancreas transplants are counted twice, both in kidney transplants and in pancreas transplants.

[b]Date on intestine transplants was not collected prior to April, 1994. At that time, information was collected retrospectively for transplants performed from January 1990 to March 1994.

Table 3.2

Patient Survival Rate for Transplants in the United States from October 1, 1987 to December 31, 1997 (in percentages)

	Patient survival rate			
	1 year	2 year	3 year	4 year
Kidney	93.7	90.9	88.1	84.9
	97.3[a]	96.0[a]	94.5[a]	93.8[a]
Pancreas	92.0	89.2	86.7	84.3
Liver	81.7	78.2	75.5	73.1
Heart	83.5	79.4	75.9	72.3
Lung	74.0	65.0	57.2	49.6

Source: United Network for Organ Sharing, 1997 Annual Report of the U.S. Scientific Registry of Transplant Recipients and the Organ Procurement and Transplantation Network.
Note: Data are based on UNOS Scientific Registry data as of September 14, 1999.
[a]Living-related donor transplant survival rate.

As can be seen from Table 3.1, the number of organ transplants performed in the United States annually increased from 12,618 in 1988 to 21,990 in 1999. Between 1988 and 1999 a total of 211,007 transplants were performed. Kidney transplants constitute the largest number among all organ transplants performed, followed by liver and heart transplants. Because of the improved transplant procedures, antirejection drugs, and improved quality of care following transplants, the survival rate among transplant recipients has also increased. Table 3.2 provides data on the patient survival rates for transplants between October 1987 and December 1997.

Among kidney transplant recipients, the four year survival rate is 93.8 percent for patients who received a kidney from a living, related donor, while for other kidney transplant recipients the survival rate is 84.9 percent. The lowest four year survival rate of 49.6 percent is among lung transplant recipients. Today, many transplant recipients live long and productive lives.

One of the major problems confronting the transplant community is the shortage of available organs for transplants, creating a long waiting list among patients. Table 3.3 shows that the number of patients registered on the national transplant waiting list increased from 16,026 in 1988 to 72,255 in 1999. In fact, the number increased steadily every year during this period. Since there are more patients than organs available for transplant, every year many patients die while they are waiting. Table 3.3 also reports on the number of patients who died while awaiting transplant. In 1999 alone, 6,000 patients died while awaiting an organ transplant. Organ donation rates have remained constant over the past several years, while the number of patients on waiting lists has continued to grow. Thus, increasing the supply of available organs for transplants in the United States is viewed as one of the major challenges within the transplant community. Later in this chapter, we discuss attempts that have been made thus far to increase organ donation rates. We also examine many policy alternatives that have been proposed as well to increase the supply of organs available for transplants.

National Government and Public Policy

The traditional definition of determining death (i.e., cessation of respiration and circulation generally observed by the absence of breath or pulse), made removal of organs from a dead person very problematic because the organs would also be dead from lack of oxygen and thus useless for transplant purposes. To remove organs when a person's circulatory system was still functioning could lead to a charge that death was caused by removal of the organs and could therefore be considered murder. Even when technology was available to artificially sustain both respiration and circulation, the problem was still present. Before organs could be removed and death could be declared, such technologies had to be withdrawn. However, removal of artificial respirators would also lead to lack of oxygen to organs making them again unusable for transplants. During this time, the vital role of a brain stem in a person's ability to breathe was not well understood, and the medical technology was not available to measure brain activities (Kurtz and Saks 1996).

To address this problem, the President's Commission for the Study of Ethical Problems in Medicine and Biomedical and Behavioral Research articulated a concept of brain death that came to be known as the "whole-brain standard" (Truog 1997). In 1981, Congress passed the Uniform Determination of Death Act that adopted this concept, and it reflected the new consensus that was reached by the medical and legal community on the definition of brain dead. The law provided that a person is considered dead when (1) an individual has sustained either irreversible cessation of circulatory and respiratory functions or (2) irreversible cessation of all functions of the entire brain, including the brain stem has occurred (Witmer and Knoppel 1996). Over the past few decades, the concept of brain death has become well established within the medical community to facilitate the procurement of transplantable organs. In recent years critics have charged that the concept of brain death is incoherent in theory and confusing in practice, and they have argued for the abandonment of the concept (Truog 1997).

In response to the public's concern over organ shortages, the Congress of the United States moved to establish a national policy regarding organ trans-

Table 3.3

Number of Registrations on the National Transplant Waiting List and the Number of Patients Removed from the Waiting List at Year End, 1988–1999

	1988	1989	1990	1991	1992	1993	1994	1995	1996	1997	1998	1999
Patients on waiting list[a]	16,026	19,095	21,914	24,719	29,415	33,394	37,684	43,937	50,130	56,716	64,423	72,255
Patients who died while on waiting list[b]	1,494	1,659	1,958	2,351	2,573	2,883	3,053	3,414	3,896	4,313	4,855	6,125

Source: United Network for Organ Sharing Web Site, October 2000 [http://www.unos.org].
[a]Data based on snapshot of the United Network for Organ Sharing (UNOS). Organ Procurement and Transplantation Network (OPTN) waiting list on the last day of each year.
[b]Data based on UNOS, OPTN Scientific Registry as of July 15, 2000.

plantation. In 1984, Congress passed the National Organ Transplant Act (NOTA) calling for the creation of a national organ-sharing and procurement system through the National Organ Procurement and Transplantation Network (OPTN) to be administered by the U.S. Department of Health and Human Services (DHHS). The law also made funds available to provide federal grants for organ procurement agencies, and it called for the development of a national scientific registry of transplant recipients and the establishment of the Task Force on Organ Transplantation (Gorsline and Johnson 1994). The act also prohibited the purchase and sale of organs in the United States. The OPTN contracted with the United Network for Organ Sharing (UNOS) to manage organ distribution and establish a scientific registry.

The UNOS is a private corporation and as such has its own bylaws and operating procedures. However, they apply only to UNOS members and not to OPTN members. Membership in UNOS is not a requirement for membership in the OPTN. The UNOS also maintains a national waiting list for organs (Witmer and Knoppel 1996). Organ procurement organizations (OPOs) coordinate the organ procurement process. Each OPO is assigned a specific service region. Once a health care provider refers a potential organ donor to the OPO, the procurement team assesses the eligibility of the potential donor, approaches the family for its consent, and organizes the retrieval of the organ. The OPO is also responsible for educating the community about organ donations and developing a good working relationship with health care practitioners in hospitals (Wrone 1999). NOTA also charged the secretary of the DHHS with the responsibility of periodically evaluating and issuing regulations concerning organ allocation and distribution policies.

The Task Force on Organ Transplantation that was charged with the responsibility of studying various issues related to organ transplants made a final report in April of 1984. The task force recommended that all medical professionals should voluntarily help identify prospective donors and contact the appropriate OPO, and required request/routine inquiry laws and accompanying protocols be implemented in all hospitals. The task force also recommended a development of a single, national system to facilitate access to organs and organ sharing (Gorsline and Johnson 1994). According to the task force, human organs that are donated for transplantation are a public trust and as such it recommended that government regulations should ensure the equitable allocation of organs among all patients and that priority should be given to those most in need based on sound medical judgment.

By 1986, the DHHS had not issued any transplant regulations so the transplant centers voluntarily followed UNOS and OPTN policies. In 1987, UNOS adopted a liver allocation policy that allocated livers on a local-regional-national basis according to several medical emergency categories. The policy included a safeguard status called UNOS/STAT for patients who had only twenty-four to forty-eight hours to live. Under this policy, a liver not needed locally could be allocated directly to the most urgent patient anywhere in the country.

Until the enactment of the Omnibus Budget Reconciliation Act of 1986, membership in the OPTN was voluntary. This new law required hospitals that perform organ transplants to be members of and abide by the rules and requirements of OPTN as a condition for participation in Medicare and Medicaid programs. However, implementation of the law was delayed till 1988 when in March of that year the DHHS published its final rules that included the requirement that Medicare/Medicaid-participating hospitals that perform transplants, and designated OPOs, must be members of and abide by the rules and requirements of OPTN. However, OPTN cannot unilaterally impose a policy that changes the terms of a national policy already subject to federal oversight.

In 1990, the language of NOTA was rewritten to require that the OPTN help organ procurement organizations in the nationwide distribution of organs equitably among transplant patients. Ironically, the same year, the UNOS board changed its liver allocation policy by eliminating UNOS/STAT. Under the new policy, the sickest patients no longer receive national priority for livers because under this policy organs are offered according to descending medical status to all patients locally, then to patients regionally and then nationally. In 1993, a U.S. General Accounting Office (GAO) report concluded that the current allocation system favored transplant centers over the needs of the patients, and the system prevents organs from going to the sickest patients or those who have been waiting a long time. This, according to GAO, was contrary to federal law.

In 1998, the secretary of the DHHS proposed new federal rules calling for the establishment of a national system in which patients would be evaluated under nationally accepted medical standards, and organs would be matched with the neediest patients around the country and not in a particular region (Brink 1998). The proposed new rules called on the transplant professionals to develop revised policies and develop criteria (1) aimed at allocating organs first to those in the highest medical urgency status and putting less reliance on geographic considerations, (2) to be followed in deciding when to put a patient on the waiting list for an organ, and (3) for determining the status of patients on the waiting list (U.S. Department of Health and Human Services 1998a). The proposed rules created a firestorm of criticisms and protest among state governments (discussed in the section on state government), and the issue became entangled in the politics of federalism. The administration's proposal was bitterly opposed by UNOS and it heavily lobbied Congress to oppose the proposed new rules (McCarthy 1999).

In October 1998, Congress delayed implementation of the final rule until October 1999 and directed the Institute of Medicine (IOM) to conduct a review of the OPTN's policies and the proposed 1998 final rule. In July 1999, IOM issued a report that basically agreed with the proposed final rule. The IOM made five recommendations that were accepted by Donna Shalala, the secretary of the DHHS. The recommendations were: (1) to establish organ allocation areas for livers because medical factors such as organ viability can affect organ allocation, (2) discontinue use of waiting time as an allocation criteria, (3) exercise federal oversight, (4) establish an independent scientific review process through the establishment of an "expert advisory panel," and (5) improve data collection and dissemination (Hussong 1999; U.S. Department of Health and Human Services 2000). The final rules, which went into effect in March of 2000, emphasized that organ sharing must take place over broader geographic areas; however, a "single national list" system is not required (HHS issues final rule 2000). In September of 2000, the secretary of DHHS, Donna Shalala, announced that in accordance with the recommendations of the IOM, mandated by Congress, an advisory committee would be formed to provide independent review and advice about revised organ allocation policies developed by the country's transplantation network (panel to be created 2000).

However, the battle over organ allocation policy has continued as states such as Wisconsin have filed a lawsuit in federal court to prevent enforcement of the new rules. The organ wars have spilled over into Congress as it has tried to craft a policy for this very sensitive issue. Two central issues in the battle are: (1) how should the nation divvy up the scarce number of organs donated for transplants, and (2) who should have the final say over what the policy should be? The House version of the bill proposes to strip all authority from the secretary of DHHS over substantive policy issues. The Senate version of the bill would force the secretary of DHHS to share the final authority with an advisory board made up of experts (Meckler 2000a). This was opposed by several senators. Senators Edward Kennedy (D-MA) and Bill Frist (R-TN) crafted a compromise proposal that called for the creation of a oversight panel and called for the broader distribution of organs suggested by the Institute of Medicine; but, the measure has been blocked in the Senate.

During the 1990s, several other initiatives were undertaken at the national level to increase organ donations in the country. In 1996, Congress passed the Organ Donation Insert Card Act. There were two main objectives of the act. The first was to raise public awareness about organ shortages and the second was to encourage people to make informed decisions together with loved ones about being a donor (Perry 1997). In December of 1997, Vice

President Al Gore and Donna Shalala, DHHS secretary, announced a new National Organ and Tissue Donation Initiative with a goal of increasing organ donation by 20 percent within two years (Fentiman 1998; Organ donations increase 1999). The major emphasis of this new initiative was to focus on overcoming the barriers to organ donation by creating a national partnership between public, private, and volunteer organizations. The main goals of the new initiative are to (1) increase consent to donation, (2) make sure that families are asked for donations, and (3) focus on research to learn more about what works, increase donation, and improve transplant outcomes (U.S. Department of Health and Human Services 1998b). In June of 1998, as part of this new initiative, DHHS also announced a new rule designed to increase organ donation by requiring hospitals to notify OPOs of all deaths. This new initiative had some impact as the number of organ donors increased in 1998. This was the first significant increase since 1995 (Sweeney 1999; Organ donations increase 1999).

In 1999, Congress passed the Organ Donor Leave Act. The law increased the amount of paid leave available to federal employees who donate organs for transplants from seven to thirty days of paid leave in addition to the annual sick leave (Statement on signing organ donor act 1999). President Bill Clinton also proclaimed the week of April 18 through April 24, 1999, National Organ and Tissue Donor Awareness Week (Proclamation 7185 1999).

State Governments and Public Policy

The Uniform Anatomical Gift Act (UAGA) of 1968 is one of the major legislations regarding organ donations. During the 1960s, shortages of organs combined with concern about existing legal restrictions to organ donations prompted momentum for reform. In 1965, the Commission on Uniform State Laws appointed a committee to study the topic of human organ and tissue donations. The National Conference of Commissioners on Uniform State Laws drafted and approved the UAGA at its conference in 1968. By the end of the year, forty-two states had adopted such laws (Gorsline and Johnson 1994). Today, all fifty states have such a law on the books. This act made it legal to donate organs of a deceased person for the purpose of transplantation. It also provided legal protection to health care professionals from potential criminal and civil liability surrounding organ procurement. This is the law that originated the organ donor cards. Furthermore, the law also outlined the order in which persons can legally consent to donation (Witmer and Knoppel 1996).

The UAGA of 1968 recognized that individuals have a legal right to determine the disposition of their bodies and others cannot veto their decision.

Any person over the age of eighteen can choose to donate any organ. If an individual has not indicated a desire to donate, family members may donate a deceased person's organs unless there is clear indication that the deceased person did not want any of his organs donated. A potential donor can make the gift of organ donation through a will or other documents such as a driver's license signed by the donor and two witnesses. The donor can also specify a specific person to receive an organ and name a specific surgeon/physician to carry out the necessary procedure. While under the law a family member may not veto a decision made by the person to donate an organ, in practice doctors, hospitals, and organ procurement organizations invariably reject organ donations unless the consent of the deceased individual's family has been obtained first. Thus, in the United States the donation of organs must be voluntary and family members must consent to the donation (Gorsline and Johnson 1994).

The failure of the UAGA to increase the supply of available organs for transplants led to the Anatomical Gift Act of 1987 that incorporated several changes, such as the requirement that two witnesses sign a donor card or other gift documents. It also included a provision describing the method for refusing a gift of an organ. In addition, the 1987 changes required that a person designated by a hospital ask a patient if he is an organ donor and, if such is the case, to ask for a copy of the organ donation document. Such a document and the patient's answers to questions must be made a part of the patient's medical records. If near the time of a patient's death, medical records do not reveal a choice about organ donation, then hospital personnel are required to discuss the option of organ donation with the patient. The law also requires that law enforcement officers, emergency rescuers, and hospitals make a reasonable search for documents or other information to determine a person's organ donation status. The 1987 changes also emphasized placing more priority on the donor's intent over family members' objections (Gorsline and Johnson 1994).

Several states formally adopted these changes, but not all did because there was significant opposition in some states regarding the loosening of authorization and consent requirements. However, faced with the problem of organ shortages, in recent years some state governments have tried new options to increase the rate of organ donations. For example, Pennsylvania became the first state to no longer require hospitals to obtain a family's consent if the deceased had an organ donor card (Organ donations: keep that liver 1999). Pennsylvania also was the first state in the nation to experiment with economic incentives to increase organ donations. The state is planning a three-year pilot program under which organ donors will receive $300 in funeral benefits (Organ donations: keep that liver 1999). However, under this program the payment will be made directly to the funeral home of the family's choice rather than the family itself. This program has drawn a great deal of criticism. Critics have charged that the payment for funeral services amounts to paid organ donation and that the program will unduly influence poor families to donate, while the decisions of the wealthy families are likely to be unaffected by the compensation (Menikoff 1999).

As we mentioned earlier, in 1998 the DHHS proposed new federal rules designed to give priority in organ distribution to medical need rather than priority based on geographic location (Henderson 1998c). Under the existing system the country is divided into sixty-three organ procurement areas or regions. An organ is offered first to the person most in need in the local area. If no one in the local area qualifies then the organ is offered to one of the eleven multistate regions and finally to the rest of the nation (Thompson 1998). Thus, under this system a patient in most medical need located across the country often has a much lower chance of receiving an organ transplant than a patient who lives closer but actually has lower medical need. In the United States a liver travels an average of 160 miles between donor and recipient, and only 10 percent of organs leave their regional distribution area. Of the 90 percent of livers remaining in the region more than half go to the least medically urgent cases. This often results in a significant variation in waiting time for patients from one state to the next. As the DHHS considered this geographic discrimination they found that the worst cases tend to collect at large, established transplant centers in cities such as New York, Pittsburgh, Dallas, and Los Angeles. With a national system, organs are more likely to reach such centers (Fighting over organs 1998). New rules were designed to create more equitable distribution of organs across the country based on medical need. Table 3.4 provides data on the number of transplants performed by states. As can be seen, states that perform the largest number of organ transplants include California, Pennsylvania, New York, Texas, Ohio, Florida, and Illinois.

The proposed new rules formulated by the DHHS created a firestorm of protest among many states. Opponents believed that the equity argument was a smoke screen. According to them, organ transplants were down considerably in big transplant centers as the number of smaller centers proliferated. The cost of transplant per patient could reach as high as $300,000. Thus, the big transplant centers were losing a considerable amount of money and that was the real motivation behind the new rules. Furthermore, opponents also pointed out that the new proposed rules could actually drive up the costs because sicker patients require more expensive follow-up care, and they also have a lower overall chance of surviving an organ transplant (Thompson 1998). Critics also charged that the change resulting from the new rules could drive smaller trans-

Table 3.4

Number of Transplants by State, 1993–1998

	1993	1994	1995	1996	1997	1998	Total
Alabama	425	423	454	457	451	482	2,692
Arizona	225	233	206	207	212	270	1,353
Arkansas	143	131	138	121	141	111	785
California	2,373	2,370	2,512	2,548	2,596	2,634	15,033
Colorado	316	265	327	299	319	335	1,861
Connecticut	162	149	182	186	191	196	1,066
Delaware	1	1	4	2	3	1	12
Florida	641	784	1,050	1,038	1,226	1,270	6,009
Georgia	440	446	444	383	454	475	2,642
Hawaii	27	36	18	38	43	46	208
Illinois	680	851	977	982	949	955	5,394
Indiana	311	322	280	298	276	308	1,795
Iowa	207	239	151	186	190	202	1,175
Kansas	106	106	126	107	115	124	684
Kentucky	247	265	282	288	269	286	1,637
Louisiana	304	403	408	363	348	368	2,194
Maine	31	47	33	31	32	50	224
Maryland	336	351	487	540	526	616	2,856
Massachusetts	543	553	559	595	595	562	3,407
Michigan	581	636	673	650	656	712	3,908
Minnesota	678	682	713	706	711	776	4,266
Mississippi	36	61	46	53	34	57	287
Missouri	556	616	594	541	598	645	3,550
Nebraska	267	262	246	243	234	248	1,500
Nevada	50	39	29	45	70	61	294
New Hampshire	27	23	26	30	20	25	151
New Jersey	219	244	277	312	337	330	1,719
New Mexico	62	76	104	108	65	85	500
New York	1,006	1,082	1,209	1,129	1,248	1,304	6,978
North Carolina	360	546	508	553	606	663	3,236
North Dakota	34	41	31	43	27	39	215
Ohio	920	922	959	961	984	1,071	5,817
Oklahoma	227	255	241	210	168	208	1,309
Oregon	242	241	233	211	227	216	1,370
Pennsylvania	1,594	1,405	1,588	1,685	1,763	1,690	9,725
Rhode Island	0	0	0	0	37	52	89
South Carolina	168	200	167	228	196	230	1,189
South Dakota	5	15	14	17	16	29	96
Tennessee	452	391	452	495	526	550	2,866
Texas	1,300	1,318	1,401	1,356	1,427	1,534	8,336
Utah	206	201	239	229	212	240	1,327
Vermont	5	17	27	25	26	22	122
Virginia	440	483	477	564	532	521	3,017
Washington	376	387	390	426	375	449	2,403
West Virginia	32	36	36	67	73	74	318
Wisconsin	661	613	678	701	714	705	4,072
Washington DC	233	238	229	221	191	254	1,366
Puerto Rico	37	32	37	25	41	71	243
Total	18,292	19,037	20,262	20,503	21,050	22,152	121,296

Source: United Network for Organ Sharing Web Site, October 2000 [http://www.unos.org].

plant programs out of business because they would have to compete directly with large transplant centers for acutely ill patients (Henderson 1998c).

Many state governments tried to oppose and prevent the adoption and implementation of the proposed rules changes. States like Louisiana that were most upset about the proposed changes had a relatively higher rate of organ donations. The attorney general of the state of Louisiana sued the DHHS over the right to retain jurisdiction over organs donated by Louisiana donors. In fact, in anticipation of the proposed rules changes, the Louisiana legislature in 1997 had already passed a law that gave residents of Louisiana first crack at organs donated within the state (Walters 1998). The state of South Carolina in 1998 had adopted a similar law. The South Carolina attorney general also threatened a lawsuit if the U.S. government sent locally donated human organs to other parts of the country (Henderson 1999d). The states of Oklahoma, Wisconsin, and Texas passed similar laws (Organ donations: keep that liver 1999; Fighting over organs 1998; State law makers approve 1999).

Transplant wars have erupted between states because the new rules have pitted organ recipient states against organ donor states. Wisconsin, fearing that new federal rules will let Chicago hospitals take a disproportionate share of donated organs, in collaboration with states such as North Dakota, South Dakota, and Minnesota, tried to exclude Illinois from a new organ-sharing network. The primary reason for this is the fact that Wisconsin has one of the nation's highest rates of organ donation, while Illinois has a relatively low rate of organ donation (Shapiro 2000; Medicine 1999).

In the summer of 1999, UNOS made some changes in the liver allocation policy based on the new federal rules, giving higher priority to patients with the most urgent medical need. The only exception is that livers must be offered first to "Status 1" patients (persons who are suddenly struck by liver disease and have a week or less to live) within the region first. This brought the transplant network closer to the philosophy of the DHHS. Preliminary research suggests that the new rules had some effect as the waiting time for the sickest liver transplant patient was reduced from five to three days (Henderson 2000b).

However, the battle over the new rules has continued since 1998. When the rules took effect in March of 2000, the DHHS ordered all hospitals in Wisconsin, as well as other hospitals across the country with organ transplant programs, to prepare for enforcement of a new system (to be phased in) for ranking patients on a transplant waiting list. This would require university hospital in Madison to ship more organs out of state. Wisconsin Governor Tommy Thompson filed a law suit against the federal government in U.S. District Court in Madison seeking an injunction to prevent enforcement of the new rules. The suit argued that the DHHS's new rules, which ordered

UNOS to send organs to more of the sickest patients regardless of where they live, would essentially strip the authority from the private agency running the nation's transplant program to decide how organs should be allocated (Milfred 2000). The state was unsuccessful in blocking the new rules because in November of 2000 the U.S. District Court dismissed Wisconsin's law suit. Ironically, President George W. Bush, who was elected to the presidency in November of 2000, named Governor Tommy Thompson to head the DHHS. As the secretary of DHHS, Tommy Thompson has the power to undo the new rule he had opposed. But, if Bush opts to continue the Clinton administration's broader sharing policy, Thompson also could find himself in the awkward position of enforcing those rules.

Courts and Public Policy

In the area of organ transplant and organ donation, the court's role thus far largely has been confined to the issue of whether property rights exist in the human body. Do property rights exist in cadavers and living organs and tissues? Such issues were not as significant in earlier centuries because parts of a dead person's body had little use for living persons since organ transplants were almost unheard of. However, with the development of immunosuppression agents to prevent organ rejections, better surgical techniques and follow-up treatment, doctors and biotechnicians have developed uses for human tissues and body parts that were inconceivable in the past. As a result, human body parts and tissues have become a very valuable commodity today.

Property Rights and the Dead Body

Under the common law the basic presumption was that there were no property rights in a dead body. However, certain court opinions did recognize that there were certain rights and duties respecting the sanctity of the body. American courts generally have rejected the idea that absolute property rights exist in the human body but at the same time, courts in general also have granted "quasi property rights" in corpses that are vested in the next of kin. However, such right is recognized as a limited right for the purposes of disposal and so forth, and the right ceases to exist after burial or cremation (Swain and Marusyk 1990). For example, in *Sanford v. Ware* (1950), the Court of Appeals in California held that although there is no property right in a commercial sense of the dead human body, the right to buy and preserve the remains is recognized and protected as a quasi property right. Similarly, in *Cohen v. Groman Mortuary, Inc.*, (1964) the California Court of Appeals found a quasi property right to the possession of a corpse for determining who had custody for burial purposes. The Missouri Court of Appeals in the case of *Rosenblum v. New Mt. Sinai Cemetery Association* (1972), held that while a person is responsible to bury a deceased person, he has no right of ownership of the corpse in the sense that the word "property" is generally used. In a broader sense of the term property, such a person does have a quasi property right for the possession and control of the body for the sole purpose of a decent burial (Gorsline and Johnson 1994). American courts in general also have recognized the right of a person to supervise the disposition of their remains by a will or through a contract. If a deceased person fails to exercise this right, their family may exercise it. Under certain circumstances, the rights of the coroners and medical examiners to examine and dissect the body may limit the right to disposition.

However, it is important to emphasize that not all courts recognize the idea of quasi property rights in the dead body. As we have discussed earlier, the amendments added to the UAGA in 1987 that several states adopted included changes designed to relax the rigid requirements of the original 1968 act. The amended UAGA granted the coroner a limited amount of discretion to procure organs for transplants and required the coroner to make reasonable efforts to notify the appropriate persons and obtain their consent for donation. However, if the coroner failed in his efforts to obtain consent, he was authorized to remove the organs or fetal tissue (O'Carroll 1996). This was somewhat equivalent to the "presumed consent" concept, that is, if reasonable efforts to obtain consent fails, one can assume consent.

There were several attempts made to challenge the constitutionality of such presumed consent provisions. In the 1985 case of *Tillman v. Detroit Receiving Hospital,* the Michigan Court of Appeals rejected the petitioner's claim of right to privacy on substantive due process ground by ruling that the privacy right ends with the death of a person to whom it is of value, and the estate or next of kin cannot claim privacy right. The presumed consent provision of Georgia's UAGA was challenged in the case of *Georgia Lions Eye Bank, Inc v. Lavant* in 1985 on the grounds that it constituted unconstitutional taking of private property. In this case, an eye bank had removed the eyes of an infant who had died of sudden infant death syndrome without notifying the parents. The Georgia Supreme Court rejected the petitioner's constitutional claim, but while it recognized that the parents had quasi property rights in the dead body, it ruled that it did not amount to constitutional protection. The Florida Supreme Court in *State v. Powell* rejected a similar challenge in 1986. The courts have also rejected a claim for interference in property rights of corpses (Powhida 1999; O'Carroll 1996).

As the above discussion indicated, the courts have been generally consistent in denying absolute individual claims to property rights in dead bodies while at the same time recognizing quasi property rights in dead bodies, largely for burial purposes. The courts had also ruled that such quasi property rights in dead bodies did not amount to the constitutional protection guaranteed in the due process clause. However, a dramatic shift was signaled in 1990 in the case of *Brotherton v. Cleveland*. In this case, the coroner had permitted the removal of a deceased person's corneas despite the fact that the deceased person's wife had explicitly rejected a request to make an anatomical gift based on the husband's aversion to such procedures. The refusal was well documented. The Sixth Circuit Court ruled that the surviving spouse had a protected property interest in her husband's corneas, and that the coroner had violated the due process protection. It further ruled that the plaintiff's interest in the body constituted a legitimate claim of entitlement protected under the due process clause (O'Carroll 1996; Powhida 1999). That same year, the same Sixth Circuit Court in the case of *Whaley v. Tuscola* (1995), involving a similar issue as in *Brotherton v. Cleveland,* held that Michigan law did provide the next of kin with a constitutionally protected interest in a deceased relative's body. In this case, a coroner's assistant who also owned and operated an eye bank, had an agreement with the hospital where he performed autopsies under which he would remove corneas and sometime entire eyeballs of the deceased without the consent of the relatives and sell them out of his eye bank. The court further ruled that the next of kin has the right to possess the body for burial and prevent its mutilation (Powhida 1999; O'Carroll 1996). If other courts hand down similar decisions regarding presumed consent provisions, it will have a significant impact on the relaxed and less rigid standards adopted in the 1987 UAGA amendments that many states had adopted.

Property Rights in Living Organs and Tissues

In the past, property rights have existed in living bodies under many different circumstances. For example, once upon a time, a woman's body was considered the property of her husband. Under the institution of slavery, ownership of another living human being was recognized as a right. In fact, under slavery a slave owner had the right to profit from a slave's body. Fortunately, such property rights are no longer recognized today and are not part of law. However, certain types of body tissues and fluids such as blood, hair, and semen are legally bought and sold in most countries, including the United States. Such practices give rise to various rights traditionally associated with property rights. Various courts are divided as to the sale of blood, for example. Is it the sale of a product or sale of a service? If blood is a product, then a hospital or a blood bank can be held liable if the blood is defective.

However, if it is classified as a service, they may not be strictly liable for defective blood (Gorsline and Johnson 1994).

Developments in biomedical technology involving human tissues are raising many new legal and ethical questions that policy makers will have to address in the future. Many of these developments allow for-profit organizations to make products such as drugs and diagnostic tools that earn them large amounts of money and profit. Thus, human tissues that once had very little monetary value now have become very valuable. This has led some to argue that perhaps some limited property rights in human body parts should be recognized (McLean 1995). Everyone, including the tissue donor, should share the profit generated from a product developed out of human tissue. However, others have argued that a property right approach to the use of human tissues could lead to serious problems. They raise concerns about the adequacy of current ordinary commercial consent procedures to protect more vulnerable members of society if a market in human body parts is permitted and about the unintended consequences, such as the potential for sacrificing safety standards for commercial profits (O'Neill 1996). Thus far, the courts have consistently refused to recognize property rights in a living human body (Swain and Marusyk 1990).

The case of *Moore v. Regents of University of California* in 1990 dealt with the issue of property rights in tissue extraction from a living human being. In this case, a patient, John Moore, was diagnosed with hairy-cell leukemia and was treated at the UCLA Medical Center. Over several years, the physician removed samples of blood, bone marrow, sperm, and skin every time Moore visited the Center for treatment with an explanation that this was necessary for his health. However, in reality the physician was removing these samples to supply them to a researcher for commercial development and was compensated for it. The patient was unaware of this. When Moore found out, he sued for conversion of his property along with a lack of informed consent, fraud, and deceit. The California Supreme Court acknowledged that since Moore had not given his informed consent, he had a valid cause of action against the physician for breach of fiduciary duty and negligence for failure to obtain consent, and his ownership rights could be vindicated through such a claim. However, the court held that Moore could not claim an ownership interest in the patented cell line and its resulting products because the patented cell line was legally and factually distinct from Moore's cells (Bergman 1992).

With the dramatic developments taking place in the field of genetics, the issue of property rights in tissue extraction is going to become even more important in the future. We examine this issue in more detail in the chapter on genetics research and health care.

Organ Procurement and Allocation: Problems

The well-publicized case of baseball legend Mickey Mantle in 1995 raised questions about how best to allocate scarce organs for transplants. Mantle was diagnosed with end-stage liver disease caused by hepatitis, liver cancer, and years of alcohol abuse. He was placed on the waiting list and after two days he underwent transplant surgery, while the average waiting period for a liver transplant was sixty-seven days. According to his doctor, Mantle did not receive any preferential treatment. Rather, it was his grave medical condition that placed him on top of the list under the policy of giving highest priority in organ allocation to those in most urgent medical need. Mickey Mantle died two months after the transplant (Carlstrom and Rollow 1997). Is giving highest priority to those who are the sickest the best way to allocate organs? Should someone else on the waiting list that was younger and had a better prognosis for longer survival have received the donated liver?

One of the problems with the current system of organ procurement and allocation is mistrust. The general public expresses a strong concern for equity and fairness in allocation of organs for transplants. This is perhaps not too surprising given the fact that organ transplants can run into hundreds of thousands of dollars depending upon the type of transplant. The general public often fears that given the high cost of organ transplants only the rich would receive such transplants. For example, in a U.S. Gallup poll, 88 percent of the respondents expressed a preference for the principle of fairness and equality in organ distribution, and 81 percent expressed the belief that medical need should be the only criteria used in selecting organ recipients and not social or economic factors (Lamb 1993). On the positive side, the cost of kidney transplants has dropped so significantly that it is cheaper to have a transplant than to stay on dialysis for more than two and a half years (Henderson 1999e).

According to published studies, another concern over the allocation of organs for transplant is that African Americans, women in general, and the poor have a harder time gaining access to some kidney transplants. For example, compared to whites, African Americans were 32 percent less likely to let it be known that they were interested in a transplant, 44 percent less likely to complete pre-transplant workup, and 50 percent less likely to move up to a waiting list and actually receive a kidney transplant (Henderson 1998f). Even though the chances of success are generally much greater if the organ comes from a person of the same race, especially with bone marrow transplants and skin grafts, few African Americans choose to donate their organs (Sabir 1996). African Americans on a kidney waiting list wait twice as long as whites for a first transplant, even when factors such as blood type, age, immunological status, and so forth, are taken into account. Some have suggested that a program of directed donation in which African Americans can donate their organs specifically for African-American recipients could ease the problem (Arnason 1991).

As far as the transplant community is concerned the most important problem today is the shortage of organs for transplants. One ironic thing with respect to organ transplants is that public opinion polls have consistently demonstrated a strong support in the American public for organ donation and willingness to donate organs for transplants, yet, in reality, only a few actually donate organs, resulting in a shortage of organs for transplants. In surveys, over 80 percent of respondents supported organ donation, and almost 70 percent indicated that they were likely to want to donate their own organs after death. Fewer than 20 percent of all Americans fill out an organ donor card or otherwise indicate their preference for organ donation prior to their death (Anderson 1995). Furthermore, half of the families that are approached at the time of a relative's death refuse to donate (Sade 1999; Price 1999; Kurtz and Saks 1996). The reasons may include stress surrounding a loved ones death, misperceptions about transplants, mistrust of the medical community, lack of understanding of the notion of brain dead, and doubts about the equity of the organ allocation system (Sade 1999).

The gap between the number of patients in need of organ transplants and the number of organs available is wide. The result is that thousands of patients in need of an organ transplant die every year while they are waiting for organs to become available for transplant (Delong 1998; Sade 1999; Price 1999).

Table 3.5 provides data on the number of living and cadaveric donors from whom organs were recovered for transplants. A comparison of the data presented in Tables 3.1, 3.3, and 3.5 reveals the nature of the problem. In 1999, there were 21,990 transplants performed in the United States (Table 3.1) while the number of donors from whom organs were recovered that year were only about half—10,505 (Table 3.5). During the same year, there were 72,255 patients on the waiting list for a transplant, and 6,125 of them passed away while waiting for an organ. As the data in these tables indicate, the number on the waiting list has increased much more rapidly than the number of donors has. Of nearly 2.4 million deaths in the United States each year, only about 10,000 to 15,000 bodies are considered medically eligible for organ recovery (Delong 1998). As can be observed from Table 3.5, of the 10,505 donors in 1999, only 4,662 were living donors, while 5,843 were cadavers.

Despite various policies implemented by the national and state governments to increase organ donations, the problem of organ shortages has persisted. Some cite barriers to efficient organ procurement as reasons for organ shortages. Some of the problems cited include OPOs lack of compliance with UNOS' guidelines, lack of coordination, financial barriers, legal issues,

Table 3.5

Cadaveric and Living Donors Recovered in the United States, 1988–1999

	Cadaveric donors recovered	Living donors recovered	Total	Percent increase from previous year
1999	5,843	4,662	10,505	3.4
1998	5,802	4,361	10,163	7.6
1997	5,476	3,972	9,448	3.5
1996	5,418	3,707	9,125	3.6
1995	5,358	3,446	8,804	7.3
1994	5,100	3,102	8,202	5.6
1993	4,861	2,904	7,765	9.5
1992	4,520	2,573	7,093	2.1
1991	4,526	2,425	6,951	4.8
1990	4,509	2,124	6,633	11.9
1989	4,011	1,918	5,929	0.4
1988	4,081	1,826	5,907	
Total	59,505	37,020	96,525	

Source: United Network for Organ Sharing Web Site [http://www.unos.org].

Note: Double kidney, double lung, and heart-lung transplants are counted as one transplant. Numbers are based on United Network for Organ Sharing Scientific Registry as of April 30, 1999.

and difficult decision-making protocols involved in organ donation (Dewar 1998).

According to Kurtz and Saks, nine factors hinder organ donations in the United States. These factors include: failure to sign written directives by individuals, failure to locate written directives by emergency personnel, uncertainty on the part of the general public about the circumstances and timing of organ recovery, failure of medical personnel to recover organs on the basis of written directives, failure to approach family members about organ donation, inefficiency on the part of organ procurement organizations to secure referrals, failure to place donated organs by organ procurement agencies, failure to communicate pronouncement of death to relatives, and failure to obtain adequate consent from family members of the deceased (Kurtz and Saks 1996). Various individuals have advocated several policy alternatives and strategies to address the problem of organ shortages. In the next section, we discuss some of the major policy proposals and examine the pros and cons of each.

Policy Proposals to Address the Problem of Organ Shortages

The current system of organ procurement in the United States is based on the principle of volunteerism and informed consent. Organ donation is viewed as a voluntary gift of life. Altruism is the primary characteristic of such a system. Upon a person's death, even when that person has expressed a desire to donate an organ either through a signed donor card, will, or other documents, the general practice is to seek the consent of the family members for donation of organs. Concerns that the current practices have failed to yield sufficient numbers of organs to match the increased demand and need have prompted discussion of various policy alternatives to increase the number of available organs for transplant. Some of the proposals are perceived as too radical to be likely to be taken seriously, while some others have been experimented on and advocated more seriously.

Conscription

Under the conscription system no person is allowed to opt out of donating an organ after death. Conscription is accomplished through the nationalization of cadavers, and harvesting of organs from all medically eligible bodies. Conscription transfers ownership and autonomy of one's body from the individual to the state. Chinese law has allowed harvesting of organs from executed prisoners since 1984 if the prisoner's body is not claimed, the prisoner has consented, or the prisoner's family has consented. In fact, executions sometimes are deliberately blundered in an effort to keep the prisoners alive until their organs can be removed (Jensen 2000). According to several reports and studies, the requirement of consent is often ignored and prisoners' executions are conveniently scheduled to meet the specific transplant needs. Experts estimate that two to three thousand organs are obtained from prisoners every year. The Chinese government has repeatedly denied allegations of such practices. However, Amnesty International and many other human rights organizations have expressed concerns about such practices and Human Rights Watch/Asia has reported existence of clear evidence of the prevalence of such practice in China (Chelala 1997).

All democratic societies find conscription, as a policy alternative to increase organ donation, simply unacceptable. Such a practice would raise serious ethical, political, and legal questions in most Western countries. To Westerners, such a policy violates in the most profound way human rights, human dignity, and the notion of individual autonomy.

Mandated Choice

As we discussed in the previous section, an overwhelming majority of Americans express support for organ donation but only about 20 percent sign organ donor cards. One suggestion to remedy the situation is the policy of mandated choice. Under such a policy, individuals would be required to state their preference regarding organ donation when they renew their driver's licenses, file income tax, or submit other legal documents required by the state. Individuals can express either their desire to donate organs or their opposition to donating their organs after their death, but they must make a choice (Dewar 1998). A central registry would keep a record of registrants' choices and the registry would be consulted when the need for organ donation arose. The reasoning behind such a policy is that it would force everyone to express their choice, and family members would be more likely to consent to organ donation if the deceased person had clearly expressed a desire. Such a system can also allow family members to concur in advance with a donor's decision, which would be binding in case the need for organ donation arises. Proponents also argue that such a policy would allow families to make deliberate decisions about organ donations in a calm atmosphere rather than in the emotionally charged atmosphere following death (Anderson 1995).

According to critics, there are several problems with the mandated choice strategy. One of the problems is that a decision made at the time of inquiry, that is, when applying for a driver's license, filing income tax, and so forth can be very different from a decision made at the time of death (Dewar 1998). Forcing people to express a choice also goes against the notion of volunteerism and individual autonomy. Perhaps more important, there is no guarantee that such a policy will increase the supply of organs because there is always the possibility that a large number of people may express their opposition to organ donation, particularly if they feel that they are forced to make a choice against their will. A strong public support will be essential for such a policy to have a chance to be successful. In a statewide poll about mandated choice methods, conducted in Texas, 80 percent of respondents opposed such a method of organ procurement because the harvesting of organs would occur for the convenience of others rather than the donor (Dewar 1998). Some persons may also fear that they will not receive full medical treatment or they may be allowed to die prematurely to recover their organs.

Rationing

Proponents of rationing organs argue that there are many goods rationed in the United States such as hunting permits, oil drilling leases, cellular phone services, and radio frequencies, among others. Price alone does not dictate the allocation of these commodities. Some other entity, such as a government agency, determines how certain limited resources will be distributed. Limited resources can be rationed in a variety of ways including lotteries, first come, first served basis, coupons, and so on (Carlstrom and Rollow 1997).

Given the fact that the need for organs is much higher than the supply of available organs for transplants, some have argued for rationing organs as the only way to address the problem. Rationing can be accomplished, according to the proponents, in a variety of ways. One alternative is to ration organs to those who had consented to be donors themselves. In other words, those who have not opted to donate organs will be disqualified from receiving an organ transplant, or at least they will be placed behind those in the waiting list who have opted to donate their organs. Proponents argue that such a system addresses the free rider problem (people who are willing to be organ recipients without being willing to be organ donors themselves), it would be fair (willingness to receive organ matched by willingness to donate organ), and it would encourage more people to become organ donors (Eaton 1998). However, there are several problems associated with such a proposal. One of the problems is that a person's lack of expressed willingness to donate an organ may be more due to inaction rather than a conscious and deliberate decision never to donate and become a free rider. Critics argue that limiting one's access to a particular treatment based on presumed moral blameworthiness is a harsh punishment. Furthermore, opponents also argue that such a policy would lead to a waste of organs due to "ineligibility" of suitable recipients, that is, one who meets all the medical criteria for an organ transplant but is considered ineligible because she has not expressed a willingness to donate organs. The matching of donor and organ recipient is not straightforward. Not every available organ is suitable for every recipient. Furthermore, obtaining the consent of children and those who are either incapable or have a diminished capacity for making autonomous decisions would be highly problematic. Transplants for children under such an arrangement would be problematic because children, due to their size, can utilize organs only from other children (Eaton 1998).

Organ Swapping/Trading

Some have argued for allowing trading or swapping of organs to increase the supply of available organs, especially with respect to kidney donations from live donors. Only about 7 percent of kidney donations from live donors come from nonrelated individuals (mainly spouses) because kidneys from nonrelated donors generally are not good matches. One of the alternatives proposed to address this problem is to allow trading of organs, that is, allowing patients to receive a well-matched kidney in exchange for a kidney donation from a spouse, relative, or a close friend that can be used by someone else. According to proponents this would increase kidney donations from both related and nonrelated sources (Carlstrom and Rollow 1997).

In the past swapping organs was deterred not only by legal and ethical concerns but also by scientific obstacles. However, progress in medical technology has given donations from living donors a boost. In the past, most organ donations came from cadavers. Less invasive laparoscopy techniques and faster recovery time, combined with better antirejection drugs, have given a momentum to the organ swap/trade movement. More doctors as well as ethicists are becoming comfortable with the idea of swapping organs as long as everyone, particularly the donor, understands what is involved. According to ethicist Robert Veatch, "Live donor swaps are acceptable, provided the donors give informed consent and the donation doesn't significantly risk shortening life" (McMenamin 2000). Some have come to view the use of such a barter approach as promising.

Critics of the organ swap/trade approach argue such an arrangement is quasi contractual, and to allow it would ultimately lead to for-profit transactions in organs, undermining the current system of organ procurement and donation that is based on the concepts of the gift of life and altruism. According to opponents, even though no money changes hand, it is nonetheless a prototypical market transaction because the only reason Recipient A receives an organ in a swap is the contractually agreed on "price" of inducing Recipient A's relative to donate a kidney to Recipient B. Current federal law criminalizes a variety of organ transfers and prohibits transfer of any human organ for value consideration (Menikoff 1999). However, some doctors are ready to challenge the prevailing view. Thus, if organ swaps were to take place, the issue is certainly likely to end up in the courts.

Change Definition of "Brain Dead"

A majority of organs for transplants come from cadavers. One factor that limits the number of organs available for transplants from dead persons is the dead donor rule. This is the ethical and legal rule that requires that donors should not be killed in order to obtain their organs. In other words, removal of organs alone cannot cause the death. This rule is at the heart of society's commitment to respect for human life (Robertson 1999).

The dead donor rule is the key factor in determination of death. As we discussed earlier, the United States and most European countries have followed the concept of "brain dead" to determine the time of death. This means that a person is declared dead when tests show that irreversible cessation of circulatory and respiratory functions have occurred or there is a cessation of all functions of the entire brain. This was the definition that was adopted for determination of death in 1981 with the passage of the Uniform Determination of Death Act. Prior to this time, cessation of respiration and circulation observed by the absence of breath and pulse was the standard used for determination of death. One reason for this change in the definition of dead in 1981 was to increase the availability of organs for transplants.

Faced still with the shortage of organs for transplants, some have proposed to change the definition of dead to the notion of "neocortical death," or what is often referred to as higher-brain death. The present definition relies on cessation of functions in the entire brain, including the brain stem. The brain stem is the portion of the brain that controls the vegetative functions such as respiration, heart rate, body temperature, blood pressure, and so forth, in the human body. The neocortex of the brain, the cerebrum, controls conscious thought, self-awareness, and the human body's interaction with the environment. According to the proponents who want to change the definition of brain dead, if the neocortex of the brain no longer functions, if a person no longer controls conscious thoughts but their brain stem still functions, why should we consider such a person alive (Anderson 1995)? According to proponents, adoption of the higher-brain dead definition would yield more transplantable organs, especially from the 15,000 to 25,000 people who currently exist in a permanent vegetative state who have functioning brain stems but little or no higher-brain function. Proponents argue that the time has come to reconsider the legal meaning of death in order to use organs from patients in a persistent vegetative state who have no possibility of recovering (Hoffenberg et al. 1997; Anderson 1995). However, opponents of this proposal see two major problems. One is that diagnosing neocortical death is not easy to do because brain scans for patients in a persistent vegetative state show severely depressed but not total absence of energy metabolism in their cortex. Such people react to sound and they can cry and smile, even though such reactions are often considered reflexive. Nonetheless, it is difficult to believe that most people would accept the notion that such individuals are dead. Another problem is that once one accepts the idea that a dead person can still have some brain function, how does one decide how much brain function must be present in determining death? In other words, the cutoff point between the dead and the nondead will be extremely difficult (Anderson 1995; Hoffenberg et al. 1997).

Another proposal is to change the dead donor rule to allow the retrieval of vital organs from anencephalic infants before they suffer whole brain death. Organs for transplants in children are in short supply since transplants in children can occur only with organs obtained from children due to the organ size factor. According to the proponents of this approach, since anencephalic infants have only a brain stem and lack consciousness, even with aggressive treatment they do not survive long. Relaxing the dead donor rule can be justified on the ethical ground of beneficence to the potential recipient and the absence of harm to the anencephalic donor (Robertson 1999). Opponents point to the fact that it is difficult to diagnose anencephaly, raise concern about the risk of mistaken diagnoses, and argue that only a small number of children would benefit. Opponents also raise fear of the slippery slope, that once an exception is made to the dead donor rule it will be easier to make other exceptions in cases of people living in a permanently vegetative state or people with severe, irreversible mental illnesses (1999).

The University of Pittsburgh Medical Center adopted a new protocol in 1993 to expand the pool of cadaveric donors. The protocol is designed for patients who want to forgo life-sustaining treatment in order to donate their organs. They can insist that their respirator be turned off, but it would have to be off long enough to cut off the supply of oxygen to the patient's brain cells, leading to brain death. However, lack of oxygen would also cause sufficient damage to vital organs to make them unusable for transplant. Under the new "Pittsburgh protocol," death is declared once the patient has experienced two minutes of cardiac arrest. According to this alternative definition, death can occur not only when the brain is dead but also when there has been "irreversible cessation of circulatory and respiratory functions." Removal of organs begins immediately after death is declared (Anderson 1995).

The opponents argue that this violates the spirit and letter of the Uniform Determination of Death Act, and heart functions can be restored well after a two-minute stoppage. Removing organs before brain death and before the circulatory system has irreversibly stopped could subject the transplant team to prosecution for murder, because the removal of organs and not turning off the respirator would be the actual cause of death (Anderson 1995).

Presumed Consent

The current system of organ donation in the United States is often referred to as a "contracting in" or "opting in" system. In such a system the law requires that donors and/or relatives must positively indicate their willingness to donate organs for transplants. One of the policy proposals to increase the supply of organs for transplants is to switch from a "contracting in" system to a presumed consent system. In a presumed consent system, it is assumed that a deceased person has consented to organ donation, that is, "opted in," unless the person, while alive, has explicitly stated their opposition to organ donation and has consciously decided to "opt out" of the system. In a strong presumed consent model, a clearly expressed will of the deceased is the sole criteria used for objection to organ removal. In a weak presumed consent model, the next of kin may also object to removal of organs (Gorsline and Johnson 1994).

Arguments in favor of the presumed consent model of organ donation include: (1) Such a system protects individual rights because persons have a chance to express their objection to organ donation through a relatively simple mechanism. (2) Relatives do not have property claims of the body of the deceased, and any claim asserted by the relatives is weaker compared to the claim of the person in need of an organ transplant (Kennedy and Sells 1998). (3) Such a system would free up the family from having to make a difficult choice under stressful circumstances. (4) The presumed consent model would produce more organs for transplants (Anderson 1995). Opponents of the presumed consent model advanced many arguments against adoption of such a system in the United States: (1) As we have discussed earlier in the chapter, several state governments adopted a presumed consent model under the amendments to the UAGA for a limited purpose, that is, a coroner's authority to remove organs under certain circumstances. Family members have challenged the validity of the strong presumed consent model. While the courts have generally upheld the constitutionality of such a program, courts in the 1990s in some cases ruled that such presumed consent practices are in violation of the due process clause of the Constitution. (2) A dramatic change in public policy could invoke such major unease that people might turn away from the whole concept of organ transplant (Kennedy and Sells 1998). (3) A strong presumed consent model could undermine faith in the U.S. health care system (Anderson 1995). (4) A widespread opposition to the presumed consent model by the general public is another possibility. Public opinion polls have already provided evidence to suggest that the general public is not very receptive to the presumed consent model. In a Gallup poll conducted in 1990, only 39 percent supported presumed consent (Dewar 1998; Anderson 1995). (5) The current system of organ procurement shows a great deal of respect for the wishes of the donor and recognizes the value of deferring to the wishes of the relatives, because they are affected the most by the death of a loved one and they are the ones who have to live with the decisions they make. A strong presumed consent model would give the state complete control over the body of the deceased at the instant of death, and such a move would be unwise (Anderson 1995). (6) In a quasi or weak presumed consent model the relatives would still have to make an emotional decision in a very stressful environment whether or not to object to organ removal (1995). (7) It will be impossible to inform all citizens and make them all aware that unless they explicitly express their objection to organ donation, it will be presumed that they have given their consent to organ donation. For a variety of reasons, people may fail to explicitly express their objections to organ donation, or fail to opt out. This will undermine the very concept of "informed" consent. Finally, there is no strong evidence to suggest that a presumed consent model will result in an increased supply of organs. The empirical evidence is mixed in several countries in Europe that have adopted presumed consent models. In fact, in recent years the trend in Europe is to move away from the presumed consent model (Gorsline and Johnson 1994; Jensen 2000). Brazil repealed the presumed consent model soon after its adoption due to strong opposition from the general public, as well as from the medical community (2000).

Financial Incentives

Another proposed alternative is to provide financial incentives to increase organ donations. Such financial incentives can take a variety of forms. For example, in return for organ donations, monetary compensation can be made in the form of cash to the donor's family, a donation to the donor's favorite charity, or a tax deduction to the survivor's family (Dewar 1998). Along this line, in 1983 H. Barry Jacobs proposed a plan for brokering human kidneys. According to the plan, his company, International Kidney Exchange Ltd., would charge between $2,000 and $5,000 for its services, the kidney recipients would pay for acquisition costs, and the kidney donors could price their kidneys up to $10,000. Many people strongly criticized the proposed plan (Gorsline and Johnson 1994). Congress passed the National Organ Transplant Act in 1984 prohibiting the sale of organs.

Another approach advocated is to establish a market in organs. Under this approach, like any other market, organ suppliers make financial payments to those who make premortem commitments to have their organs collected at death or to family members who give permission to remove organs postmortem. The difference between financial incentives and a market in organs is that in an organs market, prices for organs are determined by supply and demand. In contrast, market forces do not determine the amount paid to the organ donor under a financial incentive plan. The price is more or less set in an arbitrary manner. Markets in organs will be more efficient because the organ procurement organization will be motivated by a profit incentive. The organ procurement organizations will have incentives to procure more organs and acquire them in a cost-effective manner. In times of shortages, organ donors would benefit because procurement organizations will pay higher prices for organs (Barnett and Blair 1996).

According to proponents, markets in organs would provide many advantages. First, it will address the problem of organ shortages by increasing the supply of organs available for transplants (Epstein 1993). Second, an advantageous side effect may be to reduce human rights violations by limiting, if not eliminating, organ trade on the black market (Jensen 2000). Third, a market in organs enhances individual autonomy by letting individuals make ultimate decisions about their bodies and deemphasizes paternalism (Blumstein 1993).

Several arguments are advanced against the establishment of markets in organs. The arguments against markets in organs include the following. First, markets in organs will not increase the supply of organs (Blumstein 1993; Jensen 2000). Second, a market in organs will reduce altruism in society, and allowing people to sell their organs may diminish their respect for themselves (Gorsline and Johnson 1994; Jensen 2000). Third, a market in organs will have very negative consequences for the poor because it will induce the poor to sell their organs out of need, which itself constitutes coercion. It would lead to the exploitation of poor for the benefit of the rich who can afford to have organ transplants (Gorsline and Johnson 1994). Organs should be allocated by medical criteria only and not by financial considerations (Blumstein 1993). Markets in organs would lead to unfair allocation of organs. Fourth, matching donors and recipients will be difficult under such a system because of information and timing problems. Fifth, since the courts have ruled that only quasi property rights currently exist, selling organs would pose a major legal and constitutional challenge (1994). Sixth, according to U.S. public opinion polls, the financial incentives alternative receives the least support among the general public as a way of increasing organ supply (Dewar 1998).

Future of Organ Transplants: Human Cloning and Xenotransplantation

Medical science has advanced tremendously since the first successful transplant, and today, kidney, liver, and heart transplants have become routine. However, increases in the number of organ transplants will depend on the available supply of organs in the future. In the previous section, we examined various policy proposals to increase the supply of organs. Today, science is also working on developing alternative strategies to increase the supply of organs.

Human Cloning

One conceivable alternative is the possibility of human cloning to provide self-compatible cells or tissues for medical use, especially transplants (Savulescu

1999). Human cloning could serve as a source of stem cells that could be used in gene therapy but especially in bone marrow transplants. Cloning can also be the source of organs and tissues for transplant purposes. A recent success in the cloning of a sheep named Dolly in Great Britain has raised the possibility of human cloning. Such a possibility also has raised concerns among political leaders around the world, and many have spoken about a global moratorium on such research, particularly research into "reproductive cloning," that is, cloning to produce a fetus or live birth (Dickson 1999).

The advantages claimed for such cloning, including providing a new source for organs and tissues for transplants, freedom to make reproductive choices, freedom of scientific inquiry, gene therapy, prevention of genetic disease, and replacement of deceased loved ones, among others. The arguments presented against human reproductive cloning include potential misuse and abuse, violation of a person's individuality and autonomy, eugenic selection, safety concerns, and turning people into a means to an end (Savulescu 1999). The whole issue of genetic research and cloning is addressed in the next chapter.

Xenotransplantation

Xenotransplantation, seen by many as a potential solution to the problem of organ shortages, involves the transplantation of cells, tissues, and whole organs from one species to another. Interest in animal-to-human transplants has increased significantly in the scientific community due to shortages of human organs available for transplants (Institute of Medicine 1996). Biologists are rushing to develop farm animals as an alternative source for organs, and they envision organ farms where pigs, sheep, and other animals one day may be raised not just for their meat but also for their organs (Allen 1995). Transplantable organs include kidneys, lungs, hearts, and liver. The most promising possibility for animal-to-human organ transplant is pigs because pig and human organs are similar in size and structure (Check 2000). Pigs also are easier and cheaper to rear than baboons or chimpanzees and could provide an infinite supply of organs (Pigged out 1998). Furthermore, proponents argue that there are fewer ethical problems involved in the use of pigs because they are more distantly related to humans than other primates. Also, pigs give birth to as many as twelve piglets at a time, and they are already being slaughtered for food (Sinha 1999). Many other species are on the endangered list and could not satisfy the high demand. There are several companies racing to develop pigs for organ transplants (Fisher 1996). Only recently, for the first time, five pigs were cloned from the cells of an adult swine (Travis 2000). The FDA has decided to permit some clinical trials of pig-to-human transplants. The agency is proceeding very cautiously with significant oversight of the clinical trials. However, some have expressed concern that xenotransplantation is moving ahead too quickly (Randal 1998).

The advantages claimed for xenotransplantation include the potentially infinite supply of organs, avoidance of some of the legal and ethical questions that surrounds the use of human fetal cells, and medical benefits to be gained in treating some diseases. According to recent research, transplanting very small amounts of pig brain tissue seems to benefit some patients with severe Parkinson's disease (Seppa 2000).

Critics have argued that there are several problems associated with xenotransplantation, including the important issue of public perception. It could conflict with people's beliefs and/or ethical norms (Witt 1998). Thus, the question remains whether the public will ever accept xenotransplantation (Melton 1999). Another concern that has been expressed is the possibility that transplanting pig organs into humans would transfer or introduce new viruses into the human species. It also may compromise the human immune system. Molecular biologists are working on trying to identify potential troublesome viruses within pig DNA so they can be eliminated from the breeding herd (Lanza and Cooper 1997). Finally, the biggest challenge to the transplantation is the rejection of a graft or an organ by the recipient's immune system. The very fact that pigs are much further removed from the human species also increases the potential for rejection. In human-to-human organ transplants, new antirejection drugs have significantly increased the survival rates among recipients. However, in animal-to-human transplants, even with antirejection drugs, hyperacute rejection occurs within minutes of the grafted organ being introduced, with the host's blood and organ being starved because the blood starts to clot (Clark 1999). Currently scientists are experimenting with a variety of strategies to address this problem, including the possibility of inserting human DNA into the donor pig and fooling or tricking the recipient body into accepting the foreign organ as a human organ (Pool and Tauss 1998).

Organ Transplants, Values, and Public Policy

The field of organ transplant has come a very long way. Improved surgical techniques, better antirejection drugs, and better follow-up treatment have contributed to increased survival rates and longevity among transplant patients. Organ transplants have become routine and are increasingly viewed as legitimate medical therapy. Organ transplants have not only prolonged but saved the lives of many patients. The number of organ transplants increased significantly in the United States in the 1990s. While the number of both cadaveric and living donors has increased over the years, the number of people waiting to receive an organ transplant has also grown much more rapidly, resulting in major shortages of organs available for transplants. As a result, thousands of people die every year while waiting to receive an organ transplant. Critics have charged that the current organ procurement policy in the United States, based on voluntary donation and informed consent, has failed to produce enough organs to meet the current demand. To increase the number of organs available for transplants a variety of proposals has been advanced. As we have discussed in this chapter, each proposal carries with it claims of advantages and disadvantages. Should we follow any of these policy proposals? Would any of these alternative policy proposals eliminate the problem of organ shortages? Would increase in organ supply come at a price? Are we willing to pay that price? Answers to these questions to a great extent depend on one's view of the human body.

The scientific view of the human body has often tended to take a mechanical approach in which the human body is viewed as a set of parts that can be manipulated, analyzed, and enhanced. The field of genetics is the ultimate reflection of this view (Andrews and Nelkin 1998). Margaret Lock, an anthropologist, once described the scientific view of the human body as "reified, isolated, decontextualized, and abstracted from real time, actual location and social space" (Lock 1993, 370–371). Such a decontextualized and objectified view of the human body allows science to extract, use, manipulate, and patent body tissues without reference to the person involved. In fact, this view of the human body is often implanted among doctors from their early days of medical school. John Langone, a medical reporter who was allowed to be participant-observer in the gross anatomy class at the Harvard Medical School, provides an example. Before students started dissecting a cadaver, the head of the anatomy department said to the students,

> Do no ask the identity of the cadaver you are dissecting. They are owed their anonymity. They are paupers and professors, and it makes not a bit of difference whether we know who they were. Approach your investigation of the dead with, yes, reverence and dignity. I do not tell you this out of any belief that the body is the repository of the immortal soul, for that is a personal thing. Respect is owed, rather, on sound moral-humanistic grounds. But do not ask who they were. Their identities and their past lives make no difference and will serve no purpose. (Langone 1994, 4–5)

In other words, the anatomy lab is not a sociology class but a body shop, a site of a crash course in human demolition (Langone 1994). Thus, according to the scientific view of a human body, body parts can be extracted like a mineral, harvested like a crop, or mined like a resource. That is why, for example, the physician who patented the cell line from his California patient referred to his patient's body as a "gold mine," and pathologists referred to the collection of 50,000 blood samples at the Centers for Disease Control and Prevention as a "treasure trove" (Andrews and Nelkin 1998). Scientists point to all the medical successes that have resulted from investigation and scientific use of the human body.

The social view of the human body provides a very different perspective of the human body. According to this perspective, social conception of the human body helps establish community identification and encourages socially responsible behavior and a set of acceptable priorities for group behavior. A person's control over her body is important for the construction of the sense of well-being, to establish a sense of identity, and to convey a sense of values to others (Andrews and Nelkin 1998). That is why, even when we view the dead body of a total stranger, we do not view it simply as a collection of body parts but rather as a human being. We cannot help but wonder who he was, what kind of person he was, what kind of life he had lived, or whether he had a family, among other things.

People often express their values through their body. They display their identification with the community by the way in which they display and manipulate their bodies. Tissues such as blood and hair are important in social rituals of many cultures as well as for establishing religious identity. Different societies' burial practices also reflect community values (Andrews and Nilkin 1998). That is why some courts in recent years have begun to recognize the social view of the human body. Those who subscribe to the social view of the human body argue that without some limits placed on the research and scientific use of the human body we are headed toward social disaster.

Thus, in the modern age of biotechnology we are confronted with two often conflicting views, especially in the Western liberal democracies. On one hand, we are devoted to scientific, technological, and medical progress and our strong belief in private property, commerce, free enterprise, and personal autonomy and choice, including freedom of contract. On the other hand, is our belief in the notions of decency, propriety, sanctity of a person's bodily integrity, personal identity and human dignity. Can we strike a balance between these conflicting belief systems? Or must one view give way to the other?

We argue that we need to strike a balance between the two belief systems. What that means in the field of organ transplant is that organ procurement policies must be consistent with applicable values of protecting and promoting human dignity, personal autonomy and choice, mutual obligations, health care as a social/public good, creating and maintaining a healthy society, and a holistic approach to health care and physician training. We believe that public policy consistent with these values is the current organ procurement policy that is based on the principle of voluntarism and informed consent. Such public policy protects and promotes human dignity by respecting the worthiness of human beings, that is, dignity as intrinsic worth. Human dignity is one of the few values that philosophers agree on even though they disagree on the reasons for respecting the worthiness of human beings (Spiegelberg 1970). The concepts of volunteerism and informed consent respect individual autonomy and the emphasis on fair and equitable allocation of available organs, and recognize the principle of health care as a social/public good. Voluntary organ donation as a gift of life to another person also recognizes a sense of obligation a person feels to help others. However, such a sense of obligation is not forced on individuals. The current policy recognizes and shows respect for varying cultural and religious values in a pluralistic society such as ours. A social view of the human body promotes a holistic approach to health care, including emphasis on preventive care that can help build a healthy society.

Do living donors present a problem for the "do no harm" principle in medicine, since one can argue that a person is harmed by the loss of the relevant organ? Also, the principle of totality argues that while it is acceptable to amputate a diseased limb or organ for the good of the body as a whole, it prohibits the removal of healthy organs because it would threaten the functional integrity of the body as a whole (Lamb 1993). How can the donation of organs and tissues be justified from the living donors? Part of the answer lies in the fact that body tissues such as blood and semen are replaceable. With respect to the donation of irreplaceable organs such as kidneys, there is a strong consensus in the scientific community that the risk involved in donating a solid organ like a kidney is minimal. Furthermore, as long as a person is not coerced into donating organs, donation is strictly voluntary and is motivated by the value of altruism (and not motivated by the value of suicidal or homicidal intentions or financial gains). Thus, to provide a gift of life to another person is acceptable. In fact, many religions view such an act as the highest expression of noble virtues. However, obligatory harvesting of organs or undue pressure to donate is not justified, even if it is designed to benefit others. Thus, not only the voluntary nature of the act but also informed consent (the person donating an organ fully understands the risks and consequences) is essential (Lamb 1993). That is why live donations from minors and incompetent persons are questionable, because one cannot be sure that the donation is fully voluntary or the donor is capable of giving "informed" consent.

With respect to cadaveric donors, the principle of volunteerism and informed consent (with few exceptions such as coroner's authority) must also be maintained. A person who indicates willingness to donate an organ upon death by signing a donor card or through a will or other such document, provides for such a voluntary act and fulfills the requirement of informed consent. If a person fails to express her wishes during her lifetime, consent should be required of the next of kin. Relatives are the ones most affected by the death of loved ones, they are the ones who have to live with the decisions they make, and they are the ones who know and can most effectively articulate the values of the deceased person as well as their own values.

The various policy alternatives proposed to deal with organ shortages are unacceptable because they violate many of the values we have outlined. The policy of conscription and mandated choice goes against the values of individual autonomy and human rights. The presumed consent policy proposal appears to be designed more to fool, trick, mislead, and manipulate people into donating their organs, and there are serious questions whether, under such a system, organ donations would occur in a truly informed consent environment. Given the fact that there is a shortage of organs for transplants, rationing is inevitable. Currently, rationing is done on the basis of organs being allocated to the sickest people first. Despite some of the problems associated with this as an allocation principle, the proposal to ration organs by allocating them to only those who have pledged to donate their own organs in return, if the need arises, as a way to increase organ donation, is unacceptable because it relies on forced mutual obligation. The proposal to allow organ swapping borders on commercialization of organs. The policy proposal to change the definition of "brain dead" not only raises legal and ethical issues, but also appears to be conveniently designed for the sole purpose of making it possible to harvest more organs. Commercialization of organs and establishing a futures market in which individuals are allowed to sell their organs for money is simply a step in the further objectification of the human body. The economic language of supply, demand, contracts, exchanges, compensation, economic incentives, barter, and so forth, is founded in the economics conception of human beings as a commodity. A market in organs goes against the social view of a human body and violates the values of human dignity. But, if individuals are autonomous and free to make choices, why can they not be allowed to sell their organs? Aren't people free to decide what they want to do with their own bodies? The answer lies in the fact that individual autonomy and individual rights are not absolute, and society often places reasonable limits on such rights. Allowing individuals to sell their organs for money would violate the concept of human dignity by diminishing self-respect. For example, cannibalism—eating of human flesh, living and dead—is prohibited in almost all societies because such a practice treats the human body as mere meat, just as sales of organs would treat the human body as simply a collection of body parts to be bought and sold in a marketplace. This denies the very essence of being a human worthy of respect and dignity. Western liberal democracies, along with their belief in science and progress, also presuppose a civil society in which human beings are accorded the respect they deserve.

How, then, do we address the problem of organ shortages? First, it is important to recognize that short of conscription and forced donation on the part of all adult citizens, none of the policy alternatives discussed, including markets in organs, will meet the demand for organs. Such policies may increase the number of available organs but they will not do away with the shortages. Second, we should do more to increase the voluntary donations through outreach and education programs. Third, in the future, xenotransplantation may alleviate the problem of organ shortages, assuming the general public comes to accept the practice. Fourth, given the shortages of organs some form of rationing is inevitable. We should focus our discussion on the criteria that guide allocation of scarce organs. Fifth, science may be able to prolong life but science as yet is unable to prevent death. Thus, death is still inevitable.

As Kass has argued, biomedical science has progressed to the point where the newly dead, or not quite dead but brain dead people (i.e., neomorts) can be kept in their borderline condition through artificial respiration and circulation for a variety of medical uses. All it would require is to change the definition of death from death of the whole brain to death of the cortex, that is, higher brain dead. The technology for maintaining neomorts is already available and proposals to undertake such body farming is being discussed in private among scientists. An emporium or farms of neomorts can be used for physician training, experimentation, or drug testing, and could provide an indefinite supply of blood, marrow, skin, hormones, antibodies, and spare parts for transplants (Kass 1992). Is this the kind of future we want? We hope not.

Study Questions

1. How do different cultures and religions view organ transplants? How can public policies of different countries regarding organ transplants be classified?
2. Write an essay in which you describe the history of organ transplants. Be sure to include in your discussion some of the major developments or breakthroughs in the field of organ transplants.
3. Discuss national government's public policies regarding organ transplants in the United States. What is the "politics" of organ transplants?

4. Discuss the role of state governments in the development of organ donations and transplant policies.

5. What role have the courts played in shaping organ donation and transplant policies? How have the courts looked at issues of property rights regarding dead bodies, and living organs and tissues?

6. What are some of the major problems with respect to organ donations and allocations in the United States?

7. What are some of the proposed solutions to address the problems of organ shortages for transplants in the United States? What are the advantages and disadvantages of each proposed policy?

8. What are some of the promises and problems of xenotransplantation? Should xenotransplantation be encouraged?

9. What values, if any, should guide development of public policies in the areas of xenotransplants, stem cell research, and human cloning?

CHAPTER 4

Genetic Research and Health Care

The possibility of cloning human beings challenges Western beliefs about creation and our relationship to God. If we understand God as the Creator and creation as a completed act, cloning will be a transgression. If, however, we understand God as the Power of Creation and creation as a transformative process, we may find a role for human participation, sharing that power as beings created in the image of God. (Cohen 1999, 7)

Today we are learning the language in which God created life. We are gaining ever more awe for the complexity, the beauty, the wonder of God's most divine and sacred gift. With this profound new knowledge, humankind is on the verge of gaining immense new power to heal. (Clinton 2000)

Medical science is on the brink of making death infinitely avoidable—a lifestyle option, no less. This alone makes our era unprecedented. But the changes it will wreak are not just physical, with the prospect of all of us living to be several times great-grandparents. The spiritual consequences of effectively eternal life are immense, too. If death isn't inevitable, might religion, so much of which is rooted in the fear of death, disappear? And with it, could morals become redundant and what seemed to be the most joyous development in history end up leading us instead to a time of spiritual emptiness and misery? (Margolis 2000, 6)

God alone is the master of human life and of its integrity. (Pope John Paul II 1983)

The events of 2000 in the biological sciences, built upon more than a hundred years of research, promise to affect human life as profoundly as other scientific developments. As we entered the year 2001 some recalled the Stanley Kubrick movie, *2001 A Space Odyssey*, which was based on the book by Arthur C. Clarke. It depicted a world in which space travel was as common as going to the nearest shopping mall. But as we actually entered that year, space travel was still a far-off possibility. In 1969, man first walked on the moon; 1972 was the last time we were there.

But we will not be able to escape the implications of genetic research. It will affect our ability to withstand disabling and life-threatening diseases. It will enable us to regenerate our body parts. It will extend human life spans. It will likely enable us to reproduce ourselves. We may have truly, as President Clinton said, unlocked the book of life.

The question is what should we do with our new knowledge because, as in many areas, it can be used for good and for bad. It raises questions of public policy and personal ethics. Perhaps nowhere can this be better seen than in one area of genetic research: cloning.

Along with space travel science fiction has addressed cloning and reproductive technologies. Aldous Huxley, in *Brave New World,* told of a world of genetic engineering, where almost everyone was born in a test tube and their places in society were set for life. The movie, *The Boys from Brazil,* tells the story of refugee Nazis after World War II who try to clone a whole group of Adolph Hitlers. *Jurassic Park,* both the book by Michael Crichton and the movie directed by Steven Spielberg, tells the story of the cloning of dinosaurs. Like in other Crichton science-based novels (e.g., *Timeline*), the cloning experiment goes awry. Robert Heinlein's character Lazarus Long not only lives longer than most people but also gets cloned.

Defining Terms

Let us begin by defining some terms. DNA stands for deoxyribonucleic acid, which is the molecular structure that carries genetic information from one generation to another. A second important concept is the gene. Genes are segments of DNA that code for specific traits, more specifically the synthesis of proteins, the real workhorse of genetic transmission. Chromosomes are threadlike substances in cells that carry genetic information. There are forty-six in humans, set up in pairs, half contributed by the father and half by the mother. It is the mapping of genes on chromosomes, the studying of their functions, and their manipulation that form the heart of genetic research.

We should also understand that, in a sense, mankind has always engaged in some kind of genetic engineering (BioFact Report n.d.). The "old-fashioned" way is through natural selection. This is the basis for the theory of evolution, identified most closely with Charles Darwin. The basic idea is that over a period of time, those organisms that are the most suited or adapted to their environment will survive, what Darwin called the "survival of the fittest." Species with genes most favorable to a particular environment pass those genes on to their progeny. Evolution occurs when genetic information is imperfectly transmitted or there are genetic modifications or mutations and those are passed on to future generations.

A second type of genetic engineering might be called unnatural selection or selective breeding. This is the basis for animal husbandry. Scientists and farmers try to improve their stock or products selecting those specimens that have particularly attractive qualities, such as cows that give more milk or horses that run faster, and breed them. Classical genetics, based on the work of Gregor Mendel is based on selective breeding. Classical genetics has its bad side, eugenics, which we consider below.

The third and more scientifically based type of genetic engineering is genetic manipulation. Here scientists affect the actual genetic makeup of humans, animals, or plants to achieved desired results. Genetic manipulation has been the basis of the scientific developments that hold such promise (and terror to some).

History of Genetic Research

The history of genetic research begins with a nineteenth century Austrian monk, Gregor Mendel, who experimented with various characteristics of peas (Henig 2000). Mendel was interested in the evolution of plants and their variations. He focused on seven characteristics of peas (such as height) and manipulated them using well-developed scientific methods. Based on his research, he developed two laws of what became known as classical genetics. His first law, the law of segregation, stated that genes come in pairs, but that during reproduction they are split up, with each parent contributing half of the offspring's genetic makeup. Some genes are recessive while others are dominant. The offspring expresses the characteristics of the dominant gene. Only when the offspring has a recessive gene from both parents will that recessive characteristic be expressed. Mendel's second law, the law of independence, states that other genes do not affect genes and the expression of their characteristics.

Mendel published his work in 1866, but it was not rediscovered until 1900. By the early twentieth century, a number of human afflictions were established as inherited. It was not until the 1930s that Mendelian genetics was given a central role in evolutionary theory. Other scientists in the twentieth century undertook genetic research using fruit flies and bacteria rather than peas.

The German scientist Walter Fleming formulated the term "chromosomes" in the 1880s to describe a component of cells. In 1903, Walter Sutton, an American biologist, published a paper in which he theorized that chromosomes carry an individual's genetic makeup that can be inherited. In 1913, Sturtevant started constructing the chromosome map for fruit flies, a project finally completed in 1951.

DNA was first discovered in 1869. In the 1940s, much was learned about DNA. Genes produce enzymes that influence cells. Oswald Avery showed that DNA was the part of chromosomes that affected heredity. The search was then on to establish the structure of DNA.

This discovery was made by the American scientist James Watson and the British scientist Francis Crick (building on the largely unappreciated work of Rosalind Franklin). Their article in the April 25, 1953 issue of the British science journal *Nature* began with these understated words: "We wish to suggest a structure for the salt of deoxyribose nucleic acid (DNA). This structure has novel features which are of considerable biological interest" (quoted in Double-teaming the double helix 1998). The story of the discovery of the structure of DNA is wonderfully told by Watson in the *Double Helix* (1997).

DNA was first produced in a test tube in 1957 and by 1959 the genetic code was discovered, a series of proteins in a particular sequence. In 1972, a recombinant DNA (rDNA) molecule was produced for the first time. rDNA is the process of manipulating genetic makeup to produce a new substance (or species). A year later, an rDNA drug was approved for diabetics.

Genetic research soon produced practical applications. It has been used to develop new types of crops, such as corn seed that is highly productive and cows that produce more milk, both controversial (Tokar 2001). In the late 1980s, DNA evidence was used for the first time to convict someone of a crime. In the 1990s and 2000s, DNA evidence was used to release innocent prisoners from death row. Gene therapy has been used to cure a patient of a disease.

Genetic research, apart from the ideas discussed above, has gone in two related directions: mapping the genetic code and cloning.

The idea of completely mapping the genetic code of humans began in 1988 and picked up steam in 1990. The United States, through the National Institutes of Health (NIH), funded a project that was the equivalent of landing a man on the moon. The human genome project was a $3 billion international effort with the completion goal of 2005. In 1998, a private company, Celera, announced that it also would undertake the project and beat the publicly-funded team. In June of 2000, the groups made a joint announcement stating that they had completed the project, well ahead of schedule (though in reality, neither team had mapped the entire genome by that time) (Wade 2000b).

Perhaps the most controversial of genetic research projects is cloning, the replication of an individual using the cells of that individual. One of the original scientists behind cloning was the German Hans Spemann. In 1902, Spemann took a two-cell salamander embryo and split it apart. He was then able to grow new salamanders from each cell. Spemann found that only very early embryo cells would allow continued growth. In 1928 he transferred the nucleus of a cell to another salamander cell that did not have a nucleus and then grew it to a full-sized salamander. In 1938, Spemann wrote up the results of his decades-long research. He proposed an experiment to transfer the nucleus of a differentiated or more developed embryo into a fertilized egg without a nucleus. He also suggested the possibility of cloning from cells of adults. In 1952, Robert Briggs and Thomas J. King were able to accomplish Spemann's vision with tadpoles. The term cloning was first used in 1963 by the British scientist J.B.S. Haldane (Thinkquest.org).

Several episodes related to cloning created something of an uproar. In 1977, Karl Illmensee claimed to have cloned mice from early embryos. However, no one was able to replicate his work and Illmensee was accused of fraud, losing his research grants. In 1978, Robert Rorvik published a book, *In His Image: The Cloning of a Man,* in which he claimed that an American millionaire had had himself cloned (Kolata, 1998).

By 1984, scientists were able to accomplish cloning of mammals from embryo cells; 1996 was the breakthrough year when "Dolly" the sheep was born from udder cells of an adult sheep. In 1998, Japanese scientists announced the cloning of a calf from an adult cow. And in 2000 the possibility was raised of cloning a species near extinction to prevent that catastrophe (Zitner 2000).

Genetic Research: An International Perspective

As with many of the other health policy issues considered in this book, the international community has considered issues related to genetic research. Much research in this area has been conducted outside the United States and has raised many of the same questions. The two major areas of concern have been stem cell research and cloning. Great Britain has fairly liberal legislation, while France (with its largely Catholic religious makeup) is much more restrictive. In January 2001, for example, the British parliament adopted regulations permitting stem cell research. More specifically, they approved the use of human cloning and the use of destroyed embryos for such research (Ethicist 2001). Germany prohibits the use of embryonic stem cells (Cohen 2001).

Many nations, including the United States, have formed commissions to consider the various issues involved in such research (Knowles 2000). One problem, typical in considering legislation across a number of countries, is that important definitions differ. For example, the definition of "embryo" differs from country to country. The commissions attempted to develop a set of principles to guide their deliberations and recommendations. Many of these principles are found in U.S. legislation and regulations. These include:

- Respect for human life and dignity.
- Quality, including safety, of medical treatment.
- Respect for free and informed consent.
- Minimizing harm and maximizing benefit.
- Relief of human suffering.
- Freedom of research.
- Noncommercialization of reproduction. (Knowles 2000, H-6)

Many of the laws have *restrictions* on the use of fetal tissue. These include the *consent* of the donors, a *time limit* for the research (that is, after the embryo has developed past a certain point, it cannot be used for stem cell research), a limit on embryos used, and regulatory oversight. Also, a good argument must be made that only human embryo tissue meets the research needs (Knowles 2000).

A number of nations have placed restrictions on stem cell research or banned it completely. The European Commission's policy is to not fund such research and it has urged its member nations to not fund it either. As of August 2001 (when President George W. Bush made his decision on funding of stem cell research, see below), nine members banned it. France and Germany have actively pushed for international bans. Such research is allowed in parts of Australia and research on stem cells from placentas or umbilical cords is allowed in the People's Republic of China. Guidelines passed in Japan allow the use of research with stem cells only from embryos that would have been discarded. Singapore also allows such research (U.S. stem cell decision 2001).

The Canadian government is considering allowing stem cell research but with many of the same restrictions discussed in the United States (MacKinnon 2001). MacKinnon describes the proposed legislation:

> First, although using leftover embryos from IVF [invitro fertilization] clinics would be allowed, after that, there would be severe restrictions. No embryo could be created from donated egg and sperm just for research. And no embryo could be created by cloning. Canada isn't just proposing to ban these procedures, it wants to criminalize them with heavy fines, even jail terms. Setting up a kind of regulatory regime that research scientists just haven't seen before.

Foreign nations have agreed that some practices are unacceptable. These include human cloning for purposes of reproduction, the creation of hybrid or cross-species individuals, cross-species implantation, implantation into a woman of an embryo used in research, and commercialization (Knowles 2000).

Applications of Genetic Research

Genetic research, like much scientific research, was based on both basic scientific questions and applications. The basic scientific question, put simply, is how humans work. Genetic research focuses on the most elemental components of humans and other species. That work will continue and we will learn more about our world and ourselves. That is the basic function of science.

One intriguing finding is that scientists used to think that the human genome had as many as 120,000 genes. Announcements in 2001 suggested a much lower number, 30,000 genes. This suggests interaction among genes and the possibility of faster development of gene-based drugs, and also that much more of the genome has been patented (see below) (Pollack 2001).[1]

But applied science and technology has more practical goals: how to put the information to work to better humanity, make a profit, or both. The human genome project has led to four types of analyses to take advantage of the new knowledge and techniques (Wade 2000b). One task is to identify the genes on the genome. The second is to conduct similar inquiries on other organisms, looking for similarities that can be used to understand human genes. The third is to map the proteins. And the fourth is to compare humans to see how small changes may produce differences in disease patterns. There are five basic applications of genetic research to health care: genetic medicine, genetic therapy, genetic testing and counseling, stem cell research, and cloning. Technically, cloning is not a health issue; use of the technique will not improve the health of a sick person. On the other hand, it can, theoretically, improve the health of a community. Genetic research has much potential and much to commend it. But it also is controversial, creating important ethical issues, including what it means to be a human.

Genetic Medicine

One application of genetic medicine is to understand the causes of such human diseases as Parkinson's disease, cystic fibrosis, multiple sclerosis, and diabetes (Wilmut 1998). Scientists are searching for the genes (most likely a combination of genes) that lead to such diseases. They are also searching to discover how cells are turned on to fight diseases and repair tissue.

We should note that one very important payoff of the human genome project is that much of the research will be conducted using computers to sequence the genome, thus significantly cutting back on the time it takes to do the research. This already has started to produce results (see Chang 2000). For example, SmithKline Beecham used computer sequences to find the gene that produced an enzyme implicated in Alzheimer's disease. Another company, prior to the availability of the knowledge base derived from the human genome project, took two years to find the suspected gene (Chang 2000). Indeed, the human genome project has led to a new strategy of genetic medicine: finding a gene and exploring whether it causes a disease and then looking for ways to treat it. The older way is to start from the disease and see if there is a genetic cause for it.

As an early example of how the genome project will help foster genetic medicine and thus benefit us, consider the story told by James Shreeve (2000):

> In a briefing at the National Institutes of Health in Bethesda, Md., Dr. Klausner showed slides of cells taken from two women. The slides told identical stories: the cells in the women's lymph glands were bloated, diffuse and dividing out of control. Using the slides, the doctors had diagnosed B-cell lymphoma in both women. Both were given a 45 percent chance of survival.
>
> Then Dr. Klausner flashed a second set of images on the screen, showing what these two women's cancers looked like from the genomic perspective. Scientists conducting a research study had washed solutions containing the women's lymph cells over lymphochips, bits of glass about the size of a nickel that had been studded with thousands of short strands of DNA representing known human genes. What resulted were patterns of red and green dots, like a grid of traffic lights, revealing which genes were active and which were dormant. Neither pattern looked anything like the one seen in healthy lymph cells. But they didn't look like each other, either. Down at the molecular level, where cancer originates, the chips showed that the women actually had two quite different diseases, caused by different mutations in their genetic codes.
>
> By comparing their lymphochips with those from other cancer patients, the scientists predicted that one woman might actually have an 80 percent chance of survival; the other, a grim 20 percent. The wider meaning is that with the genome finished, researchers in other studies can now compare such patterns to begin investigating what leads cells to run amok in cancer in the first place.

This kind of knowledge will lead to the development of genetic pharmaceuticals, much more powerful, perhaps, than anything we have now (Wade 2000c). Cloning from animals could be used to make these pharmaceuticals. This is an area where the private sector is highly involved. Pharmaceutical companies, both the mainstream and the new biotechnology companies, are working on these new and powerful drugs (Lemonick 2001).

As an example of the possibilities, research is being undertaken directed at HIV (human immunodeficiency virus) and AIDS (acquired immunodeficiency syndrome) patients. While there is no vaccine for HIV, there are drugs, based on genetic research, that inhibit the virus from invading healthy cells (Park 2001). Drugs are being developed that attack only malignant tumors, as opposed to current radiation and chemotherapy modalities that kill surrounding cells as well (Brownlee 2001). Inhibitors are being developed that will delay if not suppress the development of Alzheimer's disease (Nash 2001).

An important aspect of the development of genetic medicine is the promise not only of developing more effective medicines but of doing so more quickly and cheaply. Prior to genetic research, drugs either were based on natural substances or developed in the laboratory. They were then tested on animals followed by clinical trials with humans. The results of first the animal and then clinical trials are then submitted to the Food and Drug Administration (FDA) for approval. Most drugs do not pass the animal/clinical testing stage. The time from first development of the drug to final FDA approval has taken as long as fifteen years and cost upwards of $500 million a year, though the time has been shortened to as little as five years recently. With the advent of genetically-based pharmaceuticals, the hit and miss nature of drug development is considerably reduced. "One way to do it is to limit trials to those people most likely to respond to a given drug. This too is governed by genetics" (Lemonick 2001, 63).

One of the more exciting applications of genetic medicine and pharmaceutical research is designer drugs. Such drugs are crafted toward an individual's genetic makeup, unlike broad-spectrum drugs that treat all people with the same disease in the same way. Additionally, genetic research will enable physicians to prescribe appropriate doses for individuals. In other cases, some drugs may not be used because of the impacts or side effects that they have. Genetic research will thus enable doctors to target drug use more precisely (Swint 2000).

Realizing the potential of genetic medicine will require considerably more research. The genome project needs to be completed (that is, not all genes have been mapped). More important, much more research needs to be done on proteins that act in response to genetic instructions. This new field, structural genetics, has the goal of setting forth the structure of proteins. Doing so will make it easier to design appropriate drugs. Some of the drugs used for those suffering from AIDS or HIV are based on structural genetics (Duncan 2001; Pollack 2000).

One company, Human Genome Sciences Inc., announced in September 2000 that it had successfully tested a wound-healing drug, developed first for people suffering from leg and foot ulcers. There are potential applications of the drug, a protein that encourages tissue growth, for cancer, diabetes, and other illnesses (O'Connor 2000).

A related development in genetic medicine is cloning. One possibility is the cloning of animals, creating transgenic (cross-species) animals that can produce new medications and, perhaps, body parts. Breeding such animals has, humorously, been called "pharming" (Pennisi 1998). In early 2002, two companies reported that they successfully cloned a pig (Stolberg 2002).

Genetic Therapy

> Medicine is on the brink of a new era—that of molecular genetic medicine. As in the case of previous conceptual and technical revolutions, we are witnessing the early stages of a quantum change in the way in which we understand and confront human disease. Like previous revolutions associated with the development of the sciences of human anatomy, pathology, medical pathology, microbiology, and chemical pathology, the revolution of molecular genetics is opening doors to new and definitive approaches to therapy that were previously only the stuff of dreams and scientific fantasy. This approach has come to be called "gene therapy." . . . Interestingly, the birth and evolution of gene therapy has been, if not unique, certainly one of the more unusual scientific developments in modern biomedicine. It has become a dominant concept in the treatment of disease long before it has given its first compelling evidence of true clinical effectiveness. It is, nevertheless, an established, powerful, and inexorable driving force in modern medicine. (Friedmann 1999, 1)

Of all the developments emanating from genetic research, gene therapy offers, perhaps, the most promise. As the basic science of genetic research has developed, we have learned more and more about the genetic bases of many diseases. Gene therapy offers the possibility of eliminating those diseases. Examples of diseases that are genetically-based include PKU, hemophilia, and cystic fibrosis (Laurence 1999). The therapy is then the physical repair of the faulty gene.

The science behind gene therapy is conceptually simple, though it has been difficult in practice and required several different strands of research. First, we needed the basic understanding of genetics. This began with Gregor Mendel's research in the nineteenth century. Second, it required that scientists be able to understand the specific genes that underlie the disorder. The human genome project was very helpful here. Third, there had to be some way to make the genetic correction. This was the development, at least at the present time, of recombinant DNA or rDNA. Related to this was the need to find a delivery mechanism. The most common mechanism is viruses, because of their ability to penetrate cells to their genetic makeup. The viruses are subjected to DNA manipulation, the rDNA, and injected into the cells. In the process of preparing for the therapy, the bad genes are eliminated and the good genes placed in the carrier virus (Wade 1999b). As early as the mid-1960s, scientists had determined that viruses could transmit genetic codes into another organism (Friedmann 1999b).This is not the only mechanism for gene therapy, as what has been called "naked gene transfer" may also work. But viruses remain the mechanism of choice for most of the clinical trials (see Friedmann 1999a). Finally, there had to be trials, both human and nonhuman, of the safety and efficacy of gene therapy.

By the 1980s the process of transfer had been significantly improved and by the early and mid-1990s, reports emerged of this promising technology that would offer quick results. Clinical trials involving humans, so vital in establishing safety and efficacy, began in 1989. By mid-1995, more than a thousand patients were involved in some 200 studies in the United States and abroad. But many of these studies proved disappointing in that the effectiveness of gene therapy was much more limited than the hyped promise (Friedmann 1999b).

One important development has been the interest of the private sector in gene therapy. Academic venues and the private sector will continue to work together to develop the new technology. This is because of both the massive amount of money needed to carry on trials and the implementation on a regular basis of gene therapy but also because of the creativity and risk involved in developments in this field (Friedmann 1999b). The conjoining of academia and the private sector provides both great potential and great risk.

Gene therapy is still in the clinical trial phase. As such, the trials require considerable oversight of how they are conducted. Permission and review takes place at both the local and national levels (Wivel and Anderson 1999). At the local level, permission is required from two bodies. The first is an institutional review board, which makes sure that subjects of human experimentations such as gene therapy are protected. In particular, these boards are concerned that participants or patients provide full consent to the clinical trial and that they are aware of the risks involved. The second local body, the institutional biosafety committee, is concerned with the specific use of recombinant DNA technology. At the federal level, an advisory committee within the National Institutes of Health was involved in developing guidelines and the FDA has the regulatory authority over the procedure (Wivel and Anderson 1999).

There have been mixed results in the use of gene therapy, understanding that this is in the very early stages of use. An experiment with fetal cell transplants to treat Parkinson's disease was canceled because it did not appear to help older sufferers and produced harmful side effects in younger ones (Kolata 2001). Another experiment, involving animals, successfully employed stem cell bone marrow to rebuild heart muscles and heart blood vessels (Wade 2001a). Two other animal experiments saw success with Alzheimer's-related symptoms and diabetes-related symptoms (Weiss 2001b).

Gene therapy thus has promised a great deal and delivered a bit. Thompson describes the history of clinical trials to date as high hopes combined with harsh lessons (Thompson 2000). Nevertheless, gene therapy has the potential to alleviate, limit, or eliminate a number of disorders, ranging from AIDS to cancer (the most common disease targeted for gene therapy research) to yellow fever. Clinical trials will continue under increased government supervision. And the promise of gene therapy makes it potentially one of the most important developments in the biomedical fields for the twenty-first century.

Genetic Testing and Counseling

A third, related application is in genetic testing and counseling. Knowing which gene, or genes, causes a specific disease allows for testing whether an individual's genetic makeup possesses the potential for a disease. Those with the genetic potential for disease may then be treated to make sure the potential does not actualize itself. For example, drugs can be designed to inhibit the genes from expressing their potential. Another possible alternative is gene therapy. In this case, doctors, knowing the genes that may cause the disorder, repair them so they do not produce the disorder through the instructions given to proteins. For example, there have been clinical trials of gene therapy for people suffering from hemophilia and cancer. There have been reports of the successive treatment of newborns with faulty immune systems who would otherwise have died (Kolata 2000; Stolberg 2000d). Gene therapy has been used to retard the progression of Alzheimer's disease. In one case, a woman's skin cells were modified to stimulate the growth of nerve cells and then inserted in her brain (Okie 2001).

Related to gene therapy is genetic counseling of people whose genetic makeup suggests possible future problems. Prenatal screening is one place where genetic counseling is likely to have a tremendous impact. One important aspect of genetic testing is that it is still in a primitive stage. It is likely that the interaction of multiple genes (especially given the new low estimate of the number of human genes) is responsible for particular diseases. Further, there may be an interaction between a person's genetic makeup and environment that leads to the expression of a disease or disability. The fear is that the claims for what genetic testing can do may outstrip what it can actually do. Even then, therapy is more difficult than diagnosis (see Holtzman and Shapiro 1998).

Couples seeking to have children may undergo genetic counseling to see if they possess an unfavorable genetic background. Based on this genetic testing and counseling, the couple may choose to have children and take the risk or may decide to avoid having children with the affected parent. This could lead to adoption or use of other types of reproductive technology.

Sometime in the future, it may be possible to select a genetic makeup for a child that has desired qualities, from the mundane, such as eye color, to the more specific, such as a particular ability or quality, like height or the ability to play the piano. This is, in a sense, the positive side of eugenics, which, as mentioned earlier, is already being practiced with breeding animals. There have been some attempts at doing this with humans.

In the late 1970s, concerned about the declining quality of the human gene pool and human interference with natural selection, Robert K. Graham began a gene pool, a sperm bank for Nobel Laureates. The repository closed in 1999, but some 200 children were produced as a result (Plotz 2001). Plotz asks why we should be concerned about this "experiment."

> Why shouldn't we leave it alone? Why should we want to know any more about it? Partly because it's a fascinating riddle—did it live up to its grand promise?—but also because the repository is not simply a peculiar histori-cal footnote. We are entering a new age of eugenics. Cloning is months away, not decades. It is a guide to the future. Scientists will soon be ma-nipulating embryonic genes, knocking out diseases, adding immunity, good looks, who knows what. Building better babies will soon become a sci-ence. Eugenics will be chic again (though surely not by that name). As reproductive law scholar Lori Andrews puts it, "private eugenics" has re-placed public eugenics. Almost no one subscribes to Graham's civic inter-est in improving the American "germplasm." But it has been replaced by a very widespread consumer interest: How can I improve my own child?. . .
>
> The repository and its children matter because they preview this world to come. Graham promised parents smarter, better children than they could have naturally. He used the best science of his time (sperm storage and artificial insemination) to preserve and replicate what he saw as the most valuable genes in the world. New-genics will try to do much the same thing—though more precisely, more microscopically, more scientifically. (Plotz 2001)

Two articles in the *New York Times* illustrate very nicely the use of genet-ics to improve humans. The first story (Goode 2001) tells of research into the equine genome beginning in 1995. The research could be used, as has been in at least one case, to detect a genetic defect in horses bred from a particular line. Another use of such research is to improve the quality of racehorses. As with human genetic research, trying to find the simple marker that leads to a particular trait is difficult:

> Heredity, researchers have found, appears to exert a stronger influence in determining performance in sprints, like those run by standardbred trotters, than over the longer contests typical of thoroughbred races.
>
> The genetic legacy passed on by sire and dam, however, does not translate into a single trait, but a complex mix of abilities and characteristics— speed, stamina, drive, efficiency of movement, the composition of muscle, heart, lung and limb.
>
> And there is no one biological recipe for success. Champion thoroughbreds come in all shapes and sizes. They are tall and short, stocky and slim. Some are exemplars of textbook equine conformation; others exhibit flaws that would make a veterinarian shudder. Secretariat appeared as a resplendent, muscle-bound giant. Seabiscuit, the legendary racehorse of the 1930's and the protagonist of a recent best-seller by Laura Hillenbrand, looked more like a cow pony.
>
> Few if any of the traits that combine to produce exceptional performance, scientists say, are likely to be governed by one powerful gene acting alone. Instead, they are probably influenced by many genes of smaller effect acting together.
>
> Nor are genes the whole story. Training, nutrition, expert veterinary care and a variety of other environmental influences go into transforming raw talent into victory. Thus, the chances that scientists will ever find a "speed" gene, or that individual owners will be able to use genetic screens to "buy the game," as Mrs. Chandler put it, are remote. (Goode 2001)

Three days later, the *Times* printed a story about the possibility of genetic enhancements for Olympic athletes (Longman 2001). This raises important questions that the International Olympic Committee (IOC) is only just beginning to consider. The deliberations of the IOC should be placed in the context not only of advances in genetic sciences but also efforts by the committee to ban the use of performance-enhancing drugs. Just as the FDA has jurisdiction over pharmaceuticals and has assumed jurisdiction over cloning, the two present problems to the IOC.

Questions facing the IOC and the larger society include whether genetic enhancement ought to be forbidden and whether it can used in the case of a disease or injury. Are athletes similar to race cars where you keep advancing the capabilities and technology of the machine? What if someone is the product of genetic manipulation at birth? Would, could that person be banned from competitive sports?

Of course the science of genetic manipulation is still in the early stages and the health risks and unknowns are great. Nevertheless, the potential is there. This can be seen in the announcement in early 2001 that a genetically altered rhesus monkey had been created (Genetically modified monkey created 2001). Such monkeys, much closer to humans than mice, will be injected with genes that will produce diseases such as HIV or diabetes and then experimented on to find ways to block the disease at the genetic level. Preimplantation genetic diagnosis can already be used to screen embryos for some 400 health conditions. The diagnoses can then be used to determine whether a specific embryo should be implemented in the mother. In one reported case, the mother had a genetic predisposition that would lead to the onset of Alzheimer's disease at a fairly early age. The couple wanted children but did not want to pass on the genetic condition. The embryos were screened and one without the genetic condition was successfully implanted in the mother (Krieger 2002).

Stem Cell Research

Stem cells are cells that have not differentiated and thus can continue to reproduce themselves creating lines of stem cells. The most abundant supply of stem cells is in early stage embryos, generally available from the use of reproductive technology such as in vitro fertilization. Such fertilization is designed to assist women who are having problems getting pregnant. The technologies produce an abundance of embryos, only a few of which are implanted in a woman. The rest are frozen and stored. Such cells can be induced into producing new organs or new tissues such as nerve cells (National Bioethics Advisory Commission 1999). Research on stem cells (mostly animal) dates to the early 1960s: The oldest of stem cell treatments has been the transplantation of stem cells to help produce blood in cancer patients (Chapman, Frankel, and Garfinkel 1999).

There are different types of stem cells. One, as mentioned, is embryonic cells that derive from embryos. A second type are embryonic germ and fetal stem cells from aborted fetuses. A third source is adult stem cells, from fat tissue, bone marrow, and other body tissues (Chapman, Frankel, and Garfinkel 1999). The great virtue of embryonic stem cells, apart from their ability to reproduce themselves, is that they are multipotent. That is, they can be influenced to grow into many different kinds of tissue cells, whereas adult stem cells are much more restrictive in the kinds of cells they can become. Thus, the potential for replacing worn out organs is tremendous. Apart from replacement of organs, stem cells may be used to treat diseases such as Parkinson's, Alzheimer's, cancer, and diabetes.

The major questions related to stem cell research is the source of the stem cells and whether there should be public funding for such research.

Cloning

The most advanced use of genetic research is cloning, the creation of a new being from the genetic makeup of another. The announcement in 1998 of the birth of "Dolly," a cloned sheep, set off a major eruption of concern about the implications of cloning. The method used for cloning Dolly is relatively inefficient. By 2000, scientists in the United States and Japan announced a much more efficient technique. In the case of Dolly, scientists used reproductive tissues. In the more recent case, scientists used skin cells from the ears of a bull. After allowing the cells to grow under laboratory conditions for a few months, the nuclei of the cells were removed and placed into the eggs of a cow. The nuclei of the cow cells had already been removed. The new injected cells were then placed in the uteri of cows and were successfully grown and birthed (Wade 2000a). Alexander (2001) states that the first stages of human cloning may have occurred in 1998 and 1999. Further, Alexander asserts that the technology for cloning is fairly simple. The barriers to cloning are not technological, but political and ethical. While we will discuss the ethical and policy issues below, there are some practical applications of cloning, apart from the ego-driven desire of some to preserve their genetic makeup.

Wertz (1998) describes three such scenarios. In the first scenario, the teenage son of a couple, their only child, is killed in a car accident. Because of cancer-related problems, neither parent can reproduce through natural means. Rather than make use of a donor or adopt a child, they decide to clone from themselves.

The second scenario also involves an only child who dies as a teenager. The parents decide they want another child that is as much like the lost one as possible. In this case, they have a cell from their daughter that has been stored and frozen.

The third scenario involves a genetically inherited disease. The wife's family is strewn with breast cancer. The husband comes from a family whose members live long lives. The couple decides to avoid the possibility of breast cancer by cloning from the husband, though preimplantation genetic diagnosis could also be tried.

There are other perspectives on the cloning of children who have died, such as the second scenario. Thomas Murray's (2001a) 20-year-old daughter was murdered in late 2000. He teaches medical and scientific ethics and testified before Congress in 2001 that he would never consider cloning his daughter, though he missed her greatly. "Cloning," he wrote, "can neither change the fact of death nor deflect the pain of grief." The new child might have the same genetic makeup but would grow up in different circumstances;

it would not be the same child. Murray points out that cloning technology is still relatively primitive and there are many more failures than successes. Further, even the "successes" have been incomplete, including abnormalities and premature aging. He offers a thought experiment:

> Perhaps the best way to extinguish the enthusiasm for human cloning would be to clone Michael Jordan. Michael II might well have no interest in playing basketball but instead long to become an accountant. What makes Michael I great is not merely his physical gifts, but his competitive fire, his determination, his fierce will to win. (Murray 2001a)

These exciting developments in genetic research have tremendous potential, but it may be years before that potential is realized. Consider the following timeline published by the *Chicago Tribune* on its Web site after the announcement of the completion of the genome project in June 2000:

> Possible Advances in Genetic Science
> 2002–2003: Mapping of entire human genome 100 percent complete
> 2002–2010: First tests of genetic screening against risk of cancer, diabetes, and strokes
> 2015: Medical treatments tailored to the genetic makeup of each individual available
> 2025: Doctors able to correct genetic flaws, controlling some congenital diseases
> 2050: Many diseases cured at molecular level before they arise
> Average life span reaches 90–95 years
> Increased knowledge about human population and aging genes
> (Future of genetic research 2000)

Arguments Against Genetic Research

As we have seen, the benefits of genetic research are potentially boundless. Nevertheless, each of the five areas discussed raise important questions. Some involve access to the available benefits. Others raise the possibility of discrimination and loss of insurance. Some raise questions about oversight and safety of research and clinical trials. Still others raise important and controversial ethical questions.

Genetic Medicine: Problems of Access

An important question related to genetic medicine concerns access. Because the United States lacks universal health insurance the benefits from genetic medicine may be limited to those with insurance, especially the more generous programs.

Further, as more people have become enrolled in managed care organizations (see Chapter 7), there is some doubt whether managed care will cover the new treatments. There is a tendency for such organizations not to cover what might be labeled "experimental medicine" or clinical trials. Some patients' bill of rights proposals and legislation address this issue.

Gene Therapy

Some very serious questions have been raised about gene therapy. As we saw earlier, gene therapy is still in the clinical trial phase and subject to institutional oversight, such as human subjects review committees. In the early 1970s, a human gene therapy operation occurred with two German girls suffering from a metabolic error. The operation was conducted without appropriate and vigorous scientific protocols, including follow-up, so no conclusions could be drawn about the safety or effectiveness of the therapy (Friedmann 1999b). Martin Cline of the University of California at Los Angeles conducted another gene therapy transfer in Israel and Italy. But the university's human subjects committee did not approve Cline's operation and his work was terminated (Friedmann 1999b).

In general this institutional oversight appears to have worked well. By 2000, nearly 400 studies had been conducted, involving over 4,000 people. The first documented success of gene therapy was announced in the spring of 2000. Three French infants were born with deficient immune systems. Scientists at the NIH added corrective genes to the babies that allow them to live normal lives (Kolata 2000). There also were reports in 1999 of treating hemophilia patients and rejuvenating heart cells. In the case of the hemophilia patients, a private company, Avigen Inc., and scientists at the Medical Center at Stanford University and Children's Hospital in Philadelphia were involved in the trials (Fisher 1999).

But the course of the clinical trials did not always go smoothly. Jesse Gelsinger suffered from a genetic deficiency that limited his body's ability to metabolize ammonia. He took part in a gene therapy trial that took place at the University of Pennsylvania Medical Center. In clinical trials such as this, research subjects are often divided into groups and given different dosages of the treatment to test for efficacy of the treatment as well as for safety. Gelsinger, an 18-year-old, was in the group getting the highest dosage (Wade 1999b). Jesse was told that he would not personally benefit from this first stage clinical trial, but that the trial would help test first the safety and then efficacy of the treatment. The family was, apparently, not told about problems with the procedure, a clear violation of patient consent guidelines (see Gelsinger 2000).

Gelsinger and another patient were given the highest dose of the virus (in this case, the virus that causes the common cold). In September 1999, shortly after being administered the virus, Jesse Gelsinger died. It was not clear what the cause of death was or whether the high dose of virus was the cause, though that is likely. Three other patients receiving similar treatments apparently experienced adverse side effects (Stolberg 1999). In any event, that clinical trial stopped after Gelsinger's death (Wade 1999b).

A second death during a gene therapy experiment made the news in 2000. In this case, the experiment was conducted at St. Elizabeth's Hospital in Boston by a team from Tufts University and a North Carolina company, Vascular Genetics Inc. In this trial, a gene was inserted into the patient that would make a particular type of growth factor leading to the growth of blood vessels. Additionally, another patient participating in the trial had a small tumor that became enlarged (Hilts 2000b).

What made this incident more troubling was that the death of one patient and the tumor growth in the second were not immediately reported to the FDA. The second patient, because of the tumor and history of smoking, should not have been a participant, and was not told about the presence of the tumor. The FDA sent a warning letter to the researchers in May 2000. The trial, like the University of Pennsylvania study, stopped.

Yet a third unfortunate incident came to light in early 2000. Some twenty children were given gene therapy, this time at Baylor Medical College in Houston. The virus used, the delivery mechanism, was the same one employed in the Arizona trial mentioned above. In this case, the children were suffering from brain cancer. Unlike the Arizona case, the virus may have exposed the children to hepatitis C and the AIDS viruses. Again, the FDA investigated the incident.

In still another incident, three patients died in a gene therapy experiment at Beth Israel Hospital in 1999. That incident was also not reported to the NIH. Scientists, apparently, were unaware or uncertain of the reporting requirement. In any event, Beth Israel responded to Gelsinger's death and the subsequent reaction by FDA to shut down all of the University of Pennsylvania's gene therapy trials, by closing down its trials (Hilts 2000a).

Even more disturbing was the result of a survey by the NIH. The survey asked scientists using this particular virus whether they reported adverse events. The survey found that of the 600-plus events that occurred, only thirty-nine were reported, a reporting rate of less than 6 percent (Stolberg 2000c).

Concerns raised by the reports of adverse consequences included the lack of completely informed patient consent, the failure to inform the appropriate government oversight bodies, such as the NIH's Recombinant DNA Advisory Committee (RAC) and the problems associated with commercial companies participating in the trials. RAC's role has been downgraded and reports were made to the FDA (Stolberg 2000a). For example, the Gelsingers were unaware that monkeys had died after similar treatments and that other patients had had adverse reactions to the treatment. In the case of the University of Pennsylvania clinical trials, the FDA was not informed of previous problems (Gelsinger 2000; Stolberg 2000a). Another problem is that the biotechnology field in general has spawned commercial businesses by scientists and some think this conflict of interest may distort openness about risks (Stolberg 2000a). The problems raised have caused government agencies and even one professional society to take action.

Insurance and Eugenics

As our ability develops to associate health problems and potential health problems with an individual's genetic makeup, other policy questions naturally arise. While still in an elementary stage, genetic risk assessment is becoming increasingly available. Genetic screening can point to individuals who may be at an elevated risk for an adverse health condition sometime in the future. As of February 2001, over 1,000 genetic mutations have been identified, resulting in about 1,500 disorders (Peltonen and McKusick 2001).

There are other issues to consider also. If someone has a genetic predisposition for a disease, where does health insurance fit in? There are two questions that can be raised here. The health insurance company wants to know what its potential liability is from its customers. If a subscriber is aware of a genetic problem, is there not some obligation to inform the company of that? Or should there be an obligation for all of us to undergo genetic screening? Does a health insurance company have the right to protect itself and its investors against possible future health problems (see the discussion in Longman and Brownlee 2000)?

From the standpoint of the subscriber, allowing genetic screening reports to be sent to a health insurance company could result in being turned down for insurance. Given the problems of people without health insurance (see Patel and Rushefsky 1999, Chapter 5), the consequences of such a decision would be enormous (see Cantor 2000 for a general discussion of such issues).

Perhaps worst of all is when genetic screening produces a false positive, a test result indicating the presence of certain genes when those genes or mutations are not in fact present. Then the individual faces the possibility of discrimination based on a false test. As we shall see below, public policy at both the federal and state levels have focused on this issue.

Genetic testing and counseling can lead to the unpleasant side of genetic engineering, eugenics. With eugenics the attempt is made to eliminate specimens or species that have undesirable traits. Eugenics was practiced by Nazi Germany in its attempt to eradicate Jews. In the United States, it was the basis for social Darwinism, the idea that refusing to assist poor people would lead to their disappearance and improve the "stock of humans." It forms the basis for killing mentally retarded people or at least making sure that they cannot reproduce.

The problem here is determinism, the notion that some characteristic is based solely on genetic makeup, perhaps even a single gene. This is essentially the argument of the very controversial book by Richard Herrnstein and Charles Murray (1994), *The Bell Curve.* They assert, after a very exhaustive statistical analysis, that intelligence is largely inherited and, furthermore, that intelligence differences between the races are largely genetic in character.

There are several problems with this line of research as exemplified by Herrnstein and Murray. First, there is little basis in genetic research for racial differences. At most, racial differences, so important socially, are based on about .01 percent of our genetic makeup (Angier 2000). A second problem is that while some characteristics, such as skin or eye color, are influenced by a single gene, personality characteristics, including intelligence, are affected by thousands of genes. Third, the environment influences the expression of many traits that are genetically based. For example, while there may be a single gene that determines height, a malnourished child is unlikely to realize the full potential of that gene. Intelligence, a much more complex characteristic, is likewise affected by nurturing in the early years (Angier 2000).

The Storm over Stem Cell Research

One of the most controversial issues, that welled up in 2001, relates to stem cell research. To recall, stem cells are the cells from embryos or adults that can be induced to create new organs. These organs can be used for transplants, helping to alleviate the national shortage of donor organs. Stem cells can also be used to regenerate tissue, such as nerve tissues in paraplegics or brain tissues for those suffering from Parkinson's or Alzheimer's disease.

The major source of stem cells is embryos donated by couples undergoing infertility treatment. These are then grown in laboratory conditions for about a week and the stem cells are extracted from the growing embryos (Bailey 1999). Bailey (1999, 35) describes how stem cell research and cloning might be applied to humans:

> Using cloning technology, doctors might one day take the nucleus of one of your skin cells. Put it in a human egg from which the nucleus has been

removed, and allow that cell to divide to the blastocyst stage. They would then take out the stem cells from its inner cell mass and dope them with the appropriate hormones and proteins to turn the stem cells into, say heart tissue, which could then be used to repair your ailing heart. Using your own cells in this way would mean that your immune system wouldn't reject the newly engrafted tissues, since the tissues would be a perfect match.

There are two related issues here. First is the embryo that is used, whether from one's own tissues as Bailey describes above, or from a donated embryo (the current source of most stem cells), a human? Pro-life advocates view any fertilized embryo as a human, with all the guarantees of life and liberty as any other human. Thus, they see stem cell research, in its present form, as akin to abortion. The views on abortion and stem cell research are the same. The president of the American Life League, a pro-iife organization, stated the position very clearly: "It doesn't matter if it's done in the womb or a petri dish, it's still killing" (quoted in Bailey 1999, 36). The U.S. Conference of Catholic Bishops opposes both stem cell research and the funding of such research, though many Catholics support such research (Salter 2001).

Complicating these arguments is the report in 2001 that an embryo was created expressly for the purpose of using stem cells (Zitner 2001). This is close to the case of the parents who had a child that had developed leukemia. A treatment for childhood leukemia is bone marrow transplants. But no satisfactory match could be found for the child. So the parents decided to have another child in the hope that the new child would match the older one. Here genetic research played a role. The son was conceived via in vitro fertilization and the cells from the newborn's placenta and umbilical cord were transplanted into the older child. As described, the embryos were tested and those that matched the older child but would not have leukemia were implanted. As reported in July 2001, the older child was doing better (Belkin 2001). Going even further into controversy and tying stem cell research and cloning together, researchers in Massachusetts reported that they cloned human embryos for the purpose of harvesting stem cells (Stolberg 2001b; Weiss 2001d).

Those who argue this position state that embryos from miscarriages could be used instead. There are two problems with this stance. First, miscarriages are not planned, and thus the supply of miscarried embryos for stem cell research would be random. Second, miscarriages occur because there are medical problems either with the mother or the embryo (Andrews 2000). That would not make these embryos good candidates for stem cell research.

Others see the importance of stem cell research, including the scientific community working in this field, and do not think that embryos warrant those protections. They argue that the embryos would be abandoned anyway and not come to term.

The scientific community has weighed in on the debate, arguing that the promises of stem cell research are potentially enormous. Further, reports by the National Academy of Sciences and the NIH that appeared in 2001 asserted that research on both embryonic and adult stem cells should continue and that at present the focus of research should continue on both lines, with stem cells having potentially the greater payoffs (Committee on the Biological and Biomedical Applications of Stem Cell Research 2001; National Institutes of Health 2001).

Alternative sources of stem cells are beginning to appear. A study in 2001 found that stem cells from placentas were, like embryonic stem cells, capable of transforming into other types of cells (Wade 2001b). Human fat also appears to be a good source of stem cells, though apparently not as flexible as embryonic stem cells or cells from placenta (Grady 2001). Until an alternative supply of stem cells with human applications, say from pigs or from adults, becomes readily available, human embryo stem cells will remain the source of choice.

Religions and the religious community have also weighed in, because stem cell research raises the question of when life begins (Niebuhr 2001). Jews and Muslims have what is called the "forty day rule" (Weiss 2001d). That is, according to those two religions, life does not begin until the embryo is forty days old. Under this conception (pun intended!), week old embryos (blastocysts) are not human and therefore use of those relatively undifferentiated embryos would not be forbidden. Christianity has had a mixed history of when life begins. It was not until 1588 that the Catholic Church declared that life began at conception. Three years later, a new pope rescinded this view and it remained unchanged until 1869 (Weiss 2001d). The church's position is that the embryo becomes human at conception.

There are two other issues related to stem cell research that are discussed below. The first, given the controversy over the source of embryonic stem cells, is whether the federal government should fund such research. The other is the very interesting question of who owns the stem cells and genes; this is the issue of commercialization of genetic medicine.

Arguing over Cloning

An editorial by J. Bottum (2001) in the *Weekly Standard*, a conservative publication, stated the arguments against cloning. Bottum argues that the prohibition of cloning is not just a conservative political issue. It could unite radical environmentalists, who distrust technology, with religious conservatives. Bottum then summarizes the arguments against cloning:

Those reasons range from the extraordinarily high incidence of deformity among cloned animals, to the familial confusion that will be engendered by reproducing oneself as one's own child, to the likely psychological damage to the person created by cloning, most fundamentally, to the fact that moving from the begetting of our children to the manufacture of our descendants is a radical and perhaps irreparable dehumanization.

Wachbroit (1997; see also Pence 1998) addresses many of the issues raised by Bottum (and others). For example, Wachbroit does not see the issue of familial confusion as anything to worry about or that the psychological harm that Bottum is worried about would be any different from a child growing up, say, in an impoverished family. We would not, Wachbroit says, say that the poor child should not be born.

Wachbroit points out that cloning falls between reproductive technologies such as in vitro fertilization and genetic engineering. From his perspective, genetic engineering, with its greater applications than cloning, raises more difficulties. Genetic engineering is the deliberate attempt to produce a better, or at least different, human being. Wachbroit argues that that should be our major concern.

Genetic Research and Public Policy

Policy at the National Level

Gene Therapy

Agencies in the federal government began looking at many of the issues raised by recombinant DNA studies and gene therapy. The question was how to evaluate the clinical studies and decide on their effectiveness. The agencies included two advisory committees of the NIH and the FDA, which as we saw above, have regulatory authority over medical procedures and devices. In general, oversight of gene therapy trials is conducted by the federal agencies as well as local review agencies.

All of this raises questions as to how well the FDA, which has regulatory authority, and the NIH, which has funded much of the research, were monitoring gene therapy experiments and clinical trials. NIH has advisory committees (Wivel and Anderson 1999), and the federal government has issued rules that all adverse events be reported (Stolberg 2000b). The Senate Committee on Health, Education, Labor, and Pensions subcommittee on public health held hearings in May 2000.

The American Society for Gene Therapy (ASGT) addressed the problems of the clinical trials. In December 1999, the society issued a statement supporting the "public reporting of patient adverse events in gene therapy trials" (American Society of Gene Therapy 1999). The ASGT statement, responding to the NIH proposed rule, asked for clarification of the term "adverse event" and reconciling of RAC's and FDA's definition of adverse event. ASGT also asked that patient confidentiality be protected and that a process be developed to gather, analyze, and publicize the data sent from researchers.

In response to concerns about financial conflicts of interest, ASGT issued the following statement:

> In Gene Therapy trials, as in all other clinical trials, the best interest of the patients must be always primary. International, national and institutional guidelines on standards of care must be rigorously followed, approved protocols strictly adhered to, serious adverse events promptly reported to all appropriate regulatory and review bodies. Relevant federally and institutionally established regulations and guidelines in financial conflicts must also be abided by. In addition, all investigators and team members directly responsible for patient selection, the informed consent process and/or clinical management in a trial must not have equity, stock options or comparable arrangements in companies sponsoring the trial. The American Society of Gene Therapy requests its members to abstain from or to discontinue any arrangement that is not consonant with this policy. (American Society of Gene Therapy 2000)

In December 2000, the Clinton administration proposed a set of rules that would require increased oversight of gene therapy research (Weiss 2000b). The regulations would require immediate reporting to the NIH of adverse reactions believed to be caused by the treatment, though that left it up to the researchers to decide whether the treatment might have caused the reaction. Adverse reactions not caused by the treatment would be submitted to a NIH committee as part of an annual summary report.

The next month, the Clinton administration, with three days before it left office, proposed a set of rules regulating gene therapy experiments (Weiss 2001a). The FDA proposed allowing it to issue public information about gene therapy tests and about xenotransplantation, where animal organs are transplanted into humans. The regulation would permit FDA to provide considerable information concerning the tests, such as complete description of the field trials, safety test results, copies of informed consent forms, monitoring procedures, updating safety records, and any disciplinary actions (Weiss 2001a).

Stem Cell Research

To recall, there are two major public policy issues related to stem cell research. First is the issue of the status of a frozen embryo. Is it a human life, a person entitled to all the protections available in the United States to any citizen, including the right to exist? The process of harvesting stem cells calls for the destruction of embryos. Should we neglect the value of that life to save other lives?

A related, very much intertwined, issue has to do with funding for stem cell research. Such research is expensive, and while the private sector has been heavily involved in funding research in the biotechnology area, most of the fundamental research is still funded by the public sector, largely the federal government. The major funding agency here is the NIH. The question of the nature of the stem cell research and funding are intricately tied up. If stem cells come from humans, the research should not be conducted, at least according to pro-life advocates. If that is not the case, then the funding should continue.

In 1974, Congress placed a moratorium on research involving living human fetus tissue. In 1975, the Department of Health and Human Services (DHHS), after issuing regulations concerning the protection of human research subjects (including fetuses), issued regulations that research on and the funding for research on dead fetuses was acceptable. The allowable research would still be conducted under state and local regulations, which vary dramatically (Flannery and Javitt 2000).

In 1987, NIH requested approval for the experimental transfer of fetal cells into a human brain as a means of alleviating Parkinson's disease. The response of the DHHS was to issue a moratorium on funding of such research. DHHS then convened an expert panel to consider the issue. Upon taking office in 1993, President Clinton ordered the lifting of the moratorium. Later that year, Congress passed legislation permitting the funding of transplantation of fetal tissue as long as the appropriate consents were obtained (Flannery and Javitt 2000).

In 1995, some members of Congress tried to include a rider in the DHHS appropriations bill prohibiting funding any research with human embryos. The amendment was included in legislation in 1996 and subsequent years' appropriations bills. A supplemental FY 1999 appropriations bill contained a prohibition of funding for stem cell research if the stem cells were the result of deliberate procreation (that is, created for the purpose of the research) and if the process of obtaining the cells posed undue risk. For example, the embryos could not be destroyed for the purpose of conducting the research (Flannery and Javitt 2000). Embryos that had been developed through in vitro fertilization and with the consent of the donors could be used. Opponents of the amendments argued that such prohibitions stifled critical development in this area.

In 1995, President Clinton created the National Bioethics Advisory Commission (NBAC). In November 1998, scientists at the biotechnology company Geron announced that they had extracted stem cells from human embryos. That set off a furor. Clinton asked the NBAC to examine the ethical issues (Bailey 1999; Parens 2000). The concerns expressed by the president involved policy, legal, medical, and moral issues.

Stem cell research is clearly related to one's view of when life begins (Ethicist 2000). As the NBAC report put it, the controversy over stem cell research (and especially the source of those stem cells) involves two important ethical principles: cure disease and protect human life (NBAC 1999). So to some extent, our perception of what an embryo is and what protections it should have colors our views of what sources can be used. In the United States, at least, the consensus seems to be that embryos created for the explicit purpose of research should, at the very least, not be publicly funded. But there are other sources of stem cells, say from miscarriages or discarded embryos in the course of fertilization treatment, where the appropriate stance is less clear and room for compromise exists (NBAC 1999).

The NBAC recommended that miscarried and leftover embryos from fertilization treatment be the only source of stem cells. The commission also recommended that the ban on federally funding of stem cell research be partially lifted to allow the use of discarded embryos. The commission called for full informed consent on the part of the potential donors. Related to that, the commission said that payment to potential donors should remain prohibited. Also, the commission called for a panel that would oversee federally funded stem cell research. Such a panel would review the protocols for deriving stem cells, approve stem cell lines, maintain a database of approved sources, and provide guidance for agencies that sponsor research to consider ethical issues. The NBAC also called for the supplementation of the national review by local, institutional review boards (NBAC 1999).

In January 1999, the DHHS issued a statement from the general counsel stating that because stem cells could not themselves develop into humans, they did not fit the definition contained in the congressional ban. Pro-life advocates and the National Conference of Bishops denounced the decision, and seventy members of the House of Representatives sent a protest letter to President Clinton.

The federal government also has some regulatory authority over stem cell research, especially the FDA. FDA's regulatory authority in this area derives from its authority to regulate "biological products, a drug or a medical device" (Brady, Newberry, and Girard 2000, B-4). This jurisdiction is based on several pieces of legislation, including the Food, Drug and Cosmetic Act and the Public Health Service Act (Brady, Newberry, and Girard 2000). The FDA has a regulatory process under which it approves medications, and this has been extended to include biological products. Thus these biological products have to meet the same requirements as pharmaceuticals in terms of clinical testing, safety, and so forth.

The definition of a drug under the Food, Drug and Cosmetic Act certainly includes the application of stem cell research and biological products: "articles intended for use in the diagnosis, cure, mitigation, treatment, or prevention of disease in man or other animals and articles (other than food) intended to affect the structure or any function of the body of man or other animals" (Brady, Newberry, and Girard 2000, B-7).

The FDA has no overall framework for its regulation of biological products. As part of President Clinton's reinventing government effort, the FDA announced in 1997 that it would try to develop a framework for regulation in this area that would protect public health and not stifle innovation. This framework revolved around the idea of public health and safety. Those products that posed the most risk to humans would receive the most scrutiny and regulation. Those that posed little risk would receive more cursory oversight. Implementation of the framework began in 1998. The process, which is being phased in, is supposed to ensure appropriate standards for clinical testing of the products. As with other drugs, the regulation of biological products is still carried through on a case-by-case basis, with the FDA being granted considerable discretion in carrying out its functions (Brady, Newberry, and Girard 2000).

Apart from funding by the NIH, the federal government supports stem cell research in other agencies, such as the Environmental Protection Agency (EPA) and the Department of Veterans Affairs (DVA). EPA, to take one example, uses stem cells to determine whether some chemicals cause genetic birth defects that lead to cleft palates. Research at DVA centers have, for example, studied genes that are found in children with a type of stomach cancer and compared them with genes in normal cells (Eiseman 2000). The federal government also funds tissue banks that collect and store fetal tissues that are the products of abortions. At this point, the federal government does not appear to be funding the use of stem cells that are the product of in vitro fertilization (2000).

As mentioned before, the DHHS ruled that stem cell research was not covered by the congressional ban (Meyer 2000). However, policies often change when new administrations come into office. In 1989, President George H. W. Bush continued a ban on federal funding of stem cell research. President Clinton lifted the ban and Congress has allowed it. President Bush's son, George W. Bush, took office in January 2001. He announced that he was opposed to federal funding, though not to the purpose of the research.

He was also pressured by pro-life groups to reimpose a ban. On one hand, Senator Strom Thurmond (R-SC) has supported stem cell research, because he has a daughter suffering from diabetes. Likewise, Senator Gordon H. Smith (R-OR) has a relative suffering from Parkinson's disease. He too favors stem cell research. President Bush's secretary of Health and Human Services, Tommy G. Thompson, also supports stem cell research, though he did not state a position on federal funding (Stolberg 2001a).

President Bush requested that the NIH examine stem cell research. In June 2001, NIH issued a 200-plus-page report documenting the importance of stem cell research, though not addressing the question of federal funding (McQueen 2001; NIH 2001). The report suggested that research on both embryonic and adult stem cells was necessary and that embryonic cells might present more flexibility in applications than adult stem cells.

President Bush agonized over the decision as stem cell research dominated the headlines in the spring and summer of 2001 (Chen and Zitner 2001). *Newsweek*'s July 9, 2001 cover story on the debate declared it the "stem cell wars" and "cellular divide" (Begley 2001). He held six formal meetings to discuss the issue in July and August 2001. Participants included leaders of the Right to Life Committee, the U.S. Conference of Catholic Bishops, the Juvenile Diabetes Research Foundation, bioethicists Leon Cass, Daniel Callahan, and LeRoy Walters, the president of the University of Texas M.D. Anderson Cancer Research Center, and representatives from the NIH (Seelye and Bruni 2001).

The politics of stem cell research crossed party lines. Many Republicans, like Strom Thurmond, Orrin Hatch, and Nancy Reagan (whose husband, former President Ronald Reagan, suffers from Alzheimer's disease) supported stem cell research. Sixty-one U.S. Senators sent letters to the president asking him to fund stem cell research (Alvarez 2001). Thirty members of the House of Representatives sent similar messages to the president (Thomas and Clift 2001). Yet other conservatives pressured the president to bar federal funding, if not ban some of the research (Toner 2001).

Pope Paul II became involved in the debate as well. During one of his trips to Europe, President Bush met with the Pope who asked him not to allow stem cell research to continue. This added to the pressures facing the president because he was trying to solidify the Catholic vote for Republicans in general and for his 2004 reelection campaign in particular (Simpson 2001). Indeed, religious, financial, and health interests were combining and clashing in interesting ways.

The president finally made his decision, after much public agonizing and consulting, in August 2001. In a televised speech to the nation, President Bush began in a didactic mode, explaining what stem cells are, how they are derived, and the potential benefits from such research. He also looked at the issue of when a human life begins. The president then announced his decision. Federal funding would be limited to stem cell lines that remained in fertility clinics. He stated that some sixty such lines existed throughout the world and believed they would be adequate for research purposes (Goldstein and Allen 2001). The stem cell lines were in private biotechnology companies and universities in five countries: the United States, Israel, India, Australia, and Sweden (Stolberg 2001c).

The president's decision was initially hailed as an artful compromise: permitting federal funding of stem cell research on already existing lines. Republicans on the whole supported the president's decision and while Democrats were unhappy about it, Republicans who supported federal funded, such as Orrin Hatch, accepted the decision (Chen 2001; Hook and Brownstein 2001). The public strongly supported Bush's decision, though they also thought that it was motivated by political considerations (Keen 2001).

But Bush's decision did not go uncriticized. Conservative Republicans such as Tom DeLay of Texas, the House whip, was one such critic; House Speaker Dennis Hastert of Ohio did not praise the president (Chen 2001; Hook and Brownstein 2001). Roman Catholic bishops were very critical and the Southern Baptist Convention was unhappy though quiet (2001).

The decision was also faulted from the other side, that it placed too many constraints on funding for stem cell research. Here scientists took the lead. They questioned whether the sixty stem cell lines that the president referred to were sufficient for the research that needed to be done, and there were questions about the ready availability of those sixty or so lines (Chen 2001). Some of the lines were owned by private companies, some were in other countries. Some of the lines might prove unsuitable or unsustainable. To scientists working on stem cell research, this was the equivalent of "telling mathematicians they can pursue their studies but they can never use numbers bigger than 10" (Connolly, Gillis, and Weiss 2001).

Another problem was that a University of Wisconsin foundation, the Wisconsin Alumni Research Foundation (WARF), holds a U.S. patent on embryonic cell lines, both the cells and the method of extracting them. The foundation has granted rights to a private research company, Geron Corporation. This gives both the foundation and the company intellectual property rights. The NIH began negotiating with the foundation, which indicated its willingness to facilitate stem cell research by others. But the patent does question the wide availability of stem cell lines (Stolberg 2001d).

Underlying the uneasiness of scientists about the implications of President Bush's decision was the announcement by the president during that speech that he had established the Advisory Council on Bioethics and appointed Dr. Leon Kass to head the council. Kass had been consulted by the president during the course of the decision making phase and had a great impact on the president's decision. Kass is against human cloning and the use of embryonic stem cells for research, preferring an emphasis on adult stem cells; he also opposes in vitro fertilization (Belluck 2001; Bush appoints Dr. Leon Kass 2001).

The president's decision did not end the debate over funding of stem cell research, though it did temper the debate. Both those opposed to any funding and those in favor of more expanded funding decreased their efforts, but hearings by two Senate subcommittees were still planned for September 2001 (Goldstein 2001; Kornblut 2001). Republican Senator Arlen Specter of Pennsylvania proposed legislation to permit broader stem cell research funding (Kornblut 2001).

The president was adamant that no stem cell research would be funded beyond what he would allow. Further, the administration was considering banning privately-funded stem cell research (Connolly 2001b). The administration also quickly announced that money for such research would become available in early 2002 (Stolberg 2001c).

The effort to expand federally-funded stem cell research was derailed, as were many other policy efforts such as a patients' bill of rights, by the terrorist attack of September 11. But the issue will likely resurface in 2002.

There are two interesting aspects to the controversy over stem cell research. One is the question of the nature of life and when life begins, something that pervades all genetic research. Right to life groups were now arguing that life begins at conception, even if conception takes place outside of a woman's body through in vitro fertilization. Most of the embryos produced as a result of this reproductive technology are destroyed. One estimate is that some 100,000 children were born as a result of in vitro fertilization and that about 600,000 embryos may well have been destroyed. Very few of those embryos would provide stem cells for research. Those opposed to abortion have left the fertilization process alone. But the controversy over stem cell research has raised this issue (Wade 2001c).[3]

The other interesting aspect of the stem cells debate and President Bush's decision is his consultation with bioethicists. It was mentioned above that one bioethicist the president consulted, Dr. Leon Kass, opposed cloning, stem cell research, and in vitro fertilization. Daniel Callahan, another bioethicist consulted, has made a name for himself as a strong advocate of the limits to health care (see, for example, Callahan 1995; 1998). In his 1998 book *False Hopes* Callahan argues that genetic medicine is based on a deterministic model of disease; that is, disease is a function of genetic defects and can be cured if the guilty genes are discovered. Further, he argues that modern medicine seeks to attain "perfect health." What he calls for is steady-state or sustainable medicine. By this he means, among other things, an acceptance of aging and dying. Thus, when consulted by President Bush on stem cell research, his skepticism about genetic medicine would undoubtedly have come through.

One other point needs to be made. In some ways, the Bush decision is less restrictive than the Clinton policy (Murray 2001b; Wade 2001d). This may be the great irony of stem cell research politics.

Cloning

The FDA has asserted its authority over cloning. The regulation of genetic therapy and gene transfers (including xenotransplantation, the transfer of genetic material from animals to humans) is certainly within the FDA's jurisdiction, but cloning may be another matter.

The FDA first asserted its authority shortly after the announcement of the cloned sheep Dolly in February 1997. Jurisdiction was based on a 1993 notice that the FDA had, under current law, the authority to regulate somatic cell therapy and gene therapy products (FDA 1993). FDA also has the authority to regulate drugs and devices designed to provide a diagnosis, therapy, or cure, or affect bodily functions. Under the authority of several pieces of legislation, FDA has to give preapproval for clinical trials and approval for use.

The 1997 document stated that because cloning was a tissue-based product (somatic cell nuclear transfer), it came under FDA jurisdiction (FDA 1997). In March 1997, President Clinton issued a ban on the use of federal funding for cloning.

In 1998, the FDA sent a letter informing institutional review boards (boards that review research involving human subjects) that FDA had jurisdiction over research involving cloning. Further, it said that any such research would have to be submitted as an "investigational new drug application" (Nightingale 1998). Additionally, the letter, written by FDA associate commissioner Stuart Nightingale, stated that because of questions raised about cloning, the FDA would not approve any such applications.

In March 2001, another letter was sent to the research community, again asserting FDA jurisdiction. This letter, written by Kathryn Zoon, director of the Center for Biologics Evaluation and Research, restated FDA's position:

> Clinical research using cloning technology to clone a human being is subject to FDA regulation under the Public Health Service Act and the Federal Food, Drug, and Cosmetic Act. Under these statutes and FDA's implementing regulations, before such research may begin, the sponsor of the research is required to: submit to FDA an IND [investigational new drug

application] describing the proposed research plan; obtain authorization from a properly constituted institutional review board (IRB); and obtain a commitment from the investigators to obtain informed consent from all human subjects of the research. Such research may proceed only when an IND is in effect. Since the FDA believes that there are major unresolved safety questions pertaining to the use of cloning technology to clone a human being, until those questions are appropriately addressed in an IND, FDA would not permit any such investigation to proceed. (Zoon 2001a)

The FDA's concerns, as Dr. Zoon testified before Congress in March 2001, were twofold. First, most cloning attempts fail. For example, Dolly was the 277th attempt. Second, even for those few attempts that succeeded, there were a large number of abnormalities. Safety, including that of the mother, was the focus of FDA's repeated assertion of authority (Zoon 2001b).

But FDA's authority over cloning has not gone unchallenged (Weiss 2001c). The FDA sees clones as biologic products and thus under its jurisdiction. Others suggest that this is reading too much into what a biologic product is. Further, cloning gets into issues of reproductive rights and right to life issues of cloned embryos. Several bills in Congress in 2001 would ban cloning. The legal issues remain unsettled.

If the administrative arena for dealing with these issues is complicated, the legislative arena is even more complex. As it developed through 2001, the cloning debate took three directions. "In essence, the debate over whether to clone humans has itself been cloned" (Munro and Serafini 2001, 1104).

One thread of the debate sees cloning used for reproduction purposes, for which members of Congress seem to be, by and large, opposed. The second thread of the debate is "therapeutic cloning," where embryos are cloned for research and lifesaving purposes. The third direction is the commercial use of cloning (Munro and Serafini 2001).

The politics of cloning in and around Congress are interesting. Much of the debate appears to be within the Republican Party and pro-life and pro-choice groups do not line up in an obvious way on these issues. There are a number of bills proposed to deal with cloning, though passage is uncertain.

Clearly, the cloning issue intertwines with the abortion issue. To pro-life groups, all life is sacred. Cloning has a high failure rate and even the successful ones used in therapeutic cloning results in the destruction of the embryos (Munro and Serafini 2001).

Public Opinion and Cloning

Where does the public stand on cloning? A February 2001 survey by the firm of Yankelovich Partners found the public decidedly against cloning for any reason. Ninety percent of those surveyed thought that cloning was a bad idea and 88 percent said cloning should not be allowed. Sixty-nine percent said that cloning was against God's will (Carbon copies prohibited 2001).

Those surveyed were asked why they were against cloning. Thirty-four percent said it was because of their religious beliefs, 22 percent said it "interferes with human distinctiveness and individuality," 22 percent said because cloning would be used for questionable purposes, and 14 percent said that the technology was too dangerous (Carbon copies prohibited 2001, 44).

The Courts: Whose Genes Are They?

Another issue related to genetic research has to do with commercialization and patenting (Allen 2001; Cooper 2001; Thompson 2001). The issue of patenting begins with a U.S. Supreme Court decision in 1980 that allowed General Electric to patent bacteria that eats oil. In 1991, one of the pioneers of genetic research and medicine, Craig Venter, filed a patent for DNA fragments (Allen 2001). In 1999, a company that held the patents on breast cancer genetic mutations demanded that researchers use the process that they had patented for a fee (2001).

Genetic medicine has enormous financial potential and one way to reap that potential is to make use of the patent system. Think of the profits that would be made if a drug that could prevent Alzheimer's disease came on the market. Private companies and some public organizations have been issued patents for genes or for portions of genes. This sounds like organizations or individuals are being given a patent on a portion of a human.

Hylton (2001) tells the story of John Moore who had a form of leukemia that focused on his spleen. His doctor had the spleen removed and had Moore come in for periodic follow-ups, during which he would give samples of sperm and blood. Moore was then asked by his doctor to sign a contract giving up his rights. The doctor patented the cells from Moore's spleen and sold them to a genetics research company. When Moore found out he sued, but lost the case. Hylton (2001, 105, emphasis in original) describes the results:

> But when his case went before the California Supreme Court in July of 1990, the judges weren't impressed. As far as they were concerned, Moore didn't have any right to sue Goldie [Moore's cancer doctor] for stealing his cells because the cells didn't belong to Moore in the first place. They might have come from his body, and they might have contained his DNA, but that didn't mean they were *his*. On the contrary. According to the judges, Moore's cells couldn't belong to him because if they did belong to him, then Goldie couldn't have a patent on them. "Moore's allegations that he

owns the cell line and the products derived from it are inconsistent with the patent," the majority wrote, adding the he "neither has title to the property, nor possession thereof" and concluding that "the patented cell line and the products derived from it cannot be Moore's property."

John Moore didn't own his own body.

But the reasoning behind patenting is a bit more complex. A blood sample is not patentable. But something that is produced as a result of human manipulation can be patented. That is the case for genes. Getting them requires a complex effort at isolating and then purifying the substance. The use of computer technology has made it easier to detect the genes on the genome (Cooper 2001).

Gene patenting is not the only issue. Companies are interested in patenting the proteins that are the messengers or workhorses of DNA (see Shadid 2001). On one side of the debate is a consortium of private industry and academic centers that is proposing to map the protein structures and then place them in a public database. On the other side are some small biotechnology companies that want to patent the proteins and reap the financial rewards (2001).

The patenting issue raises important policy questions (Cooper 2001; Thompson 2001). First, patenting genes, as in other areas, is an important incentive for research (Cooper 2001). It allows researchers to reap the rewards of their work. On the other hand, how the patent is used also can stifle further research. If the patent holder keeps the patented gene to itself, then the course of research may be inhibited. Further, much of the work behind the discovery was done with public funds and in publicly funded laboratories (Thompson 2001). Therefore, perhaps the patented gene ought to be made more widely available.

The government office that issues the patents is the U.S. Patent and Trademark Office (PTO). By March of 2001, PTO had issued some 1,000 patents, with another 10,000–plus pending (Thompson 2001). Thompson (2001) argues that the patent office is the only government agency regulating the industry and is unequipped for the task.

Patents can be either upstream (referring to drugs or genetics) or downstream, "the test tubes, the original cell that's torn apart to look for the genes, and the genes themselves" (Thompson 2001, 13). It is the downstream products that are of concern. This is because if a company wants to produce a drug or test, there has to be a search to see if the appropriate gene or genes have already been patented. This, Thompson points out, gives companies an incentive to patent as many genes as possible and has resulted in numerous lawsuits. Thus the development of drugs or tests is restricted.

Given both the legal and scientific chaos created and the publicly funded nature of much of the research (the Human Genome Project cost about $15 million), Thompson argues that Congress should give the PTO more authority, particularly to issue conditional patents and decide how the patents should be used. Further, he proposes that the exclusive right to the gene should be limited and that noncommercial researchers be given access to it.

An interesting application of patenting concerns Sharon and Patrick Terry (Allen 2001). They discovered that their two children had inherited a mutation from both parents that led to a disease known as pseudoxanthoma elasticum (PXE). PXE could lead to blindness and premature death. The Terrys then began to try to find out which gene was responsible for the disease. They began collecting samples of DNA of people with the disease to assist scientists in discovering the gene. The discovery came in 2000 at the University of Hawaii. The researchers applied for a patent and the Terrys were listed as codiscoverers. The Terrys' purpose was to ensure that their children and others suffering from the disease would benefit from the research and that it would not just provide profits for companies.

The States: Genetic Testing and Counseling

Public policy has begun addressing issues related to genetic counseling and testing. One issue has to do with privacy or confidentiality. The other issue has to do with discrimination against people with problematic genetic makeup (Cooper 2001). The Rehabilitation Act and Americans with Disabilities Act provide some protection, but no court decisions have been handed down yet (Jeffords and Daschle 2001). Some twenty-eight states have laws prohibiting insurance discrimination based on genetic makeup (America's next ethical war 2001; Heath 2001). The federal Health Insurance Portability and Accounting Act (HIPAA) of 1996 indirectly addresses this issue (Cooper 2001). It forbids insurance companies (including health maintenance organizations) from denying health insurance to someone with a genetic predisposition who changes jobs if that person had health insurance in the previous job. The flaw in the law is that it does not control the rates for health insurance. HIPAA also forbids discrimination against someone because his or her genetic makeup predisposes him or her to some disease unless there is evidence of the presence of the disease itself.

A bill banning genetic discrimination by employers and insurers has been proposed in the House of Representatives since 1995. In July 2001, a House subcommittee held hearings on the issue. In the Senate, Majority Leader Tom Daschle (D-SD) proposed the Genetic Non-Discrimination in Health Insurance and Employment Act. The bill, a version of which was defeated in the Senate in 2000, would prohibit insurers from denying coverage, raising premiums, or disclosing results (without permission of employee) and ban employers from using genetic research in making employment decisions. President George W. Bush supported the concept, though disagreeing about rights to sue (Heath 2001).

As with cloning, the public is clear about privacy issues and health insurance. A poll taken in 2000 found that very large majorities were against sharing genetic information with insurance companies and the government (Discrimination from gene map 2001; see also Andrews 2001). Their concerns appear to be warranted.

Some employers, a very small number, are already using genetic testing on applicants or employees. The most prominent case so far concerns the Burlington Northern Santa Fe Railway Company. In response to employees who claimed carpal tunnel syndrome, the company required genetic testing of those employees to see if they had a predisposition for the disability. If this were the case, the company might be able to claim limited or no liability. In the particular case, the company asked for blood samples but did not ask the employees for permission to do the genetic testing. In response, the Equal Employment Opportunity Commission sent a letter to the company saying it was investigating a charge of discrimination under the Americans with Disabilities Act. As with other policy areas related to genetic research, the legal issues are not settled (Lewin 2001).

One gene researcher, Craig Venter who founded the research company Celera, argues that human genome research may solve the nation's health insurance problems:

> Once we've sequenced all of our genomes, we will all be uninsurable because we all have genes in our genetic code that would indicate a propensity for some disease in the future. This is probably the single, best justification for nationalized health insurance. (Quoted in Cooper 2001, 182; see also Andrews 2001)

Genetic discrimination may also appear in the workplace. Again, if someone possesses a genetic tendency toward a health condition, that would affect an employer's health costs. Proving that the work environment did not cause the condition but that the genetic makeup was at fault could save the employer considerable money. Screening people for specific (or even general) genetic predispositions can result in discrimination. Thirteen states have enacted legislation forbidding such discrimination (Oregon, Arizona, Texas, Iowa, Missouri, Wisconsin, Illinois, Michigan, North Carolina, Rhode Island, Vermont, New Hampshire, and Maine) (Cooper 2001).

States also have addressed stem cell research. Twenty-six states have passed legislation explicitly regulating stem cell research (see Table 4.1).

State legislatures, in deciding how and whether to engage in such regulation, consider four broad areas: the source of the cells, the extent of parental informed consent, privacy issues, and commercialization (Andrews 2000). States differ drastically in what is allowed. For example, as Table 4.1 shows, nine states ban research on embryos developed in the laboratory (in vitro fertilization). Some of the laws also might apply to cloning (2000). Some federal courts have looked at state bans and declared them unconstitutional, largely because they were too vague (2000). There are also state and federal laws prohibiting women who donate fetal tissue from specifying who the recipient will be.

Another concern is privacy. For fetal tissue to be acceptable for research or transplantation, the tissue must be tested to ensure it does not carry genetic defects or genes that may lead to a disease. Thus, information about the parents would also be known. A few states address this issue.

Commercialization is one of the more troubling issues. A number of states (see Table 4.1) ban payment for embryos. There is also model legislation, known as Uniform Anatomical Gift Acts, that virtually all of the states have adopted in one form or another. The legislation was originally designed to prohibit the sale or commercialization of organs, such as kidneys. It has been applied to stem cell research. The laws basically forbid women from getting pregnant to donate the embryo tissue in return for payment (Andrews 2000).

Genetic Research, Values, and Public Policy

Advances in genetics are leading to changes in how we view humans and how biomedical research is conducted. Peltonen and McKusick (2001) argue that we are experiencing a paradigm shift in this complex field. We have discussed some of these changes, such as the new focus on proteins and the requirement of keeping track of those with genetic susceptibility to diseases. Much work is still necessary in this still infant field (2001). Peltonen and McKusick indicate some of the implications of genetic research for health care:

> We are rapidly advancing upon the postgenomic era in which genetic information will have to be examined in multiple health situations throughout the lives of individuals. Currently, newborn babies can be screened for treatable genetic disease. . . . Perhaps in the not-so-distant future, children at high risk for coronary artery disease will be identified and treated to prevent changes in their vascular walls during adulthood. Parents will have

the option to be told their carrier status for many recessive diseases before they decide to start a family. For middle-aged and older populations, we will be able to determine risk profiles for numerous late-onset diseases, preferably before the appearance of symptoms, which at least could be partly prevented through dietary or pharmaceutical interventions. In the near future, the monitoring of individual drug response profiles with DNA tests throughout life will be standard practice. Soon, genetic testing will comprise a wide spectrum of different analyses with a host of consequences for individuals and their families—an issue worth emphasizing when explaining genetic testing to the public. (Peltonen and McKusick 2001, 1229)

Not everyone looks so fondly on genetic research. One of the most powerful arguments urging caution about these new developments has been made by Andrews (2001). For example, she argues that genetic testing leads to many important privacy concerns (see Chapter 5 of this volume) and the possibility and realization of discrimination. She notes that everyone has at least five genetic defects and thus is at risk of losing health insurance if genetic testing takes place. This, she argues, as mentioned above, might be one of the strongest arguments for health insurance.

Andrews (2001) also notes that the quality of laboratory testing, counseling, and medical education dealing with genetic testing and counseling needs to be much higher than it is. She warns us about genetic determinism, that genes can account for all human health and behavioral disorders and that the promise of genetic medicine outstrips the reality.

Genetic research is perhaps the most complex of the areas discussed in the book, with its five different dimensions: medicine, therapy, counseling and testing, stem cell research, and cloning. It should be no surprise, therefore, that the seven values necessary for a healthy republic are important in this area.

The first value is protecting and promoting human dignity wherever possible. Genetic research raises important questions about the nature of life and what it means to be a person. Genetic medicine can lead to a deterministic view of life, that we are merely the result of our genetic makeup. But humans are more than just the sum of their genes. The environment plays an important role in our health and well-being, in interaction with our genes. The genome project, it has been declared, is the book of life, as if once we have completely explored all the intricacies of the genome we will know all there is to know about life, health, and death. Maybe a better metaphor is that the genome is an index rather than the book. It is where we can begin to find out what it means to be human.

The element of genetic research that clearly raises the question of the

Table 4.1

Bans Under the Embryo and Fetal Research Laws and Abortion Laws by State

	IVF embryo research banned	Research on dead aborted conceptus banned	Research on dead aborted conceptus okay with woman's permission	Bans payment for IVF embryos for research	Bans payment for IVF embryos for any purpose	Bans payment for aborted embryos for any purpose
Alabama						
Alaska						
Arizona		*				
Arkansas			*			*
California						
Colorado						
Connecticut						
Delaware						
District of Columbia						
Florida	*				*	
Georgia					*	*
Hawaii						
Idaho						
Illinois					*	
Indiana		*				*
Iowa						
Kansas						
Kentucky						
Louisiana	*				*	
Maine	*				*	
Maryland						
Massachusetts	*		*	*		
Michigan		*		*	*	
Minnesota	*				*	
Mississippi						
Missouri						*
Montana						
Nebraska						
Nevada						*
New Hampshire						
New Jersey						
New Mexico						
New York						
North Carolina						
North Dakota	*	*		*		*
Ohio		*				*
Oklahoma		*				
Oregon						
Pennsylvania	*		*		*	
Rhode Island	*		*		*	

South Carolina				
South Dakota	*			
Tennessee		*		*
Texas			*	
Utah			*	*
Vermont				
Virginia				
Washington				
West Virginia				
Wisconsin				
Wyoming				

Source: Lori Andrews. 2000. "State Regulation of Embryo Stem Cell Research." P.A.B in National Bioethics Advisory Commission. (2000). Rockville, MD: National Bioethics Advisory Commission.

Notes: IVF is *in vitro fertilization* or created in a laboratory. Conceptus is a fertilized egg, embryo, or fetus.

dignity of humans is the issue of patenting stem cells and genetic material. The patent system was created to allow researchers to reap the harvest of their work. But their work consists of elements of humans.

Additionally, there are privacy and discrimination concerns that states and, to a lesser extent, the federal government, have addressed. Genetic testing and counseling can be important, but if it reveals a genetic defect and that defect becomes known, the consequences can be harmful to the person.

Genetic testing and counseling have the potential to lead to eugenics. Eugenics, by definition, downgrades the dignity of those who do not meet one's criteria of perfection. Should those shown to have genetic defects be prevented from being born? How serious would the genetic defects have to be to make that kind of decision? Is society willing to pay the costs of treating the severely disabled newborns?

The second value is the right of access to adequate health care. This value plays out in several different directions. The major problem is that the United States does not have a system of universal health insurance coverage. Loss of coverage because of genetic makeup is simply not an issue in countries with such a system. So this value strongly supports antidiscrimination laws. Further, as mentioned above, if we all possess some genetic defects, then either no one should get coverage because of what might be a a an expensive preexisting condition, or everyone should be covered. We are all in the same boat.

A related point is that the benefits of genetic medicine will be given to those whose insurance will cover treatments. Those without such insurance clearly will not benefit. This is another argument in favor of universal access.

A related value is that health care is a social or public good. This means that people are entitled to adequate care, not necessarily all care that is theoretically possible. Genetic medicine has the potential to treat, cure, or even prevent diseases that today we can only, at best, alleviate. This does not mean that everyone is entitled to all possible genetic treatments, or that organs should be continually replaced once stem cell research reaches fruition. There are limits to what a society can afford. Whether we have reached those limits is an interesting question.

Khoury, Beskow, and Gwinn (2001) argue that public health issues need to be researched to realize the potential of genomic medicine. Specifically, they mention research in health services, epidemiology (the study of disease patterns in humans), and communications.

We also argue that more emphasis should be put on the value of prevention. Much of the promise of genetic medicine is to prevent the possibility of disease hidden in one's genes from being expressed. To the extent that genetic medicine is capable of doing this, it certainly transforms the nature of medicine.

Another value is the idea of holistic medicine, treating not just the disease but the person. This is, as pointed out in the introduction, an important aspect of Eastern medicine. It is also important in looking at the implications of genetic medicine.

As we have mentioned in this chapter, genetic research can lead to a deterministic view of people: our genes, our selves. The danger is forgetting the person and focusing on the disease and even more on the genes that contributed to or caused the disease. There are other types of treatments for ill health, and alternative medicines that might be employed.

Our last value concerns educating physicians, particularly future physicians. The implications of genetic research on the practice of medicine are enormous. However, changes in how physicians and other medical providers are trained and will practice are in their infancy. As yet, there is little evidence that genetic medicine, gene therapy, and so forth have made much difference in the practice of medicine (Billings 2000). It appears that ignorance and misunderstanding about genetic research, its practical applications, and its dangers characterize much medicine today:

> Hundreds of genetic tests are available today, thanks to the gradual unveiling of the human genetic code, and doctors are ordering them in ever increasing numbers. Yet surveys confirm that most doctors and other health care professionals understand woefully little about genetics or genetic tests.
>
> They don't know who should get tested. They don't know which tests are most useful. And they fail miserably at interpreting and communicating genetic test results, wrongly reassuring people at risk and scaring people who have little to fear.

As a result, some people are not getting the preventive care they should. Others are being advised to pursue unnecessary follow-up tests or perhaps even surgeries, and entire families are more confused or afraid than they were without the technology. (Weiss 2000a)

Reevaluating training and practice over the next five years is thus crucial (Billings 2000) (see Chapter 8 of this volume).

Genetic research is a nice example of what Deborah Stone (2002) calls a "policy paradox." A paradox is something that can be seen in two opposite ways at the same time. In this case, genetic research, in all its manifestations (genome project, cloning, therapy, counseling, patenting) has an almost unlimited potential for good. Yet at the same time, it presents threats (ethics and religion, the nature of humans, determinism, privacy, discrimination, insurance). It is both good and bad at the same time. The science of genetic medicine, though still in its infancy, has surpassed public policy's ability to control its path. We have, metaphorically, let the genie out of the bottle. Or to use a different metaphor, one provided by the editorial cartoonist Joe Heller (2000), referring to the map of the human genome: "Once you unfold one of these things it's never the same."

Notes

1. Barry Commoner (2002) argues that the DNA basis of genetic research is inherently flawed. One of the reasons for this statement was the discovery that humans had some 30,000 genes rather than the predicted 100,000+. To Commoner, this means that there are an insufficient number of genes to be able to differentiate humans from other species.

2. This section is based on the following sources: Dolan DNA Learning Center, n.d.; Kolanta 1998; National Academy of Sciences, n.d.; and Thinkquest.org, n.d.

3. The difficulties in deciding when human life begins and the abortion issue can be seen in the Unborn Victims of Violence Act. It would make it a federal crime to kill a fetus (unborn) person as part of a crime. Some twenty-three states have such legislation and the bill passed the U.S. House of Representatives in April 2001. Pro-choice groups oppose the bill because they believe it will provide a statutory basis for declaring a fetus/unborn child as a human with full human rights. This could lead to prohibiting abortions. Pro-life groups say that the federal and many state bills specifically exempt abortion. See Brogan (2001) and Eilperin (2001).

Study Questions

1. Genetic research, and scientific research in general, can become controversial and challenge existing beliefs. For example, the idea that the earth revolves around the sun (the heliocentric theory) rather

than the sun revolving around the earth (the geocentric theory) contradicted teachings of the Catholic Church when Galileo proposed this theory. Similarly, today some see the Darwinian idea of evolution as challenging religious beliefs. Does genetic research pose comparable problems? That is, do the results of genetic research challenge our view of the nature of humans?

2. One of the criticisms of genetic research, such as cloning, gene therapy, and genetic screening is that it allows us to "play God." That is, modern medicine is beginning to enable us to change how people develop, say by screening out genetic-based diseases. Some people were disturbed by the story of the mother with a genetic disposition for Alzheimer's disease who screened embryos until one without the gene was implanted in her. Others were disturbed about the couple who screened their embryos until they found one that would be a good bone marrow match for their child suffering from leukemia. How do you feel about these efforts? Write an essay in which you consider what it means to be human and how genetic research does or does not change this view.

3. When does life begin? Some see life beginning at the moment of conception. Others see life beginning, at least for legal purposes, at birth. Write an essay in which you explore how different religions answer the question about when life begins. Why do these religious views differ? Should religious perspectives be allowed to determine what kind of scientific research is conducted?

4. In the summer of 2001, President George W. Bush announced his decision allowing embryonic stem cell research to continue only on existing lines. Why did he have to make this decision? What was the basis for the decision? In what ways will the decision impede or promote stem cell research? What was the reaction of the scientific community to the decision? Do you agree or disagree with the president's decision? Why?

5. Continuing with the stem cells issue, some scientists and other advocates argue that stem cell research has the potential to cure or prevent diseases, such as Parkinson's disease, Alzheimer's disease, diabetes, and nerve damage leading to paralysis (think of the actor Christopher Reeve). Write an essay in which you discuss the tradeoffs between undertaking this research and the destruction of embryos necessary for embryonic stem cell research to be conducted.

6. A number of states within the United States have attempted to limit or prohibit embryonic stem cell research and cloning. Why do states think that such action is necessary?

7. Most nations that have considered cloning have banned it. But stem cell research seems to be different. Some oppose it (especially research involving embryonic stem cells), while others have placed little constraints on it. Why do countries differ in their public policies toward genetic research?

8. As indicated in the chapter, some fear that genetic research could lead to discrimination based on genetic makeup. Should employers be allowed to screen their employees and prospective employees for genetic faults that might lead to diseases in the future? Should employers be allowed to refuse employment to someone lacking the proper genetic background? Should insurance companies be allowed to screen workers and their families who would be covered by the plan? Should they be allowed to refuse to cover such people, or charge higher premiums for such people?

CHAPTER 5

Privacy of Medical Records and Confidentiality

The protection guaranteed by the amendments is much broader in scope. The makers of our Constitution undertook to secure conditions favorable to the pursuit of happiness. They recognized the significance of man's spiritual nature, of his feelings and of his intellect. They knew that only a part of the pain, pleasure and satisfactions of life are to be found in material things. They sought to protect Americans in their beliefs, their thoughts, their emotions and their sensations. They conferred, as against the government, *the right to be let alone—the most comprehensive of rights and the right most valued by civilized men.* To protect that right, every unjustifiable intrusion by the government upon the privacy of the individual, whatever the means employed, must be deemed a violation of the Fourth Amendment. (Justice Louis D. Brandeis's dissent in *Olmstead v. U.S.* 277 U.S. 438 [1928])

Many people would be surprised at just how exposed they are. Millions of individual records float around these days in a vast electronic network that serves both commerce and scientific research. The information zips around the country, speeded by computers at every stage. Computers help diagnose disease, monitor patients, organize data about their conditions, and transmit the information to managed care networks, medical research networks, pharmaceutical benefits managers, and other outposts of America's increasingly wired health care system. Along the way, thousands of eyes scan this data. The eyes may belong to health researchers seeking improved treatments, or to corporate managers bent on slashing costs, or to drug company marketers looking for new customers. Some of the records are even available through the Internet, part of the $40 billion medical information industry. In the Information Age, as confidences are entrusted to anonymous datamongers, we are all becoming a little like Blanche DuBois: We rely on the kindness of strangers. (Allen 1998a)

Access to medical information is about power. Obviously, access to this information conveys power over people, but it can also enhance medical research and improve public health. Second, there is no longer such a thing as a simple medical record. Each of us has a fluid kind of dossier that is neither open nor closed but is more or less available to a variety of people and institutions. Third, information is now multifunctional, and the privacy of that information will depend on its use. Finally, fair information practices are needed to cover a multitude of situations. These include consent procedures for release of information, notification of who sees your information, access to your own information, and redress for violations of the rules. (Schwartz in Goldman, Schwartz, and Tang 2000)

One of the growing health issues for the twenty-first century is medical privacy. There are three developments that have led to an increasing concern about medical privacy: computers and the Internet, advances in genetics (see Chapter 4), and the advent of managed care as the major type of health care delivery organization (see Chapter 7) (Allen 1998b).

Allen (1998b) sketches out the conjoining of computers and managed care. First, he points out that computers are used in a variety of ways, not just for storing of health information. For example, computers can be used to monitor the progress of patients, and to assist in diagnosing diseases in patients, and the information is shipped to entities such as pharmacy benefits managers and health insurers. Pharmacy benefits managers could use the data to see if doctors are prescribing more than a health plan wants and insurers and managed care organizations can use the data to identify expensive patients. During the transmission and storage of data, lots of people can have access to it. Managed care organizations want the data to either, as Allen (1998b) puts it, improve the quality of care or cut costs.

The concern for privacy, particularly medical privacy, became more important with the advent of high-powered personal computers and the Internet in the late 1980s and early 1990s (Demorsky 1990; Wood 1991). For example, a 1993 survey of members of the Healthcare Information and Management Systems Society (HIMSS) found that more than 50 percent of those surveyed were hoping to computerize their records over the next five years. Much of this was fostered by President Bill Clinton's priority on health care reform (a priority that would be defeated) (Lumsdon 1993). The Clinton plan called for everyone to have a health identity card (Hasson 1993). Similarly, a 1994 article in *The Economist* decried the primitive state of medical records and the coming automation of those records (Automating health care 1994; see also Bergman 1993).

One way of understanding the changes taking place in medical care and how it relates to information, information technologies, and privacy is to consider how much medical care has changed. Paul Starr's (1982) *Social*

Transformation of American Medicine tells the story of the development of medicine and the medical profession in the United States. From Starr's sociological standpoint, what physicians successfully accomplished was to establish medicine as a profession and to give that profession autonomy in making medical decisions.

Starr's work ends in the early 1980s. Much has changed since then. The advent of managed care in its various forms (see Chapter 7 of this book) has led to a significant change in the organization of medical care in the United States. Physicians have lost some of their autonomy and the old ideal of individualized practice, the *Marcus Welby* ideal, has disappeared. What has replaced it, though incompletely, is the industrialization of medical care. That industrialization requires new forms of management and information. As Kleinke (1998) points out, because the old fee-for-service, third-party reimbursement system was not focused on cost control, information was not critical and thus information systems were not rationalized. Under a system dominated by managed care, information becomes more critical though development of a rational system has been slow.

Medical privacy is a subset of the privacy issue. Other privacy issues involve financial transactions and protection from police authorities. In 1999, Congress passed the Gramm-Leach-Bliley Act removing the wall of separation between investments, insurance, and banking companies. One of the requirements of the act was the establishment of federal privacy regulations and notifications of privacy protections that companies provide (Lyons 2001). In 2001, companies sent information brochures to their customers describing their privacy policies. Some 1 billion such brochures were sent out (O'Harrow 2001b).

An interesting feature of many of these policies is what was known as the "opt-out" feature. These notices require that if the customer does not want his financial information shared, he must fill out a form specifically denying access (Safire 2001). The "default" position is not filling out the form and thereby allowing the sharing of information. The privacy notices have been criticized for being deliberately hard to understand (O'Harrow 2001b). Privacy advocates prefer what is known as an "opt-in" provision, whereby the default position is not permitting the sharing of information unless the customer sends in the form (Safire 2001).

The criminal justice area also raises privacy issues. The Fourth Amendment protects against illegal search and seizures. In *Mapp v. Ohio* (1961) the U.S. Supreme Court placed the exclusionary rule, that evidence illegally obtained cannot be used in a criminal case, under Fourth Amendment protection (Janda, Berry, and Goldman 1995). Over the years, and particularly during the Rehnquist court, those protections have become narrower.

However, the Supreme Court issued an important decision in 2001. The case *Kyllo v. U.S.* concerned the use of a high tech imaging device to see if Kyllo was growing marijuana in his house. Kyllo was doing so and was convicted. The Court, by a 5–4 decision, argued that a search warrant was needed in order to obtain information from inside a private house, even if, especially if, the information-gathering was done from outside the house. The Court was reaffirming the importance of privacy (Safire 2001; Walsh 2001).

Privacy in Other Countries

Other countries and international institutions have addressed issues of privacy (Le Bris and Knoppers 1997). Perhaps the place to start is with the Universal Declaration of Human Rights, adopted by the United Nations in December 1948. The Declaration, an aftermath of World War II and the Nazi Holocaust, begins with "recognition of the inherent dignity and of the equal and inalienable rights of all members of the human family is the foundation of freedom, justice and peace in the world" (Universal Declaration of Human Rights 1998). Article 12 of the Declaration specifically addresses privacy:

> No one shall be subjected to arbitrary interference with his privacy, family, home or correspondence, nor to attacks upon his honour and reputation. Everyone has the right to the protection of the law against such interference or attacks. (Universal Declaration of Human Rights 1998)

The International Covenant on Civil and Political Rights, adopted in 1966, affirms, as does the Universal Declaration of Human Rights, the inherent dignity of humans. Article 17 of the International Covenant makes an almost identical statement concerning privacy:

> 1. No one shall be subjected to arbitrary or unlawful interference with his privacy, family, home or correspondence, nor to unlawful attacks on his honour and reputation.
> 2. Everyone has the right to the protection of the law against such interference or attacks. (International Covenant on Civil and Political Rights, http://www.tufts.edu/departments/fletcher/multi/texts/BH498.txt)

A third such document is the European Convention for the Protection of Human Rights and Fundamental Freedoms (Le Bris and Knoppers 1997). Signed in 1950, again an aftermath of the Holocaust and the World War II, Article 8 of the Convention states:

1. Everyone has the right to respect for his private and family life, his home and his correspondence.
2. There shall be no interference by a public authority with the exercise of this right except such as is in accordance with the law and is necessary in a democratic society in the interests of national security, public safety or the economic well-being of the country, for the prevention of disorder or crime, for the protection of health or morals, or for the protection of the rights and freedoms of others. (Council of Europe 1950)

As Le Bris and Knoppers (1997) point out, there are differences between the three documents. All affirm the essential worth of humans and privacy as a fundamental right. But the Universal Declaration and the International Covenant see privacy as a passive right, the right to be left alone in Brandeis's terms. A more affirmative view of privacy is found in the European Covenant. Here, the right to privacy is foremost and intrusions upon it are seen as exceptional cases. The European Commission on Human Rights and the European Court of Human Rights in their interpretations of the European Covenant have also moved toward a more positive perspective on privacy (Le Bris and Knoppers 1997). Law in Europe and in Canada, which normally sees a separation in private from public law, has increasingly narrowed this separation (Le Bris and Knoppers 1997; Schwartz 1997).

Schwartz (1997, 393) characterizes the European laws as comprehensive focusing on "data collection, storage, use, and disclosure." Further, European nations have regulatory agencies and a regulatory process for overseeing protection of data. Schwartz (1997) says that despite the virtually universal insurance coverage in European nations, which might make many privacy protections unnecessary (because one cannot lose insurance), there is special protection for medical information.

The German constitution contains a special protection for medical information to protect personal autonomy. France and Germany also have strict legislative protections for medical information (Schwartz 1997). For example, German law forbids in the absence of patient consent the transfer of information to "clearinghouses" (1997, 399).

European laws directed at genetics and privacy tend to be targeted at specific areas, rather than be all encompassing. Such laws have been directed at the use of genetic information in employment decisions and prenatal screening (Schwartz 1997).

In general, European law provides a higher degree of protection of privacy of medical information than the United States does. This is true even with the issue of the Health Insurance and Portability Act (HIPAA) rules.

Some recent constitutions have explicitly included the right of protection of personal information and access to that information. South Africa and Hungary are good examples of this. In other countries where such a right does not exist explicitly in constitutions, courts have founded that right in legislation. Ireland and India are good examples here (Banisar and Davies 1999).

Privacy in the U.S. Constitution

From a legal standpoint, there is no right to privacy stated in the U.S. Constitution, though many other countries do have such a constitutional right (see Table 5.1) (Banisar and Davies 1999).

Advocates of medical privacy argue that privacy should be considered a fundamental human "right to control our own personal information" (Flaherty 1995). In 1998, the Human Rights Campaign called for federal legislation enacting privacy protections that would be a floor rather than a ceiling (Human Rights Campaign 1998). The campaign also said that federal law should not preempt state law, where state law is stronger than federal. At the same time, the Human Rights Campaign stated that privacy law should not hinder needed research, but personally identifiable information should not be included.

The idea of a right to privacy, though not specifically stated in the U.S. Constitution, has a long history in English as well as American law. One could argue that one of the issues the colonists were concerned about was Britain's claim to be able to search houses. The Fourth Amendment was written with this in mind. British law has long recognized the privacy of personal property (Sykes 1999).

Perhaps the first mention of a right to privacy came in an article in the *Harvard Law Review* by Warren and Brandeis (1890). The right of personal protection and to be secure in one's possessions is as old as English common law and embodied in the First Amendment of the U.S. Constitution. The Fourth Amendment views, indirectly, the prototypical privacy violation as a search of a diary without the author's permission (Rosen 2000). Warren and Brandeis traced the development of law in this area. First was the physical protection of person and property. Then came what they called the "right to life" (not to be confused with the abortion-based view of a right to life). The industrialization of the country in the late nineteenth century led inevitably, they wrote, to the need for an expanded definition of privacy to include "right to be let alone" (Warren and Brandeis 1890). They refer specifically to newspapers and photography as necessitating this new right.

The first time such a right was referred to in a U.S. Supreme Court case was in 1928, *Olmstead v. U.S.* (277 U.S. 438, 478). The case, which dealt with wiretapping, contained a dissent (which opened this chapter) by now-Associate Supreme Court Justice Louis D. Brandeis, asserting this right to

Table 5.1

Explicit Constitutional Right to Privacy Provisions

Countries with	Countries without
Argentina	Australia
Belgium	Austria
Brazil	Canada
Bulgaria	France
Chile	Germany
People's Republic of China (limited)	Greenland
Czech Republic	India
Denmark	Ireland
Estonia	Malaysia
Finland	Norway
Greece	Singapore
Hungary	United Kingdom
Iceland	United States
Israel	
Italy	
Japan	
Korea, Republic of	
Latvia	
Lithuania	
Luxembourg	
Mexico	
Netherlands	
New Zealand	
Philippines	
Peru	
Poland	
Portugal	
Russian Federation	
Slovak Republic	
Slovenia	
South Africa	
Spain	
Sweden	
Switzerland	
Taiwan	
Thailand	
Turkey	

Source: Banisar and Davies (1999). "Global Trends in Privacy Protection," ed. *John Marshall Journal of Computer and Information Law* 18 (Fall). Nexis-Lexis.

Note: This list does not differentate between strong and weak protections, nor does it consider the laws that almost every country has passed that protected some form of privacy.

be left alone. The importance of Brandeis's (and Warren's) view of privacy is that it transformed the concept into a much broader one than the founders envisioned.

While there are a number of cases and federal laws that rely on this notion of a right to privacy (see the summary in Standler 1997), the first U.S. Supreme Court case that asserted that there was a constitutional right to privacy came in *Griswold v. Connecticut* (1965). That case concerned a Connecticut law that made it illegal for a person to buy contraceptives, even if the person was married. The justice who wrote the majority opinion, William O. Douglas, asserted that various provisions of the Constitution's Bill of Rights created this right to privacy (see discussion in Sykes [1999], 85–87). The First Amendment allows for freedom of religion and expression (speech and press). The First Amendment also guarantees a right of association and protection of groups of interest* (Allen 1997). The Third Amendment forbids the military from quartering soldiers in a person's home without the person's consent. The Fourth Amendment provides that people shall "be secure in their persons, houses, papers, and effects." The Fifth Amendment states that a person cannot be deprived of his or her liberty or property without due process and that the use of eminent domain (not a phrase that appears in the U.S. Constitution) shall be accompanied by appropriate compensation. It also relates to privacy because it forbids people from testifying against themselves.

Perhaps the most important amendment for the constitutional assertion of a right to privacy is the Ninth Amendment. It reads in its entirety: "The enumeration in the Constitution, of certain rights, shall not be construed to deny or disparage others retained by the people." This is an important statement. It recognizes that the framers of the Constitution understood that they should not limit themselves or the people to rights only listed in the Bill of Rights. That was one of the objections made by the Anti-Federalists to the adoption of the original constitution. It also underlies and undercuts arguments made against "judge-made" rights.

The totality of the amendments create what some have argued is a fundamental right to privacy. This is so for two reasons. There are standards for determining whether a right is a fundamental one. The first standard is whether that right is an inherent part of the United States' history and practice. Additionally, the right claimed must be an intrinsic part of justice and liberty. The idea here is that if the right did not exist or were eliminated, justice and liberty would be diminished (Kaminer 2001).

In the very controversial hearings and vote over President Ronald Reagan's

---

*The term "interest group" was not used at that time.

1987 nomination of Judge Robert Bork to the U.S. Supreme Court, one of the issues leveled against Judge Bork was that he not only opposed a right to privacy but argued that people had only the rights specifically listed in the Bill of Rights. Bork's nomination was defeated for this and other reasons.[1] *Griswold v. Connecticut* then became the foundation eight years later for *Roe v. Wade,* the decision that established a right to an abortion.

Two features of the Constitution have played a role in privacy law (Cate 1997). The first is that the Constitution provides rights for the people, but generally only against government action. It has taken federal and state legislation and court decisions allowing that legislation to permit governments to take actions protecting privacy rights from invasion by the private sector.

Second, constitutional rights are often negative in nature. That is, they do not obligate government to take action but do limit government from doing things to infringe on the people's rights. Another way of looking at these two features is that they promote limits or constraints on government (Cate 1997).

Understanding Privacy

We can define privacy using the definition given by Justice Brandeis in one of the quotes that opened this chapter: the right to be left alone. Standler (1997) defines privacy as:

> the expectation that confidential personal information disclosed in a private place will not be disclosed to third parties, when that disclosure would cause either embarrassment or emotional distress to a person of reasonable sensitivities. *Information* is interpreted broadly to include facts, images (e.g., photographs, videotapes), and disparaging opinions.

Alan Westin (1967, 7; see also Cate 1997, 22) has offered one of the classic definitions of privacy: "Privacy is the claim of individuals, groups or institutions to determine for themselves when, how and to what extent information is communicated to others." Cate (1997) notes that there are four values that underlie this definition of privacy: autonomy, release from public roles, self-evaluation and decision making, and limited and protected communication.

Rosen (2000) sees privacy as the ability to control how and when we present various components of ourselves to others. The lack of privacy creates the possibility that we will be treated as celebrities, being judged on the basis of pieces of information about us taken out of context rather than knowledge of who we really are.

One of the major concerns of privacy advocates, especially concerning medical privacy, is that if communication between a patient and provider is not kept privileged (confidential) the patient may not be fully forthcoming about her problems. This is of particular concern in the mental health field or from someone suffering from a disease such as HIV/AIDS.

Another issue associated with privacy is that there are costs to providing those protections. Richard Posner (discussed in Cates 1997) argues that privacy may be used to conceal something about oneself and thus to provide incomplete or misleading information. One of the rationales behind the Health Insurance and Portability Accountability Act of 1996 (see below) is that people were afraid of losing their health insurance because of a preexisting condition. Thus the Act was passed to deal with that problem. The other way of dealing with that problem is not seek treatment for it or get treatment without disclosure. One could argue that this constitutes fraud. Posner argues that there are transaction costs to privacy (such as giving credit) and this is inefficient.

But there are also costs to limiting privacy. Rosen (2000) points out that workers under constant electronic surveillance are less productive and less psychologically healthy than workers who are not so watched. The loss of privacy also inhibits the development of intimate relations and individual personality (2000).

Posner essentially argues that information should be available or transparent (Rosen 2000). If we are concerned about being misjudged, as Rosen argues, then we should be willing to make more, rather than less information about us available. But Rosen argues that Posner and others are really talking about secrecy rather than privacy. Also, Rosen asserts, Posner and others see people as wearing what are effectively masks; we are different people or show different aspects of ourselves to people in different situations. This is misleading. But Rosen argues that wearing these masks is necessary to correspond to different situations.

Further, there is a whole range of safety issues associated with privacy. An employer would like to know the background of a prospective employee. A person would like to know whether a potential sexual partner has a communicable disease. Is the babysitter a potential threat? Is the next door neighbor a possible sexual predator? Is the physician competent? (Cate 1997). For example, in June of 2001 a Texas judge ordered fourteen sexual offenders on probation to keep a sign on their homes and in their cars warning that they are sexual offenders. One can certainly understand why neighbors would like to know the information. Yet it created a controversy because the offenders' privacy rights have been violated (Raspberry 2001).[2]

In understanding privacy issues, the underlying concern among privacy advocates, which include liberals, conservatives, and libertarians, is the notion of Big Brother popularized by George Orwell (1949) in *1984*. Orwell tells the story of a futuristic, totalitarian society where one's thoughts are not private and citizens are monitored even in their homes. While we clearly have not reached that level of monitoring, there is a sizable amount of information available about each of us. Consider the following list compiled in 1996:

- Your health history, your credit history, your marital history, your educational history, and your employment history.
- The times and telephone numbers of every call you make and receive.
- The magazines you subscribe to and the books you borrow from the library.
- Your travel history. . . .
- The trail of your cash withdrawals [especially with the advent of automatic teller machines or ATMs].
- All your purchases by credit card or check. In the not-so-distant future, when electronic cash becomes the rule, even the purchases you make by bills and coins could be logged.
- What you eat (no sooner had supermarket scanners gone on line—to speed checkout efficiency—than data began to be tracked for marketing purposes). . . .
- Your electronic mail and your telephone messages. . . .
- Where you go and what you see on the World Wide Web (James Gleick, "Behind Closed Doors; Big Brother Is Us," *New York Times* (September 29, 1996) quoted in Cate 1997, 2; see also Sykes 1999, 3–4)

A Right to Privacy

As Stone (2002) cogently points out, rights are an important and traditional way of dealing with public policy issues. Rights have a long tradition going back long before the founding of the American republic. The idea of rights can be traced to the *Magna Carta* and the English Bill of Rights. In England, as early as 1361, people were arrested for being peeping toms. In 1765, again in England, a warrant to search a house and seize papers was quashed (Banisar and Davies 1999). The French Declaration of the Rights of Man declared that private property was protected from intrusions (1999).

Closer to the American experience is the founding of the notion of rights in natural rights theory. Natural rights theory addresses the question of how we are to relate to each other in society. The theorists, such as John Locke, argued that there were certain rights that were inherent in being human, captured in Locke's phrase as life, liberty, and property and modified by Thomas Jefferson in the Declaration of Independence as life, liberty, and the pursuit of happiness. Any society, until the related idea of social contract theory, had, at a minimum, to protect the members of its society and provide these basic human rights.

The American experience put a tremendous emphasis on individual rights, rights that were guaranteed against interference by others, including government. Many of those rights became incorporated into the American Bill of Rights as interpreted by the federal (and state) courts.

Rights can be positive or normative. A positive right "is a claim backed by the power of the state" (Stone 2002, 326). A normative right is one that may not be asserted and may not be backed up by the state law. Privacy as a right can take both forms. There are laws that maintain a right of medical privacy. But there is a longer tradition that says people have a right not to have their medical information used in various ways without permission.

As we shall see below, the routes to asserting a positive right to medical privacy can take a number of routes: common law, judicial decisions, legislation, administrative rules and regulations, and presidential executive orders.

Using Stone's (2002) discussion of types of rights, we can identify the right to medical privacy as both a procedural and substantive right. It is a substantive right in the sense the person or persons asserting this right claim some specific action or entitlement. In the case of medical privacy, the entitlement is to have information contained in a medical record not widely available and used in a way that would harm that person or persons. It is a procedural right in that patients are informed of their rights and, depending on circumstances, are required to give consent before those records can be used.

Privacy concerns can take one of four forms (Allen 1997): information, personal, decisional, and proprietary. For example, decision privacy concerns those involved in making decisions about employment or insurance or decisions about reproductive choices. Physical privacy covers invasive procedures, such as genetic testing and informed consent. The last type of privacy, proprietary, is involved with ownership of genes and other parts of the body.

Confidentiality

Confidentiality has always been a hallmark of the doctor-patient relationship. Going back to the Hippocratic Oath and its modern manifestation, doctors pledge not to violate the confidentiality of that relationship. The classical Hippocratic Oath reads in part:

> What I may see or hear in the course of the treatment or even outside of the treatment in regard to the life of men, which on no account one must spread abroad, I will keep to myself, holding such things shameful to be spoken about. (translation by Ludwig Edelstein, found at Public Broadcasting System site: http://www.pbs.org/wgbh/nova/doctors/oath_classical.html).

Louis Lasagna wrote the modern version of the Hippocratic Oath in 1964. It reads in part: "I will respect the privacy of my patients, for their problems are not disclosed to me that the world may know" (found at Public Broadcasting System site: http://www.pbs.org/wgbh/nova/doctors/oath_modern.html).

Certain types of health/medical problems were particularly important. Substance abuse and mental health have long elicited confidentiality issues (see, for example Hollowell and Ethdridge 1989). More recently, the question of confidentiality for patients with HIV/AIDS raises confidentiality issues as well. State laws often require report of incidents of sexually transmitted disease.

Health Information Technology

As the opening quote indicates, information is power and control over information is a way to exercise power. Goldman (Goldman, Schwartz, and Tang 2000) points out that Justice Brandeis's view of privacy was to be left alone. She also notes that Alan Westin's (1967) view of privacy is control over information, a more proactive version of privacy.

There is a trade-off in the privacy area. As Tang notes (Goldman, Schwartz, and Tang 2000) no rights, not even those in the Bill of Rights, are absolute. In the case of privacy, the trade-off is between protecting the rights of individuals and allowing doctors, researchers, and public health officials the ability to make informed decisions. From a communitarian perspective, society has some rights that require limiting individual privacy.

Health information technology has advanced dramatically and has numerous uses. Terms as such "medical informatics" and "knowledge engineering" are being used to describe many of these private sector developments (Moran 1998, 10–11). Information technologies have become important in exploring avenues for cost control and quality care (1998).

Moran notes that where medical privacy advocates see fundamental rights, those who develop health information systems see "chaos" (1998, 13). Obtaining consent for any use of health information would create an administrative nightmare. Further, the "horror stories" such as the "push techniques" of providing information about use of drugs to manufacturers or benefits companies and then sending material to patients reminding them to refill prescriptions or try a new one, can also be used for good, not just profit purposes, particularly for at-risk populations (p. 14). Moran points out that the use of information is the only way to find out how well our health care system is working. Therefore, some kind of health information policy is needed.

The Internet

Clayton and Sheehan (1997) raise an important question relating to privacy of medical information. Say you are on a vacation and get sick; you need to go an emergency room where you are vacationing. You see an emergency doctor. It would be helpful to the doctor and you if the doctor had access to your health records. Perhaps you have some underlying disease that might affect your current illness. Perhaps you are taking some medications. That would be important information for the attending physician to know.

The emergency room doctor could telephone your personal physician. But say it is nighttime or the weekend and your physician is not available. The easiest way would be if that information was electronically available over the Internet. But if it was available over the Internet, it might also be available to others who you would rather it was not, such as employers.

The Internet promises to change the way medicine is delivered (see the November/December 2000 issue of *Health Affairs* for a discussion of E-Health). Patients will have (and have) access to health and medical information over the World Wide Web. Electronic monitoring of patients can take place over the web. The Internet will change the financing and administration of managed care organizations, such as medical claims. It may also allow the customization of health plans for employers (Goldsmith 2000; for a dissenting view of the impact of the Internet on health care see Kleinke 2000). Hodge, Gostin, and Jacobson (1999) point out that e-mail correspondence between patient and doctor is unsecured and not always reliable.

The availability of medical information in an electronic form (whether or not available over the Internet) raises privacy issues. Goldman and Hudson (2000) point out that many people are concerned about online privacy issues. About 40 percent in a survey would not give online access to their medical records to their providers and about 25 percent would not refill prescriptions online.

> Scary scenarios are envisioned, even by health care professionals: Might employers use genetic information to sort out job candidates? Might embarrassing details circulate about alcoholism, drug use or sexually transmitted diseases? Might insurers shop for the healthiest customers or charge more because of family history? (Heinlein 1996).

A study of Fortune 500 companies found that many of them used medical records in making decisions about employees. Additionally, these companies let personnel employees view the records without the permission of the employees (Nagel 1995).

Genetics

The Human Genome Project and genetic research in general creates many privacy issues. For one thing, it makes it easier to identify someone. Professor Latanya Sweeney of Carnegie Mellon University notes that someone's gender and disease can be inferred from that person's genes. Together with information available from hospitals, much private information can be gleaned. On the other hand, such information is useful in furthering medical research (Krebs 2000).

There are three elements to the physician-patient relationship that relate to genetics: patient health, patient control, and property interests (Orentlicher 1997). Patient health is aided by confidentiality and privacy because in the absence of both, patients may avoid seeking care or they may hide some disability for fear of public disclosure or loss of job or insurance.

The property interest comes about, again especially in the area of genetics, because one's genetic makeup is closely tied to one's personal identity. If genetic information is used to help or benefit someone other than the patient, property interests are raised. Orentlicher (1997) notes that this is especially the case when such information is sold, say, to pharmaceutical companies that use the genetic information or material in developing new therapies. Do patients receive a portion of any profits realized?

The third element is control. Privacy advocates argue that patients should have control over their genetic information. Genetic information may show a predisposition to a disease, such as Parkinson's or Huntington's. If such information were released to employers or insurers, it might make getting or retaining a job or insurance more difficult (there are state laws forbidding discrimination based on genetics, see below). Genetic information may also have implications for reproduction and for the health of relatives (Orentlicher 1997). Trust is thus an important component in the physician-patient relationship.

An example of how advancements in biomedicine create problems is the development of the field of clinical genetics (Pergament 1997). By definition such a doctor must have access to genetic information about patients and be able to provide counseling (Biesecker 1997). This would allow patients to make appropriate choices, say about reproduction issues, something that forwards the value of patient control (Pergament 1997). But the ready availability of gentic information can intrude upon privacy.

The confidential relationship can be broken under three conditions (Pergament 1997): if the patient's condition presents a danger to others, during court trials, and where illegal acts are involved. Pergament (1997) provides an example of a genetic condition that affects others.

His example is of a mother who is the carrier of a gene that causes hemophilia. In this particular example, the mother is diagnosed through her son. The mother's sisters may also be carriers and their children may be affected. Would disclosure to the sisters be a violation of privacy? Pergament (1997) presents data showing that though there is strong support for patient privacy in general, specific examples such as the hemophilia one show a greater propensity to disclose. In one sense, as Biesecker (1997, 115) observes, "The client in genetic counseling is an entire family."

Disclosure of genetic information may result in stigmatizing the person and family with the potential genetic disorder. This can result in discrimination in even the ability to obtain a loan, let alone employment and insurance (Pergament 1997).

Pergament (1997), writing prior to when the Human Genome Project announced its successes, warned that the one thing that will happen when the project is completed is that everyone will be seen as having genetic disorders and that there will be the development of expensive treatments for those disorders. Thus, he concludes that the present insurance system will have to be changed if everyone is at risk.

Burris and Gostin (1997) look at genetics from a public health perspective. They first distinguish between screening and testing. Screening is performed on sectors of a population to find out how widespread a disease is in that population. Genetic testing is done on individuals to see if the individual has a genetic makeup that might predispose him or her to having some disease.

They then provide three principles to help decide the impact of genetic screening. The first principle is that the screening should improve the population's health. If the presence of the gene or mutation were the most important factor in explaining the prevalence of a disorder then screening would be appropriate. They specifically mention a gene that is related to breast cancer in women. They note that most women who get cancer get it because something sets off the gene, rather than the mere presence of the gene leading to the breast cancer (Burris and Gostin 1997).

Their second principle is that screening should be just and efficient. Here they refer to the limited resources in health and suggest putting those resources where they would do the most good. This raises the question of rationing that we will address in Chapter 7.

The third principle is that screening should be acceptable to the subpopulation that would be screened. This is necessary because screening, like other public health measures, requires ready compliance.

An interesting application and parallel to genetic screening is screening for HIV. Because there is stigma attached to having HIV, as also may be true for some genetically based diseases (see, for example, Zweig, Walsh, and

Freeman 1997), states passed laws protecting privacy, confidentiality, and those with disabilities.

The kind of population screening that Burris and Gostin (1997) refer to is part of the discipline known as epidemiology. Samet and Bailey (1997) explain how traditional epidemiology differs from epidemiology that is genetically based, or molecular epidemiology. Traditionally epidemiology starts from studying exposure to something in a given population and then looking at the incidence of disease.

Molecular biology, on the other hand, is more complex, providing a stronger (though incomplete) causal linkage from exposure to disease. It includes "exposure, dose, response (mutation and functional changes) and susceptibility" to the disorder (Samet and Bailey 1997, 199).

Insurance

One important aspect of privacy, whether of genetic or other kind of medical information, is the nature of insurance in the United States. First we should note that the United States does not have a national health insurance system, as do all other major industrialized countries. Therefore, issues such as the possible loss of insurance or lack of insurance or the high price of insurance are not relevant in those countries. They are most relevant in the United States.

Because the United States relies on private health insurance (with the exceptions of Medicaid, Medicare, and other public health programs) to cover its population, people have to worry about whether they will be covered for a specific health problem or covered at all.

Further, because health insurance is private, those who provide insurance are interested in profits or at least minimizing costs. To control costs, insurance companies "experience rate" both groups and individuals (see Kass 1997, Patel and Rushefsky 1999; Stone 1999). This means that the premiums charged are based on the likelihood of claims made by subscribers and the future expense of those claims.

As Kass (1997) points out, insurance is based on risk. People buy health insurance because there is a risk that they will need medical attention and may not be able to afford it. Insurance companies try to assess or predict risks. One of the concerns of insurance companies is what is called adverse selection, a situation in which someone needs expensive medical care and seeks insurance to cover all or most of the costs. There is an incentive for such a person to purchase insurance and not inform the company about the potential expense. Insurance companies seek to reduce adverse selection by obtaining medical information.

That information could include one's genetic background (Kass 1997). A person who has a predisposition to a disorder, such as Huntington's disease or Alzheimer's or AIDS (to take a nongenetic example) would like to hide it from the insurance company. Insurance companies share medical information through a database (1997). As genetic screening becomes more accurate and widely available (particularly for disorders that have no cure or even good therapy) there might come a time when access to insurance for those with certain genetic traits becomes limited, despite protections such as the Americans with Disabilities Act and the Health Insurance and Portability Accountability Act (1997).

Horror Stories

The push for privacy in the health field has been fueled by horror stories that depict violations of medical privacy and how they have impacted individuals. These horror stories are similar to those told about managed care that have fueled much of the backlash (see Chapter 7). One such story, indicating privacy problems, appeared in February 1998. Two supermarket chains sent information about prescriptions they filled to a marketing firm, Elensys. Elensys then used the information to remind consumers to refill prescriptions, or to market new drugs (O'Harrow 1998). Other pharmacies also made use of these "drug compliance programs" (National Organization for Rare Disorders, Inc. 1998). While customers could have their names removed from such lists, most did not know of their existence. Eventually, the two supermarket chains stopped the program (National Organization for Rare Disorders, Inc. 1998).

One of the earliest horror stories took place in a hospital when an employee got into the clinical information system. With access to patient records, he then changed physician diagnoses (Gardner 1989).

Another often told horror story concerned Nydia Velazquez. When she was running for Congress in 1992, someone accessed her medical records and discovered that in 1991, she apparently had tried to commit suicide. The person who found this information sent it to a newspaper but despite the disclosure, Velazquez won the election (Hasson 1993).

The medical records of a member of a Maryland school board, indicating that the member suffered from depression, were anonymously posted on the Internet. A worker who suffered an on-the-job wrist injury authorized the release only of information relevant to the injury, but the insurance company sent her employer her complete medical file. The late tennis player Arthur Ashe, who contracted AIDS from a blood transfusion, found that his condition was made public although he had not given permission (Health Privacy Project 2001).

One of the more egregious stories concerns the young daughter of a hospital employee who obtained names and telephone numbers of patients from the hospital records. She then called patients and told them they had been diagnosed as having HIV.

Thousands of medical records from the University of Michigan Health Center inadvertently were made available on the Internet for several months. There are other stories of personal health information becoming accessible via the Internet (Health Privacy Project 2001).

A woman visited her doctor for a checkup and a few weeks later received an advertisement from a drug company about their cholesterol-reducing drug. In another case, a woman instructed her pharmacy not to give any information about her prescription drug use to her husband. They did anyway and he used the information to claim she was a drug addict and unfit to take care of their children (Health Privacy Project 2001).

The intersection of privacy, the battle over abortion, and the Internet has created its own story. An Illinois woman had an abortion that resulted in some physical injury. An antiabortion Web site published the woman's picture and medical records. The woman sued the hospital for releasing her records without her consent and the Web site for "publicly humiliating her" (Simon 2001).

Another pro-life Web site publishes pictures of women entering abortion clinics. A spokesperson for Planned Parenthood stated that this was a new weapon in the abortion wars (Simon 2001).

Public Opinion

Where does the public stand on health privacy issues? The Institute for Health Freedom commissioned a 2000 report by the Gallup Organization (Gallup Organization 2000). The survey found that medical privacy was considered very important by a large majority of those polled (78 percent). A larger majority considered only financial privacy as very important. No majority of the respondents favored giving access to medical information to any group, though the most acceptable group was pharmacists. Strong majorities opposed giving access to employers, police, insurance companies, and so forth without permission. There was also opposition to giving access without authorization to doctors and researchers. At the same time, few of the respondents knew anything about federal regulations concerning privacy. When told about the new rules, overwhelming majorities opposed national databases and personal identification numbers.

Criticisms of Privacy

While there are strong advocates for the protection of privacy, including medical and especially genetic, privacy has its critics. One line of reasoning is that rights may or may not be fundamental but they are not absolute. Even the rights contained in the U.S. Constitution's Bill of Rights have some limitations. The U.S. Supreme Court has held, for example, that the right of free speech is limited. In the classic case, the Court held that there is no right to falsely yell "fire" in a crowded theater. Further, some rights clash with each other.

Etzioni (1999) presents an intriguing argument toward privacy and medical privacy in particular from a communitarian standpoint. Communitarianism, as we saw in Chapter 1, is an ideology that seeks to reconcile radical individual libertarianism with radical social conservatism. It believes that there should be a balance between rights and responsibilities and individuals and societies.

Etzioni recognizes many of the medical privacy issues discussed in this chapter, recounting more of the horror stories found in the literature (see below). He makes two important distinctions concerning violations of medical privacy. While many of the horror stories result from the unauthorized use of medical information, which clearly violates ethical guidelines, Etzioni argues that the most serious threats to medical privacy come from authorized uses that are the result of technological changes (largely computerization and the Internet, but also the move toward managed care). It is these authorized uses that are of the major concern to him.

Second, Etzioni distinguishes between violations of medical privacy on the part of the public sector and on the part of the private sector. He argues that there are laws protecting against public sector abuses, but most of the abuses, including authorized ones, come from the private sector.

On the other hand, there are important benefits to having access to computerized medical records. These include public safety, research, cost control, quality control, and public health (Etzioni 1999, 150–155). Etzioni seeks a middle ground that would allow public benefits while still protecting individual privacy.

Etzioni also argues that one of the common remedies suggested for ensuring medical privacy is informed consent. However, he points out that informed consent is often not voluntary. Waiving rights may be a condition of obtaining insurance and once access to information is given to outside parties privacy regulations and legislation are no longer controlling. Nor does he think that self-regulation works well by itself. Indeed, Etzioni argues that self-regulation often is resorted to as a means of stemming public sector regulation.

What Etzioni recommends instead is institutional reform through a process of layering. The inner layer consists of those who directly treat the patient, who need ready access to records, and have a lesser financial interest that does not harm privacy. The intermediate level includes managed care and insurance companies. The outer level includes those very much driven by profit, such as marketers, the media, pharmaceutical companies, and prospective employers. Etzioni would allow limited access to personal health information to the intermediate level and little to the outer levels. Etzioni also supports the use of personal medical identification cards and argues that a similar layered approach could be used. Access would be limited to certain pieces of data on the card. To protect privacy, Etzioni advocates access to audit trails to see who has had access to information.

This communitarian view has not gone uncriticized. For example, Richman (2001) attacks Etzioni's perspective from a libertarian viewpoint. For one thing, Richman disagrees with Etzioni that the private sector is more of a threat to privacy than the public sector. For another, he disagrees with Etzioni's dismissal of the importance of informed consent based on an individualist perspective.

Richman argues that informed consent is still important even if imperfectly carried out. Further, he asserts that the real problem is employment-based insurance that hinders the development of a real medical marketplace. Further, Richman disagrees with the idea that communities have rights that can be balanced against individual rights.

Sykes (1999) also disagrees with Etzioni and his communitarian ideas, though from a liberal rather than libertarian perspective (Sykes also disagrees with libertarian critiques of privacy). Sykes argues that rights, such as the right to privacy, are awkward inconveniences but they are rights not just privileges. Like Richman, Sykes notes that Etzioni downplays threats to privacy from the public sector (from, for instance, having national medical health cards).

Privacy, Confidentiality, and Public Policy in the United States

National Government

Federal Legislation

A number of federal laws also address privacy issues, though there is no law that addresses medical privacy directly. The federal laws that do address privacy issues focus on financial records, communications, freedom of information, and so forth (Allen 1997). The 1967 Freedom of Information Act permits, with some exceptions, access to government files; the 1971 Fair Credit Reporting Act provided the ability to obtain and challenge credit reports; the 1974 Family Educational Rights and Privacy Act placed limits on schools' abilities to collect information as well as limit access to that information about students (Sykes 1999); the federal Privacy Act of 1974 limits use of records by the federal government (Cate 1997; Cushman and Detmer 1997); and a 1977 Privacy Protection Commission included the private sector, though most of the commission's recommendations were not enacted (Sykes 1999).

A major problem has been the growth in the number of databases collected by the government (Sykes 1999) that are used for a variety of purposes, including criminal justice. The use of social security numbers for identification purposes allows easier collection of data about a person's activities (Safire 2001; Sykes 1999). For example, during the proceedings leading to the impeachment of President Clinton, the independent counsel's office sought the book buying records of Monica Lewinsky (who the president was accused of having sexual relations with) from a local Washington, D.C. bookstore. Under threat of a court order, the records were handed over.

The Internet also poses privacy threats. The expansion of this system has provided wonderful access to information in a wide variety of areas, including medical information, and access to communities of people with similar interests or problems, including health problems. But visiting sites allows the collection of information about one's habits. Additionally, a number of sites provide access if you allow a small program (called cookies) to be placed on your computer hard drive. Though these can be removed and one can refuse to allow them on, many people do not bother to take the step.

In 1995, the Medical Records Confidentiality Act was proposed. Testifying before the Senate Committee on Labor and Human Resources, Janlori Goldman (1995) pointed to public opinion polls, government studies, and other material calling for one federal law to replace the patchwork quilt of federal legislation. The Privacy Protection Study Commission recommended federal legislation as far back as 1977. Both the Office of Technology Assessment and the Institute of Medicine of the National Academy of Sciences recommended legislation (Goldman 1995).

Goldman (1998) argues that some features of privacy legislation (at the state level and proposed at the federal level) and regulation had some elements that were relatively uncontroversial. Patients should have access to their medical records including the right to copies of those records. Easily understandable information about health information and disclosure of health information should be made available to patients. There should be safeguards protecting health information from disclosure and there should be penalties for those who disclose health information in unauthorized ways.

Other elements of a privacy policy are more controversial and there is little consensus (Goldman 1998). Consent is an important element of privacy but the controversy is whether an employer or insurers can compel consent. Privately funded research raises privacy issues and there is concern about how to protect privacy. Law enforcement access to information and federal preemption of state privacy laws are other issues.

The federal Americans with Disabilities Act (ADA) passed in 1990, and similar state laws, prohibit discrimination against someone because of disabilities. At the same time, the ADA also protects confidentiality and privacy of medical records. One major partial exception is the 1997 Health Insurance and Portability Accountability Act (HIPAA) passed in 1996. HIPAA was passed during the turbulent 104th Congress, controlled by Republicans after their dramatic victories in the November 1994 elections. The legislation addressed a problem known as "job lock," where workers were afraid of changing jobs because a preexisting medical condition might make them ineligible for health insurance even though they had health insurance in their old job. This was the portability aspect of the legislation, the ability to continue or carry health insurance from job to job (see Rushefsky and Patel 1998).

HIPAA focused on personally identifiable information. The law also provided for the development of computerized transmission of health information to make the health system more efficient. At the same time it provided penalties for unauthorized disclosure of confidential information. Further, it gave Congress (really Congress gave itself) three years to pass legislation to protect the privacy of patients. If it failed to meet the deadline, then the Department of Health and Human Services (DHHS) was authorized to issue appropriate regulations. Congress, not surprisingly, missed the deadline and DHHS began the lengthy process of issuing regulations, a process that would take several years and involve two administrations.

There have been other bills regarding privacy introduced in the House and the Senate. In the 105th Congress (1997–1998), bills by Patrick Leahy (D-VT), Jim Jeffords (R-VT) and Representative Christopher Shays (R-CT) specifically addressed medical privacy (Bazelon Center 1998). None made it out of committee. One bill, sponsored by then-Speaker Newt Gingrich (R-GA), that did win passage in the House was the Patient Protection Act. Title 5 of the act dealt with the confidentiality of medical records. Three bills on medical privacy were introduced in the Senate; again none made it out of committee.

In the 106th Congress (1999–2000) six bills were introduced in the House directly addressing medical privacy. Another five bills were introduced that contained medical privacy provisions (information from the Health Privacy Project Web site at Georgetown University). In the Senate, three medical privacy bills were introduced and another three bills had provisions that protected privacy. Some of these other bills were part of the patients' bill of rights legislation, which would have created a right to medical privacy. Typical of such proposed legislation is the Health Care Personal Information Nondisclosure Act of 1999 introduced by Jeffords of Vermont, a Republican who in spring 2001 became an independent, allowing Democrats to take control of the Senate. The bill's findings lay out the argument for a right to privacy.

1. Individuals have a right of confidentiality with respect to their personal health information and records;
2. with respect to information about medical care and health status, the traditional right of confidentiality is at risk;
3. an erosion of the right of confidentiality may reduce the willingness of patients to confide in physicians and other practitioners, thus jeopardizing quality health care;
4. an individual's confidentiality right means that an individual's consent is needed to disclose his or her protected health information, except in rare and limited circumstances required by the public interest;
5. any disclosure of protected health information should be limited to that information or portion of the medical record necessary to fulfill the purpose of the disclosure;
6. incentives need to be created to use nonidentifiable health information where appropriate;
7. the availability of timely and accurate personal health data for the delivery of health care services throughout the nation is needed;
8. personal health care data may be essential for selected types of medical research;
9. public health uses of personal health data are critical to both personal health as well as public health; and
10. confidentiality of an individual's health information must be assured without jeopardizing the pursuit of clinical and epidemiological research undertaken to improve health care and health outcomes and to assure the quality and efficiency of health care. (Health Care Personal Information Nondisclosure Act of 1999)

Some proposed legislation at the federal level directly targets genetic records, providing privacy protections. In 2001 (107th Congress), H.R. 602 was proposed by Representative Louise Slaughter (D-NY) with over 200 cosponsors and S. 318 was proposed by Senator Tom Daschle (D-SD) with eighteen cosponsors (Goldman 2001).

H.R. 602, the Genetic Nondiscrimination in Health Insurance and Employment Act would amend the Employment Retirement Income Security Act (ERISA) and other legislation. Groups such as the American Civil Liberties Union, the National Breast Cancer Coalition, and the American Society of Human Genetics support it. Of course, there are groups opposed to it as well, particularly health insurance companies (Michael Goldman 2001).

Executive Branch

As we have seen HIPAA called for Congress to develop health privacy legislation by 1999. If Congress failed to meet that deadline, then the DHHS was to issue regulations.

In 1997, Donna Shalala, secretary of the DHHS, offered five principles for protecting personally identifiable health data. The five principles were consumer control, accountability, public responsibility, boundaries, and security (DHHS 1999a). Each of these principles deserves a brief discussion.

Consumer control means that consumers have the right to access their medical records and to correct them if there are any mistakes. Accountability means that there are penalties attached to violating confidentiality rights. Public responsibility is the recognition that medical records contain information valuable to public health officials and to researchers. They also are useful in ferreting out fraud and abuse. Any privacy standards should cover how such health information can be released and used. The idea of boundaries is that health records should be used only for medical purposes. Rules should bar the use of health records, by and large, from nonhealth use, such as decisions on employment or insurance coverage. The final principle, security, covers the protection of records from unauthorized disclosure (DHHS 1999a).

In May 1998, the DHHS issued a proposed rule under HIPAA that called for administrative simplification. The proposed rule would give every health care provider a standard identification number to be used when processing claims. A second rule issued at the same time provided for a common format for electronic submission of claims. The idea is to reduce administrative costs (see DHHS 1998a). While such standardization would reduce administrative costs they also raise privacy concerns because it makes it easier to access data. A month later, DHHS proposed a rule giving employers a standard identification number (1998b). The Clinton Health Security Act, proposed in 1993, included a national health identification system, where everyone would get a card guaranteeing coverage.

Advocates of a national identification system made a number of arguments in favor of the proposed regulations. First, it would aid research and treatment by creating a database. Under such a system a doctor with a patient suffering from a rare disease could check the database for information on patients with the same disease and treatments for the disease (Stolberg 1998).

A second benefit of the national identification system is increased efficiency. This can be seen in several ways. Billing would be easier, as would finding patient records. A third benefit, related to the last, is that when patients switch health plans or providers, patient monitoring would be more easily achieved (Stolberg 1998).

Certainly an important part of the debate is the trade-off between personal privacy and the advancement of medical research. Wheeler (1999) points out that much medical research is not just clinical trials but studying medical records. Epidemiology, the study of disease patterns in human populations, is based on looking at medical records. To the extent possible, personally identifiable information is removed from records used for research purposes. Further, researchers normally have to go through institutional review boards (IRBs) designed to protect human subjects to get permission to do the work. Often, an IRB will require informed consent but exceptions are made.

In August 1998, DHHS addressed privacy concerns raised by earlier proposed regulations. It proposed rules limiting access to electronic records and to protecting against lost records (DHHS 1998c). The proposed rule called for entities that keep health records to develop a security plan and to train workers. The rule also called for the use of electronic signatures when transmitting health information to verify the authenticity of documents and identify transmitters.

In the absence of the mandated federal legislation, DHHS began the process of issuing regulations. The first attempt came on November 3, 1999 (DHHS 1999b). The proposed rule noted the fragmented nature of state laws and argued that a comprehensive federal law would increase the efficiency of the health care system. It noted that health care information is important in delivering services, understanding disease patterns, research, and so forth and, at the same, recognized public concern about the privacy of their health care information. The rule remarked on two important developments that raise privacy concerns: computers and integrated health care plans, such as managed care organizations.

Regulations have their limitations and Shalala urged Congress to address those limitations. For example, the rules do not cover records kept in paper form, only in electronic form. Nor can the regulations cover what recipients of the records do with them. The rules do not provide consumers with a right to go to court in the event of inappropriate use of medical records (DHHS 1999a).

In August 2000, DHHS announced standards for storage and transmission of electronic health information and at the same time, said that privacy protections, promulgated either by Congress or by the department, would be forthcoming (2000a).

The department received over 50,000 comments on the proposed rule. The American Medical Association (AMA) made some interesting points in rejecting the draft. Its major concern was patient consent, noting that there are very persuasive reasons why medical information containing personally identifiable information is necessary to help forward health care and research. But, the AMA observed, this need for information does not give health entities a right to it. Further, the AMA feared that patients might refuse to provide information if they knew it would be used without their permission. Therefore, the medical association recommended that if such information is to be used, it must be stripped of personally identifiable information (see James 2000).

In December 2000, during the waning days of the Clinton administration, DHHS announced its rules for protection of health information in whatever format. The rules required patient consent for disclosure of medical records, including advanced consent in the case of routine use of records. The rule gave providers the discretion to decide how much medical information to disclose to other providers treating the patient. Employers will not have access to health records without prior consent (DHHS 2000b).

The rule permitted disclosure of health records under certain circumstances. These include:

- Oversight of the health care system, including quality assurance activities
- Public health
- Research, generally limited to when a waiver of authorization is independently approved by a privacy board or Institutional Review Board
- Judicial and administrative proceedings
- Limited law enforcement activities
- Emergency circumstances
- For identification of the body of a deceased person, or the cause of death
- For facility patient directories
- For activities related to national defense and security (Department of Health and Human Services 2000c).

Privacy protection got caught up in the change of administrations. In the last days of the Clinton administration, a number of regulations were issued in a variety of areas, such as environment and health. The new Bush administration sought to stop the regulations to give itself time to review them. Such was the case with the medical privacy protection rule.

Under the provisions of the Congressional Review Act, administrations are to submit new regulations to Congress, giving Congress a two-month period in which to review the proposed rule. The Congressional Review Act was passed in 1996 as part of the Small Business Regulatory Enforcement Fairness Act. The idea for such an act was contained in the *Contract with America* (Gillespie and Schellas 1994). Republicans had long sought to place restraints on the writing of regulations, particularly those that impacted businesses. The Reagan and first Bush administrations sought mechanisms to gain administrative control over the writing of regulations (Tiefer 1994).

The Clinton administration, more favorably inclined toward regulations than its predecessors, ended this administrative strategy. But when the Republicans gained control of both houses of Congress for the first time in forty years, it enacted much of the proposals contained in the Contract.

The Congressional Review Act contains a process for reviewing regulations. Prior to the expiration of the sixty days, any member of Congress can introduce a resolution to review the rule. Appropriate committees then undertake the review and send a bill of disapproval, if that is the case, to the respective floors. Under Senate rules, such a resolution is not subject to a filibuster. If Congress passes the resolution, the president must sign or veto the bill. This is the process that the new Republican administration, the second Bush administration, said was not followed.

In February 2001, the new secretary of the DHHS, Tommy G. Thompson, issued a notice that because the process of congressional review was not undertaken, he would open the rule for comment for an additional thirty days (2001a). The Bush administration was under pressure by "hospitals, health insurers, medical equipment suppliers and drugmakers" to change the regulations (O'Harrow 2001a). These and other industry groups had made considerable campaign contributions to Republicans (2001a).

One reason for their opposition was the compliance costs associated with the privacy regulations. Estimates of the costs varied from $18 billion over a ten-year period (government estimate) to $40 billion over a five-year period (industry study) (O'Harrow 2001a).

In April 2001, Thompson announced that the Bush administration, despite some concerns, was leaving the December 2000 privacy regulations in place. Since the February announcement, the department received some 24,000 comments. While leaving the regulations in place, Thompson said the department would issue guidelines to address certain issues. These include allowing doctors to have access to needed information and to be able to consult with other physicians, preventing confusing forms from interfering with patient care (for example, allowing doctors to order prescriptions for patients over the phone), and permitting access by parents of their children's health records, with special focus on abortion, substance abuse, and mental health (DHHS 2001b; see also Pear 2001). Revising the rules would require the administration to go through the normal regulatory process (Pear 2001).

The Bush decision appears to be in line with a policy of extending privacy protections. President-elect Bush said: "As president, I will prohibit genetic discrimination, criminalize identify theft, and guarantee the privacy of medical and sensitive financial records. In addition, I will make it a criminal offense to sell a person's Social Security number without his or her express consent (quoted in "Aide Report" 2001).

The regulations met with criticism. The American Hospital Association (AHA) argued that just three of the regulations' provisions would cost over $22 billion in compliance costs over a five-year period. The AHA charged that the Clinton administration rule went further than authorized under HIPAA and the rule itself was "seriously flawed" (AHA 2001a).

More specifically, the AHA comment argued that DHHS had authority only to regulate transactions; instead the rule covered all medical information. Further, the AHA argued that requiring patient consent for all purposes could harm patient health. For example, if a physician suggested that her patient undergo surgery, she would normally send the patient's records to the hospital for admission and other purposes. Under the rule, the AHA argued, consent would be needed before such information could be sent. The AHA therefore recommended that obtaining consent be made optional and that a reasonable period of time be allowed for the withdrawal of consent. Similarly, the Healthcare Leadership Council argued that the new rule would drastically increase red tape (Medical privacy rules raise questions 2001).

Blevins and Kaigh (2001), in a paper for the Institute for Health Freedom and part of a brief for House of Representative staffers, argued the new rules do not provide much in the way of protections for patients and, further, erode some protections. They contend that the regulations do not create a right to privacy; rather they give the federal government access to patient records. A second myth they mention is that the rules guarantee that a person can restrict access to one's medical records. Blevins and Kaigh list eight ways that medical records can be used without patient authorization, similar to the list cited above. Further, they point out as others have, that once data has been disclosed to some third party, records are no longer protected under privacy rules.

In July 2001, the Office for Civil Rights (OCR) within the DHHS issued the first of several guidances promised by DHHS Secretary Tommy G. Thompson (Office of Civil Rights 2001). The guidance or standard was designed to inform those covered by the privacy regulations how OCR and the department will enforce them. The standards take the form of questions and answers (frequently asked questions or FAQS).

The regulations, originally issued in December 2000 and accepted by the Bush administration in April 2001 give covered entities (such as hospitals, physicians offices, etc.) two years to comply. They also seek to make sure that privacy does not result in too much red tape. For example, the regulations and the guidance allow family members to pick up prescriptions from pharmacies without prior consent of the patient. Similarly, emergency rooms do not need to obtain consent if the situation warrants immediate attention.

A third myth is that coercion is not used in obtaining consent. Blevins and Kaigh (2001) note that health care providers may refuse to provide services unless privacy rights are waived. Other myths include the idea that patients can get full disclosure of when their records are used and that there are effective penalties for violating privacy rights.

Further, the rules do not protect all personally identifiable health information. Specifically, body tissue, blood, and sperm are not covered. Blevins and Kaigh note that all three contain genetic material and thus genetic privacy is not protected. Finally, they point that one goal of the rules is to create a national system for electronic health information and patients will not have control over access to those records.

One interesting problem pointed out about the new federal medical privacy regulations is the issue of marketing. Perry (2001; see also Tapellini 2001) argues that the regulations allow marketing of information without prior authorization by, among others, life insurance and pharmaceutical companies.

The American Association of Health Plans (AAHP), the association of managed care organizations, was also critical of the new regulations as being too bureaucratic. Ignagni and Stewart (2001), for example, while pointing to the importance of protecting medical privacy, also noted problems with heavy-handed regulations (their own version of privacy horror stories):

> In several states we've seen well-intentioned privacy laws result in unintentional consequences.
>
> - In Maine, for example, florists were unable to deliver flowers to hospital patients.
> - In Hawaii, the state's workers' compensation program had to be shut down for three months in order to collect patient authorizations.
> - And in Minnesota, researchers were unable to conduct meaningful medical record research to improve quality because few individuals were mailing back their permission forms.

On the other hand, consumer oriented groups were much more favorably inclined toward the new regulations. For example, Janlori Goldman, director of the Health Policy Project at Georgetown University, testified before Congress praising the regulations, even urging the expansion of the regulations (Goldman 2001). Goldman argued that health privacy was very important to Americans and related some horror stories of breach of privacy. She recommended that the privacy recommendations be broadened to all entities that handle health information, and that consent be required if health information is used for marketing purposes, enhance privacy of medical records on the part of law enforcement agencies, and allow people the right to sue if their health privacy rights are violated (2001).

To complicate things even more, in December 2001, the Office of Management and Budget produced of a list of twenty-three recommendations that it suggested federal agencies might want to either repeal or change. Among the twenty-three was the privacy rule issued by the Clinton administration in December 2000 (Claybrook 2002; Office of Information and Regulatory Affairs 2001). The rule still remains in effect, subject to administration guidance and implementation, but it is clearly endangered.

Then in March 2002, the George W. Bush administration issued a proposed rule modifying the Clinton administration rule (Office of Civil Rights 2002; Pear 2002). The major change in the proposed rule was to eliminate the requirement that patients consent could disclose medical information to other providers for medical treatment and "other health care operations" including insurance companies and managed care organizations (Pear 2002). DHHS argued that requiring such consent could result in a decrease in the quality of health care. The health industry favored the proposed rule, consumer and privacy advocates opposed it (2002).

State Governments

State Constitutions

Some eight state constitutions, such as Florida's, assert this right (Cate 1997). Florida's constitution (Article 1, section 23), typical of such provisions, reads:

> Every natural person has the right to be let alone and free from governmental intrusion into the person's private life except as otherwise provided herein. This section shall not be construed to limit the public's right of access to public records and meetings as provided by law.

No state constitution addresses issues related to information privacy (Cate 1997).

State Legislation and Medical Privacy

States have addressed privacy issues and have provided for the confidentiality of medical records. States have laws that cover wiretapping and other surveillance techniques (Allen 1997). Some states also have laws that restrict access to the medical records of employees (Rothstein 1997b).

But as is typical in our federal republic, state laws are a patchwork defying easy summary (Pritts et al. 1999). All but one of the states (South Carolina) has laws protecting medical records. Half the states have privacy laws (Electronic Privacy Information Center http://www.epic.org/privacy/consumer/states.html).

Typically, state laws focus on particular health care entities, such as insurers, physicians, nursing homes, and hospitals. With the exception of a few states, such as Rhode Island and Wisconsin, no state has a comprehensive medical privacy law. Pritts et al. (1999) find that states laws are behind the times (as seems to be typical of public policy in this area). For example, few laws covered the newer forms of health care organization such as managed care organizations.

The first of the laws were passed at the beginning of the 1970s and focused on those who were discriminated against because they had a trait that led to sickle cell anemia. Beginning in the 1980s, states began passing legislation that more broadly protects against genetic discrimination.

Rothstein (1997b) notes that employers who can gather or have access to medical information about their employees have had incentives to gain such information. The major incentive is to try to reduce their health costs. There are instances where employers changed their health insurance coverage so that it would not cover or at least would limit expenses for a particular disease, such as AIDS. This is easier to do for employers who self-insure. They self-insure because it saves them administrative costs and perhaps money (that would go to insurers before being paid out). Further, self-insured companies, even those that use a third-party to administer the plan, are protected from regulation by the states under the provisions (and court interpretation) of the Employee Retirement Income Security Act (ERISA) of 1974. ERISA preempts state laws (see the 1987 case *Pilot Life Insurance v. Dedeaux*; see Kass 1997). Overall, the Health Privacy Project finds that states provide a higher level of protection and more comprehensive protection than any federal law yet proposed. Therefore, federal law should not preempt state law, especially to make state laws weaker (Pritts et al. 1999).

To summarize the Health Privacy Project findings, only seven states lack a statute providing for patients' access to their health records. Thirty-three states provide such access from health care facilities such as hospitals. Thirteen provide for access from health maintenance organizations, seventeen for insurers, and twenty-two for mental health records.

Some states also have statutes that restrict disclosure by specific entities. For example, thirty-five states restrict disclosure of government maintained records, thirty-seven restrict disclosure of managed care organization records, twenty by health facilities, eighteen by insurance companies, and seventeen by mental health workers.

A number of states have statutes that limit disclosure for specific conditions. The four major conditions are substance abuse, genetic testing, mental health, and HIV/AIDS (Pritts et al. 1999).

Most states have laws mandating that certain information be made available to researchers and insurance companies, such as the patient's zip code, birth date, ethnicity, and gender as well as the diagnosis. Most of us can be identified just knowing zip code, birthday, and gender (Krebs 2000).

A 1997 report looked at confidentiality issues at the state and federal level (Gostin, Lazzarini, and Flaherty 1997). The report notes that there are two goals related to the collection of health information. The first is to make sure that such information is available to assess the health of individuals and communities and to evaluate the effectiveness of institutions. The second goal is to make sure that the use of this information does not infringe on the privacy of individuals.

Twenty-four states have addressed issues related to genetic privacy laws. The issue is whether genetic information has the same protection as other types of medical information or whether more specific laws aimed at genetic information are necessary (National Conference of State Legislatures 2001). Table 5.2 presents the data. As can be seen, which is typical of state legislation, there is a wide variety of laws among the states). The most common protection is the requirement of informed consent before releasing genetic information. No state defines DNA samples as personal property (National Conference of State Legislatures 2001).

A Model Health Privacy Policy

In July 1999, the Health Privacy Working Group issued a report spelling out in detail what an ideal medical privacy policy should look like. It offered eleven principles for such a policy and argued that they should all be adopted together. The principles are:

1. For all uses and disclosures of health information, health care organizations should remove personal identifiers to the fullest extent possible, consistent with maintaining the usefulness of the information.

2. Privacy protection should follow the data.
3. An individual should have the right to access his or her own health information and the right to supplement such information.
4. Individuals should be given notice about the use and disclosure of their health information and their rights with regard to that information.
5. Health care organizations should implement security safeguards for the storage, use, and disclosure of health information.
6. Personally identifiable health information should not be disclosed without patient authorization, except in limited circumstances. Health care organizations should provide patients with certain choices about the use and disclosure of their health information.
7. Health care organizations should establish policies and review procedures regarding the collection, use, and disclosure of health information.
8. Health care organizations should use a balanced and objective process to review the use and disclosure of personally identifiable health information for research.
9. Health care organizations should not disclose personally identifiable health information to law enforcement officials, without a compulsory legal process, such as a warrant or court order.
10. Health privacy protections should be implemented in such a way as to enhance existing laws prohibiting discrimination.
11. Strong and effective remedies for violations of privacy protections should be established. (Health Privacy Working Group 1999, 4–7; see also Hodge, Gostin, and Jacobson 1999)

Privacy and Confidentiality of Medical Records, Values, and Public Policy

In all of these problems, of course, lie trade-offs—between privacy and progress, between the interests of industries and the interests of individuals. Much of the current upheaval seems irreversible—genetic mapping is an inevitable aspect of scientific knowledge, and the computerization of medical records is an inevitable aspect of the advance of technology. Yet it is worth remembering that some of the most difficult predicaments here are a consequence of a specific political decision: the collective American choice not to adopt a program of universal health care. Because 43 million Americans have no health insurance, and because many millions more fear becoming one of their number, a sick person in this country is threatened by information in a way that the sick in Europe or Japan or Canada are not. (Allen 1998a)

While invasions of privacy have been a problem for quite a while, four developments have increased the urgency of this concern. The first is the

Table 5.2

State Genetic Privacy Laws

State	Personal access to genetic information required	Informed Consent Required Perform or require genetic test	Obtain genetic information	Retain genetic information	To Disclose genetic information	Define as Personal Property Genetic information	DNA samples	Specific penalties for genetic privacy violations
Alabama								
Alaska								
Arizona		+			+			2
Arkansas					+			1
California					+		+	2
Colorado					+	+	+	3
Connecticut	+							
Delaware			+	+	+		+	5
Florida		+			+	+	+	4
Georgia		+			+	+	+	4
Hawaii								
Idaho								
Illinois					+			2
Indiana							+	
Iowa								
Kansas								
Kentucky								
Louisiana					+	+	+	3
Maine								
Maryland								
Massachusetts		+			+		+	3
Michigan		+						1
Minnesota								

State								Total
Mississippi								
Missouri					+		+	2
Montana								
Nebraska								
Nevada		+	+	+	+		+	5
New Hampshire	+							1
New Jersey		+	+		+		+	4
New Mexico	+	+	+	+	+		+	6
New York		+	+		+		+	4
North Carolina								
North Dakota								
Ohio								
Oklahoma								
Oregon	+		+	+	+		+	5
Pennsylvania								
Rhode Island					+			1
South Carolina		+			+		+	3
South Dakota		+						1
Tennessee								
Texas					+		+	2
Utah								
Vermont		+		+			+	3
Virginia					+			1
Washington								
West Virginia								
Wisconsin								
Wyoming								
TOTAL	4	10	5	6	22	5	16	24

Source: National Conference of State Legislatures (2001). "State Genetic Privacy Laws" [www.ncsl.org/programs/health/genetics].

computerization of medical records. This creates the possibility for easy access to millions of medical records. While steps can be taken, and have been taken, to limit this problem, the easy availability remains troublesome.

The second, related, development is the Internet. The Internet creates wonderful possibilities for making information available. Much of the research for this book was done via the Internet. The Internet makes it easier to share medical information when needed. But that same easy availability makes it easier to access and make use of information in unauthorized ways.

The third development is managed care. With the industrialization of the health care system, medical information is important for determining the best therapy in a given situation. Such information must be available to be shared, again creating the possibility of breaches of privacy.

The last development is advances in genetic research. As discussed in Chapter 4, genetic research has enabled scientists and doctors to look deeply inside humans to see the basis of many diseases. Such research has and will lead to improved therapies that seem magical to us now. But such research also opens up new layers of personal information. That information, about the potential for disorders, has created new privacy concerns.

Legislation and regulations at the federal and state levels have addressed some of these issues, such as genetic discrimination (Heath 2001; Hodge, Gostin, and Jacobson 1999). But these public policy efforts are little more than dents on the larger issue of privacy. European governments, on the whole, have a much more encompassing view of privacy and privacy protection than in the United States. Not all states prohibit genetic discrimination and there is considerable variation in protections provided (Heath 2001). Fragmentation typifies public policy in this and other areas.

At the same time, business and research interests are concerned that the protections provided will stifle research and the development of new medical therapies. Communitarians argue that privacy, like other rights, is not absolute and society has rights of its own, including the right to critical information.

Privacy raises many of the concerns and value issues discussed in Chapter 1. Our first principle is promoting the value of human dignity. Medical information is among the most personal information about individuals. Disclosure of that information, particularly unauthorized disclosure, may be embarrassing at best. At worst, there is the potential for loss of employment and insurance, and stigma from the community. Privacy affects the personal autonomy of us all.

Our second principle is that everyone should have access to adequate health care. Many of the privacy concerns, particularly those related to discrimination, would disappear if the United States had a system of universal access to health care, whatever the configuration of such a system. Then some of the trade-offs would be unnecessary.

Our third principle is dual obligation. Both the AIDS epidemic and advances in genetic medicine raise this communitarian concern of rights and responsibilities. To take AIDS as an example, on one hand, prohibiting discrimination against people with AIDS and restricting widespread availability of that information is supported by a right to privacy. However, there are times when such information is important, for example, for potential sex partners. Similarly, protection against discrimination because of one's genetic makeup (such as because of the potential for getting breast cancer or Parkinson's disease) is an appropriate public policy goal. Genetic makeup affects more than the individual. It also affects siblings, children, and other close relatives. There may be some obligation to inform or be informed about possible genetic problems.

Our fourth principle is that health care is a public good. Some of the information and products from genetic studies, such as stem cell research, may be useful in medical research.

Our fifth principle is that greater emphasis should be put on prevention than is presently being done. Here we are interested in the health of society as a whole. As Etzioni (1999) would put it, society has rights too. Too much privacy can inhibit medical care and the welfare of society as a whole.

A sixth principle relates to the education of health care providers. Particularly in the age of managed care, the privacy and autonomy of patients needs to be reemphasized. The computer revolution (including the Internet) has the potential to generate considerable efficiencies in the provision of medical care. The human element will still need to be an important part of medical education and health care delivery. But privacy and the personal autonomy that accompanies it would still be important.

Notes

1. One of the reasons why Bork was strongly opposed for appointment to the Supreme Court was his role in Watergate. President Nixon ordered the attorney general, Elliot Richardson, to fire special Watergate prosecutor Archibold Cox. Rather than do that and break his promise to the Senate Judiciary Committee to protect Cox, Richardson resigned. The number two person in the Justice Department, Deputy Attorney General William Ruckelshaus, was then ordered to fire Cox and he too resigned rather than obey the order. The number three person was the solicitor general, Robert Bork. Bork was likewise ordered to fire Cox. He did not want to and was ready to resign. However, Richardson and Ruckelshaus convinced Bork to keep his position and obey the president. They reasoned that someone had to follow the president's orders. This then became an important point of contention for those opposed to Bork's very conservative views and long paper trail (law articles and judicial decisions).

2. Raspberry (2001) wonders why, if these sexual offenders are dangerous, they are out on probation.

Study Questions

1. Is there a right to privacy in the United States? Should there be a right to privacy in the United States? If there is such a right, where is it located in the federal Constitution? Should judges be allowed to invent or develop new rights? Should legislatures be allowed to do so? On what basis might they be allowed or forbidden to develop new rights?
2. Should patients be allowed control over who has access to their medical records? If not patients, then who should have such control? How can we assure that access to medical records is not abused?
3. Let's say you are applying for a job and you have a genetic predisposition to some disease. Should you be obligated to let your future employer and insurer know about the genetic predisposition? Why would you do so voluntarily?
4. In 2002, the George W. Bush administration proposed a rule covering medical privacy. The rule relaxes some of the restrictions that were in the original Clinton administration rule. Do you agree or disagree with the new regulations? Why?
5. Should research firms be given access to your medical records so that they can discover how well treatments work, even if personal identification information is deleted?
6. Are privacy rights absolute? That is, are they superior to other considerations, such as research and treatment? Consider the communitarian critique of privacy rights: What responsibilities accompany rights? Do you agree with or disagree with the communitarian view on rights? Defend your answer.

CHAPTER 6

Health Care Rationing

With respect to health care, a nation can provide all of its people with some of the care that might do them some good; it can provide some of its people with all of the care that might do them some good; but it cannot provide all of its people with all of the care that might do them some good. (Fuchs 1998, 213)

What proportion of health care resources should go to programs likely to benefit older citizens, such as treatments for Alzheimer's disease and hip replacements, and what share should be given to programs likely to benefit the young, such as prenatal and neonatal care? What portion should go to rare but severe diseases that plague the few, or to common easily correctable illnesses that afflict the many? What percentage of funds should go to research, rehabilitation or to intensive care? Many nations have made such hard choices about how to use their limited funds for health care by explicitly setting priorities based on their social commitments. In the United States, however, allocation of health care resources has largely been left to personal choice and market forces. (Kopleman and Palumbo 1997, 319)

Rationing has never been widely accepted in the United States, though we have had experience with it. During the total mobilization that accompanied World War II, rationing was widespread. Under the Office of Price Administration (OPA), resources were diverted to the war effort. Wages and prices were controlled and the supplies of consumer goods, from automobiles to fuel to food, were controlled. Coupons were given for many of these goods. With the end of the war, rationing also ended.

But that did not mean we had no further experience with rationing in the United States. During the energy crisis of 1973 and 1974, brought on by the Arab oil embargo and price increases in retaliation for United States efforts to help Israel during the October 1973 war, some states limited days that gasoline could be purchased (by license plate numbers).

During the 1971–1974 period, the Nixon administration instituted a wage and price control program designed to stem inflation. The situation was ironic because Nixon had worked in the OPA during World War II and had left the agency with considerable doubts about government rationing.

Energy and rationing, in a sense, made something of a reappearance in 2001. As a result of increased energy costs and the California energy crisis, the Bush administration issued an energy plan under the direction of Vice President Dick Cheney that focused mainly on increasing the supply of energy. The plan called for increased drilling for fossil fuel resources in places such as the Arctic National Wildlife Preserve and the Gulf of Mexico; construction of new power plants, including those using coal and nuclear fuel; construction of new oil refineries; and construction of more power grid lines.

Environmentalists and others criticized the plan for giving short shrift to conservation (using energy resources more efficiently) and alternative energy sources. The response by Vice President Cheney was that "Conservation may be a sign of personal virtue, but it is not a sufficient basis for a sound, comprehensive energy policy" (Kriz 2001, 1560). If we understand energy conservation as a form of rationing, then the vice president was suggesting that rationing would not work. Providing more supply to meet demands was the appropriate policy.

In the health care field, there have been some attempts at rationing prior to the 1990s under the guise of planning. These programs, as were all of rationing attempts in health care in the United States, were brought on by increases in the costs of health care and the need to reduce those costs.

The major program at both the state and federal levels was the certificate-of-need programs. States passed laws requiring that hospitals and other health entities go through an approval process whenever they wanted to make a major purchase of a new piece of equipment or expand services. The programs were designed to reduce duplication and excess capacity. The villains were the third-party payment system and competition for prestige and business (Patel and Rushefsky 1999).

In 1972, the federal government entered the scene. It passed an amendment to the Medicare portion of the Social Security Act mandating a review of such purchases that involved Medicare funding. The penalty was the withholding of Medicare payments for unapproved projects.

In 1974, the federal government went much deeper into this area with the passage of the National Health Planning and Resource Development Act. This was an attempt to bring some rationality to the "accidental system" (Reagan 1999) of health care in the United States. It established local health systems agencies (HSAs) that would be the first line of approvals for expansion (states would have final approval). Theoretically, the HSAs had the power to review existing services and could, potentially, move to close them down. The reality was that for a variety of reasons, including lack of public support and provider domination, the HSAs almost never undertook to close facilities (though they did produce comprehensive studies of community health care resources) and had little impact on costs. The program was ended during the Reagan administration, though some still retained their certificate-of-need programs (Patel and Rushefsky 1999).

Rationing Defined

In defining rationing, it is helpful to make a distinction between resource allocation and rationing (Blank 1988). Both involve making choices but occur at different levels. Resource allocation occurs more at the macro level. It involves deciding how much will be spent on health care versus other societal needs, such as defense or education. Rationing occurs within the resource allocation. That is, once a decision is made about how much should go to health care, however that decision is made and whether the decision is explicit or implicit, then decisions are made about how to allocate the health dollars. What percentage of the population should be covered by health insurance? How much should go to prevention, how much should go to neonatal intensive care, and so forth (Fuchs 1998). Traditionally, in the United States, these types of decisions are made implicitly. The public sector is involved in some of these decisions, but the private sector makes many of them.

Ubel (2000) offers a very useful definition of rationing. He defines rationing as "any implicit or explicit mechanisms that allow people to go without beneficial services" (2000, 29). As such, rationing can occur at various levels. Caps put on health care spending at the national level can lead to rationing. Decisions by managed care organizations (MCOs) to include one medication in a formulary (a list of approved medications) and not another one that might be more beneficial or more costly is another example. Limiting the number of physical therapy treatments per week for hip replacement (as occurred with one of the coauthors' mother) is another example. Indeed, James E. Sabin (1998) argues that the United States has engaged in an experiment in implicit rationing through the advent of managed care. The problem Sabin sees with this experiment is that it was done without consulting those involved, including patients. Thus what has resulted is "an adversarial system of priority setting" (1998, 1003). The result is the mistrust that has fueled the managed care backlash (below and Chapter 7 of this book).

Rationing can occur at the physician-patient level, what Ubel (2000) calls bedside rationing. For a medical decision to qualify as bedside rationing, three conditions must be met (2000). First, the service that is being withdrawn or not recommended must be one that would provide some benefit to the patient. Second, the reason for making the decision must be in the financial interest of someone other than the patient. For example, if a more expensive medication were not recommended because doing so would result in some financial penalty to the physician that would meet this condition. The third condition is that the physicians "have control over the use of the medically beneficial service" (2000, 112).

Blank (1997) argues that there is a set of illusions that Americans have about their health care system that is leading to the failure of the system. Breaking those illusions will lead us to see the necessity of rationing and that we are already engaged in rationing.

The first illusion is that health care and medical care are the same. Medical care includes all the providers and institutions that seek to alleviate or remedy disease. Health care is a broader concept that looks at health outcomes in the population at large and sees reasons for those outcomes that are more expansive than medical care. The health of a population is affected by "poverty, crime, drug and alcohol abuse" (Blank 1997, x).

A second related illusion is that as we spend more money on medical care and medical technology the population will become healthier. Like the first illusion, this one equates medical and health care and suffers from the same narrow perspective. While the United States may have the best medical care system and the most advanced technology, health outcomes for the population as a whole do not match our spending on medical care compared to other countries (Blank 1997).

The third illusion is that rationing does not occur in the United States and should not occur. Blank (1997) points out that there is substantial rationing that goes on, though the phrase is not used. As discussed above, bedside rationing is fairly common. Managed care organizations ration through a variety of techniques (below). Rationing appears in the United States when a substantial portion of the population does not have health insurance and therefore has limited access to medical care.

A fourth illusion is that the changes needed in the health care system can be made painlessly. The move toward managed care and the push for managed competition were attempts to make changes with few overt costs and without discussing rationing. The belief by many that much could be saved by cutting waste and fraud also fits with this illusion (the discussion in Patel and Rushefsky 1998).

The final illusion is that health care costs can be controlled without a major government role. Here Blank (1997) mentions global budgets and fee structures that have been adopted by other nations (the section below on international perspectives on rationing).

Rationing and Rights

Another important distinction that plays a role in many of the issues discussed in this and other chapters is the nature of rights. Rights can be distinguished between negative rights, the older type, and positive rights (Blank 1988). Negative rights, which are embodied in the U.S. and state constitutions, include the right to be left alone, to not be interfered with. The idea of natural rights (John Locke) or inalienable rights (Thomas Jefferson in the Declaration of Independence) is essentially one of negative rights. The notion of autonomy of one's life becomes important here. Issues such as the right to die (Chapter 2) and medical privacy (Chapter 5) involve negative rights. Rationing is generally not a problem here.

Rationing is very much involved in the other type of right, positive rights. Positive rights are "those that impose obligations on others to provide those goods and services necessary for each individual to have at least a minimally decent level of human existence" (Blank 1988, 191). The concept of a "right to health care" involves positive rights. The push for patients' bill of rights in the United States and elsewhere is another example of a positive right (Chapter 7). Managed care in the United States and the more explicit rationing that occurs in other countries (such as Great Britain) are attempts to limit positive rights, if understood in this context as the demand for unlimited care, and save resources and costs.

There is also a tradition that rights are accompanied by obligations. This is very much in line with the communitarian view that we have discussed in other chapters (see, especially, Chapters 1 and 7). The individual rights perspective, especially accompanied by a largely market-oriented health care system, leads to the notion of a right to health care. While that has not been established in law, it is seen in the managed care backlash (below and Chapter 7), where consumer/patients argue that they were denied needed and appropriate health care. Managed care has been the major policy tool for restraining the health care system.

Blank's (1997) advocacy of rationing is compatible with a communitarian perspective. First, he argues that the problem with the American health care system is a lack of clearly defined goals. As a result, reforms are somewhat aimless. Part of the reason for the lack of goals is the failure to come to grips with the individuals and their relationships with the larger society. For Blank the appropriate goal is to "maximize the health of society, not individual medical benefits" (1997, xviii). Medicine is only one path to meeting this goal. Further, Blank argues that having such a goal means that people should become more responsible for their own health.

The former governor of Colorado, Richard Lamm, has been on almost a crusade of seeking limits, particularly in health care. His argument can be simply stated (Lamm 1998). Too much money is spent on health care, especially given the return (outcomes). A certain portion of health care is of, at best, marginal utility. Government has limited resources and publicly provided health should be limited to what can be afforded. The focus of government policy is on the entire population and not on specific individuals. The same is true for managed care plans: the focus is on the health of the group of subscribers and not on individuals. Rationing, by this perspective, is an appropriate public policy.

One question we should ask is why rationing is necessary. At one level the answer is simple. There are limited resources available and not all can be devoted to health care. In some respects, the demand for health care, or medical care, is unlimited and continues to grow. In the United States two specific reasons are mentioned as why rationing is necessary. The first is increases in the cost of medical care (Blank 1997). The United States spends more on health care than any other nation, but does not necessarily receive more for it. For example, on various measures of health the United States is below many of the European countries. In any event, increasing health care costs crowd out spending on other worthy causes. While the United States saw some moderation of cost increases in the middle and late 1990s, because of the advent of managed care and the 1997 Balanced Budget Act, cost increase reared its ugly head at the beginning of the twenty-first century.

A second rationale for rationing is the maldistribution of health care resources (Blank 1997). This is an ethical issue at several levels. First, a significant portion of health care expenses goes to the elderly. Demographic data predicts a significant increase in the percentage of the elderly population in the United States (and other industrialized countries as well).

The obvious ethical dilemma is whether we as a society should continue to devote such a high percentage of medical resources to this sector of the population. Blank's (1997) analysis focuses on high users (not necessarily the elderly) with chronic conditions. He also suggests that high users tend to be people who engage in unhealthy behaviors. They have higher rates of hospitalization, more chronic problems, and higher death rates than those who were more likely to engage in healthy behaviors (Blank 1997, 6–7).

A related issue is that a more even distribution of health care resources would allow coverage of more people. This is what Oregon did with its Medicaid program (below) and effectively what other countries have done (international perspectives section).

Another issue related to rationing is medical technology. While we discuss this in more detail below, we note here that there is kind of a medical technological imperative that leads to the development of new medical interventions that are costly and, in at least some cases, not always cost effective. Developments in genetic research (Chapter 4) promise incredible advances in our ability to understand the causes of diseases and to develop appropriate treatments for them. But those treatments are likely to be very expensive.

Rationing decisions are also made at the individual level. We might ask, for example, how people without health insurance obtain medical care. The answer tends to be that many of them put off seeking help until problems worsen, and then seek help from places like emergency rooms. This is the most expensive source of care and is clearly a waste of resources (Patel and Rushefsky 1999). Rationing, to a certain extent, includes limiting waste and inefficiencies as a way of conserving resources or freeing them up for other uses.

Another example of rationing at the individual level concerns the debate over whether Medicare should include a pharmacy benefit. Traditional Medicare does not include such a benefit, though HMOs often offer such a benefit to attract subscribers. Medicare subscribers may also purchase supplemental insurance that would include a drug benefit.

But a substantial portion of Medicare recipients do not have such a benefit. What do they do? The poorer recipients have choices. They may choose not to use the medication. They may choose not to use as much of the medication as prescribed to save money, a form of rationing, in this case stretching out the medication. A third choice reported is that some recipients have to choose between food and medication. Again, these are rationing choices.

Rationing is as much an ethical/values issue as it is an economic issue. In 1994, Norman Daniels issued a challenge to bioethicists to try to resolve four problems given the limited resources that can be devoted to health care. The first challenge is whether rationing should favor the best outcomes from medical procedures, or the fairest outcomes. The second challenge relates to priorities: Should we focus on treating those who are the most disabled? or sickest? The third challenge is the aggregation problem: Should high benefits for a few people outweigh smaller benefits to many people? The final challenge is one of procedure: Should democratic processes be used to determine priorities (as was done in the Oregon plan, see below) (Daniels 1994)?

Two important societal goals involved in rationing are distributing resources fairly (an ethics-based goal) and doing as much good as possible with those resources (an economics-based goal) (Fuchs 1998). There are problems with these two goals. First of all, fairness and goodness can mean different things (Stone 2002 on different interpretations of policy goals). Consider the goal of doing as much good, maximizing benefits.

Doing good might mean saving as many lives as possible. Or it might mean extending life expectancy. Or it might mean focusing on the quality of life. Or it might mean providing care and sympathy even if it does not affect health (Fuchs 1998). Fairness, equity, and efficiency have similar problems of interpretation and agreement.

Freedom and democracy are other important goals related to rationing, or allocation of heath resources. Democracy means that there should be public input in decisions and accountability for those decisions. Rationing or allocation decisions should not be simply technocratic (decided by a cost-benefit or cost-effectiveness analysis) nor the sole product of a committee of experts. Freedom means that patients have choices about plans and providers and providers are not unduly constrained in their practice. One of the great problems in rationing is that all these values are important and they involve trade-offs. No decision, whether implicit or explicit, is likely to be completely satisfactory.

How to Ration

In discussing rationing, it is important to note that rationing can take place in many different ways. While the United States has not engaged in explicit rationing, with some exceptions such as the Oregon plan, organ transplantation, and managed care, rationing has occurred in this country. We just do not call it that. That is why understanding the different forms rationing can take is important.

As mentioned earlier, one form of rationing is based on physician discretion (Blank 1997; Ubel 2000). Physicians decide whether an additional treatment is warranted for a particular patient. This is what Ubel calls bedside rationing. For example, physicians do not have to treat Medicaid patients. Similarly, physicians may choose to locate in more affluent areas and not in impoverished areas, such as inner cities and rural communities.

Rationing can take place through the use of prices, market mechanisms. For example, people who do not have the ability to pay, as discussed above, tend to do without, though not without harmful effects on health. Not everyone can afford or has access to health insurance.

Rationing can take place in non-price or implicit ways (Blank 1997). This is more typical of Western, industrialized countries with some kind of national health insurance system. Such rationing may take the form of queuing, waiting lines for services that are not deemed critical. In the United States, queuing is used in organ transplantation because of the shortage of available donated organs (Chapter 3). One of the promises of genetic research, particularly stem cell research, is the possibility of generating new organs without the necessity of organ donation via death. If that promise becomes reality, then rationing for organ transplantation would either be unnecessary or based on price.

Another way to ration is to set a fixed budget for health care. As we will see, countries with national health insurance plans have this tool available to them. A related technique is to either slow the development of new technology or, much more likely, limit access to technology. On a number of measures, the United States makes technology much more available than other countries, such as Canada and Great Britain.

Analytical Techniques for Rationing

Medical judgments are made on the basis of a number of different types of evidence (Mulrow and Lohr 2001). These include medical research, such as evidence-based medicine discussed below, the specifics of a patient's conditions (including the beliefs of the patient, other conditions the patient might have, and so forth), the experience and beliefs of the provider(s), the values of society, and the resources, rules, and financing of the health care system.

David M. Eddy (2001) presents a useful way to think about analytical techniques and rationing. He suggests we think of two different situations or settings. The first setting is what he calls the "open-ended or unlimited budget" (2000, 389). In this setting, providers are not concerned about the cost of treatment and patients and payers are willing to pay whatever the recommended treatment costs. In the "closed or limited budget" (2000, 389) setting, patients and payers are not willing or able to pay for all possible treatments. Then providers and plans must consider costs. As Eddy points, there is a whole range of variations of these two settings.

In both settings, providers (and plans) have to decide on how effective various treatments are and to make sure that benefits of the treatments outweigh the costs. In the limited budget setting, a further consideration is whether the treatment is worth the cost. Analytical techniques such as evidence-based medicine and cost-effectiveness analysis play an important role in these kinds of decisions.

Evidence-Based Medicine

One technique for rationing that is gaining in importance is evidence-based medicine (EBM), sometimes called "patient-oriented evidence that matters" or POEM (Slawson and Shaughnessy 2001). EBM can take the form of clinical guidelines or clinical standards (Mulrow and Lohr 2001). Advocates of this approach argue that it will save money and allow expansion of insurance and care to underserved populations. Payers can use research, EBM, to make decisions about which technologies to cover and how (Garber 2001). Slawson and Shaughnessy (2001) argue that EBM of the POEM sort does not disadvantage patients. As noted in the definition of rationing above, they distinguish between services that are necessary (and therefore should not be rationed) and those that might be beneficial and could be rationed if the benefits are small. They write:

> The true goal of evidence-based medicine and information mastery is to provide effective and efficient care to patients via a health care system that allows all people to receive basic care. To meet this goal, this system has to be reconfigured so that existing resources are used in a way that is fair and equitable to all persons (and not just patients). Costs must be considered. (Slawson and Shaughnessy 2001, 54)

The goal of EBM is to increase the value of medicine. The value of medicine is a function of its quality and its cost (Slawson and Shaughnessy 2001). The fear expressed by those critical of managed care (below and Chapter 7) is that the focus is on reducing costs by reducing the quality of medicine. But one can improve the quality of care and reduce costs (thereby raising the value of health care) by reducing misuse and overuse (2001).

An example of overuse is that patients hospitalized with acute myocardial infarction (heart attack) in hospitals with cardiac catherization facilities are more likely to undergo procedures such as angioplasty and bypasses than in hospitals without such facilities. The procedures cost considerably more than other procedures and the outcomes in terms of mortality and morbidity are not better with the more expensive procedures (2001).

An example of misuse is prescribing antibiotics for viral respiratory infections, even though such a therapy has no impact on the viral infection. Another example of misuse is errors in prescribing medications (2001).

Slawson and Shaughnessy argue that rationing must occur in the United States but we should ration services rather than people as is done (through lack of insurance coverage or access to services). Further, such rationing should focus on the larger community and not just the patient.

Rationing based on EBM would produce clinical guidelines for providers in treating their patients (Norheim 1999). Such guidelines will be acceptable if they are backed by appropriate medical science and are the result of a deliberative democratic process. There are a number of places where physicians, plan administrators, consumer advocates, and others can examine clinical guidelines at various Web sites. The National Guidelines Clearing House, at www.guideline.gov, is a joint venture of the Agency for Healthcare Research and Quality (AHRQ) within the U.S. Department of Health and Human Services (DHHS), the American Medical Association (AMA), and the American Association of Health Plans (AAHP—the interest group for managed care plans).

Norheim offers a set of criteria for assessing the importance of guidelines, the acceptability of the process for arriving at the guidelines, and for acceptability of the information produced as a result of the process. His basic point is that guidelines need to be acceptable: "Clinical decisions should be based on the best available evidence within the twin constraints of resource scarcity and public scrutiny" (Norheim 1999, 1429).

Of course, not everyone is happy with the potential for EBM as a tool for rationing. Kleinert (1998) argues that EBM should be used along with ethical values and judgment. Allowing EBM to be used at levels higher than the practitioner places the judgments of health care allocation in the hands of bureaucrats or politicians. It also removes, apart from the element of individual judgment, concern for the individual patient. Kleinert, though he does not use the term, is concerned about the reductionism inherent in EBM:

> The evidence-based line above which treatment will be funded and below which it will not (discussion of the Oregon plan, below) is a hopeless myth. The modern trend to search for precise answers in the form of numbers and probabilities can have only a limited role in human sciences such as medicine. As Amartya Sen . . . said in his excellent talk about competing concepts of equity in health care, "It is better to be vaguely right than precisely wrong." (Kleinert 1998, 1244)

Marc Rodwin (2001) sees EBM as less than fully objective with lots of political implications. He writes that there has been a strong tendency in the United States to try to seek technocratic solutions to political problems; EBM fits this pattern. However, Rodwin argues that one of the major impacts of EBM is its use by managed care organizations to reduce the power of providers, especially physicians.

> To begin with, evidence-based medicine reduces the discretion and autonomy of physicians. While in the past the authority of doctors prevented questioning of their clinical choices, with evidence-based medicine, payers and managers can ask physicians to justify their decisions, thereby reducing the clinical discretion of doctors.
>
> Moreover, when relying on evidence-based medicine, clinical choices are not justified based on clinical insight, medical training, or personal experience. Instead, they are based on data from journal articles in medicine, epidemiology, and economics, which rely on such analytical techniques as random clinical control trials, multiple regression analysis, and cost-effectiveness analysis. These methods don't require a medical education and place nonphysicians trained in social science, science, or public policy analysis on par with physicians. Relying on such studies breaks the lockhold that the medical profession traditionally has had over judging medicine.

Furthermore, evidence-based medicine has enabled payers, purchasers and governmental authorities to use their financial clout to alter the practice of medicine. Traditionally doctors defined the standard of care. Now, armed with more and better information about medical practices, payers and purchasers can deny payment for medical services they deem medically unnecessary or ineffective. In so doing, they redefine standards for appropriate medical practice. (Rodwin 2001, 440–441)

Belkin (1997, 515) calls this the "technocratic wish": that there be some scientific solution to the twin problems of cost and quality and, at the same, enhance control of providers.

Cost-Effectiveness Analysis

A second important technique of rationing is cost-effectiveness analysis (CEA) (Ubel 2000). CEA is a technique for comparing different medical services, in our case, in terms of how many lives are saved or how much the quality of life is improved. It provides one tool for examining the efficacy of medical technologies and is an important element of technology assessment.

The result of a CEA is a ratio that shows the cost of achieving a health objective. The ratio is often expressed in life years gained or quality of adjusted life years (QALY) (Ubel 2000) in the numerator of the ratio and the cost in the denominator. The ratio can be used for different types of patients (such as those with other health conditions) and for different levels of the treatment (Russell et al. 1996).

One reason why CEA is both important and difficult is the nature of medical interventions. There is a certain amount of uncertainty in any intervention. That is, medical interventions are probabilistic in nature (Fuchs 1998; Mulrow and Lohr 2001). An intervention that works in one case may not work in a similar case. Medical tests are highly probabilistic. In testing for a particular condition, say hepatitis C or the presence of HIV, some percentage of the results are going to be wrong. A test may produce a positive result (presence of hepatitis C) where the subject does not actually have the disease (a false positive), whereas a test result may show that the subject does not have the disease when in fact she does (a false negative). This probabilistic nature of medicine makes rationing decisions more difficult.

Further, Russell et al. (1996) argue that CEA should not be applied mechanistically. That is, they assert that there are other considerations that might affect clinical decision making, such as who and how many people are affected (helped or harmed) by the decision.

One example of the use of CEA on a national level can be seen in Australia (Birkett, Mitchell, and McManus 2001). Pharmaceuticals have been increasing in costs more rapidly than most other medical interventions. Australia uses CEA of medications to decide which ones to include on a list eligible for patient subsidies. Those that are accepted for the list have demonstrated their value. Proposed drugs are compared with existing medications or, if none are available for the specific indication, with nonpharmaceutical interventions. Randomized clinical trials or something approximating them are submitted to the Pharmaceutical Benefits Advisory Committee. Because new drugs are almost always more expensive than older drugs (though often more effective), comparisons are made on the basis of life years gained, QALYs gained, or deaths prevented. The study then shows the "incremental net cost of achieving each additional unit of outcome" (2001, 108). The authors judge the project a success, though at the same time they point out that such analyses have not restrained increases in drug costs.

Technology Assessment

Related to EBM and CEA is technology assessment. The former congressional Office of Technology Assessment (OTA) defined the term as "a comprehensive form of policy research that examines the technical, economic, and social consequences of technology applications" (Luce and Brown 1994, 49).

Much of the advances in the health sciences have occurred through the development of medical technology (Weisbrod 1994). These include vaccines, arthroscopic surgery, organ transplantation, reproductive technologies, noninvasive diagnostic procedures such as computed tomography (CT) scanners and nuclear magnetic resonator imaging devices (MRI), and the many applications resulting from genetic research (Chapter 4).

In general, these technological developments have resulted in increased rather than decreased costs and thus have contributed to the explosion of health care costs (Patel and Rushefsky 1999). By contrast, consider advances in computer technology. As the power and quality of computer technology have dramatically increased, costs have dropped. This has become even more apparent in the case of pharmaceuticals. Increases in drug costs have fueled the renewal of health care inflation in the early years of the twenty-first century. In 1999, expenditures on prescription drugs increased by almost 17 percent over the previous year, compared to 6 percent for physician services and 3.7 percent for hospital services. Overall health expenditures increased by 5.6 percent. Projections are that while there will be some moderation of costs through 2010, prescription medication expenditures will continue to outstrip those of other health care services (Heffler et al. 2001).

The intensive use of medical technology also distinguishes the United States from virtually all other western, industrialized countries. For example, the United States has many times more CT and MRI scanners than any other nation and the queues for operations such as pacemakers are much smaller here than in other countries (Patel and Rushefsky 1999, Chapter 7; Rottenberg and Theroux n.d.).

A recent study examined technology in the United States and seventeen other countries, focusing on the treatment of heart attack victims (Technological Change in Health Care [TECH] Research Network 2001). The United States leads the other nations particularly in the use of the more expensive, intensive technology, such as cardiac catherization, bypass surgery, and primary angioplasty. Further, the adoption and diffusion of new technologies occurred faster in the United States than elsewhere (though some other nations were close to the U.S. pattern).

Why so much more technology in the United States than elsewhere? Weisbrod (1994) argues that until recently the health insurance system contained incentives that promoted the use and paid for the development of medical technology. Other countries, with their national health care systems, placed budgetary constraints on the use of technology. The United States's decentralized system contained few if any such constraints. The purchase and use of technology has been left to individual providers. TECH research network found that countries that had "weak supply-side restrictions on the adoption of intensive treatments" saw greater growth in the use and diffusion of technology than those countries that had stronger controls, such as Canada and Denmark (TECH Research Network 2001, 37).

There have been some attempts to restrain the economic impact of medical technology. The certificate-of-need programs in the 1960s and 1970s sought to control the dissemination of technology, especially of CT and MRI scanners. More important, the development of the prospective payment system (diagnostic related groups, DRGs) in Medicare and the advent of managed care sought to have some impact. DRGs, by fixing hospital Medicare payments for specific diagnoses, encouraged providers to use less technology. Managed care, first in the form of health maintenance organizations (HMOs) and then in other types, sought to limit expenses through utilization, preauthorization, physician reviews, and financial incentives, such as limits on prescriptions and budgets for medications. All have reduced somewhat the use of new technology (Weisbrod 1994). There is some evidence that managed care places controls on use of technology and that there have been cost savings as a result. Baker and Wheeler (1998) found that there is an inverse relationship between HMO market shares and the use of MRIs. The authors are careful to say that they make no claims about the impact of lower utilization on quality of care. Further, they argue that because managed care organizations may limit the adoption of new technologies, the return on investment in new technologies may decrease. This, in turn, may reduce the development of new technologies.

The federal government has been involved in technology assessment. Congress created the OTA in 1972 "to aid in the identification and consideration of existing and probable impacts of technological application" (Office of Technology Assessment Act, PLS 92–484, 92nd Congress, 2nd session). OTA became the fourth of Congress's staff agencies (the other are the General Accounting Office, the Congressional Research Service in the Library of Congress, and the Congressional Budget Office). Its task was to conduct studies on technology-related issues. Over the course of its twenty-three year history, it issued reports at the request of Congress on a wide variety of topics. These included bone marrow transplants, cardiac radionuclide imaging, and intensive care units. OTA was terminated in the fall of 1995, a victim of budget cutting by the new Republican controlled Congress (Morgan 1995).

Another federal agency that engages in medical technology assessment is the Food and Drug Administration (FDA). FDA is responsible for assessing the safety and efficacy of new drugs, medical devices, and biologics. The FDA does not conduct research itself; manufacturers and developers submit research for FDA approval.

A third federal agency with some jurisdiction related to medical technology assessment is the Agency for Healthcare Research and Quality (AHRQ). Housed within the DHHS, AHRQ's basic mission is to fund research on health outcomes.

Much of technology assessment in the United States is carried out by the private sector, mainly universities and corporations (and corporations fund a considerable amount of university research). That research is used by purchasers and providers to decide whether to cover, purchase, or use a new technology. It is fair to say that in the United States there is much research being conducted but in the absence of some overall authority, decisions which affect society as a whole are made in a very incremental, fragmented form.

There are ten steps in the technology assessment process (though there is considerable variation in how those steps are taken (National Information Center n.d.). The ten steps are: identify assessment topics, specify the assessment problem, determine the locus of assessment (that is, who is going to undertake the assessment), retrieve available evidence, collect new primary data, interpret evidence, synthesize evidence, formulate findings and recommendations, disseminate findings and recommendations, and monitor impact. As can be seen, technology assessment is a long, difficult, expensive process.

Luce and Brown (1994) conducted an analysis of how hospitals, HMOs, and third-parties use technology assessment. Hospitals use technology assessment to look for new technology, to control costs, and to make purchasing decisions. HMOs use the technique to make purchasing decisions and to decide what technologies to cover. Third-party payers use it to inform their coverage decisions and to distinguish between state-of the-art technologies and experimental ones (covering the former and perhaps not the latter).

Of course, the major question behind these three techniques is whether advances in medical technology are worth the cost. Two studies of medical technologies do suggest they are beneficial. The first one, by Cutler and McClellan (2001), examined technology dealing with five conditions: heart attack, low birthweight babies, depression, cataracts, and breast cancer. Their benefit-cost analysis shows that benefits outweighed costs for the first four of the conditions. For the fifth condition, treatment of breast cancer, the costs and benefits were about equal (for a discussion of politics and technology evaluation in regard to breast cancer treatment, see Mello and Brennan 2001).

The second study, by Kleinke (2001), finds that major developments in pharmaceuticals during the 1990s were responsible for improvements in the health of cancer, AIDS, and heart disease patients, as well as low birthweight babies. Life expectancy also has risen. While Kleinke admits that the new medications are more expensive than older ones, they are also more effective. The increased cost for innovation is the price we pay for progress.

Rationing and Ethical Perspectives

Apart from questions about how to ration are issues of the principles on which rationing should be based. The principles come from the field of ethics, and ethicists and philosophers have examined the fairest or most just way to ration. Within the American context, those who have written along these lines have decried the health care system as fundamentally unjust. The injustice derives from the employer-based health insurance system, the lack of universal coverage, and decentralized decision-making. This is compounded by the advent of managed care and the rationing that is inherent in it (below) (Emanuel 2000).

The focus of those writing about justice and health care is access to health services and allocation of health resources. Emanuel (2000) offers four principles to guide allocation decisions (they apply specifically to managed care organizations). The first is that whatever allocation of health resources is made should result in improved health. The second principle is that members of managed care organizations should be fully informed about allocation decisions. This coincides with the idea of the autonomy of individuals, a principle that also lies at the heart of privacy issues (Chapter 5). The third principle is that members should have the opportunity to consent to the allocation decisions. This supports the autonomy view and also the perspective that democratic participation is important. The final principle is the minimization of conflicts of interests. This relates to financial incentives that may lead to certain allocation decisions (the discussions about managed care below and in Chapter 7). A fifth principle to complement the first four is to allow grievance procedures for denial of services (allocations). We address this issue in the next chapter.

One interesting part of Emanuel's (2000) discussion is how to apply or implement these principles in managed care organizations. He suggests that a market approach is one way to do so. Members and prospective members, under a market system, would have a choice of plans that would offer differing sets of benefits and providers (differing allocations of health resources) and would make the choice of plan on an annual basis. The accepted name for such a plan is managed competition. While there are examples of plans that approximate managed competition, most employees do not in fact have such choices.

Further, there are weaknesses to this form of market allocation. It is based on individual choice and not collective decision making and it calls for a single choice to cover complex issues (Emanuel 2000).

Cookson and Dolan (2000) examine a different set of principles for invoking justice in rationing decisions. Their paper focuses on principles for deciding who should get health care and when (2001, 323). The first principle is need, but one problem with the principle of need is that it means different things. This ranges from immediate threat to life, to immediate ill health, to lifetime ill health, to immediate and lifetime capacity, to benefit from treatment. In addition, there are degrees of need. This is no simple principle.

Their second principle is maximization. Again there is variation here. Maximization, very much economically based with its utilitarian focus, can mean maximizing the health of the entire population. Or it might mean maximizing the well-being of the entire population, which would include nonhealth factors.

The third principle is egalitarianism. This principle would have us use health resources to reduce inequalities in health care. This might mean ensuring that everyone gets to live a "similarly long and healthy life" (Cookson and Dolan 2000, 327). Or it could mean giving people the opportunity to live such a life.

The ideas of justice and fairness are at the heart of Kopelman and Palumbo's (1997) analysis. They explore four theories of justice: utilitarianism, egalitarianism, libertarianism, and contractarianism. They find that all four theories of justice provide rationales for redistributing health care resources to children. They argue, as does Emanuel (2000), that the inefficiencies of the market does not make it a good mechanism for allocation of health resources.

Health Care Rationing: International Perspectives

Before looking at systems in other countries, it is helpful to understand that the public sector in the rest of the Western, industrialized world provides for more coverage of health services than in the United States. This may be called the "international standard" (White 1999). Components of this standard include covering virtually all of the population (universal coverage) and "medically necessary" (White 1995, 6) services (plus drug benefits for defined populations). Financing is based on contributions to a system, rather than premiums to an insurance plan offered by an employer or by Medicare (in the case of the Part B portion of the program). Those contributions are related to income (ability to pay). Financing is also based on general revenues. The countries that White studied control costs through regulation. There are fee schedules and, for the most part, global budgets. All of the countries try to control technology development by limiting investment in new technology. This can be accomplished through licensing, direct budgeting, and fee schedules (1995).

The contrast between the international standard and the U.S. health care system is dramatic. More people are covered in other countries and there is more regulation of health care in those countries. At the same time, the other countries have done a better job of controlling costs. The closest the United States comes to the international standard is the Medicare program, at least until the consensus underlying Medicare frayed under budgetary pressures (Oberlander 1998; Marmor 2000).

Great Britain

Compared to the United States, other countries, such as Great Britain, engage in much more explicit rationing. The origins of the British National Health Service (NHS) go back to 1911 when limited medical coverage of low-income workers was mandated. The coverage only covered workers (and not the workers' dependents) and then only for general medical care. The combination of dissatisfaction with the limited system, the hardships suffered during World War II, and the community spirit that was raised in fighting the war led to the passage in 1948 of the NHS (Graig 1999). Among Western, industrialized countries, Britain has the only health care system that truly could be called socialized medicine.[1] The expectation was that British citizens would receive all the health care they needed and wanted. Expectations easily exceeded the capacity of the system to perform (Newdick 1997).

The system's response was to set limits. For example, Britain has one of the lowest ratios of physicians to populations among the Western industrialized nations (Graig 1999). Access to technology has also been limited. In 1993, the United States had more than four times as many CAT scanners proportionate to the population in Great Britain and about four and a half times more magnetic resonance imaging (MRI) machines in 1995 than Britain. Similarly, health expenditures as a percentage of gross domestic product was twice as high in the United States (13.6 percent) as in Britain (6.7 percent) in 1997. The United States spent $4,090 on health care per person in 1997 as compared to $1,347 in Britain (Graig 1999). On a number of health care statistics, outcomes in the two countries are about the same (1999). The difference in spending is that it is pretty much controlled in Britain (rationed) and much less controlled in the United States.

Rationing, or resource allocation, is divided into three sections through a "top-down" budgeting process to regional health and district health authorities, to primary care services, and to community-based service (Graig 1999, 159). The largest section is from the central government (NHS) and covers eight regional and about a hundred district health authorities (Graig 1999; Newdick 1997). This pays most physician and hospital services and is based on population, market forces, projected health needs, and the size of the elderly population (1997). The health authorities, in turn, make allocations to doctors and hospitals via contracts for specific services (1997). Clinical discretion (1997), or what Ubel (2000) calls bedside rationing, is also included, though not explicitly in rationing. Funding is largely from general tax revenues.

User fees are not charged for most services, the major exception being dental care and pharmaceuticals (Graig 1999; Newdick 1997). The NHS does not cover all services, in particular long-term care.

Rationing occurs even in the case of pharmaceuticals. A 1999 survey by the British National Schizophrenia Fellowship found that many psychiatrists were withholding prescriptions of newer medications to treat the illness because of insufficient funding:

> The survey found 16.4% of psychiatrists said their prescribing was affected by lack of funding; 15.6% by "personal cost concerns"; 8.9% by a fixed allocated budget; and 4% by a restriction on patient numbers. Another 8% were added to the total—representing half of the psychiatrists who said they were subject to prescribing directives—bringing the total to 53%. (Dean 1999, 657)

Dean (1999) argues, echoing Kleinke (2001), that though the cost of new drugs is considerably higher than for older drugs they replace, the costs of older drugs included more than just the drugs themselves. The failure to work as well as the newer ones leads to social problems such as additional hospital care, social services and, sometimes, imprisonment. Thus a complete cost-benefit analysis might support using the newer drugs (discussion above).

The private sector has a role to play in delivering services in Britain. Citizens cannot move or opt out of the system (which can be done in Germany but not in Canada; Graig 1999). Those who wish elective surgery and wish to avoid the long queues (a form of rationing), can go to the private sector. Graig (1999, 163) quotes Aaron and Schwartz in describing the difference between the two sectors: "the private patient pays to avoid waiting, the NHS patient waits to avoid paying." There has been an increase in the percentage of the British population with private health insurance. The move toward private insurance, much of it provided by employers, indicates dissatisfaction with the National Health Service. Most particularly, it indicates some unhappiness with the rationing endemic to the British system (1999).

In 2001, the British Medical Association issued a report studying the entire British health care system (NHS and the private sector) (British Medical Association 2001; see also Report urges more honest approach to rationing 2001).

One relatively new and incomplete way that Britain tries to ration health care is through the use of techniques such as CEA and EBM. Both are a function of observations in Britain as well as in other countries (including the United States) that there are wide variations in the practice of medicine. The British Department of Health has funded research to develop evidence about the most cost-effective procedures and develop guidelines for clinical practice (Newdick 1997). To date, EBM has had a limited impact on the NHS.

The Royal College of Physicians has recommended that a national council for heath care priorities be created. Such a council would provide a forum for debates over rationing. Klein (1998) questions what such a forum will do and whether it will be useful and productive. Broader rationing decisions are much more difficult to make than are decisions about more narrowly tailored issues. The narrower issues concern approval of a new technology or recommendations about a particular therapy. Klein (1998) concludes his article by saying that the best or at least most realistic way of making decisions is on a case-by-case basis. Such a procedure is known within the public administration and public policy literature as "muddling through" (Lindblom 1959) For Klein (1998) and Hunter (1995), the appropriate way is to base rationing on clinical decisions (bedside rationing) that are determined by the openness of decision making between patient and provider (transparency). Trying to do top-down rationing in a very explicit fashion, as Britain has talked about and some European countries are doing (below), will ultimately prove harmful.

Mechanic (1997) likewise favors elegant muddling. He argues that explicit rationing has a role in setting national priorities, setting provider reimbursement rates, doing cost-effectiveness analyses, and so forth. But there are significant reasons why explicit rationing should not be done. One reason is that explicit rationing is done in a bureaucratic setting. Medical care may change, leading to the need for new standards, but bureaucratic decisions are hard to change. A second reason is that the process of making decisions concerning medical care at the clinical level is variable and depends on the state of technology, the physician/patient relationship, and so forth. Mechanic (1997, 85) writes that "Medical care is a process of discovery and negotiation, not simply the application of technical means."

The third argument Mechanic raises against explicit rationing concerns differences among patients. Rationing decisions, based on such things as clinical guidelines and EBM do not take account of differences among patients on severity of disease, socioeconomic characteristics, and so forth. A fourth related argument is lack of flexibility. Mechanic (1997) uses an example of an HMO that contracts with a bone marrow transplant facility and steers its patients to that facility regardless of where the patient lives.

The final argument Mechanic (1997) makes against explicit rationing is the possibility of political manipulation. Rationing at levels higher than the provider/patient level is always a political phenomenon (Klein 1998) that brings in outside forces and causes political and social battles.

For Mechanic (1997), implicit rationing, with its ability to respond to patients' needs and differences and to changes in medical understanding, is to be preferred, as long as it done in an open and fair way.

While there has been significant discussion of rationing as it concerns the NHS (as articles in the *British Medical Journal* indicate), not all agree with the rationing policy. Light (1997, 112; see also Klein 1998) describes rationing in the NHS:

> The NHS rations by delay to get on waiting lists, and then on the waiting lists themselves, and then with the further wait after an appointment has been made. It rations by undersupply of staff, doctors, machines, facilities, etc; by undercapitalisation of run down facilities; by dilution of tests done and services received; by discharge earlier than desirable; and by outright denial to even have the chance to wait or be undertreated.

Light argues that rationing is not inevitable and that there is not a bottomless pit of health needs. This is the argument that Callahan (1998), among others, makes: that the demand for health care is virtually unlimited. Light argues that this is a question that should be answered empirically rather than merely asserted. If he is correct, then rationing in the NHS may not be necessary.

This argument is supported by Frankel, Ebrahim, and Smith (2000). They contend that the idea of unlimited demand for help is based on the aging of the population, development of new medical technologies, and rising expectations. But the view that unlimited demand exists is founded on assertions rather than empirical data. Their discussion of the evidence suggests the NHS does meet demands. Further, they point out that the debate over rationing and the NHS began during a recession. Where there does appear to be some mismatch between demand and meeting that demand is in elective surgery, particularly for hip replacement and cataract surgery. Even here, Frankel, Ebrahim, and Smith argue that demand can be met with just a little bit more effort by providers. What they do see as driving the rationing debate and the view that there is unlimited demand for medical care services is what they call the "social construction of pessimism" (2000, 43). To some extent, Frankel, Ebrahim, and Smith write, this pessimism is based on the self interest of providers who are unhappy with the NHS.

Further, Light (1997) argues (as does the American public, see Patel and Rushefsky 1998) that there is a considerable amount of waste which if eliminated would also obviate the need for rationing. Various inequalities, such as clinical variations in practice and differences in access for certain sectors in society, force unnecessary rationing.

Light (1997) is particularly critical of the private sector, which, he writes, is allowed to cherry pick (a claim sometimes made about managed care organizations in the United States particularly with regard to Medicare; see Patel and Rushefsky 1999). This means that insurance companies seek healthier people with easier cases; the NHS thus has sicker, more chronically ill patients. Further, the waiting times for surgery are about thirty times higher in the public sector than in the private sector. One reason for this is that surgeons limit the amount of work they do for the NHS and devote more time to privately paying services. If changes were made in these areas, Light argues, rationing would be unnecessary.

While the discussion in Great Britain over the future of the NHS is based on a relatively explicit discussion of rationing, Britain is hardly the only country facing issues related to rationing. Other countries, including the United States, are attempting to address the problem of "growing demands and constrained resources" (Klein 1998, 959). In the fall of 1998, an international conference on priorities in health care, the second, was held in London. It produced a number of reports and articles (Klein 1998). For example, Soren Holm (1998) examined how attempts at rationing in European countries, such as the Netherlands, Norway, and Sweden were based on the process for arriving at priorities. But the second phase of reports from the Scandinavian countries focused on problems with the process. One problem was that there was difficulty in figuring what the purpose of a health care system is. The various possible goals (from equality in access, equality in status, meeting needs, treating disease, improving the health of a population) are fuzzy and unclear and there are trade-offs among them. The conclusion one gets upon reading the conference papers and the debates that occurred in the middle and late 1990s in England and elsewhere is that rationing does occur, but the basis for it is unsettled. For example, it appears that age is the basis for some rationing in Britain (Rivlin 1999 and references cited therein).

One problem that faces the British NHS is a lack of resources to meet demand for services (Hope 2001). This can be seen in the deficits with which the NHS operates and the long queues (waiting lists). The British Medical Association (BMA) argues that the gap is actually much greater than is apparent:

> However, the gap between funding and need is even greater, as it also includes demands that are identified but explicitly not met as a result of rationing decisions and unmet needs or health problems, which have not yet been clearly identified or translated into a demand for treatment. (British BMA 2001, 22)

In 2000, the British government, addressing this underinvestment, committed itself to providing more resources with a goal of achieving equality with other European nations by 2005 (that is, increasing spending up to the average in Europe) (BMA 2001). One factor leading to the increased funding was a report by the World Health Organization ranking national health systems on a series of indicators based on outcome, patient satisfaction, and financing. Britain came in 18th. The United States, by comparison, ranked 37th (BMA 2001). But as the BMA (2001) argued, more resources and stable levels of funding would greatly help the system.

Canada

> Canada's system of universal public insurance for health care . . . expresses the fundamental equality of Canadian citizens in the face of disease and death and a commitment that the rest of the community, through the public system, will help each individual with these problems as far as it can. (Evans, 1992, 740)

The Canadian health care system presents a different model of health care than Great Britain or the United States (Patel and Rushefsky 2002). Whereas the British system could rightfully be considered socialized medicine, the Canadian system, officially known as Medicare, can rightfully be considered a national health insurance program based on a single-payer system. In many ways, the Canadian system resembles the American Medicare program. Physicians are paid on a fee-for-service basis through negotiated fee schedules. The program does not cover certain services, such as outpatient prescriptions and long-term care. Further, among the industrialized nations, Canada spends proportionately less than some other nations. In 1998, Canada spent 9.8 percent of its gross domestic product (GDP) on health care, compared to 10.4 percent in Germany and 13.6 percent for the United States (Organization for Economic Cooperation and Development 2001).

Unlike the U.S. system, the Canadian system has in place a method for restraining expenditures. The federal government pays the provinces, which then reimburse providers. Increases in payments to the provinces are tied to the growth of the economy and the population of the province. Caps or limits have been placed on physician expenditures to prevent physicians from expanding the number of services given to patients to increase their incomes. Hospitals are given a fixed budget each year and allocate their resources based on those budgets (Graig 1999; Patel and Rushefsky 2002).

Apart from direct controls on spending through caps and global budgets, Canada controls the spread of medical technology. The provinces have to approve the purchase of new and expensive technology, such as MRI machines, which tend to be limited to academic medical centers rather than widely dispersed as in the United States (White 1995). Canada also tends to limit the number of providers, another way of limiting expenditures, and overuse (Roos et al. 1998).

One important difference between the Canadian and U.S. systems is in the value structure. While parts of the U.S. system incorporate community values in the sense that there are public programs to provide assistance to targeted groups (such as the elderly, the poor, the disabled, and children), many Americans do not have health insurance at all or have it through their place of employment. For Canadians, universal coverage and a single-payer system (which provides considerable cost savings over the more complex American system; Chernomas and Sepehri 1995) means that the entire nation is supported. For Canadians, government has a responsibility to ensure the welfare of the entire population, especially the weakest segments (Jecker and Meslin 1994, 188).

Yet the Canadian system, like those of other countries that meet White's (1995) international standard, has problems related to rationing (Walker and

Goodman 1993). Not all services are covered, there is a growing private sector, and physicians have expressed unhappiness with limits on provision of services and their income. Further, as with the British NHS, there can be fairly long waiting times (queues) for "elective" services, such as hip replacements. To exacerbate these problems, a 1990 recession led the national government to cut back on its health budget (Graig 1999).

Denmark (Scandinavia)

The late 1990s saw a focused discussion in Great Britain on rationing. Around the same time, a similar conversation was taking place in Denmark. A report by the Danish Council of Ethics (1997) proposed to explore how health care decisions were made in that country. Its term, "priority setting," was synonymous with rationing. The council stated that priority setting has always taken place but had become more important because of pressure for services, the aging of the population, and developments in medical technology (including potential developments stemming from genetic research). Such priority setting occurs at four levels: national government, counties and cities, in hospitals, and by individual practitioners. The report also listed various players or interest groups that sought to influence priority setting. These included the media, politicians, patient associations, patients and their families, providers, professional unions, manufacturers of medical products, and so forth.

Interestingly, the report talked about three cultures and the four different levels of priority setting. The distinction among these three cultures was how patients are viewed. The administrative culture is one where patients are seen as heterogeneous with lots of health care problems that need to be taken care of in a rational way. The treatment culture, typical of providers, is one where the patient has a specific medical problem that needs to be addressed. The care culture is one where the concern is not just for the illness of a particular patient but also for the patient as a being with myriad problems and needs. The significance of the three cultures is that they present conflicts in how to treat patients.

> These three cultures can provide different approaches to concrete priority-setting questions. Thus they may form the background for disagreement and conflict at the administrative level, in the ward, in dealings with the concrete patient. If you look at the question of hospitalisation time from the viewpoint of the administrator it is to be regarded in connection with the fact that shorter hospitalisation time equals treating more new patients and thus possibly reduces waiting lists. From the viewpoint of the treat-

ment provider the patient is really done with when the treatment is done with, and there is therefore no reason to keep them in hospital any longer. From the viewpoint of the care provider the question of hospitalisation time is also about whether the patient feels safe being discharged, whether the patient has a social network, etc. (Danish Council of Ethics 1997)

The Danish Council of Ethics argues that widely accepted values should underlie priority setting. The four values mentioned by the 1997 report are equal human worth, solidarity, security and safety, and freedom and self-determination. The council set as the general goal of the health care system: "Furthering health and preventing disease, fighting and relieving suffering related to the aim of ensuring the opportunity for self-expression for all irrespective of their social background and economic ability" (Danish Council on Ethics 1997). The council report continues that the basis for deciding on how to prioritize treatments should be on need. They question whether need is generated by providers and the medical industry. To move away from that type of generation, the council says need should be based on the gravity of the illness, urgency, and possible benefit to health (1997). While these three dimensions do overlap, the first two seem particularly close. The difference is that an illness may threaten death, but if the prognosis is that there is no cure or even a way to alleviate symptoms such as pain, then the need for treatment decreases.

The Danish Council of Ethics (1997) also set up four subgoals: social and geographic equality, quality, cost-effectiveness, and democracy and consumer influence.

Other Scandinavian countries also have experimented with priority setting (Danish Council of Ethics 1997). The Norwegian model sets five levels of priorities: The highest level, priority one, is addressed to those conditions that may lead to immediate consequences to either the patient or society. These include childbirth complications, emergencies, and emergency preparedness (which may be given higher priority in the United States after the September 11, 2001 terrorist attacks on the World Trade Center in New York and the Pentagon in Washington, DC). The second priority level focuses on those conditions that might prove serious at some time in the future if not treated. These include treatment of chronic diseases and some preventive programs. Level three priorities are those conditions that are not serious but the treatments have proven to be efficacious. These include treatments for such things as high blood pressure and childhood diseases. Health information and industrial health programs also come under this category. Level four priorities are for less serious conditions for which treatment is presumed to work in the sense that it improves the quality of life and a person's health.

Examples include the use of technology that has proven useful but is not as well accepted, such as ultrasound scanning routinely done on pregnant women. The final priority level, level five, is for services that are popular but whose efficacy is not well established. Examples include technology whose benefits have not been established and routine screenings of healthy persons. These services are not funded by the public system but are left to private clinics (Danish Council on Ethics 1997). The Norwegian plan provides that all those suffering from conditions categorized as priority level two will be treated within six months.

The development of these guidelines has engendered public discussion and instilled the notion that some patients should get more treatment than others (Danish Council of Ethics 1997).

But there have been problems. There is some gaming that occurs as advocates try to get particular services raised to higher levels of priority. Additionally, implementation of the guidelines has been uneven, as counties and providers have interpreted the guidelines in different ways (Danish Council of Ethics 1997).

The Netherlands has investigated a different model of priority setting. Everyone is guaranteed access to a basic set of health services. Other health services have to be paid for privately. In addition, the Dutch system sought to reduce the demand for health care through public advertising campaigns to convince people not to use the health care system unnecessarily. Further, physicians would be encouraged to reduce unnecessary prescriptions and medications by reducing some of their autonomy and changes in the payment method. The public opposed reductions in the health package, though physicians reacted more positively to the proposal. Clinical guidelines and protocols were established to categorize treatments and patients. The payment system, however, was not changed (Danish Council of Ethics 1997).

Sweden considered a model based on a set of three principles: human worth, need and solidarity, and cost effectiveness. The principles form a ranking system, with human worth at the top and cost effectiveness as third. Based on these principles, five levels of priorities were set at the political/administrative level and at the clinical level. For example, level one priorities at the political/administrative level include treatment of life-threatening diseases and illnesses that threaten permanent disability, treatment of chronic diseases, alleviative treatment of those near death, and treatment of illnesses that might reduce personal autonomy. At the clinical level, level one priorities include treatment of life threatening or permanent disabling illnesses, and at a slightly lower level, the other conditions mentioned at the political/administrative level. The priority setting exercise produced considerable debate but also considerable support. To an extent, providers tried to imple-

ment the priorities. Politicians seemed reluctant to support the recommendations (Danish Council of Ethics 1997).

Why spend all this time talking about priority setting and rationing in
other countries, particularly in Denmark? The reason for the focus is that the
Scandinavian and other countries are explicitly considering the idea of priority setting and doing so in a way that generates discussion among the public
and appropriate health and political stakeholders. In the United States, with
the exception of organ transplantion, no such discussion has taken place.

Rationing in Other Countries

Other countries were employing methods that would or could lead to rationing of health care services. In Germany, where national health insurance was
born (Graig 1999; White 1995), the government proposed to adopt "an annual health budget" (Durand de Bousingen 1999). Providers can be fined for
overprescribing or overtreating their patients. The plans give insurance companies more power to supervise treatments and prescriptions. A similar plan
was adopted in France in 1996 (Dorozynski 1997).

Some countries, such as Israel, considered budget cuts because their national health insurance programs were consistently running deficits. In the
case of Israel, sickness funds were permitted to impose copayments and to
restrict access to some services and choices of providers. Chinitz and Shalev
(1998) argue that what Israel has done is to try to be explicit about rationing
but because of opposition to changes has implicitly rationed.

Some of the problems that rationing raises can be seen in two cases in
New Zealand (Feek 1999). In 1993, New Zealand passed legislation concerning health care services for people with disabilities. Guidelines were
developed to decide who among those with end-stage renal disease (kidney
failure) was eligible for kidney dialysis. In the first case a 76-year-old man
was denied dialysis and the subsequent controversy carried over to the mass
media. Some claimed that the decision was made on the basis of budgetary
concerns, rather than clinical. The patient's family claimed age discrimination. The minister of health said the patient was not a good candidate for
dialysis because he also suffered from heart disease and prostate cancer. A
review of the case by the hospital led to the patient being put on dialysis,
though he died a year and a half later.

The second case was of a 63-year-old man with kidney failure plus dementia
and diabetes. The judgment was based on analysis of interim dialysis. Eventually the courts decided that the decision was based on clinical evidence and the
treatment was denied. The patient died a little over three weeks after dialysis
was terminated. Feek (1999) in his discussion of the two cases argued that

rationing worked, that the use of clinical guidelines combined with a review (appeals) process can produce fair and reasonable outcomes.

Bridgewater (1998) compares rationing in New Zealand and Great Britain, using coronary artery surgery as his example. His description of the British approach is one where consultant surgeons have the responsibility for deciding who gets the surgery and where they are on the waiting list. These decisions are based on "clinical priorities, available operating resources, and purchaser contracts" (Bridgewater 1998, 1251). By contrast, New Zealand uses an approach that Bridgewater (1998, 1251) describes as "more communal." Cardiologists screen or assess patients, patients are scored according to a priority system, they are assigned a likely operative mortality probability, and the information is presented at a meeting at which surgeons and cardiologists are presented. Decisions are based on agreement of the physicians.

What is interesting about Bridgewater's comparison is the discussion of how the two countries treat patients who are not immediately in danger of dying. New Zealand appears to deny the surgery to low risk patients who are not in imminent danger while Britain is more likely to treat such patients. The dilemma that Bridgewater addresses is one of limited resources that all health systems confront. Should one allow surgery for patients in imminent danger but with a high risk of dying or focus on those in less immediate danger but more likely to survive and survive well?

National Government and Public Policy

In many ways, rationing is much more difficult to talk about in the United States than in other countries. The major reason for this is that the United States does not have a system of national health insurance and therefore does not meet what Joseph White (1995) calls the international standard. Rather, the U.S. health care system developed incrementally, prodded by political forces, economic circumstances, and technological development (Starr 1982). The result is what Michael Reagan (1999) calls an "accidental system."

Thus the American health care system has different components, funded in different ways and to the extent that rationing occurs, it is generally implicit (with a few exceptions). Most physicians (providers) are in private practice. Some hospitals are publicly owned (public health service, Veterans Affairs, municipal hospitals), but most are either nonprofit or profit. The medical supply industry (including pharmaceutical companies) is privately owned. Much health research is funded by the federal government (largely through the NIH and the National Science Foundation) but a considerable amount occurs privately as well. All municipalities have public health services and there are some health services located in the nation's public schools.

Because the United States does not have national health insurance, people obtain health insurance in different ways. Looking at 1999 data, almost 67 percent of the population under 65 obtains health insurance from employment (National Center for Health Statistics 2001). This varies by racial/ethnic group. Seventy percent of whites have insurance through employment, compared to about 55 percent of African Americans, almost 64 percent of Asian Americans/Pacific Islanders, and almost 47 percent of Hispanics. A little more than 9 percent of the population is covered by the federal/state Medicaid program. Again, one can see racial/ethnic differences. Seven percent of whites are on Medicaid, 18.6 percent of African Americans, 9.2 percent of Asian American/Pacific Islanders, and 14.1 percent of Hispanics (National Center for Health Statistics 2001).

The major publicly financed health insurance programs are Medicare, Medicaid, and the new State Children's Health Insurance Program. Between the three programs, more than 74 million people are covered. There were 39.2 million Medicare enrollees in 1999 (most of them over 65, but some disabled), some 40.6 million Medicaid recipients, and about 2.7 million children enrolled in S-CHIP (National Center for Health Statistics 2001; HCFA.gov Web site, SCHIP status). In 2000, about 38.7 million people (14 percent of the population) were without health insurance. This represented the second straight year of decline, largely due to the expanding economy at the end of the twentieth century. Though this certainly is good news, the likelihood of continued declines in those without health insurance is slim. The economic slowdown, with the nation in a near recession by the middle of 2001, was likely to turn into a recession following the terrorist attacks in New York and Washington, D.C. in September, 2001 (Pear 2001c). Even with the good news through 2000, clearly, the international standard has not been met in the United States, nor is it likely to be soon.

One of the great ironies of the American health care system is that while it covers a smaller percentage of its population than other industrialized nations' systems, it spends more. In 1999, the United States spent $1,210.7 billion on health care, about 13 percent of gross domestic product. The federal government spent $384.7 billion on health care, about 22 percent of the federal budget, while the state and local governments spent $163.9 billion on health care, about 15 percent of their budgets (National Center for Health Statistics 2001).

In a sense, international comparisons are a bit deceptive. Jacob Hacker (2001, 2002) argues that much of the social welfare benefits in the United States are provided by the private sector. If one adds the public and private benefits together, social welfare spending is comparable to Western industrialized nations. The uniqueness of the American system is that a considerable portion of social welfare benefits are provided by the private sector. Hacker also points out, however, two important trends. First, private social benefits are eroding, and the private sector is being used as a model for transforming public sector benefits (also White 2001).

The importance of the configuration of social welfare benefits in the United States to rationing is related to the concept of fragmentation. Because there is no one centralized, locus of authority, there also is no one place that can impose rationing on the health care system. The kinds of allocations of resources done at the national level and then filtered down through lower levels of authority that typify most of the Western, industrialized countries do not exist in the United States. To the extent that rationing appears in the United States, it is has focused on relieving the pressures of health care costs.

At various times, such as the late 1970s, late 1980s, and early 1990s, there was much concern about the increasing cost of health care and health insurance (to payers such as private enterprises and government and to consumers). In the middle and late 1990s, such pressures eased. National health care expenditures as a percent of gross domestic product peaked at 13.3 percent in 1995 and dropped to 13.0 percent three years later (National Center for Health Statistics 2001). Then in 2000 and 2001, pressures reappeared. How did government and business react to increasing costs? In a sense, restrictions placed on expenditures are a form of rationing.

The Private Sector and Managed Care

The private sector responded in several ways. First, they shifted some of the costs of health care to employees through higher premiums, coinsurance payments, and deductibles (Robinson 2002). Some, particularly the smaller employers, responded by eliminating the health insurance benefit. Both cost shifting and eliminating of the benefit helped increase the number of people without health insurance (Patel and Rushefsky 1999, Chapters 5 and 6), though the economic expansion years from 1994 through 1999 did see an increase in coverage because of low unemployment and moderation of health care costs (Employment Benefits Research Institute 2001; Pear 2001c).

More important, employers resorted to managed care in what Buchanan (1998, 619) called a "payers' revolt." While we have mentioned managed care a number of times already, we have not yet defined it. Managed care can be broadly defined as

> any health insurance plan that seeks to restrain the use of health care services. Such a plan can be as simple as requiring preauthorization for a nonemergency hospital stay. It can also encompass more organized forms of provider delivery. (Patel and Rushefsky 1999, 305)

This is a broad definition and there is some disagreement about what exactly a managed care plan or managed care organization is. Such plans include the classic health maintenance organization (HMO) as well as looser forms such as preferred provider organizations and point-of-service plans. Commercial and nonprofit insurers may offer managed care plans and form managed care organizations (MCOs). Providers may offer managed care plans (provider sponsored organizations), especially hospital-based organizations. Providers may also form intermediary organizations, such as risk-bearing provider groups (RSPGs), situated between an insurer and subscriber (Noble and Troyen 1999). Further, many employers, taking advantage of administrative savings and the regulatory protections of the Employment Retirement Income Security Act (ERISA) of 1974, have self-administered plans, though they may hire companies to run the plans.

Hacker and Marmor (1999) argue that the term "managed care" is imprecise and loaded with aspirational meaning. That is, the term is used to portray a given perspective; it is sloganeering. The idea is that these organizations will manage the care of their subscribers rather than focus on restraining costs for the payers (employers or government in the case of Medicaid and Medicare). Their preferred definition is that managed care "represents a fusion of two functions once seen as separate: the financing of medical care and the delivery of medical services" (Hacker and Marmor 1999, 1036). Furrow (1997, 425) likewise describes managed care organizations as "a hybrid of insurance cost control mechanisms, and medical delivery." Hacker and Marmor state that we should focus on the financial incentives or reimbursement methods, the different organization forms, and the different management techniques used to control costs.

Further, Hacker and Marmor (1999, 1040) note that the most appropriate way to look at and compare health plans is to consider three dimensions: "managerial control of clinical decision making, risk sharing between plan and provider, and limits on patient choice of medical professional." Much of the backlash against managed care (Chapter 7) can be ultimately traced back to these three aspects.

The shift to managed care by employers easily can be demonstrated. In 1977, 96 percent of employees in private firms with health insurance were in indemnity plans. These are plans that allow employees and their dependents to use the provider of their choice and then get reimbursed for expenses. By 1988, that number had dropped to 71 percent. By 1998, only 14 percent of such employees were in indemnity plans. The other 86 percent were in some kind of managed care plan or organization (Gabel 1999).

Managed care makes use of many of the techniques of implicit rationing. Some of the techniques, while not directly related to rationing types of deci-

sions, influence physician clinical decision making and have been controversial. Two of those techniques are capitation and risk pools (Hall, Kidd,
and Dugan 2000). Capitation is payments made to providers, generally physicians, per patient regardless of the patient's utilization. Risk pooling is when
a physician's organization is given a fixed sum of money from which it pays
for defined services. If there is money left over in the pool it can be distributed to the providers.

Other techniques to control utilization include bonuses paid to physicians,
utilization reviews and preapprovals, gatekeeping, formularies, and restricted
lists of providers (selective contracting). Bonuses might be paid to physicians in a plan who keep their referrals for additional services or for medications below a specified limit. Utilization reviews look at the practices of
providers to see who is exceeding average recommendations for services.
Preapprovals require that authorization be given prior to use of a service,
such as surgery or physical rehabilitation. Gatekeeping is using primary care
physicians to screen the use of and referral to specialists (who are most expensive). Formularies are lists of approved pharmaceuticals. Those on the
list can be used without special permission. Plans may deny or pay less for
pharmaceuticals not on the list. Plans also try to limit the providers they will
use or encourage patients to pick from a list of providers (as occurs with
preferred provider organizations). Plans may restrict which hospitals and
emergency care facilities that it will authorize.

How effective has managed care been? Since its major goal has been to
provide health services and restrain cost increases, we look first at the cost
issue. Here, as with the health services or quality issue, the answer is mixed.
At first, managed care had a moderating influence on health costs. They
even seemed to have an impact on costs of other health plans. Laurence
Baker et al. (2000) found more modest increases in the premiums of health
care plans where HMO market penetration was higher (percentage of employees in health maintenance organizations).

Kip Sullivan (2000) argues that the efficiency of managed care plans
has been overrated. By efficiency, he means delivering services at lower
costs than in more traditional settings. Sullivan argues that the argument
for the greater efficiency of managed care plans over fees for service is
based on two errors. The first error is that medical costs are not the same as
total costs and, therefore, lower medical costs do not necessarily mean
lower total costs. For Sullivan (2000, 140), "Total costs are the sum of
medical costs plus administrative costs plus profit or surplus." The second
error is the claim that because HMO costs are lower therefore they are
more efficient than fee-for-service plans. To the contrary, Sullivan argues
that there are other explanations for lower HMO premiums. Two that he

mentions are cherry picking (encouraging lower-cost subscribers and discouraging higher-cost subscribers from enrolling) and cost shifting. HMOs try to eliminate costs that contribute to the larger society but not the plan itself. Examples include cross-subsidies for charitable care and academic research.

Further, Sullivan contends that the decrease in cost increases or inflation had other explanations besides the mere expansion of managed care plans. These include where the insurance industry is in the pricing cycle, lingering effects of the 1990–1991 recession, the emphasis on managed competition by the Clinton administration and other political leaders, and mergers within the industry. Additionally Sullivan claims that managed care organizations engaged in "low balling." Low balling is occurs when a health plan charges low premiums, perhaps below their costs, to gain subscribers and market penetration. After gaining a strong foothold in the health care market, plans start charging more (because their costs continue to increase) and, in some cases, leave the market when profits prove to be low or plans suffer losses. This appears to be what is happening with HMOs as they continue to move out of the Medicare market (see, for example, Carey, Ornstein, and Rosenblatt 2001; Okie 2001).

Some have argued that managed care has failed. Because of the backlash against managed care (Chapter 7), employers have been giving employees more choices and employees have been selecting less restrictive plans, such as preferred provider organizations or point-of-service plans (see, for example, Gribbin 2001). Further, large firms using HMOs are beginning to experience the highest increases, reversing the normal pattern (Neus 2001).

Courts and Health Care Rationing

A 2000 case decided by the U.S. Supreme Court explicitly tied managed care to rationing. The immediate facts of the case *Pegram v. Herdrich* were that Cynthia Herdrich belonged to a health maintenance organization that her husband's employer had contracted with for prepaid services. Herdrich went to see a physician in the plan (Lori Pegram), complaining of abdominal pains. A small mass was detected in her abdomen. The physician recommended that the patient wait for eight days when she could get an ultrasound of her abdomen in a facility owned by the HMO. Before the eight days were up, her appendix burst and she suffered from periotonitis (Bloche 2000; Hammer 2001). Herdrich sued the plan, arguing that the financial incentives the HMO put in place induced the physician to delay services. The case eventually worked its up to the Supreme Court. Part of the problem is that the HMO, like many health plans, is protected from suit under the Supreme Court's interpretation that the 1974 Employment Retirement and Income

Security Act (ERISA) exempts company plans that are self-insured from state regulation in the 1987 case of *Pilot Life Insurance Company v. Dedeaux* (we discuss this in more detail in Chapter 7).

The Court unanimously decided the case in favor of the HMO. But in doing so, the Court also essentially stated that rationing was an essential part of managed care and effectively national policy. Writing for the Court, Justice David Souter stated:

> Whether Carle [the clinic] is a fiduciary when acting through its physician owners depends on some background of fact and law about HMO organizations, medical benefit plans, fiduciary obligation, and the meaning of Herdrich's allegations. The defining feature of an HMO is receipt of a fixed fee for each patient enrolled under the terms of a contract to provide specified health care if needed. Like other risk bearing organizations, HMOs take steps to control costs. These measures are commonly complemented by specific financial incentives to physicians, rewarding them for decreasing utilization of health-care services, and penalizing them for excessive treatment. Hence, an HMO physician's financial interest lies in providing less care, not more. Herdrich argues that Carle's incentive scheme of annually paying physician owners the profit resulting from their own decisions rationing care distinguishes its plan from HMOs generally, so that reviewing Carle's decision under a fiduciary standard would not open the door to claims against other HMOs. However, inducement to ration care is the very point of any HMO scheme, and rationing necessarily raises some risks while reducing others. Thus, any legal principle purporting to draw a line between good and bad HMOs would embody a judgment about socially acceptable medical risk that would turn on facts not readily accessible to courts and on social judgments not wisely required of courts unless resort cannot be had to the legislature. . . .
>
> But whatever the HMO, there must be rationing and inducement to ration. Since inducement to ration care goes to the very point of any HMO scheme, and rationing necessarily raises some risks while reducing others (ruptured appendixes are more likely; unnecessary appendectomies are less so), any legal principle purporting to draw a line between good and bad HMOs would embody, in effect, a judgment about socially acceptable medical risk. (*Pegram v. Herdrich* 2000)

Further, Justice Souter argued that Congress effectively endorsed the incentive structure of health maintenance organizations when it passed legislation beginning in 1973 to promote HMOs. If the incentives are to be changed, Souter asserted, then Congress rather than the Court is the place to do it (Bloche 2000).

The Federal Government

The one partial exception to the depiction of the American health care system as decentralized and fragmented with considerable private participation is Medicare. Medicare is the closest the United States comes to having a system of universal coverage and meeting the universal standard (White 1995). Virtually everyone over the age of 65 is eligible for and participates in Medicare and there is considerable public funding for the program, both through dedicated, trust fund taxes for Part A (largely hospital and other institutional care) and general tax revenues for Part B (which covers out-of-institutional, mostly out-of-hospital care). Medicare also covers the severely disabled and those suffering from end-stage renal disease. Like private health insurance in the United States (including managed care plans) and some national health insurance systems in other countries, there is also recipient cost sharing, through premiums, deductibles, and copayments.[2]

Faced with significant cost increases, in 1983 the federal government adopted a system of prospective payment for hospitals known as diagnostic related groups (DRGs) (Moon 1996; Marmor 2000). Under the prospective payment system, Medicare recipients admitted to a hospital would be categorized under one of more than 500 groups or diagnoses. Each DRG had a payment schedule associated with it. That is, the hospital would receive a fixed payment from Medicare regardless of how long the patient was in the hospital. This provided an incentive to hospitals (and indirectly to doctors) to provide the least amount of treatment compatible with good care. If the hospital costs were below the payment, they kept the difference. If costs were above payments they suffered a loss. This was an attempt to restrain Medicare spending. In 1989, the prospective payment system was extended to physicians.

But Medicare has two sets of problems that relate to rationing. First, there are significant gaps in its coverage. Medicare does not cover out-patient prescription drugs, nor does it cover long-term care.[3] Neither were considered of great importance in 1965 when Medicare was created and the program reflected private health insurance coverage at the time (Moon 1996; Marmor 2000). The second problem is one that Medicare will face in the future: growing costs due to an expanded recipient population as the baby boomer generation begins to retire. The two problems are interrelated in and of themselves and also because they suggest pressure on allocation of resources. If we spend more money on Medicare, or for that matter, on the elderly and the disabled, there will be that much less for other needs. Rationing, while the phrase is not used, underlies much of the debates.

Considering the first problem, gaps in coverage, there are some alternatives for Medicare recipients. First, they can purchase "medigap" policies, which, depending on the choice taken, will cover some or all of the gaps in Medicare. Some of the medigap policies cover prescription drugs, though they cost more than the less inclusive policies. A second choice for recipients is to join a managed care plan, mainly a health maintenance organization, which includes out-patient medications as a benefit. A third choice, for recipients with low income is to take part in Medicaid, which will then cover prescription medications (and long-term care). But joining Medicaid requires that many Medicare recipients draw down on their assets (which happens largely through residency in nursing homes). A private alternative is to purchase specialized health insurance policies for long-term care or for pharmaceuticals.

The need for change is there, though there is concern about the resources required to fund these benefits. We know that Medicare beneficiaries without prescription coverage are less likely to purchase needed prescriptions than those with coverage (Poisal and Murray 2001). Further, those without prescription drugs coverage are likely to pay higher prices for their medications than those with coverage. The latter, whether in HMOs or through medigap policies, are more likely to pay negotiated prices (Frank 2001). Further, older Americans pay a larger portion of their prescription drugs costs than do those under 64 (Century Foundation 2000).

A number of proposals have been offered to include prescription drugs coverage in Medicare (McClellan, Spatz, and Carney 2000), though none have passed largely because of the costs of the new benefit. One of the problems is that spending on prescription drugs has vastly outstripped spending on Medicare in general (General Accounting Office 2000; on the fragility of long-term budget projections, see White 1999).

The debate over prescription medications for Medicare continued into 2001. The George W. Bush administration proposed a private sector approach. The administration proposed getting Medicare recipients to enroll in discount or buyers' clubs. For a small fee, recipients would get a discount on their prescriptions. The proposal was considered an interim one by the administration until more comprehensive Medicare reform could take place (Pear 2001a). As with many other policy issues, the terrorist attack against the United States on September 11, 2001 delayed consideration of many domestic issues. The prescription benefit for Medicare was one of those that was postponed.

At least prescription medication benefits were considered. The same could not be said for long-term care. Much of long-term care in the United States is financed outside of Medicare. In 1998, Medicaid paid for 44 percent of nursing home expenditures, Medicare for 14 percent, private insurance paid for 7 percent, and 31 percent was paid for out of pocket. When home health care expenditures are added in, Medicare pays for 20 percent and Medicaid pays for 40 percent (Feder, Komisar, and Niefeld 2000). Other countries have more comprehensive programs of caring for the elderly, though the financing for long-term care is usually separate from the overall national health insurance plan. There is some reliance on local financing, there is some means testing, and there is some reliance on community-based and home-based care (Merlis 2000).

There is one area where Medicare is more generous than national health insurance plans in other countries. When we discussed New Zealand, we mentioned that in comparison with the British NHS, both countries place some restrictions on the availability of kidney dialysis for those suffering from end-stage renal failure. The United States is a major exception here. In 1972, Congress passed amendments to Medicare legislation requiring that the program cover the full expenses for dialysis. It remains the only medical condition for which Medicare has made such a commitment (Nissenson and Rettig 1999).

Because Medicare spending has increased significantly, amounting to an estimated $242.7 billion in fiscal year (FY) 2001 (Office of Management and Budget 2001), and because the hospital insurance (Part A) of Medicare is paid largely through trust fund payments (the rest paid for by the recipient through cost sharing or through other insurance), there has been a politics surrounding the future costs of Medicare. Preparing for the retirement of the baby boom generation beginning about 2010 also created some pressures on Medicare. Medicare spending became part of the budget battles between the Republican-controlled Congress and President Bill Clinton in 1995 and 1996. One result was two partial shutdowns of the federal government in 1995–1996 (Marmor 2000; Rushefsky and Patel 1998). One result of the budget battles was the passage in 1997 of the Balanced Budget Act (BBA) (Palazzolo 1999).

The BBA sought to restrain Medicare in two ways. First, it reduced payments to providers, typically the major way that Medicare sought to save money. Second, it extended the prospective payment system to other institutional providers, such as nursing homes and home health care agencies (the latter of which had seen expenditures rise rapidly after Medicare started covering them).

These restraints had dramatic impacts on Medicare expenditures. Medicare expenditures in FY 1997 were $210.4 billion. The next year they rose slightly to $213.6 billion and then, for the first time in the history of the program, dropped in FY 1999, to $212 billion. Even in FY 2000, the increase in Medicare expenditures was modest, rising by only $7 billion to $219 billion (Office of Management and Budget 2001). Having said that, it also should be pointed out that home health care agencies started to pull out of the program, complaining about low reimbursements (Pear 2000). Legislation in 2000 restored some of the payments.

Perhaps more important was the emphasis Medicare put on managed care. Beginning in 1985, Medicare allowed recipients to enroll in managed care organizations, most specifically HMOs. Originally, a recipient would enroll in an eligible HMO and Medicare would pay premiums based on the adjusted average per capita cost (AAPCC) (Moon 1996). Because HMOs promised to save money, Medicare paid them 95 percent of AAPCC.

Enrollment in managed care organizations by Medicare recipients has grown but is still relatively small. In 2000, slightly more than 6 million recipients were enrolled in HMOs, about 18 percent of total Medicare recipients (HCFA 2000). Enrollment in managed care organizations is voluntary and so HMOs must offer incentives to attract recipients, such as prescription drugs coverage.

The experience with HMOs and Medicare has not been an entirely happy one. The HCFA (now the Center for Medicare and Medicaid Services, or CMS) has claimed that its HMO coverage feature proved expensive. This was because HMOs used various tactics to attract healthier Medicare recipients, leaving regular Medicare with the more expensive ones (Moon 1996; Patel and Rushefsky 1999). On the other hand, HMOs claimed that they were losing money covering Medicare recipients and started adding cost sharing to its plan. It wanted increases in payments from Medicare. This is a nice example of what Stone (2002) calls a "policy paradox": both HMOs and Medicare claimed they were losing money from HMO enrollment.

The 1997 Balanced Budget Act tried to remedy some of these problems. First, it expanded the choices available to recipients through the Medicare+Choice program. Under the new program, recipients could choose from six options: fees for service (essentially regular or traditional Medicare plus any supplemental insurance policies purchased by recipients), HMOs, point-of-service plans, preferred provider organizations, medical savings accounts, and privately contracted fees for service (Serafini 1997). Those who pushed for Medicare+Choice hoped this would be the first stage in privatizing Medicare (Gold 2001). The experience with this program has not been particularly successful.

First, despite the desire to expand choices and increase enrollment in alternative plans, there has been a decline in enrollment in plans. In 1999 and 2000, almost 200 plans either reduced services or withdrew entirely from the program. In 2001, a number of HMOs announced that they were dropping almost another half million recipients, bringing the total dropped since 1999 to more than 2 million recipients (Pear 2001b). HMOs complained that the fees paid by Medicare were too low. A second problem is that because of the withdrawals by HMOs from Medicare, recipients have fewer choices, in some cases no choices (Gold 2001). A third problem is that the BBA required reports on quality and performance of plans. This added to the administrative costs facing the plans while not producing additional payments to pay for them (2001).

The 1997 Balanced Budget Act also attempted to consider the long-term financial solvency of Medicare. It mandated the creation of a commission, the National Bipartisan Commission on the Future of Medicare, to develop proposals for reforming Medicare. A majority of the commission favored a proposal known as "premium support," but under the rules of the commission a supermajority was needed to endorse any proposals. No such supermajority emerged in favor of premium support (also known as defined contribution or voucher plan) (White 2001).

Yet if one is concerned about the future solvency of Medicare and rationing is implicit in these kinds of discussions, premium support ought to be considered. Perhaps the best way to understand the premium support proposal is to consider the difference between a defined benefit and a defined contribution plan (White 2001). This is perhaps easiest to understand in connection with pension programs.

Private pension programs were originally of the defined benefit plan (and most public employee pension programs still are). Under such programs, an employee is eligible for a retirement pension based on the number of years with the firm and on employee's income during the working years. Social Security is a defined benefit program. As long as the retired employee lives (and in some cases, such as Social Security, as long as the retired employee's spouse lives), the retiree receives the pension. If the retiree lives to an old age, and the faster growing sector of the population are those 85 and older, then the company will have to pay out quite a bit of money. The demographics of the U.S. population, which is aging, and the coming retirement of the baby boomer generation, suggests that expenditures on pension programs will increase as the recipient population increases. Medicare in its original form is a defined benefit program.

Private employers, however, have increasingly moved toward defined contribution pension programs. Under defined contributions, employers make a monthly contribution to a fund, the employee usually makes an equal contribution, and then the money is invested in stocks and bonds and so forth. Employer contributions end when the employee retires. The retirement income then depends on the contributions, the income while working (because higher income employees can put more money away), and how well the funds were invested. When the retiree dies, dependents would still be able to receive money from the accounts. Hopefully, the accounts will not become depleted before those dependent on them die.

The great virtue of defined contributions from the standpoint of the employer is that it limits the employer's obligation. Under defined benefits, the obligation can continue for thirty or more years after the employee dies. Under defined contributions, the obligation ends when the employee retires.

This same idea can be applied to Medicare and provides Medicare beneficiaries with the most choice. Under a defined benefits plan, Medicare spending on each recipient depends on how much recipients use medical services. As recipients age, they tend to use more services. Under defined contributions, Medicare will pay the same amount per recipient regardless of use of services (though some adjustments can be made for age, region, and so forth).

Under the premium support plan (defined contribution), Medicare would decide how much recipients' plan premiums are on the average (much as is done with HMOs right now) and give recipients a voucher worth that amount. Recipients would then shop around for a health plan that met their needs and enroll in the plan (approved by Medicare). Most proposals allow for some change of plans, say once a year. Additionally, the premiums charged by plans would exceed the voucher. Medicare would defray some, but not all, of the costs of the plans; that is why it is called a premium support proposal. Recipients would then have to pay the additional costs. This would require information about plans so that recipients can make educated choices.

From the standpoint of the federal government and Medicare, premium support is a good deal. It limits Medicare's financial obligations. The amount of support can be manipulated so that if the program starts costing too much, the support can be decreased. It eliminates any kind of explicit rationing choices. What Medicare will cover will depend on the plans that recipients choose. It provides greater flexibility and the potential for more choices for recipients.

While there are advantages of premium support for Medicare and its recipients, there are criticisms. First, it effectively privatizes the program (which is an advantage to those critical of Medicare and big government programs in general). The social contract that was an implicit part of Medicare when it passed in 1965 will be eliminated (Oberlander 1998). A second concern is that many Medicare recipients, especially the frail elderly, may not have the capacity to make good choices.

Oberlander (2000) argues that the bipartisan commission overstated the savings gained from moving to a premium support system. Most of the gains would come from various provisions of the Balanced Budget Act of 1997. His analysis of comparable programs, such as the Federal Employee Health Benefits Program and the similar California Public Employees Retirement

System (CalPERS), do not provide a good model of how premium support would save funds because they have experienced both small premium increases and large ones. Further, the Medicare experience with HMOs has not been happy. As discussed above, after attracting recipients, costs and cost sharing was increased, benefits were cut, and some began to withdraw from the Medicare market.

State Governments and Public Policy: Oregon and Beyond

The states are important payers of medical care services. The two major programs are Medicaid and S-CHIP (State Children's Health Program). S-CHIP was created as Title XXI under the Social Security Act as part of the 1997 Balanced Budget Agreement. It was designed to enroll children of low-income families that were ineligible for Medicaid in state plans, either through expanding Medicaid, through a separate program, or through a combination of both. As of FY 2000, more than 6.5 million children were enrolled out of an eligible population of nearly 11 million (Children's Defense Fund, n.d.; HCFA 2001). Most of the policy concern has been to expand the program.

This has partly been the case for Medicaid, the major state health care program, which is actually a federal/state program. The federal government established the program in 1965 (along with Medicare), sets overall eligibility standards, and pays at least half of the program's costs, with the states paying the remainder. Medicaid is a much more comprehensive program than Medicare, covering hospital and doctor visits, out-patient prescription medication, and nursing home costs, for example. Those covered under Medicaid include children, aged, blind and disabled people, and those eligible for assistance under the Temporary Assistance for Needy Families welfare program. In 1998, there were over 40 million recipients and Medicaid expenditures totaled more than $142 billion (Bureau of the Census 2000). During the 1980s and 1990s Medicaid eligibility was expanded to include covering low-income pregnant women (Patel and Rushefsky 1999, Chapter 3).

But costs have been a perennial problem with Medicaid, particularly for the states but also for the federal government. Reimbursement rates, fixed by the states, always have been lower than for Medicare or private insurance. Two efforts in particular have been employed or proposed that look like rationing. One of them is our old friend managed care. Beginning as far back as 1981, the federal government granted waivers to states to engage in demonstration and research projects. This allowed states to mandate enrollment of Medicaid recipients in managed care. This was encouraged by the Clinton administration, which issued rules making it easier for states to move recipients into managed care (Patel and Rushefsky 1999). By 1998, more than 50 percent of Medicaid recipients were enrolled in managed care plans (Bureau of the Census 2000). This compares quite favorably with Medicare managed care enrollment. Of course, Medicare recipients are encouraged to enroll rather than mandated. The results have been mixed, with some states finding cost savings but others not. One reason is that managed care plans tend to not enroll the more costly Medicaid recipients, such as the elderly and the disabled (Patel and Rushefsky 1999).

A second idea is a proposal stemming from the National Governors Association (NGA) in 2001. The NGA proposed restructuring Medicaid into three categories (Holahan 2001). The first part would be those required to be covered under Medicaid. Their required benefits would remain the same and cost sharing with the federal government would remain the same. Recipients in this category would not have be faced with any cost sharing.

The second category is a rather large one. It includes optional benefits (such as prescription drugs and hospice services) for the mandatory Medicaid population and all services for optional recipients. Cost sharing up to 5 percent of a family's income could be imposed on the optional population groups. Federal matching grants would be even larger than in the first category and benefits could be quite generous, equal to those in S-CHIP.

The third category is a kind of residual category. The NGA proposes that Medicaid be allowed to provide benefits to any targeted group. The benefits can be limited possibly to drug or catastrophic expenses and federal matching grants would be at the rate of the first category.

An important element of the proposal is that of all Medicaid spending only 35 percent is absolutely mandated by federal law to be spent on the mandatory population for mandatory benefits (Holahan 2001). The proposal would therefore allow states considerable flexibility in paying for services for Medicaid recipients. Holahan (2001, 18) argues that the proposal allows states to "underfund Medicaid, possibly reduce coverage and certainly not expand much despite new opportunities in the current program structure to do so." The fear is that despite incentives to expand coverage (because much of the costs would be absorbed by the federal government) states could reduce coverage to save money (Holahan 2001; Park and Ku 2001).

In August 2001, the George W. Bush administration announced a new Medicaid waiver program designed to expand the number of insured persons. The proposal is based on the NGA proposal (Park and Ku 2001). Park and Ku's (2001) analysis of the proposal suggests that states could reduce benefits to currently covered populations and increase cost sharing as a way to save enough to cover more people. The proposal, however, does not require the states to actually extend coverage. Therefore, states could absorb the savings (2001). The reduced benefits and/or increased cost sharing could adversely affect the health of targeted populations.

The proposal is, in a sense, similar to the one major example of explicit rationing in the United States, the Oregon experiment.

The Oregon Plan

The most explicit attempt at rationing as a means of meeting budget restraints has occurred in Oregon (though not all agree that the Oregon plan was ultimately about rationing, see below). The story begins in 1987 when the state of Oregon, facing a cost crunch as well as a concern about the uninsured, adopted a "below-the-line" policy (Jacobs, Marmor, and Oberlander 1999, 167). Under such a policy, the state would presumably not pay for treatment. The decision in 1987 was to not pay for some organ transplantations on the grounds that they were not cost effective, it was expensive, and the money could be used to extend care to the uninsured (Brown 1991). That same year, 7–year-old Coby Howard was denied a bone marrow transplant to treat his leukemia and he died. While this obviously created controversy, leadership in Oregon decided to extend the idea to its Medicaid program.

The Oregon Health Program (OHP) required first that there be some process by which the cutoff would be decided. In 1989, the Oregon legislature created a commission to propose such a plan. Hearings, town meetings, and a telephone survey were conducted (Brown 1991). The commission produced a list of some 1,600 procedures and explained where the cutoff would be. Quality of life considerations were part of the process (Hadorn 1991 for a description of the process). The list and procedure were likewise controversial. For example, the plan required waivers from the HCFA and the George H.W. Bush administration rejected the plan on the basis that it violated the provisions of the 1990 Americans with Disabilities Act (Ham 1998). A new, smaller (about 800 items), and more acceptable list was produced. Presumably the list and the rankings were determined on the basis of analysis, but it appears that more political judgments were made. The congressional OTA report stated that little analysis was actually used in making up the list (Jacobs, Marmor, and Oberlander 1999).

The Oregon Health Plan was finally implemented in 1994. It rank-ordered some 743 medical conditions and set a bottom line on funding. Since then, the list has been revised every two years (Leichter 1999). For example, drug addiction and mental health services were added. Ham (1998) argues that the list has been revised as evidence has developed about the effectiveness of various treatments. Guidelines have also been developed that allow treatment of below-the-line conditions if warranted. The law also included an employer mandate, requiring all employers to offer insurance to their employees. However, the inability to obtain a waiver from ERISA led to the demise of the mandate (Ham 1998).

Oregon has moved most of its Medicaid recipients into managed care, also a way to save some funds. Managed care organizations can offer below-the-line services but do not get reimbursed for them. There also have been complaints by consumer advocates that Medicaid recipients have trouble getting access to services through their managed care plan (Ham 1998).

As a result of funds saved, Oregon was able to extend Medicaid coverage to all its citizens living at or below the poverty line, a number in excess of 100,000 people. Until recent changes in Medicaid law (Patel and Rushefsky 1999, Chapter 3), income at the poverty level generally excluded people from state Medicaid coverage.

The Oregon plan has generated considerable controversy, criticism, and praise. Some have also argued that the essence of the plan has been misunderstood. The controversy stems from the notion of denying care to a large number of people. After all, some 170 medical conditions are denied Medicaid funding. Rationing was being imposed on the back of the poorest sector of the population (Leichter 1999). There was also criticism of the process by which the list of conditions was compiled. For example, those who developed the list had to reduce over 10,000 diagnoses into the 700-plus conditions (1999). And certainly the list had to go through several iterations before the state legislature accepted it.

Despite the criticisms, there has also been much praise for the plan. Norman Daniels (1991) argues that the Oregon plan is quite fair. To Daniels, most rationing in the United States is rationing by people, those who lack health insurance. By contrast, the Oregon plan rations by service (also Leichter 1999). Some services that are quite costly are not very effective. Therefore, funds can be used to help more people and fund more effective services. Aggregate well-being is being improved, even though some currently covered by Medicaid might not be able to get some needed or desired service. Even then, the reality is that managed care plans do provide some of those services. Further, there are provisions in the Oregon plan that allow treatment of an uncovered condition if that condition would exacerbate the health of the patient. Most uncovered conditions are treated (1999).

Perhaps the most trenchant analysis of the OHP was by Jacobs, Marmor, and Oberlander (1999). They point out, first of all, that the rationing or prioritizing aspect of the plan generated very little savings, perhaps 2 percent over a five-year period. Moving recipients into managed care produced savings of about 6 percent. Expansion of Medicaid to a wider population was largely financed out of general revenues and tobacco tax money. The reason for the small amount of savings was both the politics within Oregon and con-straints placed upon the plan by the federal government. Further, Jacobs, Marmor, and Oberlander point out that even with the prioritizing, the Medicaid program in Oregon was more generous than what Medicaid normally offers. They note, as does Leichter (1999), that below-the-line conditions were often treated any-way. One reason that they both mention is something called "comorbidity." A patient may have symptoms from more than one condition and it is virtually impossible to separate out treatment of those conditions.

The most important comment made by Jacobs, Marmor, and Oberlander (1999) about OHP is that the emphasis on rationing and prioritizing was used politically to generate support for the program, largely the expansion of the population served. They write:

> The operational Oregon Health Plan bears little resemblance to the pro-gram envisioned either by promoters or critics during the national debate over its adoption. The political strategies of reformers were crucial in shap-ing the Oregon surprise. Reformers used the rhetoric and public discussion of rationing to mobilize citizen support, involve medical providers and other interest groups in the process, and establish a new mechanism for political accountability. Ultimately, this helped maintain a broad political coalition that has paradoxically made it harder for politicians to ration medical care and easier to raise funds for the state's poor. (Jacobs, Marmor, and Oberlander 1999, 176)

Health Care Rationing, Values, and Public Policy

Rationing in health care is a fact of life, but one that seldom explicitly in-forms policy discussions. Discussions over the future of the Medicare (in-cluding solvency and expanding benefits), the uninsured, managed care and so forth all touch upon rationing. But even the United States, with its $12 trillion economy and world-class medical facilities and professionals, can-not afford to do everything for everyone.

Rationing occurs whenever a doctor decides that some treatment should not be given (bedside rationing) or an HMO decides not to include a treat-ment or a pharmaceutical as a covered benefit. What the United States lacks are mechanisms for discussing and making rationing decisions. This dove-tails nicely with the basic features of the American health care system: un-planned and fragmented authority. Other countries, covering many more of their citizens through national health insurance programs, have mechanisms for making allocation decisions. We putter or "muddle" along (Lindblom 1959; Lindblom and Woodhouse 1993).

But even if we engage in implicit rationing, however it is done in the United States, the principles we have discussed can help us achieve a healthy republic and informed decision making. The first principle is that we should protect and promote human dignity whenever possible. That means, in the context of the subject of this chapter, that we should not ration on the backs of the elderly or the frail or the weak. Some of the techniques we have discussed have the potential to favor some over others. For example, cost-effectiveness analysis, with its emphasis on quality of adjusted life years can be used to suggest that a treatment should not be given to an elderly person because there are few of these years remaining. On the other hand, if a person is going to die in about the same amount of time with or without the treatment, perhaps forgoing the treatment is reasonable.

The second principle is that everyone has access to adequate health care. This does not mean that everyone should have access to every possible treatment; the key word is adequate. The United States clearly fails this goal. The American health care system does not meet the international standard (White 1995). Some progress has been made as more people, especially children, have been covered by publicly funded programs such as S-CHIP.

The problem is the United States's implicit rationing is via the price mechanism. Those who have the funds or the employment coverage or the public coverage will have health insurance. Those who do not, about 14 percent of the population, have to get by as they can (Patel and Rushefsky 1999, Chapter 5; see also various issues of the *Journal of Health Care for the Poor and Underserved*). While it is possible to get health care even without insurance (for instance through hospital emergency rooms), that is not the optimal way to obtain care. The lessons of rationing from other Western, industrialized nations and the Oregon plan are that we should ration services rather than people. Adopting this perspective would require covering the entire population and then making decisions about what an adequate package would be. The history of health care in the United States makes it unlikely that this will occur soon.

Health care as a public good follows from the third principle. While we support a system of universal coverage, that coverage should be limited. There is where rationing comes in and this is what the international standard involves. There is a potential for the demand for health care to eat up more and more of our resources (although the demand for health care may be high, it is not unlimited). At some point, the trade-offs have to be made. Again, we have done this in the United States, but implicitly. Managed care has been one solution, though an incomplete one, to this problem.

The fourth principle is that people have a certain amount of responsibility for their own care. This requires the adoption of a healthier lifestyle, including diet and exercise. While we have not conquered death, there are preventable causes of ill health. Reducing those through individual decisions will reduce the pressures on our health system.

Related to the previous principle is the emphasis on preventive care. Some of the great miracles of modern medicine have been through prevention, such as the development of polio vaccines. This should be an important principle for managed care, now the dominant form of health care organization in the United States. The incentives, however, are not quite there. The benefits of preventive care accrue some time in the future and are not necessarily directed to a specific managed care organization. This is a perspective that needs to be changed.

Finally, the training of providers needs some revision. Much of medical care is based on personal experiences of physicians, their reading of the literature, discussions with other providers, and so on. More focus can be placed on evidence-based medicine and clinical practice guidelines. But at the same time that we use these techniques, we must remember that they apply to populations rather than to specific individuals. It will be the task of the providers, particularly gatekeepers, to apply guidelines tempered by individual differences and individual experiences.

Notes

1. In the United States, the term socialized medicine has been used to defeat national health insurance proposals, going back to the early years of the twentieth century (Starr 1982). Socialized medicine refers to a situation where the government owns the institutions, such as hospitals, and providers are essentially employees of the government. In the United States, the proposals for national health insurance only involved paying for access to medical care.

2. For a detailed description of Medicare, see Moon (1996).

3. Medicare covers some nursing home care, but only care that directly follows a hospital visit and only for a short time.

Study Questions

1. Virtually all Western, industrialized nations have some form of national health insurance and therefore a right to health care. Do you think that people in the United States should also have a right to health care? What arguments might be made in favor of such a right? What arguments might be made against such a right?

2. Write an essay discussing why the United States does not have national health insurance. Include in your essay a discussion of whether you believe the United States should or should not have such a program. Defend your answer.

3. Is rationing of health care necessary? Is it more necessary in some nations than in others?

4. If rationing is necessary, what would be the best way to do it? What values should underlie a rationing plan? Is it necessary to have a rationing plan? Would rationing be less painful and more efficient if we just "muddled through"?

5. In the United States, rationing is done through prices and through managed care organizations. How effective have these two mechanisms been? What improvements or changes might make these two mechanisms more effective?

6. In Chapter 7 we discuss the patients' rights movement, especially in the United States. Given managed care organizations' role in rationing of health care, what changes might make managed care organizations effective and still retain support among patients and providers?

CHAPTER 7

Patients' Bill of Rights

The rapid growth of managed care is not primarily due to enthusiasm for this approach on the part of patients or providers. Patients have had mixed reactions to managed care; they like the low co-payments and reduced paperwork but view some managed-care practices as emphasizing cost control over quality. In fact, there is widespread concern among the public, physicians and legislators about the effect of managed care on the quality of care. (Dudley and Luft 2001, 1087)

According to Deborah Stone (2002), rights are major tools of public policy. That is, they are generic solutions to public policy problems (also Rushefsky 2002). Interest groups have mobilized around the idea of rights; examples include the civil rights movement, the women's movement, the disability movement, and so forth (Stone 2002). Rights, Stone (2002, 325) argues, are a "way of governing relationships and coordinating behavior to achieve collective purposes." Rights are one way of resolving conflicts in systems and can work together with other such policy tools such as rules and sanctions.

The idea of rights has developed out of two interrelated traditions (Stone 2002). The more important tradition is the positive one and leads us to a definition of rights: "a claim backed by the power of the state. It is an expectation about what one can do or receive or how one will be treated . . . by invoking the state's help if necessary" (Stone 2002, 325). As an example, civil rights legislation, such as the Civil Rights Act of 1964, guarantees the right to equal treatment in public accommodations, employment, and so forth. Violations of those rights can and has led to government action to enforce them.

The other tradition is the normative one. Here, Stone (2002) argues, people can have rights that they do not actively seek and the government may not enforce and the source of those rights lies somewhere other than state enforcement. Stone argues that these types of rights are intertwined. She uses the example of the Declaration of Independence, which affirmed that there were certain inalienable rights that came from nature and from God. Despite this origin of rights, the positive tradition of rights was embodied in the Bill of Rights to the U.S. Constitution. And those rights have been subject to interpretation and expansion. Again, Stone (2002) uses the example of a right to privacy. The phrase does not exist in the Constitution but originates from judicial interpretation. We discussed privacy rights in Chapter 5. This chapter should be viewed as another example of the use of rights in health care.

Stone (2002) makes an important distinction among two types of rights that is useful in our discussion of patients' rights. One such type is procedural rights, which describe the process by which something is done, such as how decisions are made. Substantive rights focus on "specific actions and entitlements" (Stone 2002, 328). Substantive rights can be further subdivided into positive and negative. Positive substantive rights are entitlements to some kind of benefit provided by a second party. Negative substantive rights are rights to do something without restraint from some second party (Stone 2002).

Legal rights have three elements if they are to be realized (Stone 2002). The first is some formal statement of the right. There must be some law, contract, rule, or court decision that either explicitly or implicitly states what the right is. The first ten amendments to the Constitution are known as the Bill of Rights. They have a constitutional status which gives them superiority over other rights. Courts can and have interpreted the Constitution to give additional rights (such as the right to privacy and a right to abortion), though this has been very controversial.

There also must be some kind of grievance process by which rights are directed. This can occur through courts or some kind of review procedure inside or outside the organization (Stone 2002). Finally, there should be an enforcement mechanism. Stone (2002) writes that the primary enforcers of rights are the people claiming the rights.

This also leads to a brief discussion of another policy tool, rules. Rules have shown to be important in many of the chapters in this book. Privacy laws set forth rights but also rules by which those rights are to be observed. Rules have been established for distributing the limited amount of available organs for transplantation. In the same sense, rules, which are forward-looking, set down what rights patients may have. This returns us to the first of the three elements.

This somewhat abstract discussion sets the stage for this chapter's topic, patients' rights. The idea of rights that patients have is not particularly new. Hospitals for years have given patients a list of their rights. To take one example, Cox Health Systems, located in Springfield, Missouri, where the authors live, lists the following patients' rights: access to care, respect and dignity, privacy and confidentiality, personal safety, information, consent, refusal of treatment, transfer and continuity of care, hospital charges, hospital rules and regulations, identity and status of providers, spiritual counseling, freedom from seclusion and restraint, and the right to file grievances (information from Cox Health Systems Web site: [ww.coxhealth.com/Patients/patientrights.htm].

The current debate over patients' rights also originates from the issue of medical malpractice. Medical malpractice itself has a long history dating back to Code of Hammurabi about 2200 B.C. and English common law (of a somewhat more recent vintage) (the discussion in Patel and Rushefsky 1999). These developments, plus the growth of medical malpractice law in the United States, especially during the 1960s and 1970s, established that patients did have the right to sue doctors (and other health institutions such as hospitals and nursing homes). The most controversial portion of the debate over a patients' bill of rights at both the state and federal levels has been whether health maintenance organizations (HMOs) and other managed care organizations (MCOs) could be sued. Most of the debate over patients' rights concerns not so much the more well-developed field of malpractice but denial of benefits, a more unsettled issue that is directly related to rationing (discussed in the previous chapter).

Patients' Bill of Rights: International Perspective

While a patients' bill of rights has engendered much controversy and a fair amount of legislation and court decisions in the United States, it is not solely an American issue. When looking at other countries, it is important to remember that Western, industrialized nations meet what White (1995) calls the international standard. These countries have virtually universal coverage, mandatory contributions to the system, centralized regulatory authority, and controls over use of new technology. Patients' rights outside the United States are likely to be much different from those inside the United States. Further, because of the largely decentralized nature of the American system, the debate over patients' rights takes place at the state and national levels. In other countries, the national government sets the standards.

In 1994 the WHO (World Health Organization) Consultation on the Rights of Patients adopted a set of principles for patients' rights that the European members were supposed to adopt (WHO/Europe 1994). The document was grounded, first of all, in international agreements (also briefly discussed in Chapter 5), such as the United Nations Charter, the Universal Declaration of Human Rights, and the European Convention on Human Rights. Changes in health care systems also created some urgency for patients' rights protections. These include the increasingly impersonal and bureaucratic nature and complexity of the systems.

The consultation distinguishes between social rights and individual rights. Social rights include the obligation of society to provide, making use of the public and private sectors, "reasonable provision of health care for the entire population" (WHO/Europe 1994, 2). Societal obligation also includes equal access to health care and the elimination of discrimination. Two points need to be made here. First, the social obligation differs dramatically from the U.S. situation. No such obligation exists for the entire population, though there are some obligations for certain sectors of the population, largely through Medicare. Second, the document makes clear that what is "reasonable" varies from nation to nation.

The specific individual rights that the document covers are "integrity of the person, privacy and religious convictions" (WHO/Europe 1994, 3). The consultation also points out, in good communitarian fashion, that individuals have responsibilities as well as rights. These include active participation in treatment and diagnoses and making sure that all necessary information is imparted to providers. The document also recommends patients allow themselves to be subjects (with appropriate consent) to clinical teaching to help promote the future training of health care providers.

The consultation then goes into more detail about those rights. It becomes clear immediately that the European view of patients' rights differs noticeably from those at the center of debate in the United States. Consider the following two rights:

5.10 Patients have the right to relief of their suffering according to the current state of knowledge.

5.11 Patients have the right to humane terminal care and to die in dignity. (WHO/Europe 1994, 7)

As we saw in Chapter 2, such rights are very controversial in the United States and are not any part of the patients' bill of rights controversy here.

By 2000, nine countries (Denmark, Finland, Georgia, Greece, Iceland, Israel, Lithuania, the Netherlands, and Norway) had passed patients' rights legislation. Patients' charters were passed in France, Ireland, Portugal, and the United Kingdom. A patients' bill of rights was held up in France by concerns over malpractice awards (Weber 2000). Forty-three other nations that comprise WHO/Europe had not enacted any patients' rights law (WHO/Europe 2000; see also Saltman and Figueras 1998). Because the Copenhagen conference was seen as having little impact, a European network was established to promote patients' rights (Richards 1999).

The Danish Council of Ethics, in their 1997 report on priority setting, took a close look at patients' rights. In 1995, the Danish Medical Association called for the adoption of patients' rights. The Minister of Health prepared such a bill that same year and by 2000, Denmark, as noted above, had passed such legislation. The reasons for considering and adopting patients' rights legislation is the change in consumer perspectives. Rather than people being passive recipients of medical care, they became consumers, demanding more say in their treatment (Danish Council of Ethics 1997).

The council distinguishes between litigatory and substantive rights. Litigatory rights include the right to be informed about treatment, to refuse treatment, and to file grievances in the event of malpractice. The Council pointed out that these were already pretty much accepted and embodied in legislation.

It is the substantive rights that are relatively new. The council defines these as rights to specific services or a specific quality of service. This is a bit closer to the American debate on patients' rights, though litigatory rights play an important role as well. The council noted that the emphasis on substantive patients' rights conflicts with the priority setting (i.e., reallocation of resources or rationing). Substantive rights would expand available health services. Priority setting sought to constrain them. Again, this is a debate that is taking place in the United States.

The council then gets more specific and considers four types of rights that are encompassed by patients' rights: a waiting time guarantee (that a person will be treated for the specific condition within a given time); concrete individual rights (such as the right to a second opinion, treatment by a specialist); a set of principles of what patients should expect; and the right to be informed about waiting lists and the criteria for being selected from the list (Danish Council on Ethics 1997). Note that the second one of these is also part of the American debate.

A similar set of patients' rights was adopted in England, Scotland, and Wales in 1991 (Patients' rights 1991). The patients' charter lists ten rights and nine national standards. Again, we should look at these within the context of the British NHS and compare them to types of rights discussed in the United States. The rights include:

> detailed information on local health services; admission for treatment within two years of being placed by a consultant on a waiting list; . . . prompt investigation into any complaint about NHS services; . . . health care on the basis of clinical need, irrespective of ability to pay; registration with a general practitioner; emergency medical care at any time; referral to a consultant acceptable to the patient if the GP thinks it is necessary, and referral

for a second opinion if patient and GP agree that it is desirable; a clear explanation of proposed treatment, including the risks and alternatives; access to health records; . . . and choice on whether or not to take part in research or teaching. (Patients' rights 1991, 1199)

The national standards are goals to be attained. These include quicker arrival times for ambulances, patients seen within thirty minutes of appointment, and so forth.

Five years later, the government replaced the patients' charter with an NHS charter. The emphasis changed from patients' rights to patients' responsibilities. Patients still had rights (including a new one requiring that patients be given information about the quality of care) but they now also had to keep appointments and treat staff with respect. One reason for doing this, according to the British health secretary, was there seemed to be some misunderstanding about patients' rights, leading at times to assaults in emergency departments (Wise 1997).

In 1998, the United Kingdom passed the Human Rights Act, which was implemented in October 2000 and incorporated the European Convention on Rights and Freedoms. Any deviation from the obligations imposed on public bodies, such as the NHS, have to be justified. One of those obligations includes the right of patients to be administered lifesaving treatment (Brahams 2000).

Brahams (2000) spells out some of the implications or questions raised by the 1998 legislation. Part of the law (and convention) requires public officials to protect life. Brahams argues that this means providing treatment to save lives or support them. She asks whether the existence of waiting lists for kidney dialysis treatment, for example, or other kinds of treatment would violate the law. We noted in Chapter 6 that one way that the British NHS rations is via queues or waiting lists. The law, Brahams implies, might call this into questions. Likewise, if there is an obligation to protect life, is this to be done regardless of the availability of resources, especially financial resources? If the patient behaves in an irresponsible manner, could that be taken into consideration? Brahams raises the questions, but to date there appear to be no answers.

Controversy over patients' rights continued to plague England. Browne (2001, 25) writes that "the Health Secretary [Alan Milburn] is eroding 'patient power.' He is getting rid of those who stand up for patients, abolishing the written rights they have and overriding the ability of doctors to protect them." In January 2001, Milburn quietly eliminated the patients' charter and abolished the community health councils, essentially the watchdog agency for patients' rights (Browne 2001). Milburn eliminated the right to a second opinion and was moving legislation through Parliament forcing physicians to give patient records to researchers regardless of the physicians' and patients' views (Browne 2001).

Countries outside of Europe were considering patients' rights. In 1995, the Supreme Court of India ruled that doctor and hospital services that were paid for by patients were covered under the 1986 Consumer Protection Act. This was seen by advocacy groups as an affirmation of patients' rights (Kumar 1995). In October 1990, the Indian Medical Association issued a patients' rights and duties charter. As described by Sharma (2000), the charter emphasizes duties rather than rights.

Other countries that have patients' rights laws or charters or are considering such steps include South Africa, Pakistan, Cyprus, Sri Lanka, Taiwan, and Kenya.

History of Patients' Bill of Rights in the United States

One of the most significant developments in health care in the United States has been the move toward managed care. It has replaced the older system, if that phrase can be used, that consisted largely of solo practitioners working on a fee-for-service basis, third-party payers (largely commercial but also nonprofits such as Blue Cross-Blue Shield) and indemnity reimbursement of patients. The fourth party to the traditional system (provider, payer, patient) was the employer. This system was a function of the birth of third-party insurance in the 1930s; wage and price controls during World War II that led employers, unable to increase wages, to offer fringe benefits such as health insurance to their employees; and the decision after the war by the Internal Revenue Service allowing employer fringe benefits (such as paying the premiums for employee health insurance) to count as a business expense for tax purposes (Starr 1982). This "accidental system," to use Michael Reagan's (1999) term, characterized the American health care system until the 1990s.

But this system had its problems. There was no universal access to insurance, even with the passage of Medicare and Medicaid in 1965. It also lent itself to increasing costs. Providers were not concerned about the cost to their patients because they knew insurance would cover most of those costs. Patients knew that also. Further, provider income could be increased by furnishing more services (the fee-for-service feature). Insurers were unconcerned because they could raise premiums, cover costs, and still be profitable. Employers were not concerned because the premiums were tax-deductible, as long as premium increases stayed reasonable.

This created what economists called a "moral hazard." Moral hazard may be defined as when "health insurance leads to excess consumption, in the sense that insured individuals will consume medical services past the point at which the marginal utility of an additional service is equal to its marginal cost" (Gaynor, Haas-Wilson, and Vogt 2000, 993; Pauley 1971). The economic incentives were all in the wrong place.

This can be seen by looking at health care costs. Total health care expenditures increased by double-digit numbers in the late 1980s and early 1990s. Costs for the business sector increased by 15 percent in 1990 and 12 percent in 1991 (U.S. Bureau of the Census 1995; Congressional Budget Office 1997). Something needed to be done to control costs. The public sector made several attempts to control costs, from state price controls to certificate-of-need programs (at the state and federal levels). The Carter administration (1977–1980) proposed controls on hospital costs; Congress did not act on the proposal.

The Clinton administration sought to control costs using two strategies. The first, the heart of the Clinton Health Security Act, was managed competition (Hacker 1997). Placing consumers in a situation where they would choose among health plans would, it was hoped, encourage them to choose cost-effective plans and the competition for customers would stimulate plans to restrain cost (Mayes 2001). The second strategy would come into play in the event that managed competition did not restrain costs: a cap on increases in health insurance premiums. This would have moved the United States closer to the international standard of closing costs. Of course, the Clinton plan was not enacted or even voted on. And the private sector focused more on managed care than on managed competition (Marquis and Long 1999).

The major program for controlling costs of federal health care programs was the introduction of the prospective payment system in Medicare in 1983, later extended to physicians in 1989 and to other health care providers, such as nursing homes and home health care agencies, in 1997. Mayes (2001) argues that these changes in reimbursement policy mandated by Congress combined with the Clinton administration influenced employers to move to managed care for their employees. For the private sector, a considerable amount of cost shifting to consumers took place through higher premiums, deductibles, and copayments for employees (Chapter 6 in Patel and Rushefsky 1999). States controlled Medicaid costs both through managed care programs and limited reimbursements of health care providers. While these programs had some impact, the pressure for cost containment continued. The pressure on health care costs is expected to increase. One can see this in the most recent figures and projections. Table 7.1 presents the data. Both the public and private sectors turned to managed care.

Table 7.1

Average Annual Growth in National Health Expenditures from Previous Year (in percentages)

	1997	1998	1999	2002[a]	2002[a]	2010[a]
National health expenditures	5.4	4.8	5.6	8.3	8.4	6.9
Hospital care	3.5	2.6	3.7	6.3	6.6	5.4
Physician/clinical services	4.6	5.5	6.0	7.4	8.0	6.2
Home health care	12.1	−3.0	−1.4	10.7	12.8	8.1
Nursing home care	6.7	3.5	2.3	6.8	7.7	6.4
Prescription drugs	10.0	13.4	16.9	17.4	15.1	11.3

Source: Stephen Heffler et al. 2001. "Health Spending Growth Up in 1999; Faster Growth Expected in Future." *Health Affairs* 20, no. 2 (March/April): 193–203.
    [a]Projected.

Defining Managed Care

In the previous chapter we defined managed care as

> any health insurance plan that seeks to restrain the use of health care services. Such a plan can be as simple as requiring preauthorization for a nonemergency hospital stay. It can also encompass more organized forms of provider delivery. (Patel and Rushefsky 1999, 305)

Hacker and Marmor (1999, 1040) note, as we pointed out in the last chapter, that the most appropriate way to look at and compare health plans is to consider three dimensions: "managerial control of clinical decision making, risk sharing between plan and provider, and limits on patient choice of medical professional." Much of the backlash against managed care ultimately can be traced back to these three aspects.

Managed care organizations use a variety of techniques to control costs. Plans may utilize formularies, a list of approved drugs that can be prescribed for subscribers. Managed care organizations also use incentives (such as bonuses) for physicians to restrain care. These can include limiting the number of prescription drugs issued in a month to incentives to keep costs down. MCOs may also limit services provided to subscribers and limit the providers the subscribers can see.

Development of Managed Care

Managed care originated from several directions. The earliest is the development of prepaid group plans (PGPs) in the 1920s and the 1930s. The idea behind these plans, of which the most prominent were the Kaiser plans, was to provide health care services for workers on a capitation basis. That is, workers would pay a monthly premium that would cover a comprehensive set of services at a time when the services were costly and providers relatively scarce. Other prepaid plans grew up in Boston, New York, and the Pacific Northwest.

PGPs became part of a national strategy for health care when Dr. Paul Elwood developed the "health maintenance strategy" in the 1960s. While the Johnson administration was unreceptive to the idea, the Nixon administration enthusiastically supported it. The result was the 1973 Health Maintenance Organization Act, providing federal funding for the development of qualified HMOs. The qualifications were loosened a few years later. The Reagan administration, eschewing a strong public sector role in health care, called for the end of federal subsidies, which Congress did in the mid-1980s (Patel and Rushefsky 1999).

Paul Ellwood and Alain Enthoven, among others, pushed the concept that became known as managed competition (Hacker 1997; Patel and Rushefsky 1999). The basic idea was that health plans would compete for patients. The Enthoven version, dating back to 1978, was what would now be called a voucher plan (Enthoven 1978; Enthoven and Kronick 1989). Health insurance would be decoupled from employment. Consumers would select from an array of premiums and would be a given a voucher that would be used to pay for the chosen health care plan premiums. Ellwood's vision was to keep the employer/insurance linkage, but organize consumers into alliances that would negotiate with provider and insurance plans (Hacker 1997).

Managed Care in the Public and Private Sectors

Large businesses were the leaders in the late 1980s and early 1990s in moving toward managed care (Bodenheimer and Sullivan 1998; Leyerle 1994; Thorpe 1997). The federal government, through the Health Care Financing Administration (HCFA) (now the Center for Medicare and Medicaid Services or CMS), began issuing waivers to states to allow them to enroll their Medicaid subscribers in managed care plans. Medicare also began allowing its recipients to enroll in managed care plans, especially HMOs, in the 1980s. The Balanced Budget Act of 1997 created the Medicare+Choice program, permitting more choice opportunities and encouraging recipients to enroll in MCOs (Marmor 2000; Palazzolo 1999). For a variety of reasons to be discussed below, Medicare+Choice has not been particularly successful to date (Gold 2001).

Data indicate that managed care has made its mark in both the public and

Table 7.2

Private Sector Enrollment in Health Care Plans (by percent of total private sector enrollment)

	1977	1988	1998
Indemnity	96	71	14
Health maintenance organization	4	18	27
Preferred provider organization		11	35
Point-of-service			24

Source: Jon R. Gabel. 1999. "Job-Based Health Insurance, 1977–1988: The Accidental System Under Scrutiny." *Health Affairs* 18, no. 6 (November/December): 62–74.

private sectors. According to the HCFA Web site (www.hcfa.gov), by 2000 over 18 million Medicaid recipients (almost 56 percent) were enrolled in a managed care organization. This is an increase of almost 41 percent since 1996. HMO penetration into the Medicare market has been considerably slower, because Medicare recipients have a choice about enrollment. In 2000, 6.2 million Medicare recipients were enrolled in HMOs, a little over 18 percent of total Medicare recipients (HCFA 2000).

Managed care penetration in the private sector has been much more significant than in the public sector. Table 7.2 shows how enrollment has changed over time. While the shift to managed care is partly a function of employers dropping the more traditional indemnity insurance, a significant factor has also been the response of employees to financial incentives, especially for those firms offering preferred provider organization or point-of-service plans (Gabel et al. 2000).

Patients/consumers are in MCOs in different contexts. As indicated above, many workers (and their dependents) with health insurance are in MCOs of some sort. We can distinguish those firms that have third-party plans and thus are regulated by the states, and those firms that self-insure and thus are exempt from state regulation under ERISA (the 1987 U.S. Supreme Court case *Pilot Life Insurance v. Dedeaux* 48 U.S. 41). To the extent that there can be any government regulation over those plans, it has to come from the federal government. The third group is those Medicare and Medicaid beneficiaries in MCOs. The federal government has authority, which may be enacted by regulatory action, executive order, or congressional action. For example, in 1998, the Clinton administration issued new rules providing that patients' rights protections be applicable to Medicare HMO recipients. The protections included the right to appeal HMO decisions through independent reviews, even up through the federal court system (Pear 1998). Any examination of patients' rights, especially the right to sue, has to look at all three situations (Polzer and Butler 1997).

The Successes of Managed Care

Managed care can be judged on the basis of two major criteria: costs and quality of care. Miller and Luft (1997) surveyed the literature on HMOs (as well as other types of managed care plans) in terms of quality of care. Overall, their analysis of the literature found mixed results; compared to the more traditional fee-for-service plans, most studies show similar or improved quality of care and others show lower quality of care.

Miller and Luft (1997) argue that there are three reasons for the mixed results. First, incentives exist within managed care plans. They write:

> Under the simple capitation payment arrangements that now exist, plans and providers face strong financial disincentives to excel in care for the sickest and most expensive patients. Plans that develop a strong reputation for excellence in quality of care for the sickest will attract new higher-cost enrollees that bring with them only average (flat) premium payments, which is a recipe for bankruptcy or at least a financially weakened organization. Just as one would not expect competitive pressures under insured fee-for-service to result in cost containment, why would one expect competitive pressures under simple capitation to result in visible quality improvements? (1997, 20)

The second reason for the mixed results on quality of care is that neither consumers nor purchasers have sufficient information to judge quality and access to care. A number of studies have found that even when quality information was available, employers (purchasers) made little use of them. Cost savings were more important (for example Hibbard et al. 1997). Avedis Donabedian, a physician and researcher, was a major advocate of measuring and improving the quality of care. In an interview with one of his former students a month before he died, Donabedian expressed his belief that prepaid health plans had the potential to improve the quality of care by integrating care given to patients. However, he also expressed dismay that so little had been done to improve the quality of care and much more attention had been paid to controlling costs (Mullan 2001). A study by Phililps et al. (2000) focused on preventive services. They found that, overall, managed care plans were no more likely to provide preventive care than other types. HMOs were more likely to provide preventive services than other kinds of managed care plans.

The major benefit claimed for managed care is better control of costs than the fee-for-service, third-party reimbursement system. Certainly the numbers seem to bear this out. The average annual growth in national health expenditures exceeded 11 percent a year between 1960 and 1988 (Heffler et al. 2001). Compare those figures with the numbers in Table 7.1. Managed care plans, particularly HMOs, obtain lower prices by cutting down on hospital utilization. Further, they are able to obtain discounts from providers (Sullivan 2000).

In that light it should be pointed out that the largest employers using HMOs for their employees are being faced with substantial premium increases for 2002. The employers expecting *only* 11 percent increases are seeing 20 to 50 percent increases. This certainly raises questions about managed care's ability to control costs. HMOs are the most restrictive of managed care plans and presumably the most likely to control costs. (Neus 2001)

Sullivan (2000) argues that managed care advocates have overstated the efficiency of MCOs, especially as compared to fee-for-service plans. He defines efficiency as meaning making use of fewer resources or being lower priced. He attributes the overstatements to two errors. The first error is to assume the total costs of managed care are the same as lower medical care costs in managed care plans. Sullivan points out that total managed care costs include medical costs plus administrative costs and profits. Using the more encompassing calculation, Sullivan finds that managed care plans are not more efficient than fee-for-service plans.

The second error is to assume that because HMOs charge lower premiums they are necessarily more efficient. Sullivan argues that this error ignores things such as cost shifting and attempts by HMOs to enroll healthier subscribers.

Problems of Managed Care

The backlash against managed care is a result of the emphasis on restraining cost increases and the impact of that effort on the quality of care given to subscribers. The issues can be simplified down to three interrelated concepts: accountability, trust, and bureaucracy.

Daniels and Sabin (1998; see also Sorian and Feder 1999) argue that accountability is a very important feature that underlies all proposals for reform. Accountability involves the "robust disclosure of relevant information about health plan benefits and performance, and 'due process' in the form of grievance or appeals procedure" (Daniels and Sabin 1998, 51). For Daniels and Sabin, one of the most important reasons for this emphasis on accountability is that market accountability is insufficient. It depends on the actions of private decision makers. Further, they emphasize the concept of fairness in the distribution of health care resources. The real issue to them is how to best use limited health resources and it is a public problem, not just a private one.

White (1999) argues that under the old fee-for-service, third-party payment system, patients placed their trust in doctors. Under managed care, they have to trust health plans. It is the new role of managed care plans that has led to the backlash. Mechanic (1996, 1998) also notes that the advent of managed care organizations has eroded trust between patients and providers. Bloche asserts that it is the financial incentives placed on providers by MCOs that lead to this erosion of trust (Patients' bill of rights 2001).

The backlash against managed care is not just on the part of consumers but also providers, particularly physicians (Rodwin 1999). One can understand providers' problems with managed care by briefly examining the main thesis of Paul Starr's (1982) masterful *Social Transformation of American Medicine*. Starr argues that much of the history of American medicine has been influenced by the desire of physicians for professional autonomy from government, from purchasers, and from employers. One can argue that the move to managed care, with its contracting for physician services and the requirements that come with those contracts, has led to the loss of professional autonomy on the part of physicians (not to mention restraints on their income). Patients' bill of rights legislation, at whatever level, is supported by physicians because such legislation results in looser restrictions on the practice of medicine. Further, physicians argue that such restrictions hurt their patients. This is an argument made by Mechanic (2000).

In particular, the rationing that is inherent in managed care (Chapter 6) erodes the trust between patient and doctor. In the important 2000 case of *Pegram v. Hedrich,* the U.S. Supreme Court upheld managed care organizations' role in rationing (Bloche 2000; Sage 2000).

One example of features of managed care organizations that cause distrust among subscribers is financial bonuses to physicians to restrain costs. Whether such bonuses hurt the quality of care is an interesting question, but it is clear that there is a perception on the part of subscribers that it might hurt the care they receive from their physicians through conflicts of interests. Disclosure of such bonuses or modifications that focus on quality of care as well as cost can reduce the perception problem (Gallagher et al. 2001).

An important element in the managed care backlash is the view of MCOs as heavily bureaucratic. The Bodenheimer and Singer stories related below can be viewed as bureaucratic problems. Further, physician perspectives that nonproviders are making or influencing health care decisions also fit this bureaucratic mode.

Ironically, one of the accusations made against the Clinton Health Security Act is applicable to managed care. The "Harriet and Louise" ad campaign by the Health Insurance Association of America (HIAA) pointed out that the Clinton plan called for the development of new government agencies that would be bureaucratic in nature (Rushefsky and Patel 1998). The irony, as Leyerle (1994) points out, is that the bureaucracy problem remains but is located in the private sector. Reinhardt (1999, 903) refers to managed care organizations as "private health-care regulators." McEldowney and Murray (2000) also make this claim. They note that the private sector is engaged in resource allocation in health, and people do not like it any better than when the public sector does it.

Managed Care and Narratives

Much of the complaints against managed care are based on stories: narratives and personal anecdotes. Stone (2002) observes that stories are one of the most powerful ways of defining problems. Stories are potent because of their humanity and their attractiveness to the media. Stories also reflect values and ideas (McDonough 2001 and Stone 2002). Sharf (2001) demonstrated how personal narratives changed the emphasis in policy, practice, and research on breast cancer. McDonough and Sharf both warn that narratives are not proof and can be misused (also Broder 2001). Rochefort (1998), on the other hand, argues that anecdotes and stories focusing on the negative function as "sentinel events" (1998, 143) indicating problems with a system and that regulation is needed to deal with those problems. The literature on agenda building, such as Kingdon's (1984) multiple streams model, emphasizes the importance of focusing events on getting issues placed on the policy agenda (also Baumgartner and Jones 1993). Stories about what came to be called "drive-through" deliveries led to federal legislation mandating a minimum two-day hospital stay for normal deliveries and a four-day hospital stay for cesarean deliveries (below).

One of the best examples of the use of narratives to attack managed care is Anders' *Health Against Wealth* (1996; see also Court and Smith 1999). The Anders book relates many stories about how HMOs denied care as a means of saving money. Chapter 1 begins with the story of a family whose infant son had a high fever. The mother called her HMO and was directed to go to the hospital the HMO used, some forty-two miles from the parents' home. When they finally reached a hospital, though not the one the HMO referred them to, the baby had to have his hands and feet amputated because of gangrene. There were two hospitals much closer to the family than either the one they were directed to or the one they eventually stopped at. The rest of the book is replete with such stories.

Two other, less horrifying, examples of narratives illustrating problems with managed care appeared in the July/August 2000 issue of *Health Affairs*. Bodenheimer (2000) tells of problems practicing medicine in the bureaucratic environment of managed care. Managed care, in California at least, often uses selective contracting, including some, but not all, providers in a plan. And in California, HMOs contract with physician groups rather than individual physicians. As Bodenheimer's practice evolved, his group contracted with three different individual practice associations (IPAs). Each IPA had a different set of hospitals, laboratories, pharmaceutical services, and specialists that they worked with. Each set of providers had different forms. His practice had to keep track of which IPA (and thus services) which patients belonged to. After some effort, Bodenheimer was able to get all his patients in one IPA (though IPAs would say that the patients belong to them and not to his practice). Bodenheimer argues that this "fragmentation of services" (2000, 205) is a critical feature of managed care, at least as practiced in California. He suggests that the traditional model of managed care, the group/staff model such as the Kaiser HMOs, is better because it integrates the services.

The other story comes from Singer (2000), a long-time advocate of HMOs. In her case, again illustrating fragmentation of managed care markets, she found out her HMO would cover her pregnancy but not pediatric care of her daughter after she was born. Even though she knew the system and how to work it, there was still the initial denial of coverage. Singer says that providers and the HMOs need to work out the kinks in the system and HMOs should learn to show that they feel their subscribers are important and valuable. Singer writes (2000, 208):

> The call [that the HMO would not cover her daughter] left me frustrated at one of the most vulnerable moments in my life. The HMO was getting a new member who would likely become very low cost and would remain that way for many years. HMO representatives could have let me know they appreciated the business. They did not. Rather than welcoming my baby, the HMO lacked adequate administrative processes to track new members and their doctors, to notify contracting hospitals of their benefit policies, and to transfer eligibility information to affiliated medical groups in a timely manner. . . .
>
> I knew enough about coverage decision making in HMOs to expect this denial to be reversed once the paperwork was processed, as indeed it was. But I was annoyed. I had complied with the rules of my coverage policy. Phone calls and letters from my HMO suggesting significant financial liability were stressful, coming on the heels of my baby's birth, when I had neither the time nor the emotional reserves to deal with such matters. When the same thing occurs to someone with a serious illness, it's not just aggravating, as in my case. It could be life-threatening.

The media, often an important actor in agenda building, has played a role in the backlash against managed care. Brodie, Brady, and Altman (1998) found that most of the media coverage of managed care has been neutral in tone, but that coverage has gotten more negative over time. Twelve percent of stories in 1990 were critical of managed care; by 1997 that was true of 28 percent of the stories. Special stories seem to have a negative tone, full of anecdotes of people having problems with managed care organizations. Overall, however, the authors argue that it would be better to focus on the performance of managed care plans than on the media.

It is easy to see how managed care attained the public agenda as MCOs encompassed more of the health insurance market (Baumgartner and Jones 1993; Kingdon 1984).

Karen Ignagni (1998), the American Association of Health Plan's (AAHP) chief executive officer, argues that managed care is a work in progress and a revolution in American health care, and the debate over managed care needs to be broadened. We should not make policy based on anecdotes and false claims such as "gag rules," and health care plans have to make better efforts to get their story out.

Broder (2001) also argues that while anecdotes may indicate that there are problems, they do not tell us the dimensions of the problems. Nor do they tell us what the appropriate solutions should be. Broder warns against going beyond independent reviews to court suits, where judges and juries would be asked to make medical decisions, though they are not qualified to do so.

Public Opinion

The public view of managed care organizations is also important in understanding the backlash. More than half of the respondents in a 1999 survey (found at the Public Agenda Web site, www.publicagenda.org) reported that HMOs had made it more difficult to get care and to see specialists when sick. Half or more of the respondents thought that HMOs had decreased the quality of care and the time spent with doctors. While many respondents felt that HMOs did help restrain cost increases, a majority saw managed care plans as mainly looking out for their profit margins. Strong majorities favored the right to sue their managed care organization (known as enterprise liability).

A 2000 survey by the Kaiser Family Foundation and the Harvard School of Public Health found that a majority of respondents had an unfavorable view of HMOs, tied with oil companies and exceeded only by tobacco companies. The percentage of respondents who thought that managed care plans were doing a good job fell from 34 percent in 1997 to 24 percent in 2000. Correspondingly, the percentage who felt that managed care plans were doing a bad job in serving consumers increased over the same period from 21 percent to 39 percent (Kaiser Family Foundation 2001). Thirty-seven percent of those who thought managed care plans were doing a bad job based that belief on their own experience. Thirty-five percent based their view on the experience of family and friends. Only 18 percent based their view on media coverage. And the public as a whole, even broken down by party affiliation, strongly favors a patients' bill of rights (Kaiser Family Foundation 2001).

Other polls showed strong support for patients' rights legislation. Surveys taken by the Gallup organization in the spring and summer of 2001, when the battle over this issue was heating up in Congress, showed large majorities favoring the passage of patients' rights legislation, including the right to sue (Moore and Carroll 2001; Moore 2001a; 2001b). The surveys showed that the public trusted the Democrats more than the Republicans or the Republican president, George W. Bush, on this issue. The surveys also showed that when confronted with information that a patients' bill of rights might raise the cost of health care the public still supports the concept. The polls also indicate that Americans did not follow the issue closely or understand it very well, including the differences between Republicans and Democrats on the issue (Moore 2001b).

Regulating Managed Care

Given the problems that many attribute to managed care, how and to what extent should government (public policy) play a role? Mariner (1999, 861) makes the important distinction between consumer protections and rights and patient protections and rights:

> Consumer rights focus on purchasing decisions before a provider relationship is formed. They are necessary to help people choose a health plan, but they are not sufficient to protect patients when they need medical care. Patient rights focus on the relationship between patients and physicians (and other providers) and the type and quality of care provided.

One typical way of looking at rationales for government intervention is through some type of market failure. Moran (1997) notes that there are new arguments for market failure related to managed care. There are concerns about access to care (though only among those who have health insurance) whether consumers have sufficient information (and can act reasonably with this information) to choose a health plan (where choice exists) and risk selection.[1]

Government has three sets of tools with which to address these problems (Moran 1997). The first is information utilities, such as disclosure of financial incentives, lists of plan providers, and so forth. Securities laws provide a good model for such a policy (Etheredge 1997; Moran 1997). A second policy tool is economic regulation over transactions. Generally speaking, this has involved either structure and financing issues at the time of licensing or continued scrutiny of financial viability.

The third tool is what Moran calls "private enforcement":

> In the private-enforcement model, a legislative framework is created in which individual aggrieved parties can bring legal actions against market participants whose behavior offends public policy. The presumption is that the cumulative effect of these legal actions creates an environment in which all of the actors behave in the manner intended by policymakers as the only means to avoid an unending stream of costly litigation. (Moran 1997, 15)

To translate this into English, Moran is saying the legislatures can create the conditions under which consumers can sue providers or insurers. The right to sue will cause all the participants in a market to behave better to avoid the lawsuits. In the case of managed care, the ability to sue health care plans (enterprise liability or enterprise medical liability) is the most controversial part of patients' bill of rights proposals.

Noble and Brennan (1999) present a useful analytic scheme for understanding regulation of MCOs. The first stage occurred during the 1970s and 1980s. The passage of the Health Maintenance Organization Act of 1973, designed to stimulate the growth of HMOs, also meant regulating them in terms of benefits offered and financing. States, the traditional and still major source of regulatory power over insurance companies (including many but not all MCOs), concentrated on financial integrity, making information available, and other regulatory techniques dealing with quality, financing, and access.

The second stage took place during the mid-1990s. In response to the kinds of stories mentioned above, states passed legislation that was clearly anti-managed care. Such laws focused on narrow aspects such as ending gag clauses, opening plans to more providers, maternity length-of-stay clauses, and so forth.

In the third stage, states continued their focus on narrow aspects that mandated benefits, such as access to obstetricians/gynecologists. The federal government, in 1996, passed legislation mandating maternal length-of-stay clauses for plans covered or protected by ERISA. Other areas of concern in this phase were gag clauses and physician deselection (termination of a physician from a managed care plan).

The fourth stage is occurring now and seeks, according to Noble and

Brennan (1999), to reconcile consumer and market concerns. Areas of legislation or proposed legislation include regulating risk-bearing provider groups, regulation and disclosure of financial incentives, newer interpretations of ERISA, and managed care liability (or enterprise liability). Noble and Brennan note that enterprise liability is the most controversial of these areas, an observation borne out by congressional deliberations (below).

National Government and Patients' Bill of Rights

As we have seen, by the early 1990s more people were enrolling or being enrolled in MCOs, largely because such plans cost less than the more conventional indemnity plans (Dudley and Luft 2001). When Bill Clinton was elected president in 1992, he made a national health insurance plan a major priority of his administration. In September 1993, President Clinton addressed a national televised joint session of Congress and made the case for his Health Security Act. At the end of October, a proposal was forwarded to Congress.

The Health Security Act was an extraordinarily complex bill. From our standpoint, it had several important features. First, all Americans would be covered either through their place of employment, through Medicare, or through state insurance pools (Medicaid would be eliminated under the proposal). Subsidies were provided for smaller businesses to encourage them to cover their employees. Subscribers would be enrolled in health care alliances (purchasing groups) that would negotiate with insurers and others to offer plans to their members. Members were guaranteed at least three choices of plans: a traditional fee-for-service plan, an HMO, or a hybrid. The Health Security Act was based on the concept of managed competition: plans would compete with each other for subscribers and that competition would ensure a high quality of care and restraints on costs (Hacker 1997).

It is beyond the scope of this book to explain why the president's proposal was defeated in Congress (Fallows 1995; Johnson and Broder 1996; Patel and Rushefsky 1999; Rushefsky and Patel 1998). But the failure of the president's plan had important consequences for a patients' bill of rights. First, the defeat of the health plan contributed to the victory of Republicans in the November 1994 elections. For the first time in forty years, Republicans controlled both houses of Congress. Republicans in general, and those in the House of Representatives in particular, such as Speaker Newt Gingrich of Georgia, Majority Leader Richard Armey of Texas, and Majority Whip Tom DeLay, also from Texas, were hostile to big government programs and to President Clinton. Republicans were less likely to support a patients' bill of rights than Democrats, and when they did support such a bill, as we shall see below, it was more modest than Democratic proposals.

Another implication of the failure of the Health Security Act was that employees would continue to be dependent on their employers for health insurance, and the move toward managed care continued. As this did, so did the kinds of horror stories related above.

Two examples appeared in the mid-1990s. The media printed stories about HMOs releasing newborn babies and their mothers in very short periods of time. The American College of Obstetricians and Gynecology recommended stays of at least forty-eight hours for vaginal deliveries and twice that time for cesarean deliveries (Anders 1996). To save money, HMOs paid for shorter stays. In response, and part of the compromises on health care that occurred in 1996, a presidential election year, Congress passed the Newborns' and Mothers' Health Protection Act in September (Pear 1996) requiring the longer, minimum stays. States also passed such legislation (below). Similar pressures were put on HMOs to allow women undergoing mastectomies to stay overnight in the hospital rather than be treated on an outpatient basis (Anders 1996; Pear 1996).

In 1996 the Health Insurance and Portability Accountability Act (HIPAA) was passed. The purpose of the act was to allow workers who changed jobs and had health insurance in their previous jobs to get health insurance in their new jobs if the new employers offered it. The legislation limited the ability of insurers to refuse coverage because of a preexisting condition. For our purposes, the importance of HIPAA was that this was the first time that the federal government entered the field of regulation of insurance companies. Heretofore, it had been left to the states to regulate insurance companies. We will return to a consideration of this federal/state divide over health insurance regulation below.

As the media attention and overall criticism of managed care organizations, especially HMOs, increased, Congress began to consider such legislation. A patients' bill of rights was first proposed in 1997 by Senator Edward Kennedy (D-MA) and Representative John Dingell (D-MI), both longtime health policy reformers. Later that year, President Clinton formed an advisory commission to recommend a patients' bill of rights. It issued its final report in 1998 (Mitchell and Pear 2001; President's Advisory Commission 1998).

The appendix to the advisory commission's report focused on a patients' bill of rights. The proposed patients' bill of rights contained eight major provisions as follows:

I.   Information Disclosure
      Consumers have the right to receive accurate, easily understood information and some require assistance in making informed health care decisions about their health plans, professionals, and facilities.

II.   Choice of Providers and Plans

Consumers have the right to a choice of health care providers that is sufficient to ensure access to appropriate high-quality health care.

III.   Access to Emergency Services

Consumers have the right to access emergency health care services when and where the need arises. Health plans should provide payment when a consumer presents to an emergency department with acute symptoms of sufficient severity—including severe pain—such that a "prudent layperson" could reasonably expect the absence of medical attention to result in placing that consumer's health in serious jeopardy, serious impairment to bodily functions, or serious dysfunction of any bodily organ or part.

IV.   Participation in Treatment Decisions

Consumers have the right and responsibility to fully participate in all decisions related to their health care. Consumers who are unable to fully participate in treatment decisions have the right to be represented by parents, guardians, family members, or other conservators.

V.   Respect and Nondiscrimination

Consumers have the right to considerate, respectful care from all members of the health care system at all times and under all circumstances. An environment of mutual respect is essential to maintain a quality health care system.

VI.   Confidentiality of Health Information

Consumers have the right to communicate with health care providers in confidence and to have the confidentiality of their individually identifiable health care information protected. Consumers also have the right to review and copy their own medical records and request amendments to their records.

VII.   Complaints and Appeals

All consumers have the right to a fair and efficient process for resolving differences with their health plans, health care providers, and the institutions that serve them, including a rigorous system of internal review and an independent system of external review.

VIII.   Consumer Responsibilities

In a health care system that protects consumers' rights, it is reasonable to expect and encourage consumers to assume reasonable responsibilities. Greater individual involvement by consumers in their care increases the likelihood of achieving the best outcomes and helps support a quality improvement, cost-conscious environment. (President's Advisory Commission 1998)

Several comments should be made about this list. First, it is very comprehensive, much more so than the European versions of patients' rights. Second, like the European ones, it includes a section on consumer responsibilities. Such responsibilities include engaging in a healthy lifestyle, participating in decisions, being knowledgeable about the features of the plan, and so forth.

Third, there is a major exclusion from the President's Advisory Commission recommended patients' rights. Section VII of the document discusses complaints and appeals in considerable detail. It calls for a fair system of internal plan review and independent external reviews. However, it did not include a right to sue the health plan. The members of the commission could not agree on such a right and, as we shall see, this has been the major barrier to passing a federal patients' bill of rights. President Clinton accepted the recommendations of the Commission and in his 1998 and 1999 State of the Union messages urged Congress to pass a patients' bill of rights. In February 1998, President Clinton issued an executive order directing several departments (Health and Human Services, Labor, Defense, Veteran's Affairs, and the Office of Personnel Management) to bring health programs within their authority, such as Medicare and Medicaid in the case of Health and Human Services, into compliance with the recommendations of the Advisory Commission (Department of Heath and Human Services 1998; Office of the Press Secretary 1998).

Republican leaders were displeased with the commission's recommendations. House and Senate Republican leaders called it another path to the Clinton health plan and the Business Roundtable saw the plan as presaging further government intervention (Marwick 1998).

Interest groups quickly became involved in the debate over a patients' bill of rights. Consumer groups such as FamiliesUSA strongly supported it. Trade groups such as the AAHP opposed them, especially the provisions on suing. Business groups tended to oppose the plan. Doctors' and lawyers' organizations supported it.

Occasionally, some of the different groups would reach a compromise. The best example of this came in 1997 when FamiliesUSA, the American Association of Retired Persons (AARP), and three of the largest nonprofit HMOs published a statement of principles for consumer rights (FamiliesUSA 1997). To keep the consensus, the statement of principles also did not include an enterprise liability provision.

Putting Patients First?

One response to the litany of complaints about managed care has come from the trade association of managed care plans, the AAHP. This is an initiative, adopted in 1996, known as "putting patients first." The initiative, and the philosophy of care that accompanies it, is designed, according to its supporters, to provide a set of criteria for judging plan performance. Further, AAHP member plans must accept the philosophy and initiative (Jones 1997). Consider two examples of how this philosophy is supposed to work. The first has to do with providing subscribers full information about a plan's policies:

> [The AAHP] broadly affirmed that health plans should (1) routinely inform members about their plan's structure and provider network; the benefits covered and excluded, including out-of-area and emergency coverage; and cost-sharing requirements; and (2) provide information about precertification and other utilization review procedures; the basis for a specific utilization review decision with which a member disagrees, whether a specific prescription drug is included in a formulary; a summary description of how physicians are paid, including financial incentives (short of disclosing specific details of individual financial arrangements); and the procedures and criteria used to determine whether experimental treatments and technologies are covered. (Jones 1997, 118)

The AAHP policy also addressed grievance procedures:

> Responding to public confusion about how to appeal an unfavorable coverage or treatment determination, the AAHP adopted a policy that (1) health plans should explain, in a timely notice to the patient, the basis for a coverage or treatment determination with which the patient disagrees, accompanied by an easily understood description of the patient's appeal rights and the time frame for an appeal; and (2) appeals should be resolved as rapidly as warranted by the patient's situation, with an expedited appeals process for situations in which the normal time frame could jeopardize a patient's life or health. (Jones 1997, 119)

Not everyone greeted Putting Patients First with open arms. One of the more interesting critiques comes from Clark Havighurst (1997a). Havighurst argues that the initiative has two goals: warding off government regulation through self-regulation and centralizing decision making. To Havighurst, the major problem is that AAHP and its member plans seek to avoid accountability for the quality of service they provide, even though they exercise responsibility for controlling costs (also Havighurst 2000a). The fiction the association and plans would like to maintain is that they do not practice medicine (Havighurst 1997b). Havighurst argues, to the contrary, that they place constraints on physician behavior. He strongly advocates enterprise liability and recommends that AAHP put acceptance of liability in its statement of principles. Indeed, Havighust (1997b) argues that they should be exclusively liable for the care of their subscribers.

Congressional Action

Despite the efforts of the AAHP to ward off patients' rights bills in Congress and in the states, the two levels of government pressed on. Hearings were held in 1998. In 1999, both the House and Senate passed versions of a patients' bill of rights, with moderate Republicans in the House defying their leaders to vote in support of patients' rights. In 2000, the Senate passed a bill that included a mild enterprise liability provision (Mitchell and Pear 2001). The Monica Lewinsky affair and the subsequent impeachment proceedings of President Clinton helped push the patients' bill of rights off the agenda during 1998 and 1999 (Rovner 1999).

The Senate patients' rights bill became known as the Kennedy-McCain-Edwards bill, co-sponsored by Edward Kennedy (D-MA), John McCain (R-AZ) who challenged Texas Governor George W. Bush for the 2000 Republican presidential nomination, and James Edwards (D-NC). A more modest alternative Senate proposal was offered by Bill Frist (R-TN), John Breaux (D-LA), and Jim Jeffords (I-VT). The Kennedy-McCain-Edwards bill passed the Senate in 2001. In the House of Representatives, the major bill (close to the Kennedy-McCain-Edwards bill) was proposed by Charles Norwood (R-GA) and John Dingell (D-MI). It passed the House in 2000. A weaker version of it passed in 2001 (below). The Senate version of the bill was stopped by a filibuster over the liability issues.

A patients' bill of rights became part of the debates during the controversial 2000 presidential elections. Vice President Al Gore, the Democratic candidate, asked whether Texas Governor George Bush supported the Norwood-Dingell bill, the one that passed the House. The Governor's response was equivocal. As president, Bush has supported a patients' bill of rights with limited enterprise liability. House Republican leaders have also tried to craft such a bill that they could take to conference. In 2001, both the Senate (controlled by Democrats after Jim Jeffords defected from the Republican Party and became an independent) and the House (controlled by Republicans) passed patients' rights bills. The major difference between the two bills was the provisions for enterprise liability. President Bush pushed the House to pass a weaker bill, hoping that the Senate version could be watered down in conference (Balz and Harris 2001; Milligan 2001). He succeeded in convincing Representative Charles Norwood (R-GA) to go along with the weaker version. Norwood, a dentist, is one of the moderate Republicans who supported a stronger right to sue provision. His unwillingness to buck the President on this issue led to passage of the Ganske-Norwood-Dingell bill in a weaker form along party lines (Goldstein and Eilperin 2001). A House-Senate conference committee will have to work out the differences and final passage of a patients' bill of rights is not assured.

Interest groups varied, as expected, at the results of the House action. The AAHP (2001) praised the House bill in comparison to the Senate bill, because it placed more restrictions on the right to sue managed care health plans. The Health Insurance Association of America (HIAA), the trade group of health insurance companies, criticized both the House and Senate bills. The major problem HIAA saw was that even the House bill allowed lawsuits in state courts (HIAA 2001). FamiliesUSA (2001b), a consumer advocacy group, expressed dismay over the House action because of the weakened provisions for enterprise liability.

The policy atmosphere changed twice in 2001. The elections of 2000 resulted not only in George W. Bush's ascension to the presidency, but narrow control by the Republicans of the House of Representatives and a 50–50 tie in the Senate. Only the presence of a Republican as president of the Senate, Vice President Dick Cheney, kept control of the Senate in Republican hands. But when, as briefly mentioned above, Vermont Senator Jim Jeffords defected from the Republican Party to become an independent, the Democrats took control of the Senate. This resulted in the return of split government and a decided advantage for those who advocated a patients' bill of rights.

The atmosphere and agenda changed again after the September 11 terrorist attack against the United States. The focus of policy became the war against terrorism, homeland security, and economic stimulus for an economy that was apparently heading toward a recession. Issues such as a patients' bill of rights or prescription drugs coverage for Medicare were pushed off the agenda, perhaps until 2002.

Provisions of Bills

While the bills were similar in most respects, there were differences among them. The bills required managed care plans to offer out-of-network options, coverage of emergency services without prior authorization and without network limitations. The bills allowed access to medications not on the plan's list of accepted drugs (a formulary) when necessary and appropriate, and access to approved and funded clinical trials. The bills require inpatient hospital stays for mastectomies as medically necessary. They specify the kind of information to be given to plan members (such as benefits, cost sharing, participating physicians, preauthorization, and appeals procedures). Gag clauses, which limit what providers can tell patients about medical care, are banned. Internal and external procedures are spelled out in great detail, though there are significant differences between the bills (Lewis 2001; Senate Democratic Policy Committee 2001). Again, notice how much more comprehensive and detailed these proposals are compared to what was being considered in Europe.

While there seemed to be a consensus on many major features of a patients' bill of rights, there also were differences. For example, the Kennedy-McCain-Edwards bill allows a woman to obtain needed care from an OB/GYN without referral or authorization from her primary care doctor. The Frist-Breaux-Jeffords bill allows women to obtain such care, but leaves out the referral/authorization provision. It also requires OB/GYNs to seek authorization for providing some services. The Frist plan does not cover Food and Drug Administration (FDA) clinical trials.

The Kennedy bill also contains some provisions not in the Frist bill. For example, it bans the use of financial incentives to limit necessary care, though it does not prohibit the use of capitation. The Frist bill contains no such prohibition. The Kennedy bill requires prompt payment of claims for covered benefits; the Frist bill does not. The Kennedy bill prohibits punitive action against providers who are advocates of services for their patients or who help in grievance procedures; the Frist bill does not. The Kennedy bill contains provisions for monitoring how MCOs review the use of medical procedures and prohibits paying employees to deny coverage to members (giving bonuses for limiting services). The Frist bill does not (Senate Democratic Policy Committee 2001). It should be pointed out that the House bill that passed is identical to the Kennedy bill in most ways, but one of the most important differences concerned the scope of the bills. The Kennedy-McCain bill covered many more people than the Republican bills, about 190 million people versus 170 million for the Republican bill (Senate Democratic Policy Committee 2001). The major reason for this is the existence of ERISA, the Employment Retirement and Income Security Act of 1974. Another difference between the Senate and House bills is that the House bills preempt state laws; that is, states would not be able to enact laws stronger than a federal bill. The Senate bill sets minimum standards, allowing standards to pass stronger protections (Lewis 2001). The other major difference concerns the right to sue managed care plans. The two issues are interrelated.

The Importance of ERISA

ERISA became law in 1974 as a way of protecting the pension plans of employees. The provisions of ERISA and its interpretations are important in understanding the debate over patients' bill of rights (Butler 2000). First, Congress sought to insure consistency in administering pension plans so ERISA preempts state regulation of pension plan claims (King 1998). The law was designed to protect the rights of workers. Second, under court decisions, health care plans and managed care plans in particular have been covered under ERISA. Thus employees in self-insured health plans do not have rights, including the right to sue MCOs under state laws (and there have been many such laws, see below). Thus, federal legislative proposals have included amendments to ERISA, especially the Kennedy-McCain-Edwards bill. The House bill and the Bush administration support a limited right to sue, while the Senate bill has a more expansive right to sue (Lewis 2001).

Enterprise Liability

The courts have played an important role in interpreting ERISA. There are two important issues related to patients' rights and enterprise liability (Coan 1996). First, the move toward managed care has shifted responsibility away from physicians to "a system dominated by integrated economic enterprises" (1996, 1023). Second is whether such plans can be sued when covered by the cloak of ERISA. Courts have stated, in upholding plans' protection from suits under the law, that ERISA both preempts state laws and also does not provide for grievance procedures (Cerminara 1998). This provides the plans with what Cerminara (1998, 25) calls a "zone of no liability."

The particular theory being used by courts is known as "vicarious liability," whereby those injured (or denied services) impute negligence to the MCOs. Coan's (1996) analysis of court decisions, which shows a mixed reading of whether MCOs are exempt from malpractice under ERISA, concludes that they should in fact not be exempt.

Havighurst (2000b) suggests that vicarious liability be the "default rule" (2000b, 8) for holding MCOs responsible for the quality of care given to their subscribers. He does so because MCOs select providers, place financial incentives and other restrictions on their actions, and make decisions about care. He calls this "corporate health care" (2000b, 13). He also argues that though malpractice reform has not improved the quality of care and is costly, it does have deterrent effects.

One of the early cases related to enterprise liability is *Darling v. Charleston Memorial Hospital* (1966) (Havighurst 2000a). In that case, the court stated that the hospital had a legal responsibility for the quality of care given its patients, even though the injury was caused by a doctor working in the hospital. It also is related to physician malpractice, which became an important issue in the 1970s and 1980s (Patel and Rushefsky 1999, Chapter 7). Abraham and Weiler recommended enterprise medical liability during deliberations over President Clinton's Health Security Act (1993–1994), though their initial proposal was limited to hospitals and other deliverers of health care services (Abraham and Weiler 1994a, 1994b).

An important case establishing that MCOs would not be protected by ERISA under enterprise liability was *Dukes v. U.S. Healthcare* (1995) (Henry

1996/1997). Here the U.S. Third Circuit Court held that ERISA did not give complete preemption protection. Henry argues that because MCOs change the relationship between insurer and provider and provider and patient, they may be liable for suit. In particular, Henry refers to both direct intervention in medical decisions and financial incentives to providers as providing a basis for making such a claim, what he calls a "tortious interference" (Henry 1996/1997, 703).

Sorian and Feder (1999) argue that a patients' bill of rights is an absolute necessity to ensure accountability and responsiveness on the part of MCOs. They suggest that an external review would be an important step. A next step would be to allow subscribers to sue MCOs in court (enterprise liability). They note that court suits are an unwieldy way of handling problems with MCOs. However, enterprise liability would produce important benefits:

> [C]ourts are needed to provide the entire system with legitimacy. By punishing miscreants, courts are a powerful deterrent for bad behavior. In all other markets, the ultimate consumer protection is the ability to go to court and be made whole. As long as health plans are shielded from liability, consumers will continue to believe that the deck is stacked against them. (Sorian and Feder 1999, 1144)

Rice (1999) argues in favor of more regulation, really microregulation, of managed care plans in the absence of more comprehensive reforms. He states that because managed care organizations "set the rules by which providers are paid and consumers receive services" (1999, 971), they should be liable for actions that result in harm to consumers. He does not necessarily see a great wave of lawsuits. Rather, the possibility of a lawsuit would be an incentive not to cut costs in a way that would result in harm.

Rodwin (1999) discusses what he sees as a "systemic problem" (1999, 1118) with MCOs. Kaiser Permanente, the prototype of HMOs, had a policy that its members could not go to court to resolve disputes with the plan. Instead, members were to use an arbitration system. However, Kaiser, in the particular case discussed by Rodwin (*Engalla v. The Permanente Medical Group*, 1997), delayed the arbitration process. Further, the HMO argued that it could run the arbitration process in such a way that would favor its own interests. The California court case, which began in 1991, dragged on until 1997. The state Supreme Court found that despite contractual or fiduciary responsibilities to its clients, Kaiser was administering the arbitration process in a very partial way. By April 1999, Kaiser began a neutral arbitration process outside the plan. Rodwin (1999) concludes that by denying there were problems, Kaiser helped ignite the backlash against managed care.

Kaiser also, apparently, made it a practice to have subscribers go through a complicated system just to see a doctor, though persistent patients were able to see a doctor the same day. This was a way of controlling (lowering demand), the queue-type tools that mark some of the health care systems of other countries. Dissatisfaction among subscribers and physicians, and a lawsuit, led Kaiser to remove the barriers (Rohrlich 2001). What is dismaying about these two examples is that Kaiser is a nonprofit HMO and has a reputation as being one of the better HMOs.

Enterprise liability can take many forms (Kelso 1999). One such model is the contracts model, in which suits can be brought for breach of contract. At the opposite end is the tort model. As Kelso points out, torts deal with how people, groups, and organizations should behave by using a reasonableness standard that is not solely dependent on common practice within a particular industry or group. Other models include product liability, medical malpractice, and breach of faith.

In addition to the bills before Congress, in May 2001 the California Supreme Court ruled that Medicare recipients could sue their HMO for denial of services. Medicare generally requires that administrative procedures be followed, but the court's majority argued that Medicare law did not prohibit suits. The ruling will likely be appealed to the U.S. Supreme Court (Dolan 2001).

The basic argument made by MCOs against enterprise liability is that the plans do not make medical decisions; doctors do (Rodwin 1999). Therefore, they should not be held responsible for medical decisions. Further, AAHP would assert that by following the "putting patients first" philosophy, grievances would not rise up to the level of court suits.

Of course, the major argument made against enterprise liability as applied to managed care is that it will, as have medical malpractice suits, raise the cost of medical care because of the direct costs of suits and because insurers will raise the costs of their premiums charged to health care plans because of the cost of the suits (Patel and Rushefsky 1999).

This is part of a larger effort to reduce the prevalence of lawsuits in the United States, an effort known as tort reform. George W. Bush as both president and Texas governor supported strong tort reforms. President Bush and many Republicans have opposed strong enterprise liability provisions, including limiting the basis for appeals and placing a ceiling on awards that courts can make. The House bill that passed in 2001 contains both those limits (Doroshow 2001).

A Communitarian View of Enterprise Liability

In Chapter 1, we argued that a communitarian view was an important perspective in understanding the health issues of the twenty-first century. The communitarian view toward enterprise liability flows from the basic idea of what a corporation is and what rights it might have. The corporation came to the fore as part of the industrialization of the United States in the post–Civil War period (Beatty 2001). One of the key events was a U.S. Supreme Court decision in 1886, *Santa Clara County v. Southern Pacific Railroad Company.*

As Rowe (2001) and others have pointed out (McConnell 1966, Mintz 2000), what *Santa Clara County* did was to proclaim corporations as persons protected by the Fourteenth Amendment to the U.S. Constitution. Thus, they were afforded all the protections that the amendment gave to real persons (though at the same time the Court refused to grant those same rights to the former slaves), including free speech (including commercial speech, with some limitations), free press, the right to peacefully assemble, and the right to lobby government.

Further, the idea of the corporation was to insulate individuals from suits and other restrictions. The corporation was responsible, but protected by the Fourteenth Amendment. Rowe (2001, 40) describes the major advantage of incorporation:

> A corporate charter bestows an extraordinary privilege—exemption from common law rules of personal responsibility. It enables the owners of the corporation to say in effect, "I didn't do it your honor. The corporation did."

However, Rowe (2001, 40) quotes U.S. Supreme Court Justice Roger Taney (of *Dred Scott* fame) stating the communitarian perspective: private property was an important value but "the community also has rights."

Rowe (2001, 42) concludes:

> If it [the corporation] is to keep the legal status of a person, then it should accept the responsibilities that we expect of persons as they mature. A corporation, declared Chief Justice John Marshall, is but "an artificial being, invisible, intangible, existing only in contemplation of law." It is a social creation, a projection of society's values and aspirations.

Mintz (2000) states the case about protections for the corporations very forcefully, using populist language:

> But bear in mind the underlying idea of the corporation: under our Constitution, the hypothetical sovereign—the people—delegated power to an entity whose proclaimed purpose was to maximize profit for the owners, who would be motivated to invest by, in part, a grant of limited liability for

the corporation's missteps. The rationale was that in pursing its selfish interest, the corporation would achieve the economic efficiencies and innovations that would serve the people. Greed, that is, can be good.

But a corporation does not serve its intended purpose when it knowingly, willfully, or recklessly kills, injures, sickens and cheats those who gave it life, and when its uses its overwhelming economic power to buy and sell those who are and would be our presidents, congressmen, and senators.

Here is where communitarianism comes in. Communitarianism is a philosophy or ideology that seeks a balance between responsibilities and rights. That is, it seeks to find a middle ground between radical libertarians who see the individual as standing apart and above society, with few obligations required, and radical social conservatives who see society as imposing obligations and moral standards on individuals (Spragens 1991/1992). People and communities have both rights and responsibilities (Responsive communitarian platform: rights and responsibilities 1991/1992). Lind argues that the framers of the Constitution did not see any conflict between individual freedoms and community. Rather they thought "both individual autonomy *and* public virtue" (Lind 1998, 13, emphasis in original) were necessary for a functioning polity.

Minow (1996, 41) argues that corporations show "a disturbing tendency . . . to impose as many costs on others (including its constituencies) as possible, and at the same time resist meaningful accountability." Bellah et al. (1991) argue that corporations which benefit from citizenship should also have the responsibilities that go with it.

If we combine these ideas we can see the communitarian argument in favor of enterprise liability. Corporations are persons. Persons have rights and freedoms. Communitarians argue that persons also have responsibilities. Corporations as persons have both rights and responsibilities. In the case of managed care, the responsibility is not just to control costs of care but also to provide a reasonable level of quality of care. When persons do not meet their responsibilities, there should be some consequences. The way to assess the consequences is through litigation.

The communitarian approach also suggests that patients not use courts as the first resort, but as the last resort. Therefore, there should be a well-developed grievance procedure with both internal and external components and time limitations. The external reviews should be independent of the health plan to ensure objectivity (for a review of state external review plans, see Dalleck and Pollitz 2000). State patients' bills of rights legislation (see below) and proposals currently before Congress provide for external reviews, though the Republican House bill calls for a less independent external review process.

Gonzalez (1998) points out that a major purpose of enterprise liability is not just to provide a remedy for someone injured (say by denial or delay of services) by an MCO, but also to deter such injuries. Gonzalez looks at a particular theory of liability, known as the "ostensible agency" theory. To qualify under this theory, the claimant has to demonstrate, first, that a patient is enrolled in an MCO at the invitation of the organization under the belief that the MCO would be providing services. Second, the claimant has to demonstrate that the MCO exercised control of the delivery of services by physicians.

There is an additional element that supports the communitarian view of the issue. A survey of privacy statutes found that one element of such laws was confidentiality (Pritts et al. 1999). This refers to confidentiality for legal purposes of the patient-provider relationship. Apparently, a number of states grant HMOs the same rights of confidentiality as physicians, thereby supporting the role that HMOs play in providing services.

Class Action Suits

An alternative to enterprise liability, where a single patient who believes he or she has been wronged sues the managed care organization, is a class action suit (Cerminara 1998; see also Havighurst 2001). Class action suits aggregate consumers in power battles with MCOs in an effort to increase their effectiveness and power. Cerminara (1998) states that structural features of MCOs disempower consumers. There is an asymmetry of information between consumers and managed care organizations, a problem that permeates much of health care. For example, it is difficult for consumers (when they have a choice of plans) to compare information about the quality of care, prices, availability of providers, and so forth. The class action suit is one way around ERISA exemptions. This is because under ERISA protections providers, insurers, employers, and the like have restructured plans creating common features (and complaints) across plans, thus creating a class of plaintiffs. It is no longer a single plaintiff versus a single plan but a class of plaintiffs versus a class of plans (Cerminara 1998).

Havighust (2001) notes two places where such class action suits are appropriate. One is a conflict of interest basic to many managed care plans: accepting responsibility for cost control but not for quality control. A second area is in disclosure, providing information to consumers (remedying the information asymmetry problem mentioned above).

Criticizing Enterprise Liability

Enterprise liability has its critics as well as supporters. Kronick (1999), for example, argues that the battle over enterprise liability is a "digression" (p. 1103). It will not result, he writes, in either improvement in the quality of care provided by MCOs as supporters hope, nor will it significantly hurt MCOs' ability to provide services as opponents fear. The most likely result is that health plans will more tightly oversee utilization decisions made by provider groups.

Moffit (2001a, 2001b) suggests that many of the problems with managed care would be better resolved by making health care more market-oriented, rather than resorting to legislating patients' rights. Giving subscribers the ability to choose providers, medical services, and plans would alleviate many of the problems. Both Moffit and Hoff (2000) argue that a patients' bill of rights amounts to a massive increase in federal regulation over the health care industry.

A related argument is that allowing enterprise liability will encourage law suits and result in massive litigation (Hoff 2000). Employers, facing rising costs because of the increased litigation, will reduce health insurance benefits. This fits into the Republican conservative move toward tort reform to decrease the number of law suits (Doroshow 2001).

The focus on litigation is captured by two editorial cartoons in June 2001. The first, by Margulies, shows a man representing an HMO holding up a patients' bill of rights proposal. He says: "If this becomes law, medical decisions will be made by LAWYERS, not the people who are qualified to make these decisions . . . ACCOUNTANTS." The other cartoon, by Kal, shows a man standing between two charts. On the left is a chart of the U.S. health care system as a labyrinth. The man says that "Every American victimized by this system" then he points to the other labyrinth, "will be able to sue in this system," the U.S. legal system.

Taylor (2001) argues that allowing suits against MCOs will raise the cost of care. He provides his own horror stories. In the first case, an HMO subscriber wanted a bone marrow transplant to treat her breast cancer. Her doctor had recommended the treatment but an outside panel recommended against it. The patient's husband raised the money for the treatment, but she died eight months after the transplant. The husband sued the HMO. During the course of the trial, evidence was produced showing that it was more profitable for the HMO to refuse to pay for the treatment than to pay for it. The husband was awarded a total of $89 million for emotional distress and bad faith on the part of the plan. The parties to the suit eventually agreed to a considerably smaller sum.

In the second case, an HMO refused to pay for a hysterectomy to deal with cervical cancer. The HMO's advisers recommended an alternative treatment that cost less. The patient underwent that treatment, plus privately paid for the hysterectomy. The woman and her husband sued the HMO, and a jury awarded $13 million in punitive damages. As with the previous case, a smaller, though still considerable settlement, was agreed to.

Taylor's point is that the Kennedy-McCain-Edwards bill creates incentives for attorneys to look for law suits and friendly courts and for health plans to approve "treatments that are not covered by their insurance contracts, are medically inappropriate, or even harmful" (Taylor 2001, 2071). To Taylor, the threat of suits will result in cost increases and a return to significant health care inflation.

Taylor then outlines the following set of linked events. The increased costs to employers will either be passed on to employees, as increases in deductibles, copayments, and/or premiums, or lead to employers dropping their health insurance coverage. Both paths would mean an increase in the number of uninsured people. Taylor looks at the experience with malpractice and finds that most people with valid complaints do not sue and many who do lack valid complaints. To Taylor, the result of the malpractice experience is higher medical costs, waste, and hiding of medical mistakes. Taylor's fear is that reformers are trying to destroy managed care and replace it with national health insurance.

Crook (2001) argues that a patients' bill of rights would do much harm. He focuses on rationing, a different if related issue, though he does not use that term (previous chapter). Every health care system is faced with the same question of how to deny patients treatment that may be beneficial though not cost effective (2001, 2074; Ubel 2000). How health systems deal with the question differs. To Crook, managed care alleviated health care inflation in part by denying care. Crook and others argue that the record of managed care in controlling costs and providing at least as good and satisfactory quality of care as the fee-for-service system has helped the nation. Like Taylor, Crook sees malpractice claims looming if a patients' bill of rights is passed. To him, lawyers' fees are deadweight, and defensive medicine (as a result of suits or threat of suits) will drive up the cost of care. He believes reform should begin by making sure that everybody has health insurance and then ensure that they have choices of plans (consumer rights, as mentioned above) that have cost consequences.

A supporter of patients' rights argues that patients' rights legislation may result in actually reducing patients' rights (Bloche 2001). The U.S. Supreme Court in *Pegram* (discussed in Chapter 6), while denying the plaintiff's suit, stated that such suits belonged in state courts. The bills backed by Republicans (including President Bush) seek to limit suits to federal courts or limit the damages that state courts could award, as is included in the bill that passed the House of Representatives in August 2001 (Goldstein and Eilperin 2001). Some have complained that the newly passed House bill may actually limit the right to sue by preempting stronger state laws (Foundation for Taxpayers and Consumer Rights 2001; Pear 2001). Bloche's point is that this and other court decisions have quietly been progressing toward removing managed care organizations' immunity from lawsuits.

For Bloche (2001), the more important problem is that financial incentives for physicians to ration will remain regardless of which version of a patients' bill of rights becomes law, if, indeed, that even happens. The Senate bill, Kennedy-McCain-Edwards bill, allows penalties and bonuses of up to 25 percent of income, while no limits are set in Republican bills.

State Governments and Patients' Bill of Rights

While there have been debates, proposals, and some votes on a patients' bill of rights at the federal level, as of the fall of 2001 no final action had been taken. The states, however, have been anything but shy about taking on the issue. Almost 600 bills were proposed in state legislatures just between 1996 and 1998 (Marsteller and Bovbjerg 1999). By 2001, most states had passed some form of patients' bill of rights, with eight states including the right to sue (enterprise liability) in their legislation. States were encouraged to move Medicaid recipients into managed care and have done so fairly aggressively. The HCFA, now the Centers for Medicare and Medicaid Services, issued waivers to states requesting permission to use managed care.

Further, the Balanced Budget Act of 1997 allowed states to move their Medicaid recipients to managed care without first seeking a waiver. In return, the states were to issue consumer protection laws for their Medicaid managed care recipients. This required that the federal government issue the appropriate regulations (FamiliesUSA 2001a). A report by the HCFA in 2000 found that protections were needed for Medicaid managed care recipients, particularly those with the most distress, those who were homeless, and those who had other kinds of health needs or were disabled (2001a). States have begun to move Medicaid recipients with disabilities into managed care. Twenty-seven percent of such nonelderly recipients had been so enrolled by 1998 (Kaiser Commission 2001).

In January 2001, the outgoing Clinton administration issued the HCFA regulations, but in April 2001 and then in Augst 2001, the regulations were put on hold and the George W. Bush administration indicated it wanted to revisit some issues that had been rejected in developing the regulation.

FamiliesUSA pointed out, in its critique of the Bush administration, that the regulations were in many ways what the president had approved of in the bill passed by the House of Representatives.

In August 2001, the Bush administration proposed an alternative set of rules (Goldstein 2001b). The Bush administration's regulations covered fewer Medicaid managed care recipients than the Clinton administration's, exempting more than 8 million people in prepaid health plans (Kaiser Commission 2001). In general, the Bush regulations require less of managed care organizations than did the Clinton regulations.

The other path the states took was to enact legislation covering managed care recipients not sheltered by ERISA. By 2001, virtually all states had passed some version of managed care legislation. The legislation covered the gamut of managed care issues, from access to emergency care to grievance procedures and right to sue. Some states, of course, had more comprehensive laws than others; this is characteristic of our federal system. Access to emergency services, direct access to OB/GYNs, and disclosure of treatment options were the most common features of such legislation. Enterprise liability, consumer assistance programs, and coverage of clinical trials were the least common (FamiliesUSA 1998). Based on 1998 data (FamiliesUSA 1998), 70 percent, or thirty-five, of the states have passed less than thirteen patients' rights protections. Four states (California, Missouri, New Mexico, and Texas) passed nine and one state (Vermont) passed ten such protections.

There are a small number of states, in addition to Texas, that allow MCOs to be sued. The nine states with specific legislative provisions allowing suits are Arizona (2000), California (1999), Georgia (1999), Maine (1999), Oklahoma (2000), Texas (1997), Washington (2000), West Virginia (2001), and North Carolina (Butler 2001; see also Butler 1997). Four other states (Missouri, New Mexico, Louisiana, and Oregon) have enacted similar legislation, but without the strong statutory guarantees allowing lawsuits contained in the previous eight states.

All nine states require that a grievance procedure within the plan and external reviews be exhausted before a case can come before the courts (Butler 2001). Typically, the state statutes provide that managed care organizations and insurers can be sued for failure to provide care in a timely fashion. Two states (Georgia and Maine) prohibit punitive damages and Maine limits noneconomic damages (2001).

The Texas situation is particularly intriguing. Texas became the first state to allow enterprise liability in 1997. The Texas Health Care Liability Act provides for common law exceptions to ERISA preemption (King 1998). More specifically, the Texas law allows suits where the provision of services is below "the standard of ordinary care" (1998, 1225). Governor George W.

Bush strongly opposed enterprise liability, at first vetoing such a bill and then allowing it to become law without his signature after it became clear he would lose this battle (Doroshow 2001; Tapper 2001). Since the law passed, only seventeen suits have been filed, eleven of which went to court (Tapper 2001). The Texas law has caps on punitive and economic damages. Some have argued that the Texas law led to an increase in premiums and a decrease in the number of those with health insurance. But the effects, if any, on costs and numbers of people with insurance have been very small (2001).

Texas has a voluntary external review system, which most plaintiffs have used.

> From November 1997 through May 2001, independent review doctors have considered 1,349 complaints. In 672 of these assessments, or 50 percent, the independent review overturned the HMO or the insurance company's original ruling. In 567 cases, or 42 percent, the independent review upheld the HMO or insurance company's ruling. In 110 cases, or 8 percent, there was essentially a split decision. (Tapper 2001)

The Cost of Enterprise Liability

One of the key questions posed by those who oppose extending liability to managed care organizations is the impact such suits might have. The impacts include drastic increases in the number of suits, high damages being imposed on the managed care organization, and increases in prices because of malpractice suits. One study that addressed this issue (Hunt, Saari, and Traw 1998) focused on members of CalPERS, the California health plan system for state and local government employees. Because the employer is a state, there is no ERISA exemption. The study also examined the Los Angeles school district's and Colorado employees' plans.

For the 1991 to 1997 period studied, sixty appeals went to the administrative hearing stage and fifteen to twenty went to court, most of those settling before the trial convened (Hunt, Saari, and Traw 1998). In the Los Angeles school district study, there were three cases that went to trial over a fourteen year period. For Colorado, there were three cases over a seven-year period (1998). Hunt, Saari, and Traw also found that the costs of litigation were extremely small. Using a private health plan's experience, the costs came to $.27 per subscriber.

An estimate prepared for the American Association of Health Plans suggested that if the Texas liability plan were adopted throughout the country, there would be cost increases to plans of between 2.7 percent and 8.6 percent. A 1999 study by the Congressional Budget Office suggested that if the

ERISA exemption were removed, premiums would go up about 1.4 percent (California Health Policy Roundtable, 1999).

In June 2001, the Congressional Budget Office estimated that the Kennedy-McCain-Edwards bill, the more ambitious of the two Senate patients' bill of rights proposals and the one that passed the Senate, would raise premiums by 4.2 percent. By comparison, the Frist-Breaux-Jeffords bill (S.889) would raise premiums by 2.9 percent (Mitchell and Pear 2001). These estimates included the total cost of the bills; the estimate of the costs of enterprise liability was generally under 1 percent. There are as yet no estimates of the bill that passed the House in August.

An interesting aspect of the debate over managed care and the major sticking point, enterprise liability, is that managed care organizations such as HMOs have been granted considerable immunity from suits (except for those subject to state regulation). Virtually no other industry is exempt from litigation (Alter 2001). In keeping with the communitarian perspective on enterprise liability and managed care, Alter argues that rather than talk about the patients' bill of rights we should call it the "HMO's bill of responsibilities" (2001, 33). That perspective envisions HMOs as constitutionally protected persons with rights and responsibilities.

Staying with the theme of rights and responsibilities, enterprise liability should be accompanied by procedures that limit abuses via the judiciary. One way to reduce the problems that afflict the medical malpractice system (Chapter 7 in Patel and Rushefsky 1999) is to mandate an independent external review before a subscriber or dependent can take a managed care plan to court, a provision of both Senate managed care bills as well as the Norwood-Dingell bill and the newly passed House version (Goldstein and Eilperin 2001). According to Weinstein (2001), three states (New York, New Jersey, and Connecticut) with such provisions have had good experience with them. When the review finds for the plaintiff, the plan generally gives in. They do so because they risk losing more in a trial. When the review finds for the plan, a suit is rarely sought. Weinstein cites statistics where external reviews are allowed (in Medicare and state regulated plans):

> The Kaiser Family Foundation has found that there are fewer than 2 external reviews each year for every 1,000 Medicare enrollees. In Pennsylvania there were fewer than 200 external reviews in 1997 among 5 million eligible enrollees. In Maryland, 255 cases from a pool of about 3.5 million enrollees were adjudicated last year under the state's external review system. In 120 cases, the plans backed down before settlements were reached. The patients won about half the remaining cases—so fewer than 70 people won relief from their health plans. (Weinstein 2001; see also Pollitt et al. 2002)

Litigation is reduced through external reviews. Thus the cost of enterprise liability is likely to be less than opponents assert.

Outlook for the Future

Kinsley (2001) argues that the Democrats' priorities are misplaced. They are seeking to help those with insurance, at best an incremental or marginal reform, while neglecting the millions who have no health insurance at all. He says this is consistent with other legislation, such as the 1996 Health Insurance Portability and Accountability Act, which helps those who have health insurance retain it. One reason why Democrats and others are doing this, according to Kinsley (2001), is that it appears to be free from the charge of "big government." The costs are passed on to the private sector via lawyers.

Angell (2001) asserts that a patients' bill of rights will lead to the erosion of managed care, and already has where legislation has been passed and consumer demands have been acceded to. She argues that the resulting cost increases from this erosion will lead to greater numbers of uninsured Americans. This is because most Americans get health insurance through employment, and providing health insurance is a voluntary practice. If it becomes too costly, this fringe benefit will erode as well. Her solution is a single-payer system, essentially Medicare for all.

It appears that at least some MCOs already have made the changes contained in the Senate and House bills, not including enterprise liability, though these changes do not appear to have stemmed from the managed care backlash (Bloche 2001; Freudenheim 2001a; Goldstein 2001a). Further, the changes seem to be in response not to consumer pressure, but to the threat of legislatively imposed regulations. Changes include greater access to emergency room care, and easier access to specialists. Those advocating enterprise liability argue that the provision still needs to be included in a patients' bill of rights because in the absence of a threat of government action, managed care plans might reduce benefits (Goldstein 2001a).

As an example of such changes, Blue Cross of California and Harvard Pilgrim Health Care announced that they would start rewarding plan physicians based on patient satisfaction and quality of care. In the case of Blue Cross, the plan promised to stop paying bonuses for physicians who cut costs the most (Freudenheim 2001b). Further, managed care itself is evolving. Employers are giving employees freedom to pick some of the looser forms of managed care, such as preferred provider organizations and point-of-service plans. Of course, those plans are less able to control costs than the more restrictive health maintenance organizations (on the evolution of managed care, see Dudley and Luft 2001).

The U.S. Supreme Court may have the last word here. The Court created some of the problems in its interpretation of ERISA in the *Pilot Life Insurance* case. In June 2001, the Court agreed to hear a case relevant to enterprise liability and a patients' bill of rights. The Illinois case concerns a woman who paid for an operation her HMO refused to cover, even though an outside doctor recommended it. Her HMO said that two other doctors recommended a less expensive operation. The issue is whether the Illinois law mandating external review is preempted by ERISA (Justices to decide 2001). A ruling in favor of the plan would strengthen the case for federal legislation requiring reviews and the right to sue. On the other hand, the Court's decision in *Pegram* may make it more difficult to sue (Bloche 2000; Sage 2000).

The prospects for agreement on a patients' bill of rights are uncertain as of this writing (October 2001). Democrats and moderate Republicans in the Senate may not want to compromise any more on enterprise liability. The Ganske-Norwood-Dingell bill, with the new Norwood amendment, passed by the House of Representatives, includes a more restrictive right to sue than the McCain-Kennedy-Edwards bill passed by the Senate. Interest groups of various persuasions were not pleased with the House action.

The consumer group FamiliesUSA complained that the Norwood amendment made the right to sue less meaningful (FamiliesUSA 2001b). Two health associations were unhappy because now insurers would face lawsuits and fifty different sets of interpretations (Health Insurance Association of America 2001). The American Association of Health Plans, the trade association of managed care organizations, complained that litigation would still be possible even if an independent outside review upheld the plan (American Association of Health Plans 2001).

A House-Senate conference will attempt a compromise. The terrorist attack on the United States on September 11, 2001 threw many policy agendas, particularly at the federal level, into disarray. Controversial proposals, such as a patients' bill of rights were pushed aside to concentrate on security concerns. It is likely to be 2002 before a federal bill is passed, if one is. The battle over enterprise liability is clearly not over.

Patient's Bill of Rights, Values, and Public Policy

The organization of heath care has changed dramatically over the past decade. Where once there were individual institutions and physicians in solo practice, almost a cottage industry, health care has become more integrated, more industrial in scope. That has placed subscribers to managed care plans at the mercy of organizations that, while having the mission of providing health care to its members, are also concerned about restraining costs. Doing so means denying beneficial services, exactly how we defined rationing in the previous chapter.

As we saw in Chapter 6, all nations engage in rationing of health care of some sort. In the United States rationing is mostly implicit. The backlash against managed care in the United States is really a revolt against rationing (and enhanced control of providers). The result has been the move for a patients' bill of rights. Other countries are also discussing and, in some cases have enacted, a patients' bill of rights. But those rights have a somewhat different origin and are much less detailed than in the United States. Further, for the most part (Canada being a partial exception here), a patients' bill of rights is the focus of the national government. In the United States, with its typical federal, fragmented political system, the states have taken the lead.

How do managed care and the battle over patients' rights fit the values we have discussed? The first value is human dignity. To the extent that patients are treated as cogs rather than as individuals, the issue of human dignity arises. Recall Sara Singer's (2000) story concerning the birth of her child. At a time when a mother and her family ought to be focused on the child, she had to traverse a complicated bureaucracy. Fortunately for her, she was familiar with managed care and was somewhat prepared to handle the additional stress. But her basic point is that MCOs need to be more patient-oriented and patient-friendly. AAHP's program of "putting patients first" needs to become a reality.

The second value, that every person has the right of access to adequate care, is not so well met by either managed care or the patients' bill of rights. As noted above by some critics of a patients' bill of rights, the focus of this battle has been on those who already have insurance. Perhaps not everything is covered as much as subscribers would like, but they do have coverage. But some 16 percent of the American population does not have health insurance coverage. This is not an issue in other nations that meet the international standard of nearly universal coverage.

Indeed, one could argue that managed care has exacerbated the problem of the uninsured. By looking for cost savings, there is an incentive to reduce cost shifting. For example, hospital charges might include some of the costs of charitable care. However, when MCOs seek to reduce costs, it is clear that they do not want to pay for the care of those who are not members of the organization. The whole battle over a patients' bill of rights is over whether managed care will cover all services that its subscribers want.

The third value is the obligation of citizens to take care of their health. We have seen some of this, especially in European countries. The Danish Council of Ethics' 1997 report included a list of responsibilities. The British government also moved to amend its charter to focus on responsibilities.

The American battle over patients' rights has, for the most part, ignored this issue.

The fourth value is that health care is a public good, something we have stressed throughout this book. This means that people should have access to adequate health care, but not necessarily all the health care people might want. There are limits to the resources that can be devoted to health care. This is a fundamental principle of rationing. It is also at the heart of much of the debate over managed care and a patients' bill of rights. Managed care seeks to limit utilization of services to save money. Hopefully, some of the savings will come from preventive care, but that is in the long run. Patients' who have grievances against an MCO are asserting that they were denied coverage of services that they should get. Sometimes that denial is inconvenient or annoying. Sometimes, that denial is life threatening. Grievance procedures have become more common, and resorting to the courts, or enterprise liability, is being advocated more and more. But the U.S. Supreme Court in the *Pegram* case has essentially said that rationing is inherent to managed care. The question is where to draw the line. It is no wonder that enterprise liability has proven to be the most controversial element of a patients' bill of rights.

The fifth value focuses on prevention as important as alleviation of illness. A patients' bill of rights addresses this value somewhat. Access to specialists, especially OB/GYNs, without prior authorization, can lead to increased preventive care. If managed care organizations have stable populations, then they should engage in prevention, especially screening for potential diseases (such as breast or colon cancer) as well as counseling their subscribers.

Managed care in some form is likely to continue to be the predominant form of health care organization in the United States in the twenty-first century. Other countries have, and are, considering some of the American innovations. A healthy republic, as we have stressed, will require health organizations and providers to deliver services. But a certain amount of compassion, and not just a focus on costs, will be required.

Note

1. Dudley and Luft (2001) argue that one of the major reasons for the cost savings from managed care plans was risk selection. Risk selection occurs when subscribers pick plans based on their predicted need for medical care. They enroll in managed care plans when healthy and thus save money on premiums, and in indemnity plans when they think they will need serious medical care and will be more likely to get it covered.

Study Questions

1. Earlier chapters considered rights. For example, in Chapter 2, we discussed a right to die; in Chapter 5 we focused on a right to privacy; in Chapter 6, the concern was a right to health care. Chapter 7 concentrates on patients' rights. Write an essay in which you explore the notion of rights including their development and different types of rights. In what way(s) are the four rights mentioned similar or different?

2. We spent some time looking at patients' rights in other countries and compared them to patients' rights in the United States. We noted differences in these rights. Why are patients' rights different in the United States than in other countries?

3. We have seen in this chapter that while the debate over a patients' bill of rights has stalled at the federal level, many states have enacted one or more patients' bill of rights. Write an essay in which you discuss why the states have been able to take action, while the federal government has found it much more difficult to do anything.

4. The most contentious portion of a patient's bill of rights is the right to sue a health plan, known as enterprise liability. Why is this provision so controversial? What would be the effect of including such a provision? Do you support or oppose enterprise liability? Why?

5. One of the barriers that states face in their patients' rights legislation is the 1974 Employment Retirement and Income Security Act (ERISA). Should the courts reverse their ruling that ERISA protects self-insured health plans from state regulation? Defend your answer.

CHAPTER 8

Medical Education and Physician Training

Men are men before they are lawyers, or physicians, or merchants, or manufacturers and if you make them capable and sensible men, they will make themselves capable and sensitive lawyers or physicians. What professional men should carry away with them from a University, is not professional knowledge, but that which should direct the use of their professional knowledge, and bring the light of general culture to illuminate the technicalities of a general pursuit.

John Stuart Mills, Inaugural Address as Rector of St. Andrew's University, 1867. (Nuland 1999, 125)

Advances in technologies have had a profound impact on societal development. However, trying to predict trends in technology is problematic. John Nesbitt has argued that to describe the future in detail is the stuff of science fiction and not science (1984). Accelerating technological changes correspondingly require rapid organizational and individual changes. One of the areas in which technological advances have had a far reaching effect is in the area of communication technology. As communication technology advanced from writing to printing to broadcasting, it produced revolutionary changes that led society into unanticipated directions. Today, the new communication technology of computerized networking, which is a combination of all previous communication technologies, is again forcing major changes in our society and steering it in new directions. The current technologies of computing, the Internet, robotics, and artificial intelligence are extending individual capabilities as never before (Ellis 2000). One area where the impact of computerized networking technology has the potential to produce revolutionary changes is in the area of health care.

For example, faster microprocessors with increased processing power have produced beneficial results for medical devices and health care information systems. Development of inexpensive lasers essential to compact discs and large-capacity storage systems has increased dramatically expanding the information/data storage and retrieval capacity of health care information systems for the purpose of searching, processing, transferring, and analyzing. The new information technology will most dramatically impact the process-management systems (the automation of business processes among health care providers, intermediaries, and customers); clinical information interfaces (the notion that all medical information about a patient should be stored electronically to be accessed whenever, wherever, and by anyone who legitimately needs it); data analysis (based on diverse input sources such as clinicians, patients, and so forth, making it possible to learn more about a patient's clinical outcome from specific interventions leading to better decision making on the part of the health care provider); and telehealth and remote monitoring (combining case management, patient information system, and remote monitoring) (Institute for the Future 2000; Detmer 1996).

It has been suggested by many that the revolution in communication technology and the information explosion in health care along with other developments in biomedical technologies have the potential to empower patients. The World Wide Web and the Internet have made access to health care information easily available to citizens and have become major sources of health care information. The development of remote sensor technology like glucose monitors and blood pressure cuffs will allow physicians to access vital information about patients remotely. Telemedicine is making it possible to consult a specialist through videoconferencing and immediate transmission of X rays and other images (Ellis 2000). However, medicine's move into cyberspace has also raised concerns about privacy and the confidentiality of patients' medical records and the potential misuse and abuse of such information (Bettelheim 2000).

Besides communication technology, advances in biomedical technology already have revolutionized the field of health care and will continue to do so in the next century. Biomedical technology has dramatically changed the way in which health care is being practiced (Weisbrod 1994). Recent biomedical research has provided many new innovations including new drugs, medical and surgical devices, and biotechnology products. Such new technologies have become major driving forces in the field of health care. Technologies that are likely to have a significant impact on the future of health care include advances in imaging, minimally invasive surgery, genetic mapping and testing, gene therapy, new vaccines, artificial blood, and xenotransplantation (Institute for the Future 2000). Our society in general always has welcomed technological innovations in medicine. However, as we have discussed throughout this book, successes and innovations in biomedical technology also bring challenges and problems. Advances in computer and biomedical technologies have affected every aspect of health care including organizational structures, administrative and management practices, and health care professionals.

One of the most important groups of professionals that will play a crucial role in the future use of these technologies is physicians. Even though physicians constitute less than 10 percent of the health care work force, the whole U.S. health care system revolves around them. They are at the heart of the health care delivery system because they determine why, how, when, and the frequency with which biomedical technologies will be used not only in the diagnosis but also in the treatment of their patients. While a variety of health care professionals, such as nurses, optometrists, and speech and clinical psychologists, among others, provide generally well-defined and restricted services, the fact remains that in many cases patients receive these services on their physicians' orders. Physicians are the ones who admit patients to hospitals, order diagnostic procedures, and determine what kind of treatments patients will receive.

Thus, it is only natural that we focus on the medical training of physicians at this point because advances in biomedical technologies are quickly creating a significantly different health care system in the United States. This in turn will require the creation of a considerably different type of physician for the twenty-first century. Creating this new type of physician will require a different focus and emphasis in the medical education and training of physicians. It will require a shift from the current disease-oriented professional education to health-oriented professional education (Jonas 1978).

Medical schools have a strong influence over the type of physicians they produce and the nature of medicine they practice because they are the ones who select who will enter medical schools, what kind of education and training they receive, and what kind of doctors they will become. Medical students, at different stages of their medical education and training are, to a significant extent, influenced (along with their own social class and background) by their social and psychological environment, what values and attitudes they acquire or develop toward moral and ethical objectives of the medical profession, and the internalization of the attitudes of the medical profession (Fredericks and Mundy 1976). There has been a slow recognition of the value of behavioral sciences to medicine. In fact, a strong argument can be made that medicine, which is generally regarded as a natural science, should be viewed more as a social science because the goals of medicine are social (1976). To understand physicians and their medical practice, one must understand not only current medical education and training but also how and why it has evolved through history (Jonas 1978).

In this chapter we examine the history of medical education and training in the United States and perceived problems in the current state of medical education and proposed reforms/solutions, and conclude the chapter with a discussion of the kind of physicians needed for the twenty-first century.

History of Medical Education in the United States

Early Colonial Period: The Seventeenth Century

A major problem faced by the European colonists in the New World was illness and diseases caused by primitive living conditions and inadequate water and food. It was common for epidemic diseases to spread thorough the settlements claiming many lives and disseminating the population. A census in 1618 counted 600 persons living in Virginia. Between 1619 and 1625, 4,749 immigrants had arrived in the colony. However, by 1725 the total population of Virginia was only 1,025 (Kaufman 1976). Thus, the need for medical care was great but there were very few well-trained medical personnel available. In fact, very few trained physicians migrated to the New World.

Many of the early colonists were what we might consider "misfits." Some of them were religious misfits who migrated to America because they were often persecuted by established churches because of their religious ideas and practices. Others were economic misfits who had left Europe in hope of achieving economic success in the New World. Still others were social misfits, including criminals who had been sentenced to life in the new colonies. There were also many political dissenters among the early settlers (Kaufman 1976).

Companies that established colonies to provide financial gains for their investors often sent surgeons to meet the medical needs of the settlers. For example, the Dutch sent "comforters of the sick" for their colonies. However, little is known about their medical training. Many factors discouraged well-trained physicians from migrating to America. These included the long and dangerous ocean voyage, problems to be faced in the new land, lifelong separation from family, and uncertainty about the future. The few physicians who did migrate and settle in the colonies were poorly trained and failures in their medical practices at home. Thus, the quality of health care in early colonial times remained poor. In the absence of sufficient numbers of physicians, often clergy, being well educated and respected, provided medical advice along with religious and moral advice (Kaufman 1976).

One way in which men who wanted to practice medicine acquired their training during early colonial times was through a period of apprenticeship, which was in keeping with the practice in Europe. Under such a system, an apprentice was indentured to an established medical practitioner, often called a preceptor, for a certain period of time, usually about eight years. The apprentice or his family paid the physician's agreed upon fee. In addition, the apprentice provided free labor and was expected to perform certain duties such as grooming the horses, cleaning the stables, and so forth. Legal indenture papers were signed between the preceptor and the apprentice. The terms of the apprenticeship were very stringent and often the apprentice would be sworn to absolute obedience to his master, promise not to marry, play cards or dice, and agree not to "frequent taverns, alehouses or play houses" (Reed 1921). The apprentice, in return, was given access to the physician's medical library and allowed to follow, observe, and learn from the physician as he tended to his patients. At the end of the apprenticeship period, the physician would issue a certificate certifying that the apprentice was capable of practicing medicine independently (Jonas 1978). Physicians produced under such a system often were poorly trained because the physician's library often was very limited and the physician himself often had limited knowledge to impart to the apprentice. Medical apprenticeship was looked upon as similar to that of a blacksmith or a painter.

It is not surprising then that American physicians made little contribution to the literature of medicine during colonial times. The first printing presses in the colonies were installed at Harvard College in 1639 and in Virginia in 1861. However, during the second half of the seventeenth century, printing presses were placed under strict scrutiny because some material of questionable theological nature had been published. The New England press was mainly publishing orthodox puritan theology. However, there were a few respectable physicians in the colonies who made some contribution to the medical literature. For example, in 1677 Reverend Doctor Thomas Thatcher published the first medical publication called *A Brief Guide in Smallpox and Measles* (Norwood 1971).

Medicine as a distinct branch of education received very little attention from the legislators. In fact, during the first century after the colonial settlements in the New World, medicine as a profession was left completely without any protection, encouragement, or recognition (Toner 1874).

The Eighteenth Century

By the beginning of the eighteenth century the situation in American colonies had improved. Hard times had given way to more prosperous times. The improved conditions in the colonies became more appealing to the upper socioeconomic classes in Europe, and European physicians started emigrating to the colonies. By 1700, many medical graduates from Europe began migrating to the colonies as instructors. They instilled in students a desire for more than an elementary medical training and over a period of time helped to improve the quality of apprenticeships. Upon completing apprenticeships, some American students went to European universities to enhance their medical educations. However, between 1607 and 1776, of the more than 3,000 physicians who practiced in America, fewer than 400 had received medical degrees in Europe (Bonner 1995). Often, certificates of attendance on the various lecture courses were written or printed on the backs of ordinary playing cards. For example, the ticket of Ralph Asheton of Philadelphia, who was a student in medicine at the University of Edinburgh for the Royal Infirmary, was made out on the back of the seven of diamonds, while his admission to the second course on anatomy was written on the back of the deuce of spades. Both were stamped with the seal of the university (Reiling 1999).

A majority of America's physicians were trained under poor apprenticeship or they were pretenders (Kaufman 1976). Homegrown apprenticeship-trained physicians outnumbered European-trained physicians who had emigrated to the colonies. The apprenticeship system as it developed in the colonies also tended to produce generalists rather than specialists (Jonas 1978).

Most of the medical profession continued to fumble in darkness, and quackery flourished throughout the colonies. Many physicians were trained through apprenticeship, and anyone could be a preceptor. All types of regulars and irregulars practiced medicine. According to one estimate, of the roughly 3,500 physicians practicing in the colonies in 1776, probably no more than 12 percent had medical degrees. New York historian William Smith compared quacks to abounding locusts in Egypt (Norwood 1971).

Under the apprenticeship system, the quality of instruction varied greatly since there was no limitation on the number of physicians who might become preceptors. Many of the preceptors themselves were poorly trained. The quality of the student also varied a great deal. In general, a knowledge of the classical languages, especially Latin, was required of medical students along with a knowledge of mathematics, English grammar, and natural history (Norwood 1971). A degree in medicine was seen as a sign of higher learning, and Latin was viewed as the visible symbol of that learning. In fact, medicine was not valued as much for its ability to cure patients as it was for the knowledge and wisdom it implied (Bonner 1995). Preceptors on average charged $100 per year to their apprentice, although the rates for apprenticeship varied throughout the colonies. Anatomical dissection and postmortem examinations were rarely available to medical students. Maintaining the standard of medical education was in the hands of these preceptors as long as no legislatures or medical societies decreed otherwise (Norwood 1971).

Colonial newspapers were often very critical of the apprenticeship system and poor training of physicians. In 1753, a New York journal, the *Independent Reflector,* bemoaned the dismal record of the quacks and pretenders. Similarly, in 1766, the *New-York Mercury* reported on the abuses inflicted by the so-called physicians of the city. Letters to the editors often expressed similar sentiments. The medical profession was in chaos and something needed to be done. By the 1760s, the desire for reform was evident among many leading physicians, and recognition of the academic deficiencies encouraged these physicians to work toward the passage of medical license legislation and to develop medical societies, which were the first steps in the development of a profession (Kaufman 1976). In fact, as early as 1735, a medical society was founded in Boston. Medical societies were established in Connecticut and New Jersey in 1766. Such societies showed significant interest in medical education reform. The New Jersey medical society even agreed that no member of the society should take an apprenticeship for a period of less than four years and that three of these years should be spent with the master (preceptor), and the fourth year must be spent in some medical college in America or Europe (1976). The Massachusetts Medical Society was established in 1781 (Norwood 1971). In many places, medical societies became the active agents in determining the standards of medical education. Later, the responsibility of determining and maintaining standards of medical education shifted to medical schools when state agencies started to accept M.D. degrees in lieu of passing an examination by a medical society.

During the first half of the eighteenth century, medicine received very little attention from legislators as a branch of formal education. Medical legislation in the colonies prior to the 1760s was an assortment of acts passed in several colonies with the main intention of providing for some protection to the general public. Statutes tended to cover things such as fee rates, quarantine, criminal neglect, and responsibilities of the practitioners, etc. The first law designed to regulate medical practice and to provide for examination of candidates for the medical profession was passed by the New York State Assembly in 1760 (Norwood 1971). This law provided for examination of medical students by the members of His Majesty's Council and physicians selected to assist them (Kaufman 1976). A similar law was passed by the New Jersey legislature in 1772.

The first medical college in the American colonies was established in Philadelphia when it opened its doors on November 14, 1765. For bachelor's degrees in physics, students had to demonstrate their proficiency in Latin, mathematics, and natural and experimental philosophy. Students were also required to undergo apprenticeships under reputable practitioners and be able to demonstrate knowledge of the pharmacy. For a doctor's degree in physics, a student had to be at least twenty-four years of age with a bachelor's degree in physics, write and defend a thesis, and publish it at his own expense. The first American medical commencement was held in Philadelphia on June 21, 1768 (Kaufman 1976). The second medical college, the King's College Medical School, was established in New York in 1767. Other medical colleges soon followed. The efforts of the Boston Medical Society led to the establishment of Harvard Medical School in 1783 followed by Dartmouth College in 1797. The fifth medical college was established at Transylvania University in Kentucky just prior to the turn of the century (Kaufman 1976).

After establishment of the medical colleges, the preceptorial system was incorporated as part of the general scheme of medical education in America. Students were required to do an apprenticeship in addition to attending certain lecture courses. The giving of systematic lectures and demonstration courses to groups of students became more common. Anatomy was the subject generally covered in such courses. However, it was not easy to make anatomical dissection and postmortem examinations available to medical students. When a medical college in Philadelphia offered such a course only ten students enrolled. Even liberal Philadelphia was not used to the idea of dissection of human bodies. There were reports of graves being robbed for cadavers for dissection and strong opposition from town people led to mob violence. The building where anatomical materials were stored and used as a classroom was attacked several times and windows were broken. Ultimately, public appeals through the press and the influence of broad-minded people prevailed, and the public became more accepting of dissection of human bodies when they were assured that the dead had not been disturbed and the cadavers used for dissection came from people who had committed suicide or criminals who had been executed (Norwood 1971).

Soon, emphasis was placed on the importance of a hospital in the training of medical students. The use of clinical material of the hospital for teaching purposes was encouraged. In 1765, Philadelphia had some of the best clinical facilities of medical instruction. The Pennsylvania Hospital was established in 1752, and it was the first and only hospital in the colonies intended solely for the care of the sick and the wounded. Philadelphia also had an infirmary connected with the poorhouses that were designed for paupers and the mentally unbalanced. In time, it became customary for attending physicians in hospitals to have their pupils receive clinical experience by dressing wounds and tending to their hospital cases. Almshouses also became popular places for students seeking bedside instructions. However, circumstances delayed the gravitation of hospital instruction in the American medical school curriculum. Except in a few metropolitan areas, it was difficult to organize and successfully support hospitals (Norwood 1971). Furthermore, during the initial stages, there continued to be resistance to the medical student participation in treating patients. In fact, the Medical College of Philadelphia in 1789 dropped the requirement of hospital attendance by medical students before graduation as unworkable. Thereafter, only intermittently were they able to demand hospital attendance before graduation (Bonner 1995).

Thus, American medical education at the end of the eighteenth century was still in a stage of infancy with few medical schools and only 312 physicians having received American medical degrees, thirty-nine of which were honorary degrees. During the eighteenth century a variety of medical degrees were awarded. One was the bachelor of medicine and another was the doctor of medicine. There were also bachelor's and doctor's honorary degrees awarded. In addition, there were the *ad eundem* degrees which meant that when a candidate held the same degree from another institution he was admitted to a degree, *ad eundem gradum*. Both bachelor and doctoral degrees of this type were also awarded. American medical education, after the independence revolution and at the close of the eighteenth century under the new republic called the United States of America, was still undergoing many changes. Organized instruction was still in a formative stage and medical schools were few and poorly equipped (Norwood 1971).

The Nineteenth Century

Seven medical colleges were in existence in the United States by 1813 and by the 1820s a degree from a medical school was the only thing required for licensure in most states (Jonas 1978). Admission requirements were minimal: an apprenticeship was all that was required for admission by all schools. Medical education consisted of a series of lectures provided over a two- to three-year period and some demonstration of techniques, especially in anatomy (1978). The advances in anatomical knowledge of the eighteenth century had led to the adoption of the surgical model of teaching students, and most medical educators had come to accept the anatomical basis of disease. Thus, there was an increased recognition of need for anatomical studies and personal experience in dissecting the human body (Bonner 1995). The new science of physiology was incorporated as part of the teaching of anatomy.

Apprenticeships remained the dominant method for practical training even though a host of new dispensaries, outpatient clinics, small urban hospitals, and private lectures were becoming available. By the 1820s, several medical schools, often loosely tied to a liberal arts college, had begun to offer lectures to supplement the apprenticeship experience. Clinical training occupied a very small place in many of the rural medical schools that were established after 1800. The academic component of the medical education was slow to develop (Jonas 1978). In fact, by the 1830s the ties between the early medical schools to academic institutions had weakened. The absence of government regulation and competition for students during the Jacksonian period kept demands made on medical students low. Overall, medical training in the United States followed closely the model of Great Britain (Bonner 1995).

The absence of licensure requirements by state governments, and the fact that the only thing required to get a license to practice medicine was a diploma from a medical school, provided tremendous financial incentives to entrepreneurs interested in making profits. This gave rise to the proprietary, that is, private, profit making medical schools. Most medical schools established in the United States after the War of 1812 were proprietary in nature. In fact, proprietary schools grew at an alarming rate. Between 1810 and 1840, twenty-six new medical schools were established, and forty-seven more were created between 1840 and 1877. Some of them did not survive. However, by 1876, there were sixty-four medical colleges in operation out of a total of eighty that had been established in the United States (Kaufman 1976). Such proprietary schools often were established by a few local physicians and chartered by states. Many small town colleges were developed by one or two leading physicians for the purpose of increasing their income through student fees and gaining competitive advantage over other local physicians who could not claim a college affiliation (1976). Overall, most proprietary medical schools existed independently without a university or hospital affiliation, which later became the norm in the twentieth century. Medical education in the United States was a mess. Admission requirements were almost nonexistent and most students who entered medical schools had only an elementary education since literacy was not necessary for admission to medical school. For example, in 1850–1851, 80 percent of the theological students and 65 percent of the law students held a bachelor's degree compared to only 26 percent of the medical students (1976). Widespread instances of diploma mills were uncovered and businessmen would sell a diploma from a college of his choice to anyone who was willing to pay (Dan 1997). A degree of doctor of medicine (M.D.) was handed out with less than a year of study with coursework consisting of a series of lectures and no actual clinical work (Weinstock 1998a). Competition was so tough that instead of competing to provide the best medical education, medical schools competed to provide the fastest, cheapest, and easiest education (Kaufman 1976).

The first half of the nineteenth century was also the age of heroic medicine. Some of the major techniques used by the medical profession included bleeding, blistering, purging, and sweating, and undergoing treatment can best be characterized as torture. Massive bloodletting was used for every major disease, resulting in patients becoming unconscious. Such treatment terrified the patients. There were also many imposters and pretenders who cast a shadow on the entire medical profession. The inadequacies of orthodox medical practices also gave rise to many unorthodox medical sects. One such sect was known as Thompsonianism, named after its founder, Samuel Thompson. He believed that cold was the primary cause of all diseases and the practitioner must restore natural heat through botanical drugs combined with steaming the patient by a fire or hot coals. Another sect was the homeopathy which believed that there were several laws of cure. The most important being *similia similibus curantur,* that is, likes are cured by likes. They believed that there was an inverse relationship between the size of the dose and the effect on the body, thus the more highly diluted the dose the more effective it is in fighting disease. By the 1870s and 1880s homeopathy had become the largest and most influential sect (Kaufman 1976).

Several in the medical profession had come to recognize the problems confronted by the medical profession and the need for reform. Various state medical societies had begun to discuss the need for reforms. A medical convention held in 1827 in Northampton, Massachusetts was attended by representatives of medical societies and medical colleges of New England. This convention proposed a set of reforms that included a bachelor's degree for admission to medical school, a minimum of three years of study in medical school, defense of a dissertation, and a requirement for examination in anatomy, physiology, surgery, theory and the practice of medicine, chemistry, and pharmacy, among other subjects. These proposed standards were so high that they were never adopted. Also, since licensing laws did not deal with medical school curriculum, they would have been difficult to enforce (Jonas 1978). Furthermore, since medical schools depended on student fees for their financial success, colleges were not interested in adopting reforms if it meant that students would go to those colleges that did not adopt such reforms. Thus, the Northampton convention failed to accomplish its objectives (Kaufman 1976).

Another convention was held in New York in 1846 that was attended by 110 delegates from sixteen states. While this convention did not have any immediate effect on the quality of education in the United States it did lead to the establishment of the American Medical Association (AMA) in 1846. The AMA's principal concern became improving the quality of medical education in the United States. It tried to steer a middle course by developing standards that were lower than the ones adopted by the Northampton convention but higher than what was prevalent at most medical colleges (Jonas 1978). The AMA pleaded with hospitals in 1848 to end what it called an obsolete system of training by allowing medical students into their wards. A year later it called for a graded curriculum, and by the 1850s it was calling for the abolition of the poor apprenticeship system that was in existence, the adoption of a competitive method of appointing professors, and requirement of instruction in physiology, pathology, and microscopy (Bonner 1995).

Most medical schools were not interested in adopting the AMA's proposed standards. In 1860, the AMA adopted a new set of standards. In order to make medical colleges and professors less dependent on student fees, it required that medical schools and professorships be privately endowed. Charles W. Eliot, after being appointed president of Harvard University in 1869, argued that the whole system of medical education in the United States needed to be reformed (Weinstock 1998a). In 1871, he advocated that students should be required to pass a written examination to graduate from medical school. His proposal was met with strong opposition. In fact, one well-known professor wrote to him to object to a written examination stating that half of the graduating class could barely write (Dan 1997).

The start of the Civil War put a hold on reforms and the situation deteriorated further before it got better (Jonas 1978). The Civil War (1861–1865) demonstrated very clearly the deficiencies of the American medical education in the mid-nineteenth century. The Civil War was a human tragedy, but more important it was also a medical tragedy. According to some estimates 110,000 Union soldiers died from wounds and another 225,000 died from diseases. Similarly, among the Confederate soldiers, 50,000 died from fighting and 150,000 from illness. Soldiers on both sides suffered from dysentery, malaria, measles, typhoid fever, tuberculosis, pneumonia, scarlet fever, and an assortment of other sicknesses (Ludmerer 1985).

The training and skills of the average physician proved to be very inadequate. Only a small percentage of physicians performed elementary examination techniques such as measuring temperature, and simple instruments such as thermometers, stethoscopes, and hypodermic syringes were rarely used even though their use was strongly advocated by major medical schools in Europe. Many doctors were unqualified to perform surgery. In fact, their first experience was treating gunshot wounds of the soldiers. Such poor practices of physicians were the result of poor medical training received by many of them in the proprietary medical schools of the country, which had minimal entrance requirements and curricula consisting largely of lectures in subjects such as anatomy, physiology, pathology, pharmacy, and chemistry. There was no sequencing of courses so that subjects were taken in logical order. Teaching methods mainly consisted of lectures given in large lecture halls. Little attention was paid to scientific subjects and when they were taught it was often without the use of laboratories (Ludmerer 1985).

Despite objections to medical school reforms, some of the early seeds of reform were planted even before the start of the Civil War. The Lind University in Chicago had established a new medical school in 1859. The university and its medical school were not dependent on student fees since both were endowed by wealthy businessman Sylvester Lind. Thus, the medical school was able to establish higher medical school standards than its competitors in Chicago (Jonas 1978; Ludmerer 1985). The Medical Department of the Lind University in Chicago (later named the Northwestern Medical School) in 1859 became the first school to begin teaching subjects in a logical and sequential order with a graded curriculum. In 1857, the New Orleans School of Medicine initiated the concept of assigning students to patients from admission to discharge in which students were required to take a medical history of the patient, do a physical examination, and report their findings to their professors. Several medical schools had begun to embrace scientific underpinnings of medicine pioneered by French and German medical schools (Dan 1997; Ludmerer 1985). The U.S. government also had tacitly acknowledged the deficiencies of the country's medical education by imposing a compulsory examination for physicians to be admitted to the army or navy's medical service during the Civil War (Ludmerer 1985). After the 1860s, hospitals increased their educational role, and some of the early medical practices such as bloodletting began to disappear.

The reform of medical schools after the Civil War can best be described as sporadic. In 1870, Harvard Medical School adopted a broad reform package that included a graded curriculum, three years of academic training, and oral and written examinations. Within a few years, medical schools in Pennsylvania, New York, and Michigan had joined the reform movement (Jonas 1978). Unlike many other medical schools of the time, the University of Michigan Medical School could claim its own building on a university campus and had professors whose salaries were paid entirely by the university. Furthermore, in 1869, the University of Michigan established the nation's first university-owned hospital. It also began to admit women to its medical school in 1870 (Markel 2000). The Tufts University School of Medicine began to admit female students in 1893 (Madoff 1993).

Further impetus for reforming medical schools was provided in the 1870s and 1880s by several states that again began passing medical license laws that had been largely abandoned during the 1840s. Originally, such laws provided for automatic licensing of anyone who possessed a medical diploma. When the weaknesses of such a provision became apparent, states amended their laws to provide for examination of all applicants for medical licenses. In 1888, only five states required an examination for a license to practice medicine. However, by 1896, eighteen more states had amended their laws to require an examination for a medical license (Kaufman 1976).

While a few medical schools were taking reform seriously, many others were still reluctant to adopt reforms. In 1871, the Committee on Medical Education of the AMA reported that very little progress had been made with respect to medical school reforms (1976). Many colleges were not reforming to a significant extent, and the medical profession continued to fail to attract the best students. In 1876, a *New York Daily Tribune* editorial argued that the most important task facing the AMA was to restrict the number of medical colleges and to prevent the graduation of fraudulent and poorly educated physicians (1976).

Some of the better medical schools formed the American Medical College Association in 1876, which adopted minimum standards for medical schools, including a graded, three-year curriculum. In addition, meeting the standards was made a requirement for membership in the association. However, in order to stay competitive, the original schools themselves failed to meet the standards and they were abandoned in 1882. In fact, the association did not meet again until 1889 (Jonas 1978). In 1894, members of the association voted to extend the medical school requirements to a four-year course of study effective with the graduating class of 1899. Thus, some reforms were taking hold by the 1890s (Kaufman 1976).

A scientific revolution was taking place in the field of medicine that has often been referred to as "the triumph of modern medicine." Pathologists had been able to identify specific diseases. In fact, bacteriological developments were taking place at a rapid pace. By the end of the century causes of many diseases such as tetanus, bubonic plague, malaria, and yellow fever were discovered. These discoveries helped increase the importance of chemistry, pathology, bacteriology, and physiology, all of which required laboratory work (Kaufman 1976). American medicine through the Civil War had predominantly reflected the influence of French medicine, which was largely characterized by keen observation and did not make use of experimentation, the hallmark of German medical research. After the Civil War, American medicine came to be under the influence of German medicine, particularly as Americans started returning from postgraduate studies in Germany. Between the 1850s and 1860s, relatively few Americans studied in Germany, but after the Civil War that number increased dramatically. Between 1870 and 1914, about 15,000 American physicians undertook some type of serious medical study in Germany. American physicians' experiences in Germany produced two results that significantly influenced development of American medical education in later years. First, they, like their German teachers, came to believe that medical phenomena are governed by chemical and physical laws and that the path to medical discovery was through controlled experiments and not passive observation of nature. Second, they came to accept a new role model, that of full-time teacher and investigator, pursuing a career in scientific research and medicine rather than practicing medicine. The career of a professor of medicine came to be viewed as important and honorable as that of a traditional medical practitioner (Ludmerer 1985). In 1893, the first modern American medical school was created when Johns Hopkins Medical School in Boston opened its doors. It was a privately endowed school and thus not dependent on student fees for its financial success. It had full-time faculty members and a four-year graded curriculum with two years spent on preclinical "basic" sciences and two years spent doing clinical work in the university hospital. The school was very selective in its admission and considered itself a resource for training medical educators and researchers (Jonas 1978). In a short period, Johns Hopkins developed an international reputation for successfully combining educational and scientific endeavors and became a model for other schools to follow.

During the late nineteenth century at most universities in the United States, original research was not considered a part of a faculty member's responsibility. The main focus was on teaching and administration, with the practice of medicine considered the most important, especially for a clinician. This began to change as the country entered the twentieth century under the influence of German research universities and other major academic centers in Europe (Markel 2000).

Thus, by the end of the nineteenth century and the beginning of the twentieth century, the American university was beginning to provide a prominent place for medicine in the country's higher education system. Prior to that, universities generally were not heavily involved in medical education. There were several reasons as to why this shift had a natural and logical progression. First, as the amount of medical knowledge proliferated it fit directly into the purview of the modern university. Medical students, like scholars in other fields, were charged with the responsibility of discovering new knowledge. Second, the modern university was the most appropriate place for employing appropriate educational techniques such as the teaching of medicine since, like many other fields, it was becoming more complex with rapid intellectual expansion. Third, the university's role as an integrator of knowledge had become all the more important in the field of medicine because medicine was becoming increasingly dependent on fundamental sciences such as biology, chemistry, and physics, which were based in universities rather than in medical schools. The fourth reason was the fact that placement of professional schools in a university setting was very appealing to another value of a modern university, that of the idea of a liberal culture (Ludmerer 1985).

The Twentieth Century: 1900s to 1970s

In 1900, the United States had 45 percent of the world's medical schools. Furthermore, the country also had the highest concentration of physicians per capita. Also, some physicians practiced medicine part-time in the evening, and some proprietary schools offered after-hours education and training. These were known as "sundown physicians and medical colleges." The performance of medical schools and the quality of physicians were highly uneven and the AMA, professional leaders, and new philanthropic organizations had begun to push for reforms of medical schools and medical education (Martensen 1995). The reform movement was growing. By the early 1900s, at some medical schools entrance standards had been introduced for admission, standard curricula had been expanded to four years, and many new scientific disciplines were being taught in new classrooms and well-equipped buildings and laboratories (Ludmerer 1991). In 1905, the AMA Council on Medical Education was created and it began to attack the low standards prevailing in the medical schools of the country. Almost all schools required only a high school diploma for admission to medical college. Before 1900, Johns Hopkins was the only medical school that required advanced work. However, by 1910 almost fifty medical schools required some college work from all its applicants (Kaufman 1976). Still, reforms of medical schools were incremental and medical education had yet to earn public trust. When the New York Postgraduate Medical School awarded Mark Twain an honorary medical degree in 1909 he remarked, "I am glad to be among my own kind tonight. I was once a sharpshooter. But now I can practice a much higher and equally as deadly a profession" (quoted in Weinstock 1998a, 7).

Reform of the American medical education was progressing but further improvements were needed to achieve high standards of excellence. The final catalyst for reform was the Flexner Report published in 1910. In 1908, Henry Pritchett, president of the Carnegie Foundation, asked Abraham Flexner, an educational reformer from Louisville, Kentucky, to study the state of American medical education. Pritchett believed that the problems with medical education were largely educational problems. Flexner himself knew very little about medical education, but he had studied the American educational system and was a vocal critic of the elective and lecture system prevalent in American colleges (Flexner 1908). He familiarized himself with literature on medical education, including classical works on European faculties, and reports of the AMA's Council on Medical Education, conferred with editors of medical journals, and spent time at Johns Hopkins. This led him to develop a view of an ideal college based on the best features of medical conditions in Germany, France, and England. Following that he visited every medical school in the United States and Canada. The Carnegie Foundation published his report in 1910 (Flexner 1910).

Flexner was shocked by what he discovered in his study of American medical colleges. He found teaching inadequate, admission standards too low, laboratories poorly equipped, and medical schools more interested in profits than well-trained physicians (Abraham Flexner: Unrestrained 1990).

In his report, Flexner found plenty to criticize about medical schools and medical education. According to Flexner, medical students were ill prepared due to a lack of laboratory exercises and adequately supervised clinical experiences. He was concerned by the fact that part-time faculty members were engaged in extensive private practices and that most proprietary schools were engaged in education for the main purpose of making money. He strongly criticized the extensive use of lectures, didactic teaching methods, and the examination system prevalent in medical schools because, he argued, such practices tended to reward memorization. To Flexner, lectures were worthless and antiquated forms of instruction. He advocated learning by doing (1990).

Flexner was most critical of the lack of a scientific basis for medical education. He argued that the teaching of medicine must be founded upon a strong basis of science, and he advocated the teaching of science under university sponsorship. He was concerned that without this sponsorship, science would not be understood in its full context. Flexner also showed his concern not just for "curative medicine" but also "preventive medicine" (Nuland 1999). To Flexner, scientific medicine consisted of two concepts. First, he recognized that basic sciences such as physics, chemistry, and biology provided the intellectual foundation of modern science. Second, he believed that the scientific method, that is, testing of ideas by well-planned experiments through which facts can be ascertained, applied to practice as well as research. He disliked the "rule of thumb" practitioner who practiced medicine by protocol. He liked the scientific practitioner (Ludmerer 1985). To Flexner, three characteristics of an ideal medical school were properly equipped laboratories, an academically qualified student body, and original research (1985).

The Flexner Report, as it came to be known, outlined steps needed to raise the American medical education to a world leadership position. His major recommendations included the following: (1) requirement for admission to medical school should consist of a minimum of two years of undergraduate college work; (2) medical education should consist of a four year curriculum with the first two years spent in the basic medical sciences and the third and fourth years spent on supervised clinical work; (3) medical schools should provide regular laboratory experiences for students; (4) medical schools should be brought into the framework of academic universities; (5) state governments should play an active role in setting minimum standards for admission to medical schools through the state licensing boards; (6) medical schools should make use of full-time teaching and research faculty to improve the quality of instruction; and (7) the annual graduation rates from medical school should be reduced from 4,500 to 3,500, and the number of medical schools in the country should be reduced from 150 to about 31 (Flexner 1910).

The strongest support for the Flexner Report came from the best medical schools in the country. Not surprisingly, the most strident opposition to the Flexner Report came from weaker schools who were not likely to survive reforms. The call for reforms in the country's medical educational system was helped further by the press. From coast to coast, editorials in newspapers demanded improvements in their local medical colleges. This put increasing pressure on the proprietary schools to close. Ultimately, the Flexner Report, the press, and the work of the AMA and the Association of American Medical Colleges (AAMC) led to a drastic reduction in the number of medical schools and improvement in the quality of medical education. In 1924, Abraham Flexner evaluated the changes that had taken place in American medical education and noted that almost half the medical colleges had disappeared since 1910, there was general improvement in facilities and laboratories, and students were taught by full-time, specially trained faculty (Kaufman 1976). Some have credited the Flexner Report for the tremendous progress made in reforms of medical schools, while others have argued that the Flexner Report deserves less credit than it has been given because many reforms already had been underway since the late nineteenth century. Regardless of how much credit the Flexner Report deserves for the reforms, the fact remains that it certainly acted as a catalyst and significantly accelerated the reforms of medical schools and education in the United States.

The period of 1910 to 1945 was a period of consolidation. By 1925, every medical school required four years of high school and two years of college education for admission. In fact, by 1945, virtually all medical schools granted the student a B.A. degree after completion of one or two years of medical school following two years of undergraduate education. The number of medical schools by 1930 had dropped to 76 from a high of 162 in 1906. Similarly, the physician-population ratio had declined from 147 per 100,000 in 1910 to 126 per 100,000 by 1930. In 1931, 75 percent of physicians were in primary care. However, by 1945 that number had dropped to 60 percent. Furthermore, state medical (licensing) boards became involved in curriculum design and establishing regulations to govern medical schools. The increase in the number of specialists also led to an increase in many specialty boards (Jonas 1978). The AMA participated in medical licensing through its Council on Medical Education by establishing a rating system for medical schools. According to the rating system, Class A schools were defined as acceptable, Class B schools were classified as needing improvements, and those schools needing complete reorganization were classified as Class C schools. In fact, as early as 1914, thirty-one states had denied Class C schools recognition. When the National Board of Medical Examiners was created in 1915, it examined only graduates of Class A schools. Schools that could not receive AMA approval were forced to close (Ludmerer 1985).

Private philanthropic foundations played a major role in some of the educational reforms following the Flexner Report. The Rockefeller Foundation's General Education Board provided major grants to medical schools that adopted the Johns Hopkins model. This encouraged many other medical schools to follow suit (Ludmerer 1985; Jonas 1978). In fact, major grants from private foundations helped establish a system of full-time faculty members engaged in teaching and research at medical colleges. Between 1913 and 1919 the Rockefeller Foundation and the General Education Board spent $8 million to support a strict full-time faculty system at Johns Hopkins Medical School (Fye 1991).

The period following the Flexner Report also saw the rise of teaching hospitals (Ludmerer 1985). For example, in 1910 three seminal affiliations between medical schools and large, well-equipped hospitals were formed. These included Washington University Medical School's affiliation with the Barnes Hospital and St. Louis Children's Hospital in St. Louis, the affiliation of the College of Physicians and Surgeons (Columbia) with Presbyterian Hospital in New York, and Harvard Medical School's affiliation with the Peter Bent Brigham Hospital in Boston. All of these affiliations were based on a model provided by Johns Hopkins (Ludmerer 1991). Such a marriage between university medical schools and hospitals was made possible by perceived advantages of such alliances. First, it was believed that such arrangements would provide better patient care. Second, hospital representatives welcomed such affiliations because they believed that the function of a hospital was no longer just to provide patient care but also was to foster research. Third, it was economically advantageous for both the hospitals and the university. Consolidation of modern medical technology and support for laboratories for clinical research provided economic efficiency (1991). The emergence of teaching hospitals had important consequences for the development of American medicine. The teaching hospital was necessary for medical education to become a university endeavor. It also brought about a change in the financing of American hospitals because of the large donations from private foundations to support teaching hospitals. Prior to this, gifts to hospitals were mostly prompted by traditional charitable and religious motives. To compete successfully for large grants from foundations, hospitals had no choice but to become teaching hospitals (Ludmerer 1985).

The reformed medical education system remained relatively stable during the Depression. Under pressure from the AMA, medical schools reduced the number of applicants accepted during the 1930s. However, World War II changed this. During the war, the number of graduates from medical schools increased significantly.

As the medical schools and their facilities expanded it became clear that private foundations alone could not support scientific research. Many viewed government support of medicine as essential if the United States was going to continue on the path of scientific research and new discoveries in medicine. In 1930, Congress created the National Institutes of Health (NIH) because of the belief that scientific research was the most important function of the federal government in relation to public health (Fye 1991). In 1937, the National Cancer Institute (NCI) was established.

World War II helped to solidify the federal government's support of medical research, which led to many new discoveries in science, technology, and medicine. After the end of World War II, the AMA was strongly opposed to the government providing financial support directly to medical schools, and it argued that medical school expansion was unnecessary because it viewed federal support as federal interference. It continued to champion private financial support of medical school and was instrumental in establishing the National Fund for Medical Education (NFME). The AMA did not object to government funding of medical research. Given the opposition of the AMA to direct federal support of medical schools, it was natural that federal funding went in the direction of support for medical research. In 1944, only about $150,000 of the NIH's total budget of $2.5 million went for medical research conducted outside of NIH. The NIH's research budget had increased to $8 million by 1947 and to $70 million by 1955. In fact, one-third of medical school budgets were derived from research grants. By 1958, the federal government was spending $600 million annually on medical schools, primarily for medical research (Jonas 1978). Thus, medical science not only received a big boost from the federal government, but it also helped usher in the era of technological revolution in medicine (Cassell 1999). An uncontrollable force of biomedical research was unleashed with its own momentum. American medical research and American medical education had become not only preeminent but the best in the world.

The 1960s and the 1970s witnessed an unprecedented growth in the number of medical schools and the number of medical school graduates. The AMA, which had continued to oppose direct federal funding for medical schools, suffered some important defeats as Congress passed laws providing federal funds, not just for the new constructions of medical facilities but also for student loans and student scholarships. By 1968, AMA had reversed its position in favor of direct federal aid to medical schools. The trend of direct federal aid to medical schools was helped further by the 1970 report titled *Higher Education and the Nation's Health* produced by the Carnegie Commission on Higher Education under the sponsorship of the Carnegie Foundation. The major conclusion of the study was that there was a shortage of health manpower, and recommended new medical schools and health services centers and increased federal funding for health sciences education (Carnegie Commission on Higher Education 1970). The 1971 Health Manpower Law for the first time provided federal money to all medical schools for general operation. In 1976 the Health Professions Educational Assistance Act extended student scholarships and loans programs. Ironically, another Carnegie Foundation report in 1976 titled *Progress and Problems in Medical and Dental Education: Federal Support versus Federal Control* warned of the impending oversupply of physicians and recommended curtailing medical school expansion. It also warned of the geographic maldistribution of physicians, and encouraged expansion of primary care programs (Carnegie Council on Policy Studies in Higher Education 1976). The fact that the 1970 Carnegie Foundation report warned about the shortages of health manpower, while another report in 1976 warned about the impending oversupply of physicians, reflects the unplanned growth in the number of physicians entering practice and the virtual absence of a comprehensive national physician workforce policy. This in turn has contributed to several problems in the U.S. health care system that include a lack of a sufficient number of primary care physicians on one hand and the need to increase access to health care for underserved populations on the other hand, pressure for escalation of health care costs, and a contradiction between workforce needs and medical education funding incentives (Noren 1997). By the 1980s, American medical education had again become the subject of many criticisms.

Medical Education in the 1980s and 1990s

Today, medical education programs that award the degree of doctor of medicine in the United States are accredited by the Liaison Committee on Medical Education (LCME). This voluntary accrediting agency is sponsored by the Association of American Medical Colleges (AAMC) and the AMA. Laws of all states recognize the accreditation status conferred by the LCME. Licensure requirements for the graduates of LCME-accredited schools are set by each state government, and LCME makes sure that medical programs meet the minimum national quality standards. However, the LCME has avoided setting specific curricula requirements for accreditation. This has led to diverse approaches in the medical education curriculum of different medical schools.

Traditionally, most students begin medical school immediately upon graduation from college. However, there are some other options available. Some students enter a combined college/medical school program that begins after high school graduation. Such programs typically combine undergraduate college and medical school curricula and are the result of arrangements between a school of medicine and a particular undergraduate college requiring enrollment in that particular college. These programs typically take six to eight years to complete with the first two years spent on undergraduate courses and premedical requirements. At different stages, a student receives a bachelor's degree and then the M.D. degree from the medical school upon completing the program (AAMC 1996).

Most curricula are problem-based rather than discipline focused. The teaching methodologies include a mixture of lectures, small group discussions, self-instruction, and laboratory experiences. Many of these new methods were adopted in the 1980s, but it is unclear whether these changes have had any impact on the quality of medical school graduates (Jonas, Etzel, and Barzansky 1990). The first two years are devoted to providing instructions in subjects such as anatomy, biochemistry, physiology, microbiology, pharmacology, pathology, and the behavioral sciences. In the teaching of these subjects, there is an increased emphasis on the interdisciplinary approach that focuses on organ systems. Also, there is an increased emphasis on introducing contact with clinical problems early in the curriculum. Topics such as bioethics, legal aspects of medicine, disease prevention, and medical sociology, among others, are often taught parallel to or intermingled with the basic and clinical sciences. The last two years are devoted to education in the clinical setting. The length and number of clinical clerkships vary from school to school depending on the field of medicine. Most students during their clerkships are assigned to a hospital clinical service. Students are provided some elective opportunities during the first two years as well as during the clinical period. Many schools require students to pass Step 1 of the United States Medical Licensing Examination (USMLE) at the end of their basic science sequence. The main purpose of the test is to assess whether the students understand and can apply key concepts in biomedical sciences. Some schools require students to pass Step 2 of the USMLE to graduate. This exam assesses medical knowledge and understanding of the clinical sciences necessary for patient care under supervision. Step 3 is administered after graduation from medical school and is designed to assess whether graduates can apply medical knowledge and understanding of biomedical and clinical science for the unsupervised practice of medicine. The USMLE was established by the Federation of State Medical Board (FSMB) and the National Board of Medical Examiners (NBME) (AAMC 1996).

For certification in a medical or surgery specialty, following the medical school (residency), postgraduate work (graduate medical work) is required to complete the specialty board certification requirements. Three years of training is required for family medicine, internal medicine, or pediatrics, while five years of training is required for general surgery. Other surgical special-ties require additional training (AAMC 1996). Thus, most medical schools require students going into a medical or surgical specialty to spend a period of three to seven years in graduate medical education.

Medical Education and Training: Criticisms and Proposed Reforms

The escalating costs of health care, lack of access to quality health care, and too many specialists and not enough general practitioners had already be-come major concerns during the 1970s (Rogers 1978). During this time, the U.S. health care system was undergoing major transformation, and the prac-tice of medicine was changing due to various cost cutting strategies such as managed care and diagnostic related groupings (DRGs) for Medicare reim-bursement to hospitals to contain escalating costs. The rapid advances in biomedical technology, new surgical procedures, discovery of new drugs, advances in organ transplants, genetics, computerization of patient's medi-cal records, and life-sustaining technologies were raising a host of difficult and complex ethical, legal, and political issues concerning quality of life, health care rationing, right to die, organ transplants, cloning, and confidenti-ality and privacy of medical records. This led many to question whether medical colleges were providing appropriate education and training to stu-dents to prepare them for medical practice in the twenty-first century.

Thus, during the 1980s and 1990s several studies, reports, and articles appeared in scholarly journals and popular magazines criticizing the Ameri-can medical educational system and advocating change and reforms. Some charged that medicine at the end of the twentieth century stood at a virtual Rubicon and the intolerable social effects of modern health care needed to be reversed (Wolf 1998). Some called the medical profession an ailing pro-fession (Noonan 2000), while others argued that medical schools themselves were suffering from ill health (Comarow 2000). Others argued that medical education was in crisis and the healing profession was in need of healers (Gunn 1999). Several reports called for improvement in medical education and training to prepare physicians for the new century. For example, in 1984, the panel on the General Professional Education of the Physicians and Col-lege Preparation for Medicine of the AAMC published a report titled "Physi-cians for the 21st Century," in which it discussed what the panel perceived to be the problems in medical education, and made recommendations to ad-dress those problems. Several other studies also examined what kind of train-ing would be necessary to prepare physicians for the twenty-first century (Patel 1999; Elam, Wilson, Wilson, and Schwartz 1995). A two-year study conducted in 1992 by the Robert Wood Johnson Foundation's Commission on Medical Education concluded that there was a need for reform in the medical educational system (Medical education 1992). A panel commissioned by the AAMC in its 1998 report also recommended that major changes be made in the way doctors were trained (Weinstock 1998b). The changes taking place in the health care system in general and the practice of medicine in particular had led to the argument that changes in the American medical educational system were needed to prepare physicians for the twenty-first century (Sheehan 1996). Therefore, improving the way medical students are educated became the major priority for the 1990s and beyond (Greenberg 1994).

Criticisms and Reforms

One of the persistent criticisms of American medicine has been that it undervalues primary care physicians. The result is that the U.S. health care system has an oversupply of specialists and an undersupply of generalists (Barzansky 2000). Facing declining federal and state support for medical education and more competition, academic medical centers have emphasized increased clinical services as sources of revenue to support their teaching and research mission. The result is that faculties with subspecialties are recruited in disproportionate numbers to enhance revenue. Medicare reimbursement policy has also tended to reward teaching hospitals for maintaining high levels of residency positions and emphasis on training specialists. To change this trend, some have argued that what is needed is to remodel Medicare funding to reduce excess residency positions and to provide direct federal funding for both undergraduate and graduate education (Noren 1997).

The overabundance of specialists and undersupply of generalists has been blamed for high health care costs as well as geographic maldistribution of physicians. According to some, what is needed is for medical schools to produce more generalists or primary care physicians to work with uninsured and underinsured and to practice in rural areas (Verby, Newell, Andersen, and Swentko 1991). Most important, emphasis on primary care is needed because prevention of illness is at the heart of primary care. Furthermore, primary care also helps avoid costly and sometimes unnecessary diagnostic and treatment interventions and thus primary care is the foundation of an effective health care system (Lee 1995). The need for an increase in primary care physicians has been emphasized in several studies. In 1992, AAMC's General Physician Task Force recommended an increase in the number of family physicians, general internists, and general pediatricians in the workforce (AAMC 1993). The concern for more primary care physicians was highlighted in a 1995 special supplement of *Academic Medicine,* which was devoted to primary care and the education of generalist physicians (Primary care 1995).

Yet medical schools have continued to produce specialists. According to the AAMC's data on the production of physicians from medical school during the period of 1987 to 1989, most medical schools graduated less than 25 percent of students who can be considered generalists and only two schools were able to graduate close to 45 percent of students with generalist leanings (Cohen 1995). Similarly, data from six medical schools in Pennsylvania from the period of 1986 to 1991 show that of the 5,244 physicians who graduated, 3,953 were trained as nongeneralists, while only 1,291 were trained as generalists (Rabinowitz et al. 1999). Thus, some have argued that part of the blame rests with medical education and what is needed is reform of medical schools' curricula. However, others have argued that producing more primary care physicians at any given medical school is not simply a matter of changing the curriculum because many variables go into a medical student's decision to choose primary care over a specialty. In the United States, one of the best predictors of high output of primary care physicians is whether the medical school is privately or publicly owned—a variable that is not subject to easy manipulation. In general, schools that historically have produced a large number of primary care physicians continue to do so (Barzansky 2000). It is possible that current and future changes in the health care system such as managed care, increased health care delivery in an ambulatory setting, increased external regulation, loss of physician autonomy, and more emphasis on health outcomes, among others, may enhance the relevance of general practice (Worley, March, and Worley 2000). However, that remains to be seen.

A second and somewhat related criticism leveled at medical education is that the clinical experiences of medical students are very limited and largely confined to an inpatient hospital setting. As mentioned above, the current Medicare reimbursement mechanism tends to reward academic health centers or teaching hospitals for maintaining high levels of residency positions with an emphasis on training specialists. One of the reforms advocated is to move the education setting from the hospital into the community (Okasha 1997). The teaching of clinical medicine should be shifted from inside the hospital to outside the hospital because the kinds of patients seen in inpatient settings are very different from the kinds of patients seen in outpatient settings, such as physicians' offices, public clinics, nursing homes, and the like. Clinical training should be better matched to the requirements of clinical practice in a changing health care environment of medical practice, health care delivery, and managed care. Critics charge that inpatient services have become anachronistic for learning clinical medicine. Increases in costs of care and the DRG system for reimbursement to hospitals in the Medicare program have led to shorter hospital stays. Often important diagnostic tests are done outside the hospitals, and the range of diseases seen on inpatient services has narrowed. Hospitals have become more concentrated with patients who need the advanced technology of intensive care units because they have multiple coexisting diseases and they have failed to respond to office treatment (Kassirer 1996).

A recent study based on visits to twenty-six medical schools and a survey of others provides some hopeful signs. According to the study, medical colleges are implementing curricula changes designed to improve training in general practice medicine with more emphasis on community-based ambulatory experiences. The community-oriented, population-based experiences incorporate approaches to primary care that are based on epidemiological evidence, emphasizing a community or population rather than individual patients. Such experiences are structured as a single block experience over several weeks in which students are matched with a specific community site and/or population on a full-time assignment. Medical schools also are shifting away from the traditional departmentally administered individual clerkships to multispecialty clerkships with increased exposure to generalist teachings and clinical experiences in community and rural settings (Hunt, Kallenberg, and Whitcomb 1999). If medical practice is to become community-based practice, it would require incorporating more social and humanistic foci in medicine.

The third major criticism of medical training is that current medical education is centered on the "what" of medicine, that is, a reductionist approach has helped produce highly trained scientists and specialists who can very competently practice a science-based and technologically complex system of medicine. Unfortunately, the critics argue, this has come at the sacrifice of the "how" of medicine, that is, a social or humanistic approach to medicine. Such an approach focuses on how medicine should be practiced in relation to the needs that it serves—community and patient needs (Guze 1995). What is needed is curricula reform that would expose medical students, especially at the undergraduate level, to behavioral and social sciences and arts and humanities. If medical students are to be provided community-based clinical experiences, it is all the more important that general practice-based and community-based teaching should incorporate cross-disciplinary studies in social sciences, economics, epidemiology, communication, sociology, and social anthropology, among others. Medical students need to learn about environmental, social, and psychological influences on health (Editorial 1994). Behavioral sciences have a lot to offer in these areas. One of the major recommendations of the Robert Wood Johnson Foundation Commission on Medical Education was that medical education must include behavioral, social, probabilistic, and information sciences because in addition to biological knowledge, physicians must have an understanding of the behavioral and social aspects of health and disease (Marston 1992). Others have argued that medical history should also be included because it can teach medical students critical thinking and information gathering skills, and it can inform the practice of medicine (Biddiss 1997). Still others have argued that medical schools also should educate students in health policy, to enable physicians to deliver better patient care and become better advocates for their patients' needs. It also will allow them to become active participants in shaping future health care systems. Such training also would allow more physicians to specialize in the administrative policy making aspect of health care, and would help them to retain a patient-centered perspective in policy decisions (Clancy et al. 1995).

Medical schools' curricula have been criticized for exposing students to a great deal of duplication in chemistry, physics, math, and biology. It is argued that medical students should be exposed more to the liberal arts and humanities because the science of medicine can be enhanced by the art of medicine, and these two are not mutually exclusive (Eichold 1999). The fact that emphasis on scientific facts in medical school comes at the expense of liberal arts and humanities has been seen as a crisis (Wolf 1997). What can a medical student learn from exposure to the arts and humanities? Proponents argue that there are many similarities between the arts and medicine. The practice of medicine requires practitioners to confront questions of the meaning of life, tragedy, the sadness of illness, pain, disease, and death, as well as experience the joys of successful treatments or cures and the beginning of new lives, among other things. The arts and humanities can help with these issues. It can also help develop self-perception and improve communication skills (Calman and Downie 1996). Literature, along with arts in various forms—drama, poetry, music, rhetoric, and religion—can help teach medical students how to live their lives as good doctors, broaden their educational horizons, and enhance personal growth. Arts and humanities can also help focus the health practitioner's attention on an area that has become increasingly important due to advances in medical technology and science—medical ethics (Gillon 2000). Teaching literature side by side with medicine can aid the learning process and address ethical and moral issues related to the modern practice of medicine (Skelton, Macleod, and Thomas 2000).

The fourth criticism of medical school education is that it has not done enough to incorporate the teaching of bioethics. It has been argued that money has become a higher consideration than basic ethical principles in medical training and practice (Rothman 1997). As we have discussed throughout this book, advances in new technologies are raising complex ethical and legal

questions about the right to die, organ transplants, cloning, privacy and confidentiality of patients' medical records, patients' rights, and health care rationing. This trend will continue with new breakthroughs in technological
discoveries. Critics argue that medical schools need to do more to educate
and train physicians to deal with the ethical and moral issues they face in
their medical practices. To be effective and caring, the health care giver will
require comprehensive character development. Great importance must be
attached to teaching ethics to ensure that medical schools produce practitioners who are not only intellectually and behaviorally competent, but are sensitive to the humane and social values of the profession (Li 2000). Proponents
of teaching medical ethics and law believe that these subjects can contribute
to the overall objective of medical education, which is to produce good doctors who will enhance and promote the health and welfare of people they
serve "in ways which fairly and justly respect their dignity, autonomy, and
rights" (Doyal and Gillon 1998). A curriculum for teaching ethics and law
has been developed in Great Britain (Teaching medical ethics 1998). Teaching ethics and professional character development can serve several objectives, including development of good and moral professional values that help
establish a good interpersonal relationship between physicians and patients,
enhance decision making by helping develop the ability to judge and ana-
·lyze ethical problems, and help to minimize the negative consequences of
ever-changing technologies by focusing attention on the ethical issues raised
by biomedical technologies (Li 2000).

A majority of medical schools in the United States teach bioethics to foster different ways of perceiving and understanding caring roles to prepare a
new generation of physicians (Fox 1999). However, how such a topic is
incorporated in the medical school curriculum varies considerably. It may be
taught as a separate course by itself, or the subject may be covered through
case study method, independent study, or a special seminar/workshop (Patel
1999). In fact, bioethics has become a growth industry, and more than 165
bioethics centers and programs, often affiliated with university medical
schools, have been established in the past thirty years. In 1995, President
Clinton established the National Bioethics Advisory Commission whose
membership has contained many professional bioethicists. However, it should
be pointed out that there are critics of the bioethics movement in medicine,
and they argue that bioethicists have a tendency to foster paternalistic values
and believe that they "know best" what is good for patients and what treatments they should receive. According to critics of the field of bioethics, such
paternalism has the potential to limit patients' choices, and bioethics, in fact,
may be hazardous to our health (Bailey 1999).

The fifth criticism of medical education and training is that the current curriculum fails to train medical students for pain management and for providing appropriate care for terminally ill patients. The care of terminally ill and dying patients will become even more important as the baby boom generation approaches old age and the twilight years of their lives. A 1997 report from the Committee on Care at the End of Life of the Institute of Medicine recommended that medical educators initiate changes in undergraduate, postgraduate, and continuing medical education to make sure health care practitioners receive the relevant knowledge and skills that allow them to care for dying patients (Field and Cassel 1997). According to the report, many doctors do not know or understand the desires of patients and their family members. Furthermore, many Americans fear a technologically overtreated and protracted death and the prospect of abandonment and untreated pain (Abbott 1998).

Surveys of medical students and practicing physicians have revealed that most of them did not receive any teaching/training in caring for the dying. Studies conducted by the AMA during 1993 and 1994 found that only five of twenty-six medical schools required a course on death and dying, and only 26 percent of 7,048 hospital residency programs offered a regular course on end of life care (Cohn, Harrold, and Lynn 1997). A group of researchers at Washington University School of Medicine in St. Louis conducted a survey of 81 physicians in training who had been out of medical school for a median time of two years. Most of the participants in the study could not correctly answer questions related to pain management that were considered to be reasonable knowledge for physicians in training. Eighty-one residents had received their degrees from fifty-five different medical schools, and only eight schools had offered a course in cancer pain management, reflecting the fact that managing chronic pain is not addressed aggressively in medical schools (Doctors lack training 1998). Another study reported that very few doctors ever discuss with their patients the issues of end of life care and treatment (Shorr 2000). Medicine needs to provide appropriate care for people with progressive diseases rather than just relying on aggressive treatments even when the diseases are incurable. The science of medicine must learn to recognize the point at which the care of patient suffering from terminal illness must move from treatment and cure to providing care for the dying. The art of medicine must take over at this point (Cohn, Harrold, and Lynn 1997).

In recent years, debates about physician-assisted suicide have prompted many organizations to develop continuing education courses to teach physicians how to provide continuing end of life care to patients (Sulmasy and Lynn 1997). The Robert Wood Johnson Foundation has provided major grants to end-of-life movements to support projects aimed at educating physicians, as well as the public, about methods to improve the care of dying patients. A $1.5 million grant from the organization led to the establishment of the Education for Physicians on End-of-Life Care Project (EPEC). The main purpose of the project is to develop a standardized curriculum for educating physicians in the care of dying patients, improving physicians' skills in areas such as communication, palliative care, ethical decision making, symptom management, and psychosocial assessment (Skolnick 1997). Other organizations involved in such curriculum developments include The American Institute of Life-Threatening Diseases, AMA, and the Center to Improve the Care of the Dying.

The sixth criticism of current medical education in the United States is that medical schools' curricula put too much emphasis on the curative model of medicine and too little emphasis on preventive care. One of the weaknesses of the curative model is that it operates on the assumption that the role of medicine begins only when patients are sick. Thus, the whole medical system is geared toward curing patients after they become sick rather than preventing illnesses from occurring. According to the critiques of the U.S. medical system, what is needed is not just a change in the practice of medicine but also a change in the goal of medicine. Rather than becoming preoccupied with biomedical progress for its own sake, we ought to strive for creating a healthy society (Callahan 1997). The goals of medicine as a healing art should be to prevent injury and disease, promote and maintain health, provide relief from suffering, and cure when possible (Hanson and Callahan 1999). The general professional education of medical students must include an emphasis on health and disease prevention. This would require incorporation of behavioral, social, and information sciences and ethics into medical school curricula (Enarson and Burg 1992). The emphasis on preventive care also underscores the need for medical schools to train more primary care providers. It would also require incorporating nutrition into medical school curricula including applied nutrition so that primary care physicians can provide better and more informed counseling to their patients. Dietary excesses or imbalances often lead to illnesses, and providing primary care physicians with training in applied nutrition will promote the goal of preventive care (Davis 1994). The National Research Council in 1985 warned that nutrition instruction in most U.S. medical schools was inadequate (National Research Council 1985). Congress passed the National Nutrition Monitoring and Related Research Act in 1990 in recognition of the importance of nutritional education in medical schools.

The seventh criticism of medical school education and training is the failure to train students in complementary or alternative medicines (CAM) such as homeopathy, chiropractic medicine, traditional Chinese medicine, and osteopathy, among others. CAM incorporates many different approaches and methodologies from spiritual healing to nutritional intervention to acupuncture (Berman, Lewith, and Stephens 2001). Many Americans, skeptical of high tech medicines and treatments, are turning to alternative medicines for dealing with their health problems. More than one-third of Americans are using alternative medicines and therapies. Over 50 percent of people in Europe and 80 percent of people worldwide use alternative medicines. There is some evidence that some forms of alternative medicines produce favorable results (Micozzi 1996). CAM is the fastest growing area in health care. In 1997, an estimated 42 percent of Americans used some form of alternative therapy. The numbers are even higher in family practices even if most patients do not mention it. Physicians need to be aware of CAM therapies so they can discuss them with their patients (Steyer 2001). Alternative medicines can no longer remain an obscure issue. During the 1990s Americans paid more visits to alternative medical practitioners than to all their primary care physicians combined, and spent nearly $14 billion on CAM therapies. In fact, between 1990 and 1997, the number of Americans using alternative medicines increased from 34 percent to 42 percent, and spending on alternative medicines increased from $14 billion to $21 billion (Lamarine 2001).

Consumers of alternative medicine often are not acutely ill, but suffer from various chronic illnesses such as headaches, back pain, digestive disorders, and the like, and they tend to have had unpleasant experiences with modern medicines (Goodenough and Park 1996). Alternative medicines also appeal to those who prefer a holistic approach to health care. According to research, compared to nonusers, alternative medicines users tend to be better educated and more often report lower than average health statuses. Users of alternative medicines also tend to view alternative medicines as more consistent with their own values, beliefs, and philosophies toward health and life (Astin 1998).

According to a nonscientific online survey conducted by Modern Healthcare on its Web site, a large majority of respondents wanted their health care providers to offer alternative treatments, more federal money spent on more research on alternative therapies, and federal health care programs and health insurance to cover the costs of such therapies. About half of the respondents also indicated that their organizations' insurance plans cover some form of alternative therapies (May 2001). Thus, critics charge that medical schools can no longer ignore the issue of complementary and alternative medicines, and future doctors must be trained in such approaches so they can better deal with their patients' needs.

The NIH in 1992, called a conference to discuss the major areas of alternative medicines. It defined seven fields—bioelectromagnetics, diet and nutrition, herbal remedies, manual healing methods, mind/body interventions, pharmacology, and biological treatments (Steyer 2001). In 1993, the Society of Teachers of Family Medicine formed the Group on Alternative Medicine, which developed curriculum guidelines for medical education in alternative medicines (Wetzel, Eisenberg, and Kaptchuk 1998). In 1995, an NIH-sponsored national conference recommended that complementary and alternative therapies should be included in nursing and medical education (Berman 2001). According to a survey of 117 medical schools in the United States, 64 percent offered an elective course in alternative medicines or included information about alternative medicines in their regular courses. Chiropractic, acupuncture, homeopathy, herbal therapies, and mind-body techniques were typical topics covered in such courses (Wetzel, Eisenberg, and Kaptchuck 1998). Thus, it appears that medical schools have responded to the criticisms and incorporated the teaching of complementary and alternative therapies in their curriculum. However, it should be kept in mind that since most medical schools have a very packed curriculum CAM courses tend to be elective (Berman 2001).

The eighth criticism of medical education in the United States is that it has failed to produce a sufficient number of minority physicians. Despite the fact that African Americans, Hispanics, and other racial minorities are becoming a larger portion of the population, with the exception of Asian Americans few of them become physicians and the number of minorities entering medical school has dropped in the last several years. African Americans constitute 12 percent of the total population in the United States, but make up only 3 percent of the total number of physicians in the country. Similarly, Hispanics compose 10 percent of the population, but they constitute only 5 percent of the physicians in the country (Report: Nation must diversify 1999). According to David N. Sundwall, M.D., chairman of the Council on Graduate Medical Education, the physician workforce needs to reflect the nation's increasingly diverse population but despite two decades of efforts to increase minority numbers in medicine, they remain underrepresented at all levels (Evelyn 1998). It should be emphasized that almost all discussions of minorities include Blacks, Mexican Americans, mainland Puerto Ricans, Native Americans, and Alaskan natives. Asian Americans, who are well represented in medical schools, are generally excluded from analyses of minority representation in medicine.

Similarly, there is a significant lack of minorities in senior faculty positions at many medical schools in the United States. According to Jordan J. Cohen, M.D., president of the AAMC, "as long as our medical school faculties have little more than a token representation from many sectors of the richly diverse American culture, the medical profession cannot truly lay claim to the ethical and moral high ground it professes to occupy" (Cohen 1998). Increasing the number of minority faculty is important because in running faculty development programs, minority physicians are more likely to be interested in research problems that are relevant to poor populations and minorities (Nickens 1996).

The history of minority recruitment at medical schools is a mixed one with some successes and several failures. After medical schools opened their doors to minorities in the late 1960s, minority graduation from medical schools increased to about 8 percent in the mid-1970s (Nickens 1996). But following these major gains, minority enrollment after the mid-1970s dropped again. Due to renewed efforts by the AAMC in the early 1990s, the enrollment of minorities again increased during the 1990 to 1995 period (Geiger 1998). Prior to 1968, only about 2.5 percent of American physicians were African Americans, and less than 0.2 percent of medical students were Mexican American, Puerto Rican, Native American, or Native Alaskan (Carlisle and Gardner 1998). However, underrepresented minority enrollment increased by 43 percent after 1986 and peaked in 1994. In fact, between 1990 and 1994, the number of new underrepresented minority students entering medical schools increased at an average annual rate of 8.3 percent (Carlisle and Gardner 1998). The number of minority students enrolled in medical schools increased from 9.7 percent in 1991 to 11.4 percent in 1993 (Mahaney 1994). Thus, significant gains were made in increasing the number of minority students enrolled in medical schools, yet their numbers were still underrepresented considering that minorities made up about 22 percent of the U.S. population (Lewin and Rice 1994). Furthermore, the numbers of minority enrollment began to decline significantly after the mid-1990s as affirmative action programs in higher education came under increased attack on both judicial and political fronts, as well as in public opinion (DeVille 1999). The elimination of affirmative action programs, either through ballot initiatives or court rulings in California, Texas, Louisiana, and Mississippi, had a major negative affect on the acceptance and enrollment of racial and ethnic minorities in medical schools across the country, but especially in those states. The number of minority applications to medical schools in those four states dropped 17 percent in 1997 compared to only a 7 percent drop in all other states (Minorities lead drop 1998). The drop in medical school applications from those four states accounted for nearly 40 percent of the overall drop in the number of applications of minority students (Hawkins 1997). Nationwide, the number of minorities applying to medical schools dropped 11 percent (Weinstock 1997). One of the suggested ways to deal with the judicial challenges to race-based affirmative action programs is to use social class instead of race as the basis for preferential admission decisions in an effort to maintain or increase student diversity in medical schools (Magnus and Mick 2000).

Why is increasing the number of minority medical students and physicians important? There are several good reasons for this. One is the fact that studies have shown minorities are more likely to work in inner cities and minority communities. Thus, increasing the number of minority physicians in the country is likely to increase access to health care by the poor and minority populations (Report: Nation must diversify 1999). Similarly, studies also have demonstrated a correlation between physicians' social classes and those of the patients and communities they serve (Magnus and Mick 2000). It is estimated that the racial minority groups will make up the majority of Americans by 2050, if not earlier. So unless we increase the number of minority physicians, access to health care for those in greatest need may get worse (Geiger 1998). Another important reason for increasing the number of minority physicians in the country is that it will help address the challenge of effectively delivering health care services to a diverse racial, ethnic, and cultural population in the United States. In the future, it will be important for physicians to understand the cultural differences and values of their patients for the effective delivery of health care services (Trevalon and Murray-Garcia 1998).

Demographics are changing in the United States as the country has become a truly multicultural society. The number of U.S. residents whose first language is not English jumped from 23 million in 1980 to 32 million in 1990. Doctors are increasingly encountering patients who speak many different languages and come from many different cultures. Language and cultural barriers between a patient and a doctor can interfere with effective health care (Brink 1998). As we have discussed in this book, patients' cultural and religious values often shape their attitudes about death, the human body, and thus how they feel about issues such as the right to die, euthanasia, and organ transplants, among others. It is important that physicians receive training in cultural values and how they influence health care issues. Yet studies have shown that very few schools offer separate courses in cultural values (Flores 2000). In the United States in 1999, only 13 medical schools offered courses on cultural sensitivity and ethnic and racial diversity (Loudon et al. 1999).

Related to the issue of cultural diversity is the role of spirituality in the healing process. Studies have shown that patients want spiritual issues addressed when they are seriously ill or dying. In a Gallup Poll conducted in 1990, 65 percent of respondents said that doctors should talk with their patients about spiritual concerns. Studies also have demonstrated that spiritual and religious commitments can have a positive effect on a person's physical and mental health care (Puchalski 1998). For example, a 1995 study by Dartmouth found that one of the important predictors of survival and recovery after open heart surgery was the degree to which patients drew comfort from their religion. Such patients were three times more likely to be alive six months after heart surgery compared to their nonreligious counterparts.

Other studies have shown that people who believe in a higher power tend to live longer, have fewer drug and alcohol problems, fewer mental and physical problems, and an overall better quality of life (Mangan 1997). In recognition of this, medical schools across the country are offering courses on the role of spirituality in the healing process. Nearly one-third of the nation's 125 medical schools offer such a course (1997). In a pioneering new program at Brown University's School of Medicine, students are being evaluated on how well they communicate and understand the moral beliefs of their patients (Mangan 1996).

Many of the criticisms of the medical schools discussed in this section are valid and as we have discussed medical schools have made efforts to address these by making changes in curricula. However, they still have a long way to go.

Physicians for the New Century: Medical Education, Values, and Health Care Policies

Between 1906 and 1992, fifteen major studies or reports made recommendations designed to improve undergraduate medical education. These studies discussed and recommended changes in the areas of medical schools' curricula, teaching methods, organization and structure, and relationship to various external organizations such as accrediting agencies and licensing boards. Some of the reforms were incorporated, while others were not due to often conflicting goals and interests of different organizations involved in medical education (Enarson and Burg 1992). Many of these studies and reports were similar in terms of recommended reforms and objectives of the reforms. The primary objectives for reforms outlined by these studies have been to better serve the public interest, physician workforce needs, to deal with rapidly increasing medical knowledge, and to increase emphasis on generalism (Christakis 1995). Some of these reforms have produced positive results. However, overall many of these reforms have failed to produce fundamental changes in the profession of medicine as a whole and the types of physicians produced. To bring about fundamental changes that will help produce physicians for the next century will require more than just tinkering with the curricula content and structures of medical schools. It will require dramatic changes in the philosophical and ideological outlook at three levels.

First, it will require a rethinking and reemphasis on the true meaning of professionalism in the field of medicine. Medical students and physicians must increasingly become aware not only of what they should know in terms of medical knowledge but also what they should be as physicians. The classical definition of professionalism consists of three major points—a high level of intellectual and technical expertise, autonomy in the practice and regulation of the discipline, and a commitment to public service (Stephenson, Higgs, and Sugarman 2001). The social basis of occupational autonomy and authority to professionals is based on the concept of a social contract between the profession and the public or the society. In exchange for autonomy and authority for self-regulation, a professional is expected to maintain high standards of competence and moral responsibility. This high standard of moral responsibility includes the notion that while a professional is not required to put aside material considerations, she is expected to subordinate personal financial gain to the higher values of responsibility to clients and to the public interest (Sullivan 2000). The very basis of the social contract between a professional and the public or society is that professionals will be altruistic and moral in their daily activities (Cruess and Cruess 2000).

Today, the medical profession has come under increasing criticism and has begun to lose some of its professional autonomy. One of the reasons for this is the fact that the managed care revolution with its managed competition, HMOs, and free market approaches has transformed the doctor-patient relationship. Traditionally, the doctor-patient relationship has been based on trust and care but it is being replaced by questions of cost and benefits. In the process, the social contract has been rewritten so that stronger and narrower interests prevail and the public has become a bystander (Sullivan 2000). The second reason is the fact that the medical profession itself deserves some of the blame because they have passively accepted these changes and because they have often cared more about personal material gains than about one of the most important aspects of professionalism and the social contract—to serve the public interest. The medical profession has failed to uphold its end of the bargain and has often failed to make decisions designed to serve the public interest. What is urgently needed is for the medical profession to reassert its authority by reclaiming the original social contract based on the concept of civic professionalism and produce physicians who serve the public interest, treat medicine as a public good, and promote the larger common good in helping build a healthy society (2000).

The second philosophical change that must occur is that the medical profession must stop relying totally on the curative model of medicine and broaden its horizons. The curative model is a clinical approach to medicine that narrowly focuses on cure as its ultimate goal (Fox 1997). The biomedical model of diseases needs to be expanded beyond the physical and biological to incorporate a more holistic approach to medical care. The underlying framework of medicine that operates from a linear, reductionist model of diseases must be broadened to include the importance of health in the context of socially based life conditions. The current operating model has produced biomechanically oriented, detached physicians who cannot communicate effectively with their patients when it should be producing physicians who are capable of reflection, imagination, and curiosity, with a capacity for introspection (Pauli, White, and McWhinney 2000). American medical professionals must recognize that medicine is more than just a science and learn to accept the Confucian precept that medicine is a humane art, that is, medicine is more than just a means to save lives. The practice of medicine also includes a moral commitment to love people and free them from suffering through personal caring and treatment (Zhang and Cheng 2000). Today, because of biomedical, computer, and information technologies, physicians are better able to care for their patients, but not with the same humanitarian sense as their predecessors. Certain qualities that make medicine a humane art such as sensitivity, compassion, empathy, and caring are not necessarily qualities that can be taught. Even though some of these qualities can be acquired through role models such as teachers and attending physicians, some of these qualities have to be in a person before they enter medical school (Langone 1994).

Thus, the third philosophical change that must occur is in the process of how students are selected for medical schools. The current selection process often is biased against the very qualities that should make for a good, caring physician. According to Gunn, the selection process for medical school is fundamentally and ideologically flawed, and is skewed toward choosing students who do not and will not think independently on important issues. As a result, medical schools end up producing physicians who are technicians rather than healers (Gunn 1999). A great majority of the members of medical school admissions and advisory committees and aspiring doctors do not see a liberal arts core curriculum as an ideal preparation for medical school. This is unfortunate because it is the mental training of the liberal arts that will endow students with the capacity to deal with life and death issues that they will confront in their practices. In medical schools, the predominant scientific model is the biological one in which patients are seen as biomechanical systems to be manipulated and fixed, and medical problems to be solved (1999). Given this, the tendency is to admit students to medical schools who have a background in the sciences and not in liberal arts or behavioral and social sciences. For example, for the 1995–1996 academic year, of the 17,357 applicants who were accepted for admission to medical schools, 10,928 (62.9 percent) had biological or physical sciences as their undergraduate majors, while 2,592 (14.9 percent) had undergraduate majors in nonscience subjects such as anthropology (155), economics (240), English (334), foreign languages (155), history (299), philosophy (101), political science (164), psychobiology (168), psychology (892), and sociology (84) (AAMC 1996).

Historically, medicine has been associated with liberal arts, but today medicine has come to be associated with the sciences. If we are to produce physicians for the needs of the twenty-first century, we need to reverse this trend and realign the medical profession with liberal arts and the behavioral and social sciences. There is evidence that some medical schools in their screening process are beginning to look for double majors—in sciences and liberal arts (Langone 1994).

To meet the health care needs of this century, we need to educate, train, and produce physicians who will be well versed, not just in the science of medicine but also in the art of medicine—the humane art of medicine. We need to produce physicians who not only will treat patients with care and compassion but also protect and promote their dignity, treat health care as a public good, view their social contract as one of mutual trust and obligation, take a holistic approach in the care of their patients, place greater emphasis on preventive care, be effective advocates for their patients and promote access to health care for all individuals, and, in the process, help build a healthy society that improves the quality of life in America. Today's medical schools do an excellent job of producing outstanding scientists and physicians, but they need to a better job of producing physicians who also are better healers (Nuland 1999).

Study Questions

1. Discuss the history of medical education in the United States. What were some of the major milestones?
2. What are some of the major criticisms of current medical education in the United States?
3. What reforms in medical education and training of physicians would you advocate to prepare physicians for the twenty-first century?

CHAPTER 9

Conclusion

Transformation of the U.S. Health Care System

The U.S. health care system has undergone a major transformation since the 1980s, and more changes are on the way. There are several factors that have contributed to this transformation. A major one is dramatic advances in the field of biomedical technologies. Most developments in the field of health care technology can be classified as replacement technology or new technology. Replacement technology replaces an old procedure with a new one, for example, the CAT scanner replaced invasive surgery as a diagnostic procedure. New technology refers to procedures that have never been performed, such as organ transplants, and to development of technologies in the areas of life extending, life sustaining, and reproduction (Wildes 1994). Lewis Thomas has provided a three-level classification of medical technology—nontechnology, halfway technology, and high technology. Nontechnology involves offering patients reassurance and providing nursing and hospital or hospice care, but offers little hope for curing diseases. Halfway technologies include organ transplants and the use of artificial organs. Such technologies are designed not to cure but to make up for a disease or to postpone death. High technologies are the result of genuine understanding of disease mechanisms and include immunization, antibiotics, and the like. It is important to emphasize that high technologies are relatively inexpensive while the halfway technologies are the most expensive (Thomas 1975).

New discoveries through biomedical research are revolutionizing the practice of medicine. Life-sustaining technologies hold out the promise of prolonging life indefinitely. Advances in the field of organ transplants have made it possible to replace almost all of the human body parts with human, animal, or artificial organs. Discoveries in the field of genetics, in areas such as cloning and stem cell research, have the potential to provide an unlimited supply of organs for transplants, designer drugs, and gene replacement therapies, and provide cures for many diseases. According to David Ellis (2000), some of the future technological advances are likely to include autonomous mobile robots running on software that possesses human levels of intelligence, superhuman sensory perception, and manipulative capabilities; intelligent mini drug and tissue manufacturing machines that can be implanted in the human body, and are capable of performing medical and surgical tasks; doctors' offices and clinics that exist only in virtual reality; and a significantly improved Internet that will connect all these devices and make it possible to remotely monitor, troubleshoot, repair, and share information.

Americans generally have welcomed technological innovations in medicine. However, they seem to have a love-hate relationship with medical technology. On one hand they applaud medical technology for saving lives and improving the quality of health care. On the other hand technology is blamed for the high cost of health care, and many Americans are weary of high tech medical interventions designed simply to prolong life (Neumann and Weinstein 1991). This is understandable because while medical technology has brought benefits it has not helped find cures for many diseases. The proliferation of medical technologies has taken place more in the area of halfway technologies than high technologies. In contrast to Great Britain and many Scandinavian countries, the U.S. government has not played a major role in the assessment of medical technology or in regulating the introduction of new technologies in the marketplace. In the United States, market forces have been most influential with respect to diffusion of high-cost technologies. The Food and Drug Administration's (FDA) main focus in the regulation of medical technologies has been in the area of safety and efficacy of drugs and medical devices and not as much in the area of assessing the cost effectiveness of medical technologies (Patel and Rushefsky 1999). The Office of Health Technology Assessment (OHTA) within the National Center for Health Services Research and Health Care Technology Assessment (NCHSR/HCTA), whose main function was to provide advice to the Health Care Financing Administration (HCFA) regarding what should and should not be covered in the Medicare program, was replaced in 1989 by the Agency for Health Care Policy and Research (AHCPR). The AHCPR's main mandate is to encourage improvements in organization, financing, and provision of health services as well as in clinical practices (Perry and Pillar 1990). Thus, at the government level there is very little assessment of medical technology from a cost-effectiveness perspective except with respect to government health care programs.

In the competitive environment of the managed care revolution, health maintenance organizations (HMOs), preferred provider organizations (PPOs), insurance companies, and employers that pay the medical bills have resorted to the capitation method of payment and primary care physicians have come to play the roles of technology gatekeepers controlling patients' access to hospitals, specialists, and medical technologies. Technology assessment is often broadly defined as a form of policy research that examines the technical, social, and economic consequences of technological applications. However, those who pay the bills take a much narrower view of technology assessments and view them largely as means of separating experimental from state-of-the-art procedures to determine whether to cover them (Luce and Brown 1994). Assessment of medical technologies, setting priorities for technology assessment, and the relationship between biomedical technology and quality of life have generated a considerable amount of discussion and debate in the United States (Donaldson and Sox 1992; Lara and Goodman 1990; Mosteller and Falotico-Taylor 1989).

The second factor that has contributed to the transformation of the U.S. health care system in the past twenty years is developments in the field of information technology. The blending of digitization, chip technology, and communications has led to the establishment of the information age, or the age of connectivity. The new information technology is helping to bring about change in many aspects of health care and medical practice. One area that information technology has impacted is the area of medical education and training of physicians. Because new information technology is providing unparalleled access to new knowledge, medical schools are confronted with the question of how best to educate and train students for the challenges of medical practice in the twenty-first century (Wagner 2000). The second area in which the information technology is having a major impact is how physicians practice their craft. The new technology of information processing and communication is making it possible for physicians to access and continually update practical knowledge, quickly record and retrieve patient information, engage in self-assessment of clinical practice, track the financial consequences of clinical decisions, integrate clinical data with outside sources, and seek computer-based decision support (Schneider and Eisenberg 1998).

The Internet also promises to radically change the practice of medicine in the twenty-first century through telemedicine and cybermedicine. In telemedicine, physicians use electronic communication and information technologies to provide or support clinical care from a distance. Telemedicine has the potential to help expand the range of health services to underserved rural and urban communities. In telemedicine, physicians communicate with other physicians for the benefit of the patients. Cybermedicine is different in that physicians set up sites on the World Wide Web and diagnose unseen patients. Internet pharmacies are beginning to provide prescription drugs either by requiring prescriptions from consumers' personal physicians, or by requiring consumers to consult with online physicians, or by providing prescription drugs without prescriptions or consultations with physicians, which is illegal (Silverman 2000). E-health is rapidly becoming a very controversial area of health care (Bates and Gawande 2000; Goldsmith 2000; Kassirer 2000; Kleinke 2000; Parente 2000; Robinson 2000).

The third factor responsible for the transformation of the U.S. health care system was the arrival of managed care in the 1980s. President Clinton's effort at overhauling the nation's health care system through his proposed Health Security Act in 1993 failed. One of the cornerstones of his reform proposal was the creation of a health care system based on managed care and managed competition.

Despite the failure of reform efforts, a managed care revolution did take hold in the private sector. New types of health service delivery organizations such as HMOs and PPOs came into being. One of the primary purposes of such managed care organizations was to cut health care costs by generating competition and managing patient care. The number of HMOs and PPOs proliferated as some of the Medicaid and Medicare patients, along with patients who were insured through their employers, were either forced or encouraged to join such health service delivery organizations (Patel and Rushefsky 1999). Today, a majority of Americans belong to some form of HMO or PPO.

The managed care revolution also led to the rise of corporate ethos that has come to permeate all sorts of health care organizations, not-for-profit as well as the for-profit sector. The traditional organizational culture of medicine based on ideals of professionalism and voluntarism has been replaced by notions of health care marketing and profit making as business school graduates have come to occupy management positions in hospitals, HMOs, PPOs, and other health delivery organizations, replacing graduates of public health schools and physicians (Wolf 1998). The rise of this corporate ethos has turned the U.S. health care system into a commercial market in which health care is viewed as a private industry to be controlled by market forces rather than a social service and a public responsibility. Today, private, investor owned health care organizations control almost all private health coverage and also a major part of publicly financed health care programs (Relman 2000).

The business philosophy that has come to dominate the current U.S. health care sector also is reflected in increased attempts by the commercial interests serving the medical-industrial complex to influence the judgment of physicians. Perhaps this is no more clearly evident than in the area of physician education. A study conducted by the watchdog organization Public Citizen has documented the relationship between medical education activities, the pharmaceutical industry, and medical education services supplier (MESS). According to the study, MESS was being paid more than $1 billion per year, largely by the pharmaceutical industry, to organize hospital presentations, symposiums, and continuing medical education programs. This also included preparing educational material for doctors, residents, and medical students. It is difficult to believe that under such circumstances MESS can provide objective, unbiased information about their financial backers' products (McCarthy 2000; Drug company influence 2000). The pharmaceutical industry is spending billions of dollars marketing products not just to doctors but also to residents in training at teaching hospitals. Teaching hospitals that are under financial strains due to declining government support are increasingly turning over parts of their educational responsibilities to the pharmaceutical industry (Relman 2000).

Health Care Policy in an Age of New Technologies

The factors that contributed to the transformation of the U.S. health care system in the last twenty years or so also have created many problems. This book has focused on some of the problems brought about by advances in biomedical technology, information technology, and the managed care revolution.

Biomedical technology is a double-edged sword. Biomedical technology has provided numerous benefits and has the potential to offer a great deal more. However, biomedical technology also raises a number of very difficult and complex ethical, economic, and political issues. Life-prolonging and life-sustaining technologies have raised a number of questions such as: Do patients have a right to refuse certain kinds of medical interventions that keep them alive in a permanent vegetative state? What is quality of life? Do people suffering from incurable diseases have a right to determine the circumstance and timing of their death? Do people have a right to commit suicide? Do patients have a right to seek the assistance of a physician in helping them end their own lives? We have addressed this topic in Chapter 2 of the book.

Chapters 3 and 4 have addressed the topics of organ transplants and genetic research that also raise many difficult questions. On what basis should we determine priorities in the distribution of available organs? How can we increase the supply of organs for transplants? What are the public policy alternatives and their consequences? Should we rely on cloning of animals to harvest their organs for transplants in humans? Should we allow cloning of humans for transplant purposes? Should we ban human cloning? Should stem cells research be encouraged by the government and should the government provide funding for embryonic stem cells research?

Advances in information technology also have raised a number of troubling questions with the most important being the potential abuse and misuse of patients' medical information and protecting the privacy and confidentiality of patients' medical records (Goldman and Hudson 2000;

Lumpkin 2000). We addressed this issue in Chapter 5. Who should have access to patients' medical records? How can we prevent misuse of such information? How can we protect the privacy and confidentiality of patients' medical records? The advent of the Internet with its e-health, telemedicine, cyberpharmacies, and cybermedicine raises the question of how we control the quality of care and the credentials of health care providers and pharmacies on the Internet. Should such practices be regulated by government or state medical boards (Silverman 2000; Fried et al. 2000; Boulding 2000)?

The managed care revolution in the private health care sector with its emphasis on cost cutting, corporate models of medicine, health care marketing, and profit making has brought about a major public backlash against managed care. Managed care brought to the forefront the issues of health care rationing and patients' bill of rights. The topic of health care rationing was addressed in Chapter 6 of this book. Rationing of health care resources is done explicitly in several European countries while a great deal of rationing of health care resources in the United States is done more implicitly in what might be called "under the table" rationing. Oregon is one state that has engaged in explicit rationing of health services in its Medicaid program. Should the United States engage in more explicit rationing of health care services and resources as a way of controlling rising health care costs? Should we ration access to expensive biomedical technologies? If so, what should be the basis of such rationing? Could we afford to continue to provide unlimited health care services to all our citizens?

Chapter 7 addressed the issue of patients' bill of rights as a means of protecting patients from denial of legitimate services by the HMOs and PPOs. What kinds of rights are patients entitled to? Should they have the right to sue their health care providers and insurers for denial of health care services or coverage of certain health care services?

Finally, in Chapter 8 we addressed the question of medical education and training that is necessary to prepare physicians for the challenges they will face in the twenty-first century. Some of the important questions are: Is the current education and training provided by medical schools adequate? If not, what are some of the shortcomings of the current system? What types of reforms are needed to improve medical education and training of physicians?

What should be our response to the new health care system of the twenty-first century shaped by biomedical and information technologies and managed care? As we enter the brave and uncharted new health care world of euthanasia, physician-assisted suicides, organ transplants, cloning, stem cells research, designer drugs, gene replacement therapies, computerized medical records, health care rationing, cybermedicine, telemedicine, and e-health, what values should guide us in formulating public policies to deal with complex and troublesome ethical, economic, and political dilemmas raised by such a new world?

The Institute of Medicine, in a 1999 report, "To Err is Human: Building a Safer Health System," blamed the U.S. health care system itself for many medical errors. A second report released in March 2001, "Crossing the Quality Chasm: A New Health System for the Twenty-first Century," recommended a broad overhaul of the U.S. health care system and called for a new vision of care in the twenty-first century that consists of a patient-centered and performance-based health care system that has the patient as the source of control, care based on continuous healing relationships, and customization of health care based on patient needs and values. The main focus of such a system should be to reduce the burden of illness and suffering and to improve the functioning and health of the people (Harris 2001; Parker 2001). A project report on the goals of medicine by the Hastings Center outlined four goals of medicine: (1) prevention of disease and injury and promotion and maintenance of health; (2) relief of pain and suffering caused by ill health; (3) care and cure of those suffering from a malady and care of those who cannot be cured; and (4) avoidance of premature death and pursuit of a peaceful death (Hanson and Callahan 1999).

Throughout this book we have argued that the formulation of health care policies in an age of new technologies should be guided by certain basic interrelated values or principles. One of the most important values is that of respecting and promoting human dignity. Modern medicine, especially with respect to biomedical technologies, has presented us with many choices (e.g., reproductive technologies). It should be kept in mind that while modern medicine already has produced and has the potential to produce many more benefits, it also poses threats to freedom of choice, self-determination, and human dignity. Thus, in formulating public policies in these areas it is essential that we create a medical, social, and political environment that respects human dignity and choice.

The second important value that must guide formulation of public policies in the field of health care is citizens' access to good health care. Thus, public policies must ensure that access to health care is provided to underserved areas and communities and that no one is denied access or left behind. Some of the modern advances in biomedical and information technology such as telemedicine and videoconferences, can enhance our ability to increase access to remote areas. But, high tech medicine also raises the prospect that poor, uninsured, and underinsured people may be left out of costly medical treatments. We need to ensure that high tech medicine is not available only to those who can afford it, and we must find a fair way to allocate scarce health care resources.

The third value that should guide health policy making is the value of mutual obligations, that is, a sense of individual and collective duties and responsibilities. In other words, the right of freedom of choice, self-determination, and the right of access to good health care must be closely aligned with duties and responsibilities on the part of the citizens. Just as citizens have a right to expect health care, freedom of choice, self-determination, and participation in democratic decision making in health care, they also have a duty and an obligation to family, community, and society. This means that as patients and potential patients citizens have a responsibility to examine their own lives, to modify their own habits and behavior, and make every effort to live a healthy lifestyle. For example, citizens who view smoking as an issue of freedom of choice and individual rights also have the duty and the responsibility to think about the consequences of their choices and the demands it places on use and allocation of health care resources.

The fourth value that should guide health care policy making is that we should treat health care not as private good but rather as a social or public good. This means placing more emphasis on community health. We need to recognize that our sometimes lopsided concern with individual rights can undermine the capacity of communities to provide for the collective well-being of its members. The reaction to the value of paternalism that was dominant in the health care system of the early twentieth century in the United States was to move in the direction of individual rights in the 1960s. As many communitarians have argued, this often has led to an excessive emphasis on individual rights and an exclusion of consideration of community values or values of common good in debates over health care policies and health care reforms. What is needed is to strike a balance between the values of individual rights, freedom of choice, and self-determination on one hand and the values of social or public good, that is, community good, on the other hand. It is important to keep in mind that while conflicts between individual good and community good often produce a great deal of tension, it is important that we explicitly recognize these conflicts in our deliberation over health care policies and find a way to resolve them.

The fifth value that should guide health care policy making is that health care policy must focus on creating and maintaining a healthy society. This means that a greater emphasis must be placed on preventive care. Despite a great deal of rhetoric about prevention, we continue to pay lip service to the value of prevention. One simple reason for putting emphasis on preventive care is that preventiing illness and disease is much cheaper than treating and curing them. True prevention will require not just training physicians in appropriate use of behavior modification of their patients but a broad educational effort at the community level that encourages citizens to engage in activities and lifestyles that prevent illnesses and produce positive health outcomes. This also requires a much stronger integration of public health services with medicine (Mechanic 1993). Government must allocate more resources for educational programs in the areas of prevention and nutrition. Medical schools also must produce more primary care physicians and as a society we must find ways to make primary care a more attractive and rewarding field to medical students. The health care system must balance the "curative" model of health care that has dominated American medicine with the "preventive" model of health care by putting more emphasis on prevention of illnesses and maintaining good health. The emphasis that is placed on the health care of the individual in our current system must be complemented by emphasis on the health status of the community or the nation as a whole. There are many environmental and lifestyle variables that are directly linked to certain health maladies and illnesses. Health care policies must address problems of illnesses caused by environmental factors and lifestyle choices.

A holistic approach to caring for patients should be the sixth value that guides health care policy making. America's health care system must move away from the "biological" model in which patients are viewed as organic systems to be manipulated and corrected when some parts break down to treating patients as a whole person that takes into consideration their cultural values, spiritual needs, and psychological well-being. The biological model of medicine leads to treating patients in a compartmentalized fashion rather than as a whole person. The science of medicine must be tempered with the art of healing.

Finally, we must make changes in the education and training of medical students to provide them with the tools necessary for the twenty-first century. At a minimum, this means that medical schools must produce physicians who have adopted the above mentioned values in their practice. It means that physicians must restore a sense of public service as the highest motive in the medical profession, reassert their professional autonomy, and become effective advocates for their patients' health and well-being.

The values we have outlined to guide health care policy making are presented as guideposts and not as precise scientific principles, and they are not necessarily based on any hard empirical evidence. We realize, for example, that the concept of human dignity is not easy to define, that there are certain inherent conflicts between individual good and the public good or between individual rights, duties, and responsibilities, and that trying to strike a balance between competing values is very complex and difficult. Just as in medicine, we do not have any magical formulas that can tell us exactly where and how to strike a perfect balance between conflicting values in formulating public policies. There are plenty of disagreements among philosophers, bioethicists, social scientists, and health care professionals over most of the issues and controversies we have addressed in this book. The values we have outlined are an important part of health care policy making and are meant to be a small piece of a larger mosaic that includes politics, compromises, bargaining, and consensus building. Policy making will never completely be a precise science of objective intellectual exercise driven by hard empirical evidence, although empirical evidence certainly should inform and enlighten policy makers. In politics, the science of policy making is always mitigated by the art of policy making. Policy making is often driven by certain underlying values either implicitly or explicitly. This is clearly reflected in the fact that even though Americans in general are enthusiastic supporters of technological advances and believe that science and technology can solve any problem, their response to policy questions on issues such as the right to die, organ transplants, and cloning, is influenced by their religious, moral, cultural, and political values. This is also clearly reflected in the public controversy over federal funding for embryonic stem cells research and President George W. Bush's policy response. This was as much a political as ethical and scientific response to strike a balance between competing and conflicting values. As we confront health care policy making in an age of new technologies, we hope that the values underlying various policy options and alternatives are at the forefront of discussion, debate, and deliberation by policy makers as well as by the general public.

Study Question

1. Discuss the transformation of the U.S. health care system in the twentieth century. What philosophy should guide the U.S. health care system?

Appendix A
Web Sites

This appendix lists Web sites of various organizations, advocacy groups, and government agencies that are involved in issues that are addressed in this book. Needless to say, the list is not comprehensive and by necessity selective. We hope that students and readers who are interested in these issues will find the list a helpful resource in obtaining additional information. We have made every effort to make this as up to date as possible. However, Web site addresses change often.

Biomedical Technologies and Ethics

Center for Bioethics and Human Dignity
http://www.bioethix.org
The Center for Bioethics and Human Dignity helps individuals and organizations deal with the bioethical challenges of our day, including managed care, end of life treatment, genetic intervention, euthanasia and suicide, and reproductive technologies. The center has a tax-exempt, not-for-profit status and is supported by gifts and grants from individuals, corporations, and foundations. The center produces a wide range of live, recorded, and written resources examining bioethical issues. The center also explores the potential contribution of religious values in Western culture as part of its work.

Georgetown University, Kennedy Institute of Ethics
http://www.georgetown.edu/research/kie/
The Joseph P. and Rose F. Kennedy Institute of Ethics, established at Georgetown University in 1971, is a teaching and research center offering ethical perspectives on major policy issues. It is devoted to research and teaching in biomedical ethics and other areas of applied ethics. The institute

also houses the most extensive library of ethics in the world, the National Reference Center for Bioethics Literature; produces BIOETHICSLINE®, an online medical ethics database; and conducts regular seminars and courses in bioethics.

University of Minnesota: Center for Bioethics
http://www.bioethics.umn.edu
The mission of the Center for Bioethics is to advance and disseminate knowledge concerning ethical issues in health care and the life sciences. The center conducts original interdisciplinary research, offers educational programs and courses, fosters public discussion and debate through community outreach activities, and assists in the formulation of public policy.

Pro Right-to-Die/Euthanasia Organizations

Compassion in Dying Federation
http://www.CompassionInDying.org
According to the Compassion In Dying Federation its mission is to provide national leadership for client services, legal advocacy, and public education to improve pain and symptom management, increase patient empowerment and self-determination, and expand end of life choices to include aid in dying for terminally ill, mentally competent adults. This organization works toward improved care and expanded options at life's end, with the goals of comprehensive, effective comfort care for every dying person, and legal and humane aid in dying if suffering is unbearable and cannot be relieved.

Euthanasia Research & Guidance Organization (ERGO)
http://www.FinalExit.org
The Euthanasia Research & Guidance Organization (ERGO), a nonprofit educational corporation based in Oregon, was founded in 1993. Its mission is to improve the quality of background research of assisted dying for persons who are terminally or hopelessly ill and wish to end their suffering. It conducts opinion polls as well as develops and publishes ethical, psychological, and legal guidelines for patients and physicians to help them prepare for making life ending decisions.

Hemlock Society USA
http://www.hemlock.org/hemlock
The Hemlock Society is the oldest and largest right to die organization in the United States, founded in 1980 by Derek Humphry, and is a not-for-

profit organization. The Hemlock Foundation funds the educational and charitable parts of the Hemlock operation. The Patients' Rights Organization (PRO-USA) is the legislative arm of the Hemlock Society. Its funds go directly into legislative efforts to change the law in favor of the right to die.

Death with Dignity National Center

http://www.deathwithdignity.org

The mission of the Death with Dignity National Center is to expand end of life choices and advance the legalization of physician aid in dying. Its main objectives are to encourage broader, more informed public discussion of end of life issues, facilitate consensus building among groups seeking better care for terminally ill patients, and promote more open, responsive policies in the United States.

Anti-Euthanasia Organizations

International Task Force on Euthanasia and Assisted Suicide

http://www.iaetf.org

The International Task Force on Euthanasia and Assisted Suicide concentrates solely on issues surrounding assisted suicide and euthanasia and addresses these issues from a public policy perspective. The goal of the task force is to influence the assisted suicide and euthanasia debate so that a patient's right to receive care and compassion will not be replaced by a doctor's right to prescribe poison or administer lethal injections.

Euthanasia.Com

http://www.euthanasia.com

This site provides information for research on euthanasia, physician-assisted suicide, living wills, and mercy killing. The group is committed to the fundamental belief that the direct killing of another person is wrong.

Compassionate HealthCare Network

http://www.chninternational.com

The Compassionate HealthCare Network (CHN) was formed in 1992. It promotes "aid in living" and opposes euthanasia by actively defending the inherent value of all human life. CHN's work is international, and comprises a network of people who provide speakers and workshops; research data pertaining to euthanasia, assisted suicide, palliative care, advance directives (living wills and protective medical documents); and videos to professionals, students, churches, the government, lay organizations, and individuals.

Citizens United Resisting Euthanasia (CURE)

http://home.netcom.com/~cureltd/

Citizens United Resisting Euthanasia (CURE), Ltd., founded in 1981, is a grassroots advocacy network that defends the rights of patients to receive medical treatment, particularly when care is critical. It is a nationwide coalition of concerned citizens of diverse professional, political, and religious backgrounds who oppose euthanasia.

Organ Donations/Procurement/Transplants

U.S. Department of Health and Human Services: Organ Donations/Transplants

http://www.organdonor.gov

This Web site provides information about organ donor cards, frequently asked questions, legislative updates, facts and statistics on organ donations and transplants, and lists and addresses of organ procurement organizations, professional health organizations, voluntary health organizations, organ and tissue organizations, transplant network organizations, and government agencies.

United Network for Organ Sharing

http://www.unos.org/frame_Default.asp

The United Network for Organ Sharing (UNOS) is a nonprofit charitable organization that provides a nationwide umbrella for the transplant community. It maintains the nation's organ transplant waiting list under contract with the Health Resources and Services Administration of the U.S. Department of Health and Human Services. Its mission is to advance organ availability and transplantation by uniting and supporting its communities for the benefit of patients through education, technology, and policy development.

Organ Watch: University of California, Berkeley

http://sunsite.berkeley.edu/biotech/organswatch/index.html

Organ Watch is an independent, human rights oriented documentation center that tracks global rumors on organs; issues reports to the media and national and international medical societies; and investigates individual complaints and allegations of organ stealing, organ trafficking, corruption of transplant waiting lists, violations of the human and medical rights of the nearly dead, mutilation of bodies of pauperized dead, and violations of national regulations and international codes on removing and allocating organs for transplantation.

The Web site contains links to information about policy, laws, and medical and science ethics as they relate to organ transplants, including material on topics such as living donations, forced donations, degrees of relatedness, incarcerated donors, sales, and brain death.

Privacy and Confidentiality of Medical Records

Electronic Privacy Information Center (EPIC)
http://www.epic.org/privacy/medical/
EPIC is a public interest research center in Washington, DC, established in 1994. Its main objective is to focus public attention on emerging civil liberties issues and to protect privacy, the First Amendment, and constitutional values. EPIC works in association with Privacy International, an international human rights group based in London, UK and also is a member of Global Internet Liberty Campaign, Internet Free Expression Alliance, Internet Privacy Coalition, Internet Democracy Project, and Trans Atlantic Consumer Dialogue.

Privacy Rights Clearinghouse
http://www.privacyrights.org/index.htm
The Privacy Rights Clearinghouse (PRC) is a nonprofit consumer information and advocacy program that offers a unique opportunity to learn how to protect personal privacy. The PRC is a project of the Utility Consumers' Action Network (UCAN), a San Diego based nonprofit membership organization which advocates for consumers' interests vis-a-vis telecommunications, energy, and the Internet. The PRC was established in 1992 with funding from the Telecommunications Education Trust, a program of the California Public Utilities Commission. From 1992 through October 1996, the PRC was administered by the Center for Public Interest Law of the University of San Diego School of Law.

U.S. Department of Health and Human Services:
Office of Civil Rights
http://www.hhs.gov/ocr/hipaa/
This Web site provides information about relevant rules and laws dealing with issues of privacy of medical records and health information. It also provides links to relevant resources in this area.

Citizens Council on Health Care: Medical Privacy
http://www.cchc-mn.org/privacy.php3
The mission of the Citizens Council on Health Care is to analyze the impact of current and proposed policy on health care access, and to define and support market-based alternatives to health care rationing. The Web site provides links to issues related to privacy and confidentiality of medical records.

Lawrence Berkeley National Laboratory's Project:
Ethical, Legal and Social Issues in Science (ELSI in Science):
Personal Privacy and Access to Medical Data Bases
http://www.lbl.gov/Education/ELSI/privacy-main.html
This site provides information about advantages and disadvantages of medical records data bases, who has access, the role of the government, and how to keep medical records and information private.

American Civil Liberties Union
http://www.aclu.org/
Look for issues of privacy and civil liberties.

Genetic Research and Cloning
National Center for Genome Resources
http://www.ncgr.org
The National Center for Genome Resources links scientists to innovative solutions in bioinformatics—through collaborations, data management, and creative software development. NCGR is a nonprofit research organization in Santa Fe, New Mexico.

Health Hippo: Research Integrity and Bioethics
http://hippo.findlaw.com/hippores.html
This site provides the latest information regarding legislations, federal regulations, and federal funding for genetics research and cloning, and provides links to other resources.

Center for Human Genome Studies: Los Alamos National
Laboratory
http://www-ls.lanl.gov/index.html
The CHGS at Los Alamos National Laboratory was established in 1988 as part of the Human Genome Project. The center's goals include high quality DNA sequencing, assembly of complete high resolution maps of chromosome 16 and regions of chromosome 5, studies at the molecular level of chromosome structure and function, and isolation of selected genes of interest. In January 1997 the CHGS became part of the Joint Genome Institute (JGI), is a merging of LLNL, LANL, and LBNL's Human Genome Centers into one organization.

U.S. Department of Energy: Human Genome Project: U.S.
http://www.ornl.gov/hgmis/
Begun in 1990, the U.S. Human Genome Project is coordinated by the U.S. Department of Energy and the National Institutes of Health. Project goals

are to identify all the genes in human DNA; determine the sequences of the 3 billion chemical base pairs that make up human DNA; store this information in databases; improve tools for data analysis; transfer related technologies to the private sector; and address the ethical, legal, and social issues (ELSI) that may arise from the project.

National Bioethics Advisory Commission

http://bioethics.gov/nbac.html
The commission was established by an executive order issued by President Bill Clinton in 1995. The commission is comprised of not more than fifteen members appointed by the president. The commission is charged with the responsibility of providing advice and recommendations to the national Science and Technology Council and to other government agencies about government programs, policies, and regulations as they relate to bioethical issues arising from research on human biology and behavior and clinical applications.

The National Human Genome Institute

http://www.nhgri.nih.gov
The National Human Genome Research Institute (NHGRI) was originally established in 1989 as the National Center for Human Genome Research. Its mission is to head the Human Genome Project for the National Institutes of Health (NIH). NHGRI is one of twenty-four institutes, centers, or divisions that make up the NIH, the federal government's primary agency for the support of biomedical research. The collective research components of the NIH make up the largest biomedical research facility in the world. NIH is part of the U.S. Department of Health and Human Services.

Patients' Rights

American Hospital Association: Resource Center

http://www.aha.org/resource/pbillofrights.asp
The American Hospital Association (AHA) presents a patients' bill of rights hoping to contribute to more effective patient care and be supported by the hospital on behalf of the institution, its medical staff, employees, and patients. The AHA encourages health care institutions to tailor this bill of rights to their patient community by translating and/or simplifying the language as necessary to ensure that patients and their families understand their rights and responsibilities.

Patient's Access Coalition

http://home.patientaccess.com/pac/
The Patient Access Coalition is a group of national patient and medical services provider organizations dedicated to ensuring that the focus of health

care be on patients and the quality of their medical care. The coalition works to ensure that people who choose managed care are guaranteed timely access to specialty care at a reasonable cost.

International Alliance of Patients Organizations
http://www.iapo-pts.org.uk
The mission of the organizations is to help build health care services with patients at the center in every country by advocating internationally with a strong patients' voice on all aspects of health care policy; realizing active partnerships with patients' organizations and other key players; and maximizing the impact of patients' organizations through capacity building.

Hospice Patients' Alliance
http://www.hospicepatients.org
The Hospice Patients Alliance was formed in August of 1998 as a nonprofit charitable organization and is a 501(c)(3) corporation serving the general public throughout the United States. The organization protects the rights of patients, their families and caregivers, the bereaved, and staff by providing information about the standards of care governing the health care provided, the services required to be provided by law, standard industry practices, and how to obtain the very best hospice care available.

Cloning

Human Cloning Foundation
http://www.humancloning.org
The objective of the nonprofit Human Cloning Foundation is to promote human cloning and other forms of biotechnology. The HCF believes that cloning technology can be used to cure diseases and prolong life. It further believes that blood can be cloned, organs can be cloned, and that infertility can be cured with the use of this new technology.

Roslin Institute, Edinburgh, UK
http://www.roslin.ac.uk
Roslin Institute is one of the world's leading centers for research on farm and other animals. It has internationally recognized programs on molecular and quantitative genetics, genomics, early development, reproduction, animal behavior and welfare, and has pioneered methods for the genetic modification and cloning of farm animals.

Appendix B
Films and Videos

Many of these films and videos can be obtained from Fanlight Productions (www.fanlight.com) and First Run Icarus Films (www.frif.com).

Genetic Medicine

Brain Candy
This is an 89-minute movie made in 1996 that has some relationship to health research. The premise of this farce is that a researcher for a drug company discovers a drug that makes people happy and quickly becomes profitable for the company. Unfortunately, it has a side effect: it makes the drug user comatose. The movie then follows the attempt of the researcher to get the company to stop making the drug. It raises questions about the profit motive of pharmaceutical companies versus what is in the public interest. In that sense, it relates to genetic research.
Paramount Pictures

The Burden of Knowledge
This documentary deals with genetic screening's capacity to find genetic defects prior to birth. The question is what to do with the knowledge of genetic birth defects. Should we let medical science decide who gets to live? What responsibility do the parents or government have? Is too much knowledge not good for us?
Fanlight Productions (www.fanlight.com)

Extreme Measures
This is a 118-minute film made in 1997 that includes a section on medical research. A doctor is attempting experiments to regenerate nerve tissue; his "subjects" are homeless people. The doctor justifies the unethical nature of the research (he clearly does not have the consent of the research subjects) on the grounds that the potential benefits to society are enormous. This parallels accusations made by right to life advocates that research on embryonic

stem cells is done, first of all, without their permission, and, second, results in the deaths of the embryos.

It raises questions about informed consent for medical research and whether embryos are humans and thus subject to the same protections as other humans.

Columbia Pictures

Gattaca

This 107-minute film made in 1997 is about a futuristic society that makes use of genetic engineering to produce genetically perfect children. There is a genetic underclass that is kept at the lower levels of society. One of them seeks to become an astronaut and he eventually succeeds. There is considerable genetic testing to screen out "flawed" people. This raises questions mentioned in Chapter 4 of this book about the eugenics movement. Eugenics is the dark side of genetics research. Should society allow this kind of genetic engineering? What do we do with the "flawed" people? There are right-to-life issues here.

Columbia Pictures

Homo Sapiens 1900

This 1999 documentary looks at the birth of the eugenics movement, which included sterilization laws in the United States and its applications in Nazi Germany and Stalinist Soviet Union. Eugenics predates the genome project, but it raises chilling questions about government's ability to determine who shall live and who shall die. To what extent do we want government to make those kinds of decisions? At the same time, should parents have the right to decide not to continue a pregnancy if it has been determined through genetic screening and counseling that the baby would be seriously deformed? Should the state have the right to tell the parents that they should not or cannot have the baby? And, if the baby is born, who will pay for its care?

First Run Icarus Films (www.frfi.com)

No Ordinary Baby

This 2001 made for TV movie on the Lifetime channel concerns a couple having trouble reproducing. Their doctor helps by cloning them and implanting the embryo into the mother. The parents and doctor try to keep secret the story of the world's first cloned baby. As discussed in Chapter 4, a number of nations, including the United States have banned cloning. What is the nature of life? Is a cloned person qualitatively different from a noncloned person? Why would someone want to be cloned or have a relative cloned?

Organ Transplants

A Heart for Jo

This short documentary, made in 1996, examines the attempt of a mother to get a heart and lung transplant for her 13-year-old daughter who has Down syndrome. The story takes place in Great Britain and Jo is denied a place on the list because of her disease, the shortage of organs, and so forth. During the course of her quest, Jo's mother meets an American woman with Down syndrome who had the operation and thrived. This video raises an interesting question about quality of life. Because Jo has a genetic condition, she is not on the list for organ transplants and this is combined with a shortage of organs. Should Jo be denied because of Down syndrome? What criteria should be used in making these kinds of rationing decisions?

Patients' Rights

As Good As It Gets

This widely acclaimed film about the romance of a successful writer with severe anxiety problems (not to mention a bad personality) and a waitress has been noted for its attack on health maintenance organizations (HMOs). The waitress has a son with severe allergies. She belongs to an HMO, but he isn't getting treatment. The writer wants to date the waitress and go on a trip with her, but she doesn't want to leave her son. The writer arranges (and pays) for a physician to come to the waitress's house (and it has been a very long time since doctors did that), examine the boy, set him up for tests, and arrange for treatment of the allergies. In the course of the examination and discussion with the doctor, the waitress (played by Helen Hunt) launches into a tirade against HMOs using very bad language. She then apologizes to the doctor, who laughs and says he thinks that is HMO's official name. Audiences loved that scene.

Rainmaker

This film, based on the book by John Grisham, is about a lawyer retained by a woman whose son is suffering from leukemia. The mother would like bone marrow treatment for her son, but the health insurance company, viewing the treatment as still in the experimental stages, refuses to cover it. The son dies and the mother sues the company. Her lawyer wins the case and the company declares bankruptcy. Should all available treatments be given to those who want them? Should insurance companies, or managed care plans, or employers decide who gets what services? Should those decisions be left to providers and patients?

Privacy

Banking Our Genes

This documentary crosses over into the genetics area. It discusses preventive medicine based on understanding our genetic makeup. But in the absence of regulation, there is the possibility that such information may be mishandled, thus raising privacy issues. What kind of control should we have over our genetic information? Do we lose that control forever in the name of science?

Fanlight Productions (www.fanlight.com)

Rationing

Dreams and Dilemmas

This documentary looks at neonatal medicine and premature infants. Neonatal intensive care is very expensive and the survivors often have severe health problems. The technology has developed dramatically, but the costs crowd out other kinds of health and medical needs. This issue also relates to right to life movements.

Right to Die

A Fate Worse Than Death

This documentary looks at decisions about whether to withdraw life support from a family member who is in a coma. The documentary discusses durable powers of attorney and living wills.

Bringing Out the Dead

This 101-minute movie made in 1991 follows the life of an emergency medical technician (EMT) in a poor section of Manhattan. At the end of the movie the EMT takes tubes out of a patient who he thinks wants to die but has been resuscitated fourteen times that day. This movie raises questions about the right to die, in this case a patient on life-sustaining technologies appears to want to die and the EMT makes his own determination that this is what the patient wants. Should the EMT or any other health provider have the right to make this kind of inferential decision? Where should government come in? For example, should the EMT be arrested for murder?

Paramount Pictures

Caring at the End of Life

This is a documentary about nurses dealing with six terminally ill patients. It raises questions such as when to end life-sustaining treatments and the role of technology in sustaining life. Are we letting technology control our decisions about how long to keep people living? How much autonomy should we give people in letting them make these kinds of decisions?

Fanlight Productions (www.fanlight.com)

Dax's Case

This is a 60-minute video made in 1985 about Donald "Dax" Cowart, who was suffering from severe burns over most of his body and wanted to end his suffering. Like the other films and videos in this section, it raises the question of whether someone has the right to end his or her own life. This case is different from some of the others because Dax was alert. His intent was clear, unlike Cruzan and Quinlan, and he was greatly suffering. Does he have the right to end his suffering? Does government have a compelling state interest in preserving a life, even given the suffering?

Available from Concern for Dying, 250 West 57th St., New York, NY

Death on Request

This documentary focuses on a Dutch man suffering from Lou Gehrig's disease (ALS) and the decision by the patient and his wife to seek euthanasia to end his suffering. The documentary shows the death of the patient as being very peaceful. This film raises the question of quality of life for a person who is suffering from a fatal disease. In this case the person is still aware and capable of making his decision.

First Run Icarus Films (www.frif.com)

Help Me Die

This documentary focuses on euthanasia. The emphasis is on personal rights and responsibilities as loved ones may want to end their pain or be allowed to die with dignity.

On Our Own Terms: Bill Moyers on Dying in America

This four-part series was made in 2000. As the title indicates, the series looks at the right to die movement in the United States, a movement which advocates patients' control over their destiny. Interest groups in the United States have had an enormous impact on public policy and life in general. Here is one that advocates control over one of life's most important decisions. Like many of the other films and videos in this section, it raises questions about government's role in this most personal of decisions and personal autonomy at a time when we have so little control over our own lives.

Fanlight Productions (www.fanlight.com)

The Switch

This 1993 made for television movie is about a motorcycle rider who becomes paraplegic. After a while he decides he no longer wants to live and asks a disc jockey he has befriended to pull the switch that would turn off the life-sustaining equipment. He sues the state of Georgia arguing that he has the right to control his own life-support system. Like many of the others, this movie questions the right of government to decide who shall live and who shall die.

The Vanishing Line

This 52-minute documentary made in 1998 follows a doctor who learns that the process of dying can be worse than death. Prolonging life when death is imminent can be painful. The documentary talks about a good death. This is similar to an episode of the television series *Northern Exposure*, where the doctor (the key character of the series) goes deer hunting with his friends to see what it is like. He shoots a deer, but the shot does not kill the deer right away. His companions tell him that he has to finish the task and end the suffering of the deer. The doctor's summary was that he could accept death, but it was the dying that got to him. Is dying worse than death? Should life be sustained no matter what?

First Run Icarus Films (www.frif.com)

She's Finally Free: Living with the Tragic Loss of Nancy Cruzan

This is a 25-minute video made in 1993 that tells the story of Nancy Cruzan who was in a car wreck in 1983 that left her in a permanent vegetative state. Here parents sought to have her removed from life-sustaining machines and the effort took eight years, gaining national attention. The major questions addressed in the Nancy Cruzan case are whether a person has the right to die, whether the relatives of someone in a permanently comatose state has the right to ask that life-sustaining technology be removed, and what interest government (the state) has in preserving life in these circumstances.

Available through the University of Akron audio-visual services.

Self-Deliverance

This short documentary is about a patient wishing to terminate his life to end his pain. He no longer wants to use drugs or machines to keep him alive. The patient looks for a hospice or doctor to help him, at the same time seeking ways of taking his own life. A unique aspect of this documentary is that the legislature of the Northern Territory of Australia was debating a bill that would guarantee such a patient the right to physician-assisted suicide. Why do different countries and even different regions within countries have different laws and customs related to dying and right to die? Should we train physicians to make these kinds of decisions?

Fanlight Productions (www.fanlight.com)

Soft Fruit

This is a 101-minute film made in 2000. Patsy is dying of cancer and wants to stop taking chemotherapy. A comedy-drama, the film concerns how Patsy and her family deal with Patsy's desire to end her life, including helping her enjoy what time she has left. Patsy decides to stop the chemotherapy. Patsy's decision is different from some of the others. Her decision to stop the chemotherapy is one that she takes without any medical personnel having to take action. But she is still effectively exercising her right to die. Why is this different from, say Dax's case or the Cruzan/Quinlan cases?

20th Century Fox

To Choose No Harm

One of the first things doctors are taught is "do no harm." This documentary deals with the wishes of terminally ill patients to die and their families' desire to go along with the patient and the conflict with doctors dedicated to keeping their patients alive. Should we change the education that doctors receive so they will be more willing to go along with patients' desires to end life?

Fanlight Productions (www.fanlight.com)

The Way We Die

This documentary deals with terminally ill patients, their families, and medical caregivers. The documentary shows how families and caregivers help patients, what the illnesses mean and do to the families, and shows the importance of helping patients remain alive even as they are dying. Isn't dying a normal part of living? Are there ways we can prepare ourselves better for the death of our loved ones and our deaths?

Fanlight Productions (www.fanlight.com)

Whose Life Is It Anyway?

This 120-minute film made in 1981 focuses on a sculptor who is hurt in a car accident and becomes paraplegic. Unable to continue his art, he seeks to get out of the hospital and die. The medical director of the hospital believes in the value and sanctity of life and tries to thwart the sculptor by getting him committed as depressed (who wouldn't be?). At a hearing, a judge decides he is not clinically depressed and allows him to refuse treatment. As with other films and videos mentioned here, does government have a compelling interest in preserving life, even if the person wants to die? What makes this case interesting is that patient is not dying and is not physically suffering. But he cannot continue his work. Does this change the circumstances compared to the Dax and Cruzan/Quinlan cases?

MGM Pictures

References

References to Chapter 1

Aday, Lu Ann. 1993. "Equity, Accessibility, and Ethical Issues: Is the U.S. Health Care Reform Debate Asking the Right Questions?" *American Behavioral Scientist* 36, no. 6 (July–August): 724–741.

"Artificial Eyes, Turbine Hearts." 2000. *Business Week*, no. 3673 (March 20): 72.

Beauchamp, Dan E. 1988. *The Health of the Republic: Epidemics, Medicine, and Moralism as Challenges to Democracy.* Philadelphia: Temple University Press.

Bellah, Robert N.; Madsen, Richard; Sullivan, William M.; Swidler, Ann; and Tipton, Steven M. 1991. *The Good Society.* New York: Alfred A. Knopf.

———. 1985. *Habits of the Heart: Individualism and Commitment in American Life.* Berkeley: University of California Press.

Berra, Yogi. 1998. *The Yogi Book: I Really Didn't Say Everything I Said.* New York: Workman Publishers.

Bezold, Clement. 1996. "Your Health in 2010: Four Scenarios." *Futurist* 30, no. 5 (September–October): 35–40.

Bloche, Greg M. 1998. "Rights and Efficiency in American Health Law." *Human Rights: Journal of the Section of Human Rights & Responsibilities* 25, no. 4 (Fall): 19–20.

Bouchard, Charles. 1995. "Person's Dignity Comes First in Health Care." *St. Louis Business Journal* 15, no. 49 (August 21): 391.

Brown, David. 1999. "Is There a Doctor Online?" *Washington Post Weekly Edition* 16, no. 44 (April 30): 67.

Burtonwood, Neil. 1998. "Liberalism and Communitarianism: A Response to Two Recent Attempts to Reconcile Individual Autonomy with Group Identity." *Educational Studies* 24, no. 3 (November): 295–305.

Callahan, Daniel. 1998. *False Hopes: Why America's Quest for Perfect Health Is a Recipe for Failure.* New York: Simon and Schuster.

———. 1990. *What Kind of Life: The Limits of Medical Progress.* Washington, DC: Georgetown University Press.

Cassel, Christine; Doughtery, Charles; Etzioni, Amitai; Evarts, McCollister, C.; Griffith, John; Cherry, Christopher. 1997. "Health Care, Human Worth and the Limits of the Particular." *Journal of Medical Ethics* 23, no. 5 (October): 310–315.

Cole, Wendy. 1999. "Seed of Controversy." *Time* 153, no. 1 (January 11): 77.

Colen, B.D. 1996. "Organ Concert." *Time* special issue 148, no. 14 (Fall): 70–74.

Coughlin, Richard M. 1996. "Whose Morality? Which Community? What Interests? Socio-Economic and Communitarian Perspectives." *Journal of Socio-Economics* 25, no. 2 (Summer): 136–157.

Cowley, Geoffrey, and Underwood, Anne. 2001. "New Heart, New Hope: Does This Tangled Knot of Titanium and Plastic Represent the Future of Cardiac Medicine?" *Newsweek* (July 25): 42–48.

———. 1997–1998. "Surgeon, Drop That Scalpel." *Newsweek*, 130, no. 24a (Winter): 77–78.

Daniels, Norman. 1985. *Just Health Care.* Cambridge: Cambridge University Press.

Dix, Anne. 1994. "New Values." *Hospital Development* 26, no. 1 (January): 11–12.

Dossetor, John B. 1997. "Human Values in Health Care: Trying to Get It Right." *Canadian Medical Association Journal* 157, no. 12 (December 15): 1689–1690.

Dougherty, Charles. 1992. "Ethical Values in Health Care Reform." *Journal of the American Medical Association* 268, no. 17 (November 4): 2409–2413.

———. 1988. *American Health Care: Realities, Rights, and Reforms.* New York: Oxford University Press.

Etzioni, Amitai. 1999."Medical Privacy in the Cyber-Age." *The Long Term View: A Journal of Informed Opinion* 4, no. 4 (Fall): 68–85.

———. 1996. *The New Golden Rule: Community and Morality in a Democratic Society.* New York: Basic Books.

———. 1993. *The Spirit of Community: The Reinvention of American Society.* New York: Simon and Schuster.

———, ed. 1995. *Rights and the Common Good: The Communitarian Perspective.* New York: St. Martin's Press.

Fletcher, Meg. 1997. "New Technology vs. Cost Control." *Business Insurance* 31, no. 31 (August 4): 21–23.

Fuchs, Victor. 1995. *Who Shall Live? Health, Economic, and Social Change.* New York: Basic Books.

———. 1993. *The Future of Health Policy.* Cambridge, MA: Harvard University Press.

———. 1986. *The Health Economy.* Cambridge, MA: Harvard University Press.

Goldstein, Amy. 1999. "Peeking Into Patients' Records: The Ways Medical Data Can Be Used Can Help—or Harm." *Washington Post Weekly Edition* 16, no. 44 (August 30): 8.

Gorman, Christine. 1999. "Drugs by Design." *Time* 153, no. 1 (January 11): 79–83.

Haste, Helen. 1996. "Communitarianism and the Social Construction of Morality." *Journal of Moral Education* 25, no. 1 (March): 47–55.

Henig, Robin M. 1997. "Medicine's New Age." *Civilization* 4, no. 2 (April–May): 42–49.

Isaacson, Walter. 1999. "The Biotech Century." *Time* 153, no. 1 (January 11): 42–43.

Jaroff, Leon. 1999. "Fixing the Genes." *Time* 153, no. 1 (January 11): 68–73.

———. 1996. "Keys to the Kingdom." *Time* special issue 148, no. 14 (Fall): 24–29.

Jenner, Bruce. 1990. "Grassroots Bioethics Revisited: Health Care Priorities and Community Values." *Hastings Center Report* 20, no. 5 (September–October): 16.

Kavanaugh, John F. 1998. "Ethical Commitments in Health Care System." *America* 179, no. 14 (November 7): 20.

Kevles, Bettyanne. 1997–1998. "Body Imaging." *Newsweek* special issue, 130, no. 24a (Winter): 74–76.

Key, Sandra W., and Marble, Michelle. 1997. "Internet Site Showcases Diagnostic Technology." 1997. *Cancer Weekly Plus* (April 21): 22.

Lamm, Richard D. 1999a. "Public Policy and the Health of the Nation." *Society* 36, no. 3 (March–April): 52–57.

————. 1999b. "Health Care for the New Millennium." *Vital Speeches of the Day* 65, no. 7 (January 15): 198–202.

————. 1993. "New World of Medical Ethics: Our Duty Lies Both to the Individual and the Population." *Vital Speeches of the Day* 59, no. 18 (July 1): 549–554.

Langone, John. 1996. "Challenging the Mainstream." *Time* special issue 148, no. 14 (Fall): 40–43.

Lemonick, Michael D. 1999. "Designer Babies." *Time* 153, no. 1 (January 11): 64–65.

Lloyd, John. 1997. "Profile: Amitai Etzioni." *New Statesman* 126, no. 4339 (June 20): 28–31.

Malinowski, Michael J. 1996. "Capitation, Advances in Medical Technology, and the Advent of a New Era in Medical Ethics." *American Journal of Law & Medicine* 22, no. 2–3 (Summer–Fall): 331–360.

Marx, Frederick J. 1999. "'E-health' Easing Connection with Health Care Industry." *Boston Business Journal* 19, no. 32 (September 17): 9.

McClellan, Mark. 1996. "Are the Returns to Technological Change in Health Care Declining?" *Proceedings of the National Academy of Sciences of the United States* 93, no. 23 (November 12): 12701–12708.

McCormick, Richard A. 1999. "Bioethics: A Moral Vacuum?" *America* 180, no. 15 (May 1): 8.

————. 1993. "Value Variable in the Health Care Reform Debate." *America* 168, no. 19 (May 29): 7.

McLaughlin, Linda A., and Braun, Kathryn L. 1998. "Asian and Pacific Islander Cultural Values: Considerations for Health Care Decision Making." *Health and Social Work* 23, no. 2 (May): 116–127.

Mellen, Sue. "Health Care Enters Cyber-Age with High-Tech 'Smart Card.'" *Boston Business Journal* 19, no. 32 (September 17): 7–8.

Menduno, Michael. 2000. "Virtual ER." *Hospital and Health Networks* 74, no. 1 (January): 20.

Miringoff, Marc, and Miringoff, Marque-Luisa. 1999. *The Social Health of the Nation: How America Is Really Doing.* New York: Oxford University Press.

————. 1995. "America's Social Health: The Nation's Need to Know." *Challenge* 38, no. 5 (September–October): 612–618.

Moukheiber, Zina. 2000. "Dr. Robot: Virtual Reality Is Set to Transform the Field of Cardiac Surgery. Welcome to Nintendo Medicine." *Forbes* 165, no. 6 (March 6): 159.

Mulhall, S., and Swift, A. 1992. *Liberals and Communitarianism.* Cambridge, MA: Blackwell.

Narain, Kamna R. 1997. "Medical Technology: Silicon Valley Leads Quest for Cost-Effective Quality." *Business Journal Serving San Jose & Silicon Valley* 14, no. 34 (January): 54–59.

Nelson, James L.; Osterweis, Mariana; and Wikler, Daniel. 1993. *Core Values in Health Care Reform: A Communitarian Approach.* Washington, DC: The Communitarian Network.

Newhouse, Joseph P. 1993. "An Inconclusive View of Health Cost Containment." *Health Affairs* 12 supplemental issue, (September): 152–171.

Newman, Otto, and De Zoysa, Richard. 1997. "Communitarianism: The New Panacea?" *Sociological Perspectives* 40, no. 4: 623–639.

Nitzkin, Joel L. 1996. "Technology and Health Care: Driving Costs Up, Not Down." *Technology and Society Magazine* 15, no. 3 (Fall): 40–45.

Nozick, Robert. 1974. *Anarchy, State, and Utopia.* New York: Basic Books.

Nuland, Sherwin B. 1996. "An Epidemic of Discovery." *Time* 148, no. 14 (Fall): 8–13.

"The Quest for an Artificial Heart." 2001. *New York Times*, July 4, p. A14.

Rawls, John. 1971. *A Theory of Justice.* Oxford: Oxford University Press.

Ruark, Jennifer. 1999. "Redefining the Good Life: A New Focus in the Social Sciences." *The Chronicle of Higher Education* 45, no. 23 (February): A13–A15.

Sandel, Michael J. 1996. *Democracy's Discontent: America in Search of a Public Philosophy.* Cambridge: MA: Belknap Press of Harvard University Press.

Schwartz, Peter. 1996. *The Art of Long View: Paths to Strategic Insight for Yourself and Your Company.* New York: Currency/Doubleday.

Schwartz, W.B. 1987. "The Inevitable Failure of Current Cost-Containment Strategies: Why They Can Provide Only Temporary Relief." *Journal of American Medical Association* 257 (January 9): 220–241.

Schilcher, Bernd. 1999. "Etzioni's New Theory: A Synthesis of Liberal and Communitarian Views." *Journal of Socio-Economics* 28, no. 4: 429–439.

Selznick, Philip. 1995. "Thinking about Community: Ten Theses." *Society* 32, no. 5 (July–August): 33–38.

Shafer-Landau, Russ. 1994. "Health Care and Human Values." *Humanities* 15, no. 5 (September–October): 32–33.

Sheppard, Robert. 2000. "Robotic Surgery and Biosensors: Breathtaking Developments in Medical Technology Are About to Change the Face of Diagnostic and Treatment." *Maclean's* 113, no. 2 (January 10): 50–53.

Spencer, Peter L. 1995. "Technology Gatekeepers: Cost Control Harms Medical Technology." *Consumer's Research Magazine* 78, no. 7 (July): 43.

Starr, Paul. 1982. *The Social Transformation of American Medicine.* New York: Basic Books.

Stevens, Andrew; Milne, Ruairidh; Lilford, Richard; and Gabbay, John. 1999. "Keeping Pace with New Technologies." *British Medical Journal* 319, no. 7220 (November 13): 1291.

Stevens, Jane Ellen. 1995. "The Growing Reality of Virtual Reality." *Bioscience* 45, no. 7 (July–August): 435–439.

Stolberg, Sheryl G. 2001. Despite Opposition, Three Vow to Pursue Cloning of Humans." *New York Times*, August 8. p. 1.

Strohl, Linda. 1999. "A Look at the Future of Medicine." *USA Weekend*, October 1–3, pp. 6–9.

Tesh, S. 1988. *Hidden Arguments: Political Ideology and Disease Prevention Policy.* New Brunswick, NJ: Rutgers University Press.

Tobias, Randall L. 1996. "Health Care in the Information Age: An Integrated System Wide Approach." *Vital Speeches of the Day* 62, no. 13 (April 15): 411–413.

"Tracking Patients in Cyberspace." 1999. *Best's Review: Life-Health Insurance Edition* 98, no. 4 (August): 82.

Trafford, Abigail. 1985. "Medicine's New Triumphs." *U.S. News & World Report* 99, (November 11): 46–53.

"Universal Declaration of Human Rights." 1997–1998. *Earth Island Journal* 13, no. 1 (Winter): 28–29.

Veatch, Robert. 1981. *A Theory of Medical Ethics.* New York: Basic Books.

Wadman, Meredith. 1997. "High-Level Ethics Committee Needed to Guide Genetics Policy." *Nature* 385, no. 6619 (February 27): 756.

Wallace-Brodeur, P.H. 1990. "Community Values in Vermont Health Planning." *Hastings Center Report* 20, no. 5 (September–October): 18–19.

Walzer, Michael. 1997. *On Toleration.* New Haven: Yale University Press.

Wiese, Calvin. 1999. "Community Health Networks." *Vital Speeches* 65, no. 21 (August 15): 658.

Wilmut, Ian. 1999. "Dolly's False Legacy." *Time* 153, no. 1 (January 11): 74–77.

References to Chapter 2

Adams, Glenn. 2001. "Care for the Dying Focus of Legislative Proposal." Associated Press State and Local wire, March 12.

"Advance Directives: An Update." 1995. *HealthFacts* 20, no. 190 (March): 1.

Ahdar, Rex J. 1996. "Religious Parliamentarians and Euthanasia: A Window into Church and State in New Zealand." *Journal of Church & State* 38, no. 3 (Summer): 569–594.

Alexander, Shana. 1997. "What Makes a Good Death." *Bioethics Forum* 13, no. 1 (Spring): 14.

"Americans Report Strong Support for the Right to Die, Survey Finds." 1997. *Fairfield County Business Journal* 36, no. 17 (April 28): 19.

Aseer, M Adil Al. 1990. "An Islamic Perspective on Terminating Life-Sustaining Measures." In Arthur S. Berger and Joyce Berger, eds., *To Die or Not to Die?* New York: Praeger Publisher, pp. 59–65.

Associated Press. 1997. "Challenge to Oregon's Assisted-Suicide Law Dies in Appeals Court." February 28. Woodlands Communications Inc. [http://www.wcinet.com/th/News/022897/National/48387.htm].

Battin, Margaret P. 2000. "On the Structure of the Euthanasia Debate: Observations Provoked by a Near-Perfect For-and-Against Book." *Journal of Health Politics, Policy, and Law* 25, no. 2 (April): 415–430.

Beeder, David C. 1999. "Assisted Suicide Laws Aren't Likely to Expand Soon." *Omaha World-Herald*, April 4, p. 2m.

Bilimoria, Purushottama. 1995. "Legal Rulings on Suicide in India and Implication for the Right to Die." *Asian Philosophy* 5, no. 2 (October): 159–181.

Birchard, Karen. 2000. "Irish Doctors Oppose Euthanasia Legislation." *Lancet* 355, no. 9217 (May 20): 1800.

Biskupic, Joan. 1997. "Oregon's Assisted-Suicide Law Lives on." *Washington Post*, October 15, p. A03.

Brock, Dan W. 1999. "A Critique of Three Objections to Physician-Assisted Suicide." *Ethics* 109, no. 3 (April): 519–547.

Brown, David. 2000. "A Picture of Assisted Suicide: Most Who Use Oregon Law Are Educated, Insured; Some Change Their Minds." *Washington Post*, February 24, p. A03.

Burnell, George M. 1993. *Final Choices: To Live or to Die in an Age of Medical Technology.* New York: Plenum Press.

Callahan, Daniel. 1997. "What Makes a Good Death." *Bioethics Forum* 13, no. 1 (Spring): 3–4.

Cantor, Norman L. 1993. *Advance Directives and the Pursuit of Death with Dignity.* Bloomington: Indiana University Press.

Cloud, John, and Donnelly, Sally B. 1999. "Painful Debate: Should Congress Prohibit 'Right-to-Die' Measures?" *Time* 154, no. 13 (September 27): 44.

Cohen, Lewis M. 1998. "Suicide, Hastening Death, and Psychiatry." *Archives of Internal Medicine* 158, no. 18 (October 12): 1973–1976.

Cousins, Norman. 1979. *Anatomy of an Illness As Perceived by the Pateint: Reflections on Healing and Regeneration*. New York: A Bantam Book published by W.W. Norton.

DeSpelder, Lynne Ann, and Strickland, Albert Lee. 1992. *The Last Dance: Encountering Death and Dying*. Mountain View, CA: Mayfield Press.

Deutsch, Anthony. 2001. "Dutch Legalize Euthanasia: Measure Is a First for a Country, Has Strict Code." *Boston Globe*, April 11, A9.

Doukas, David J., and Reichel, William. 1993. *Planning for Uncertainty: A Guide to Living Wills and Other Advance Directives for Health Care*. Baltimore: Johns Hopkins University Press.

Dresser, Rebecca. 1994. "Advance Directives." *Hastings Center Report* 24, no. 6 (November/December): S2, 4.

Dyer, Clare. 1999. "Euthanasia Campaigner to Stand in By-election." *British Medical Journal* 318, no. 7218 (October 30): 1154.

———. 1998. "UK Public Calls for Legislation Over Living Wills." *British Medical Journal* 316, no. 7136 (March 28): 959.

———. 1996. "Scottish Court Gives Right to Die." *British Medical Journal* 312, no. 7039 (May 4): 1115.

"Dying with Dignity." 1996. *Hospitals & Health Networks* 70, no. 13 (July): 12.

Emanuel, Ezekiel J. 1999. "What Is the Great Benefit of Legalizing Euthanasia or Physician-Assisted Suicide?" *Ethics* 109, no. 3 (April): 629–639.

Emanuel, Ezekiel J.; Fairclough, Diane; Daniels, Elizabeth; and Clarridge, Brian J. 1996. "Euthanasia and Physician-Assisted Suicide: Attitudes and Experiences of Oncology Patients, Oncologists, and the Public." *Lancet* 374, no. 9018 (June 29): 1805–1811.

Emanuel, Ezekiel J., and Emanuel, Linda L. 1998. "The Promise of a Good Death." *Lancet* 351, no. 9114 (May 16): 21–29.

Flemister, Carl E. 1997. "Reflections on a Good Death." *Bioethics Forum* 13, no. 1 (Spring): 11–13.

"A French Debate about Death." *Economist* 348, no. 8081 (August 15): 38.

Ganzini, Linda; Nelson, Heidi D.; Schmidt, Terri A.; Kraemer, Dale F.; Delorit, Molly A.; and Melinda, A. 2000. "Physicians' Experiences with the Oregon Death with Dignity Act." *New England Journal of Medicine* 342, no. 8 (February 24): 557–563.

"German Euthanasia Guidelines." 2000. *Lancet* 355, no. 9213 (April 22): 1440.

Gianelli, Diane U. 1998. "Michigan Next to Consider Doctor-Aided Death." *American Medical News* 41, no. 23 (June 15): 10.

Gillespie, Mark. 1999. "Kevorkian to Face Murder Charges: Latest Round in Public Debate Over Assisted Suicide." Gallup News Services Poll Releases. March 19.

Glass, Nigel. 2000. "Survey Finds Most Germans in Support of Assisted Euthanasia." *Lancet* 355, no. 9220 (June 10): 2057.

Glick, Henry R. 1992. *The Right to Die*. New York: Columbia University Press.

Griffiths, John; Bood, Alex; and Weyers, Heleen. 1998. *Euthanasia and the Law in the Netherlands*. Amsterdam: Amsterdam University Press.

Groenewoud, Johanna H.; Van der heide, Agnes; Kester, John G.C.; Carmen, L.M. de Graaff; Van der wal, Gerrit; and Van der Maas, Paul J. 2000. "A Nationwide Study of Decisions to Forego Life-Prolonging Treatment in Dutch Medical Practice." *Archives of Internal Medicine* 160, no. 3 (February 14): 357–369.

Grunwald, Michael. 1999. "House Votes to Prohibit Doctors Aid for Suicide: Bill Aims to Invalidate Law Passed in Oregon." *New York Times*, October 28, p. A01.

Haley, Kathleen, and Lee, Melinda, eds. 1998. *The Oregon's Death with Dignity Act: A Guidebook for Health Care Providers*. Portland: Center for Ethics in Health Care, Oregon Health Sciences University.

Hanson, Randall K, and Morris, Edwin B. 1997. "Living Wills and Other Health-Care Directives." *CPA Journal* 66, no. 3 (March): 53–54.

Hill, Dana. 1997. "Oregon Upholds Suicide Law." ABCNEWS.COM [http://www.abcnews.com/sections/us/DailyNews/election97_suicide.html].

Ho, Robert. 1999. "Factors Influencing Decisions to Terminate Life: Conditions of Suffering and the Identity of the Terminally Ill. *Australian Journal of Social Issues* 34, no. 1 (February): 25–34.

Hoefler, James M. 1994. *Deathright: Culture, Medicine and the Right to Die*. Boulder, CO: Westview Press.

Humphry, Derek. 1991. *Final Exit: The Practicalities of Self-Deliverance and Assisted Suicide for the Dying*. Eugene, OR: The Hemlock Society.

———. 1981. *Let Me Die Before I Wake: Hemlock's Book of Self-Deliverance for the Dying*. Los Angeles: Hemlock Society.

———. 1978. *Jean's Way*. Glendale, CA: Great Western Publishing.

Humphry, Derek, and Clement, Mary. 1998. *Freedom to Die: People, Politics, and the Right-to-Die Movement*. New York: St Martin's Press.

Ikonomidis, Sharon, and Singer, Peter A. 1999. "Autonomy, Liberalism, and Advance Care Planning." *Journal of Medical Ethics* 25, no. 6 (December): 522–527.

Jasper, Margaret C. 1996. *The Right to Die*. Dobbs Ferry, NY: Oceana Publications.

Kaap, Clare. 1999. "Swiss Allow Assisted Suicide, but What About Euthanasia?" *Lancet* 354, no. 9195 (December 11): 2059.

Kavanaugh, John F. 1997. "A Matter of Life and Death." *America* 176, no. 5 (February 15): 23.

Keigher, Sharon M. 1994. "Patient Rights and Dying: Policy Restraint and the States." *Health & Social Work* 19, no. 4 (November): 298–303.

Kevorkian, Jack. 1991. *Prescription Medicine: The Goodness of Planned Death*. Buffalo, NY: Prometheus Books.

Kissane, David W; Street, Annette; and Nitschke, Philip. 1998. "Seven Deaths in Darwin: Case Studies Under the Rights of the Terminally Ill Act, Northern Territories, Australia." *Lancet* 352 no. 9134 (October 3): 1097–1102.

Knickerbocker, Brad. 1998. "Hill Debates Right to Die." *Christian Science Monitor* 90, no. 181 (August 12): 1.

Kozlosky, Kim. 2000. "Dying Patients Explore Choices Beyond Kevorkian." *Detroit News*, February 24, p. A1.

Kubler-Ross, Elisabeth. 1969. *On Death and Dying*. New York: Macmillan.

Kuritzky, Louis. 2000. "Use of Advance Directive by Community-Dwelling Older Adults." *Neurology Alert* 18, no. 6 (February): 6.

Lane, Arline, and Neveloff Dubler, Nancy. 1997. *Bioethics Forum* 13, no. 2 (Summer): 17–21.

Lewis, Raphael. 2000. "Crowd Protests Euthanasia Meeting: World Conference Promotes Legal Assisted Suicide." *Boston Globe*, September 3, p. B3.

"Maine Logs Support for Assisted Suicide." 2000. *American Medical News* 43, no. 3 (January 24): 11.

Marquand, Robert. 1997. "Ruling Banning Assisted Suicide Will Slow, But Not End, Right-to-Die Trend." *Christian Science Monitor* 89, no. 149 (June 27): 1.

Mello, Michelle M. 1999. "Death, Life, and Uncertainty: Allocating the Risk of Error in the Decision to Terminate Life-Support." *Yale Law Journal* 3, no. 109 (December): 635–642.

McCormick, Richard A. 1997. "A Good Death—Oxymoron?" *Bioethics Forum* 13, no. 1 (Spring): 5–10.

McGovern, Celeste. 2000. "Hundreds of Australians." *Alberta Report* 27, no. 3 (June 5): 50.

———. 1999. "Brave New World." *Alberta Report* 26, no. 11 (March 8): 32.

McMahon, Patrick, and Koch, Wendy. 2000. "Oregon Assisted-Suicide Law Is not Abused, Study Finds." *USA Today*, February 24, p. 6A.

———. 1999. "Assisted Suicide: A Right or a Surrender?" *USA Today*, November 22, p. 21A.

Michel, Vicki. 1997. "Reflections on Cultural Difference and Advance Directives." *Bioethics Forum* 13, no. 2 (Summer): 22–26.

Miller, Pamela J. 2000. "Life After Death with Dignity: The Oregon Experience." *Social Work* 45, no. 3 (May): 263–271.

Minois, Georges. 1999. *History of Suicide: Voluntary Death in Western Culture.* Translated by Lydia G. Cochrane. Baltimore: Johns Hopkins University Press.

Moore, Art. 1997. "Right-to-Die Debate Returns to States." *Christianity Today* 41, no. 9 (August 11): 50.

Moore, Michael O'D. 2000. "Poll Shows Support for Assisted Suicide." *Bangor Daily News* (Bangor, Maine), September 16.

"'No' to Euthanasia." 1997. *Maclean's* 110, no. 27 (July 7): 61.

Norden, Margaret. 1995. "Whose Life Is It Anyway? A Study in Respect for Autonomy." *Journal of Medical Ethics* 21, no. 3 (June): 179–183.

Norris, Patrick E. 1997. "Palliative Care and Killing: Understanding Ethical Distinction." *Bioethics Forum* 13, no. 3 (Fall): 25–30.

Nuland, Sherwin B. 1998. "Doctors, Patients, and the End: The Right to Live." *New Republic*, November 2.

"Physician-Assisted Suicide and Euthanasia in the Netherlands: A Report to the House Judiciary Subcommittee on the Constitution." 1998. *Issues in Law & Medicine* 14, no. 3 (Winter): 301–324.

Pickard, Nancy. 1997. "My Ideal Death." *Bioethics Forum* 13, no. 1 (Spring): 14.

Potter, Van Rensselaer. 1999. "On Dying with Personhood: Socratic Death." *Perspectives in Biology and Medicine* 43, no. ii (Autumn): 103–106.

Ramsey, Paul. 1970. *The Patient as Person: Exploration in Medical Ethics.* New Heaven: Yale University Press.

Ramsey, Sarah. 2000. "UK Opposition to Euthanasia." *Lancet* 355, no. 9207 (March 11): 909.

Reibstein, Larry. 1997. "Matters of Life and Death." *Newsweek* 130, no. 1 (July 7): 30.

"A Request for Medication to End My Life." 1997. *Economist* (US) 343, no. 8022 (June 21): 23.

Rogers, Arthur. 1999. "Europe Joins Debate on the Care of the Terminally Ill." *Lancet* 354, no. 9172 (July 3 1999): 55.

Ryan, Christopher J. 1996. "Betting Your Life: An Argument Against Certain Advance Directives." *Journal of Medical Ethics* 22, no. 2 (April): 95–99.

Salem, Tania. 1999. "Physician-Assisted Suicide." *The Hastings Center Report* 29, no. 3 (May): 30–36.

Schiff, Lisa. 2000. "Another Look at Oregon's Law on Physician-Assisted Suicide." *RN* 63, no. 5 (May): 12–13.

Shapiro, Joseph P. 1997. "Euthanasia's Home: What the Dutch Experience Can Teach Americans About Assisted Suicide." *U.S. News & World Report* 122, no. 1 (January 13): 24–27.

Solovy, Alden. 1999. "The Price of Dignity." *Hospitals and Health Networks* 73, no. 3 (March) 30.

Sulmasy, Daniel P. 1998. "Killing and Allowing to Die: Another Look." *Journal of Law, Medicine & Ethics* 26, no. 1 (Spring): 55–64.

Thomasma, David C.; Kimbrough-Kushner, Thomasine; Kimsa, Gerrit K.; and Ciesielski-Carlucci, Chris, eds. 1998. *Asking to Die: Inside the Dutch Debate About Euthanasia*. Dordrecht: Kluwer Academic.

Thomson, Judith J. 1999. "Physician-Assisted Suicide: Two Moral Arguments." *Ethics* 109, no. 3 (April): 497–518.

Tonelli, Mark. 1997. "Beyond Living Wills." *Bioethics Forum* 13, no. 2 (Summer): 6–12.

Urofsky, Melvin I. 1993. *Letting Go: Death, Dying, and the Law*. New York: Macmillan.

Veatch, R.M. 1989. *Death, Dying and the Biological Revolution: Our Last Quest for Responsibility*. Rev. ed. New Haven: Yale University Press.

Verhovek, Sam H. 2001. "Federal Agents Are Directed to Stop Physicians Who Assist Suicide." *New York Times*, September 7.

Wall, Martin. 1995. "Irish Supreme Court Approves 'Right-to-Die' Case." *Lancet* 346, no. 8971 (August 5): 368.

Weber, Wim. 2000. "Dutch Proposal for Children's Right to Euthanasia Withdrawn." *Lancet* 356, no. 9226 (July 22): 322.

Weithman, Paul J. 1999. "Of Assisted Suicide and 'The Philosophers' Brief.'" *Ethics* 109, no. 3 (April): 548–578.

White, Herbert H. 1998. "Physician-Assisted Suicide: Reflections on Oregon's First Case." *Issues in Law & Medicine* 14, no. 3 (Winter): 243–270.

References to Chapter 3

Allen, William H. 1995. "Farming for Spare Body Parts." *Bioscience* 45, no. 2 (February): 73–75.

Anderson, Mark F. 1995. "The Future of Organ Transplantation: From Where Will New Donors Come, To Whom Will Their Organs Go?" *Health Matrix: Journal of Law Medicine* 5, no. 2 (Summer): 249–310.

Andrews, Lri, and Nelkin, Dorothy. 1998. "Whose Body Is It Anyway? Disputes Over Body Tissue in A Biotechnology Age." *Lancet* 351, no. 9095 (January 3): 53–57.

Arnason, W.B. 1991. "Directed Donation." *Hastings Center Report* 21, no. 6 (November–December): 13–19.

Awuonda, Moussa. 1996a. "Swedish Organ-Donation Drive Set for Success." *Lancet* 347, no. 9012 (May 18): 1401.

———. 1996b. "Swedish Organ Law Takes Effect." *Lancet* 348, no. 9019 (July 6): 54.

Baer, Nicole. 1997. "Canada's Organ Shortage Is Severe and Getting Worse." *Canadian Medical Association Journal* 157, no. 2 (July 15): 179–183.

Barnett, Andy H., and Blair, Roger D. 1996. "A Market for Organs." *Society* 33, no. 6 (September–October): 8–17.

BBC News, 1999. "The History of Xenotransplantation." August 19 [http://news.bbc.co.uk/hi/English/sci/tech/newsid_425000/425120.stm].

Bergman, Helen R. 1992. "Rationing Health Care: Social, Political, and Legal Perspectives, Notes, and Comment: Case Comment: Moore v. Regents of The University of California." *American Journal of Law & Medicine* 18, no.1–2 (Spring–Summer):127–145.

Blumstein, James F. 1993. "The Use of Financial Incentives in Medical Care: The Case of Commerce in Transplantable Organs." *Health Matrix: Journal of Law Medicine* 3, no. 1 (Spring): 1–30.

"Body Shop." 2000. *The Christian Century* 117, no. 19 (June 21): 669.

Bosch, Zavier. 1998. "Spain Celebrates Leading the World in Organ Donation." *Lancet* 351, no. 9119 (June 20): 1868.

———. 1999a. "Spanish Organ Donation Is Increasing." *Lancet* 353, no. 9151 (February 6): 476.

———. 1999b. "Spain Leads World in Organ Donation and Transplantation." *Journal of American Medical Association* 282, no. 1 (July 7): 17.

———. 2000. "Spain Widens Donor Pool by Updating Organ Laws." *Lancet* 355, no. 9199 (January 15): 212.

Braun, Kathryn L. 1997. "Death and Dying in Four Asian American Cultures: A Descriptive Study." *Death Studies* 21, no. 4 (July/August): 327–360.

Brink, Susan. 1998. "The Feds Demand Transplant Equity." *U.S. News and World Report* 124, no. 13 (April 6): 27.

Caplan, Arthur L., and Coelho, Daniel H. eds. 1999. *The Ethics of Organ Transplants: The Current Debate.* Amherst, NY: Prometheus.

Carlstrom, Charles T., and Rollow, Christy D. 1997. "The Rationing of Transplantable Organs: A Troubled Lineup." *CATO Journal* 17, no. 2 (Fall): 163–178.

Carnall, Douglas. 2000. "Transplant Organs." *British Medical Journal* 320, no. 7250 (June 17): 1678.

Check, Erika. 2000. "Cloning Pigs for Parts." *Newsweek* 136, no. 9 (August 8): 49.

Chelala, Cesar. 1997. "Prospect of Discussion on Prisoners' Organs for Sale in China." *Lancet* 350, no. 9087 (November 1): 1307.

Clark, Cathy, and Boyles, Salynn. 1997. "Japan Seeks Guidance from Organ Recovery Experts." *Blood Weekly* (November 3): 13–14.

Clark, Margaret A. 1999. "The Little Piggy Went to Market: The Xenotransplantation and Xenozoonose Debate." *Journal of Law, Medicine, and Ethics* 27, no. 2 (Summer): 137–156.

Cowley, Geoffrey, and Underwood, Anne. 2001. "New Heart, New Hope." *Newsweek* 137, no. 26 (June 25): 42–49.

Csillag, Claudio. 1997. "Brazil's Law on Organ Donation Passed." *Lancet* 349, no. 9050 (February 15): 482.

———. 1998. "Brazil Abolishes 'Presumed Consent' in Organ Donation." *Lancet* 352, no. 9137 (October 24): 1367.

"Daniel Canal." 1998. *U.S. News & World Report* 125, no. 1 (July 6): 18.

DeLong, James V. 1998. "Organ Grinders." *Reason* 30, no. 6 (November): 57–59.

Dewar, Diane M. 1998. "Allocating Organ Transplant Services: What Can Be Learned from the United States Experience." *Review of Social Economy* 56, no. 2 (Summer): 157–174.

Dickson, David. 1999. "Human Cloning Is Dolly's Debatable Offspring." *UNESCO Courier* (Spring): 32–33.

Dorozynski, Alexander. 1998. "France Celebrates Opt Out Register for Organ Donation." *British Medical Journal* 317, no. 7153 (July 25): 234.

Eaton, Stephanie. 1998. "The Subtle Politics of Organ Donation: A Proposal." *Journal of Medical Ethics* 24, no. 3 (June): 166–170.

Epstein, Richard A. 1993. "Organ Transplants." *American Enterprise* 4, no. 6 (November–December): 50–57.

Fentiman, Linda C. 1998. "Crisis in U.S. Organ Transplant System Intensifies." *Issues in Science and Technology* 15, no. 2 (Winter): 30–31.

"Fighting Over Organs." 1998. *Economist* 347, no. 8066 (May 2): 26–27.

Fisher, Lawrence M. 1996. "Down on the Farm, a Donor." *New York Times*, January 5, p. D1.

Fox, Renee C., and Swazey, Judith P. 1992. *Spare Parts: Organ Replacement in American Society*. New York: Oxford University Press.

Gardels, Nathan. 1994. "Nearer to the Dust." *New Perspective Quarterly* 11, no. 1 (Winter): 2–3.

Gorsline, Monique C., and Johnson, Rachelle L.K. 1994. "The United States System of Organ Donation, the International Solution, and the Cadaveric Organ Donor Act: And the Winner Is. . . ." *Journal of Corporation Law* 20, no. 1 (Fall): 5, 46.

"Heartless Japan." 1996. *Economist* 341, no. 7990 (November 2): 37.

Henderson, Charles W. 2000a. "U.K. Launches Organ Donor Promotion." *Blood Weekly*, August 17–August 24, p. 13.

———. 2000b. "Waiting Time Drops for Sickests Patients Under New Liver Policy." *Transplant and Tissue Weekly*, May 28, n.p.

———. 1999a. "Kidney Removed from Internet Auction." *Transplant Weekly*, October 18, n.p.

———. 1999b. "Center Monitors Illegal Trafficking in Human Organs." *World Diseases Weekly*, November 15, p. 28.

———. 1999c. "Canadian Government Takes Steps to Organize Organ, Tissue Donation." *Transplant Weekly*, November 1, n.p.

———. 1999d. "State May Sue U.S. Government Over Organ Transplant Rule." *Transplant Weekly* March 29, n.p.

———. 1999e. "The 'Break-Even' Cost of Kidney Transplants Is Shrinking." *Transplant Weekly*, May 31, n.p.

———. 1999f. "Organ Transplant U.S. Studies Give Organ Transplants Mixed Reviews." *Transplant Weekly*, October 19, n.p.

———. 1998a. "Organ Donation Supported by Religion, According to Newly Released Guide." *Transplant Weekly*, September 21, n.p.

———. 1998b. "Government Organ Transplant Waits May Be Reduced Due to Policy," *Transplant Weekly*, October 19, n.p.

"HSS Issues Final Rule on Organ Allocation." 2000. *Registered Nurse* 63, no. 2 (February): 12.

Hoffenberg, R.; Lock, M.; Tilney, N.; Casabona, C.; Daar, A.S.; Guttmann, R.D.; Kennedy, I.; Nundy, S.; Radcliffe-Richards, J.; and Sells, R.A. 1997. "Should Organs from Patients in a Permanent Vegetative State Be Used for Transplantation?" *Lancet* 350, no. 9087 (November 1): 1320–1321.

Hussong, Sharon. 1999. "Administrative Developments: DHHS Issues Organ Allocation Final Rule." *Journal of Law, Medicine & Ethics* 27, no. 4 (Winter): 380–382.

Institute of Medicine. 1996. *Xenotransplantation: Science, Ethics, and Public Policy.* Washington, DC: National Academy Press.

Jensen, Troy R. 2000. "Organ Procurement: Various Legal Systems and their Differences." *Houston Journal of International Law* 22, no. 1 (Spring): 555–585.

Kaas, Leott R. 1992. "Organs for Sale? Propriety, Property, and the Price of Progress." *Public Interest* no. 107 (Spring): 65–86.

Kennedy, I., and Sells, R.A. et al. 1998. "The Case for Presumed Consent in Organ Donation." *Lancet* 315, no. 9116 (April 30): 1650–1652.

Kmietowicz, Zosia. 1999. "More Doctors and Donors are Needed for Transplantation in the U.K." *British Medical Journal* 318, no. 7180 (February 6): 350.

Kurtz, Sheldon, and Saks, Michael J. 1996. "The Transplant Paradox: Overwhelming Public Support for Organ Donation vs. Under-supply of Organs." *Journal of Corporation Law* 21, no. 4 (Summer): 767–806.

Lamb, David. 1993. "Organ Transplants, Death, and Policies for Procurement." *Monist* 76, no. 2 (April): 203–221.

Langone, John. 1994. "The Making of a Good Doctor." *America* 170, no. 3 (January 29): 4–7.

Lanza, Robert P., and Cooper, David K.C. 1997. "Xenotransplantation." *Scientific American* 277, no. 1 (July): 54–59.

Lock, Margaret. 1993. *Encounters with Aging.* Berkeley: University of California Press.

Loerner, Brendan. 1997. "The Kidney Heist." *U.S. News & World Report* 123, no. 16 (October 27): 16.

Long, Clarisa. 1998. "The Future of Biotechnology: Promises and Problems." *American Enterprise* 9, no. 5 (September–October): 55–58.

Martin, Shelley. 2000. "Transplant Queues Grow as Donor Numbers Wane." *Canadian Medical Association Journal* 162, no. 12 (June 13): 1728.

McCarthy, Michael. 1999. "US Panel Suggest Changes in Organ Allocation." *Lancet* 353, no. 9176 (July 31): 405.

McConnell, John R. 1999. "The Ambiguity about Death in Japan: An Ethical Implication for Organ Procurement." *Journal of Medical Ethics* 25, no. 4 (August): 322–325.

McLean, Sheila. 1995. "Human Tissue: Ethical and Legal Issues." *British Medical Journal* 310, no. 6992 (June 3): 1423–1424.

McMenamin, Brigid. 2000. "Swap Meet." *Forbes,* June 12, p. 136.

Meckler, Laura. 2000a. "Debate in Congress, Wisconsin Lawsuit Add Complexity." *Associated Press State and Local Wire,* April 4.

"Medicine: Wisconsin Wants All Its Own Organs." 1999. *Time* 154, no. 9 (August 30): 20.

"Milestone for Heart Recipient." 2001. *Newsday* (August 2): p. A08.

Milfred, Scott. 2000. "Dyole Files Lawsuit to Stop Organ Policy." *Wisconsin State Journal,* March 21, p. 3B.

Melton, Lisa. 1999. "Inroads Made into Transplantation Problems." *Lancet* 354, no. 9 (October 9): 1272.

Menikoff, Jerry. 1999. "Organ Swapping." *Hastings Center Report* 29, no. 6 (November-December): 28–33.

Mirza, Darius F., and Gunson, Bridget K. 1994. "Policies in Europe on 'Marginal Quality' Donor Livers." *Lancet* 344, 1480 (November 26): 1480–1484.

Murray, Barbara. 1998. "Human Organs for Sale?" *U.S. News & World Report* 124, no. 9 (March 9): 10.

Nichols, Mark. 1999. "Wanted: Spare Parts: A Lack of Donated Organs Leaves Patients at Risk." *Maclean's*, May 3, p. 56.

O'Carroll, Thomas. 1996. "Over My Dead Body: Recognizing Property Rights in Corpses." *Journal of Health Law* 29, no. 4 (July–August): 238–254.

O'Neill, Onora. 1996. "Medical and Scientific Uses of Human Tissue." *Journal of Medical Ethics* 22, no. 1 (February): 5–7.

"Organ Donations: Keep That Liver at Home." 1999. *State Legislatures* 25, no. 7 (July–August): 13.

"Organ Donations Increase Following National Initiative and New Regulations." 1999. *Health Care Financing Review* 20, no. 3 (Spring): 127.

"Panel to Be Created to Assess Proposed Changes in Organ Policies." 2000. *Medical Industry Today*, September 28.

Perry, Patrick. 1997. "Congress Gets into the Act." *Saturday Evening Post* 269, no. 5 (September/October): 46.

"Pigged Out." 1998. *Economist* 364, no. 8052 (January 24): 17.

Pool, Robert, and Tauss, Marc. 1998. "Saviors." *Discover* 19, no. 5 (May): 52–57.

Powhida, Alexander. 1999. "Comment: Forced Organ Donation: The Presumed Consent to Organ Donation Laws of the Various States and the United States Constitution." *Albany Law Journal of Science & Technology* 9: 349–372.

Price, Joyce H. 1999. "A Dearth of Donor Organs." *Insight on the News* 15, no. 24 (June 28): 41.

"Proclamation 7185–National Organ and Tissue Donor Awareness Week." 1999. *Weekly Compilation of Presidential Documents* 35, no. 15 (April 19): 667.

Randal, Judith. 1998. "Xenotransplantation Moving Ahead Too Quickly for Some." *Journal of the National Cancer Institute* 90, no. 5 (March 4): 348–350.

"Religious Views on Organ/Tissue Donations and Transplants." 2000. *LifeSource Web Site* [http://life-source.org/index.html].

Robertson, John A. 1999. "The Dead Donor Rule." *The Hastings Center Report* 29, no. 6 (November–December): 6–14.

Sabir, Nadirah Z. 1996. "A Second Chance." *Black Enterprise* 26, no. 7 (February): 26.

Sade, Robert M. 1999. "Cadaveric Organ Donation." *Archives of Internal Medicine* 159, no. 5 (March 8): 438.

Savulescu, Julian. 1999. "Should We Clone Human Beings? Cloning As a Source of Tissue for Transplantation." *Journal of Medical Ethics* 25, no. 2 (April): 97–95.

Seppa, N. 2000. "Pig-Cell Grafts Ease Symptoms of Parkinson's." *Science News* 157, no. 13 (March 25): 197.

Shapiro, Joseph P. 2000. "Life in Limbo: The Transplant Wars." *U.S. News & World Report* 128, no. 16 (April 24): 26.

Sinha, Gunjan. 1999. "Organ Cowboys." *Popular Science* 255, no. 4 (October): 68–73.

Spiegelberg, Washington. 1970. "Human Dignity: A Challenge to Contemporary Philosophy." In *Human Dignity: This Century and the Next*, eds. Rubin Gotesky and Ervin Laszlo, 61–62. New York: Gordon and Breach, Science Publishers.

"State Lawmakers Approve Organ-Allocation Bill." 1999. *McKnight's Long-Term Care News* 20, no. 11 (August 3): 11.

"Statement on Signing the Organ Donor Leave Act." 1999. *Weekly Compilation of Presidential Documents* 35, no. 38 (September 27): 1817.

Swain, M.S., and Marusyk, R.W. 1990. "An Alternative to Property Rights in Human Tissue." *Hastings Center Report* 20, no. 5 (September–October): 12–15.

Sweeney, Rosemarie. 1999. "Number of Organ Donations Increases in the United States in 1998." *American Family Physician* 59, no. 10 (May 15): 2701.

"The Quest for an Artificial Heart." 2001. *New York Times* (July 4): A14.

Thompson, Dick. 1998. "Transplant Distribution: The Government Wants a New System for Doling Out Donated Organs. Oh, What a Ruckus It's Causing." *Time* 152, no. 14 (October 5): 56.

Travis, John. 2000. "Cloned Pigs, Down on the Corporate Farm." *Science News* 157, no. 13 (March 25): 197.

Truog, Robert D. 1997. "Is It Time to Abandon Brain Death?" *The Hastings Center Report* 27, no. 1 (January–February): 29–37.

"UK Analysis of Racism in Organ Donation." 2000. *Lancet* 355, no. 9205 (February 26): 732.

U.S. Department of Health and Human Services. 1998a. HHS News Release. March 26. Health Resources and Services Administration [http://www.hrsa.dhhs.gov/Newsroom/].

———. 1998b. HRSA NEWS: National Initiative Fact Sheet. June 17, Health Resources and Services Administration [http://www.hrsa.dhhs.gov/Newsroom/].

———. 2000. *Improving the Nation's Organ Transplant System.* Washington DC: Government Printing Office.

Walters, Jonathan. 1998. "Whose Organs Are They?" *Saturday Evening Post* 270, no. 6 (November–December): 70.

Witmer, Kathleen A., and Knoppel, Christopher L. 1996. "Organ Donation: A Collaborative Commitment." In *Trends in Organ Transplantation,* eds. Barbara A. Helene Williams and Doris M. Sandiford, 3–21. New York: Springer.

Witt, Clara J. 1998. "Animal-to-Man Transplants." *World Health* 51 no. 4 (July): 30.

Wrone, Elizabeth. 1999. "Commentary: Evaluating the Efficiency of Organ Procurement." *Health Services Research* 34, no. 4 (October 1999): 75–78.

References to Chapter 4

Alexander, Brian. 2001. "(You)²." *Wired* 9, no. 2 (February): 120–135.

Allen, Arthur. 2001. "Who Owns My Disease?" *Mother Jones* 26, no. 6 (November/December): 52–57, 88–89.

Alvarez, Lizette. 2001. "61 Senators Call for Stem Cell Research." *New York Times* (July 21).

American Society of Gene Therapy. 1999. "Reporting of Patient Adverse Events in Gene Therapy Trials: Statement from the American Society of Gene Therapy." Statement of Savio L.C. Woo before the Recombinant DNA Advisory Committee, December 14 [http://www.asgt.org/position_statement/adverse_events.html].

———. 2000. "Policy of The American Society of Gene Therapy on Financial Conflict of Interest in Clinical Research." (April 5) [http://www.asgt.org/policy/index.html].

"America's Next Ethical War." 2001. *Economist* 359, no. 8217 (April 12): 21–23.

Andrews, Lori B. 2000. "State Regulation of Embryo Stem Cell Research." In National Bioethics Advisory Commission 2000, pp. A-1–A-20.

———. 2001. *Future Perfect: Confronting Decisions About Genetics.* New York: Columbia University Press.

Angier, Natalie. 2000. "Do Races Differ? Not Really, DNA Shows." *New York Times* (August 22).

Bailey, Ronald. 1999. "Petri Dish Politics." *Reason* 31, no. 7 (December): 32–39.

Begley, Sharon. 2001. "Cellular Divide." *Newsweek* 138, no. 2 (July 9): 22–27.

Belkin, Lisa. 2001. "The 'Made-to-Order' Savior." *New York Times Magazine* (July 1).

Belluck, Pam. 2001. "Trying to Balance Science and Humanity." *New York Times* (August 11).

Bettelheim, Adriel. 2001. "Embryo Research." In *Issues in Health Policy: Selections from the CQ Researcher*, pp. 157–173. Washington, DC: CQ Press.

Billings, Paul. 2000. "Applying Genetic Advances: Where Do We Go from Here?" *GeneLetter* 5, no. 12 (December) [www.geneletter.com/12–01–00/features/future.html].

BioFact Report. (n.d.). "Types of Genetic Engineering" [http://www.biofact.com/cloning].

Bottum J. 2001. "Against Human Cloning." *The Weekly Standard* 6, no. 32 (May 7).

Brady, Robert P.; Newberry, Molly S.; and Girard, Vicki W. 2000. "The Food and Drug Administration's Statutory and Regulatory Authority to Regulate Human Pluripotent Stem Cells." In National Bioethics Advisory Commission 2000, pp. B-1–B-12.

Brogan, Pamela. 2001. "Abortion Foes Win House Vote." *Springfield News-Leader* (April 27).

Brownlee, Shannon. 2001. "Cancer: Smart Bombs for Targeting Deadly Tumors." *Time* 157, no. 2 (January 2): 72–74.

"Bush Appoints Dr. Leon Kass as Chair of Council on Bioethics." 2001. Kaisernetwork.org (August 10).

Callahan, Daniel. 1995. *Setting Limits: Medical Goals in an Aging Society.* Washington, DC: Georgetown University Press.

———. 1998. *False Hopes: Why America's Quest for Perfect Health Is a Recipe for Failure.* New York: Simon & Schuster.

Cantor, Charles R. 2000. "The Impact of Genetics on Insurance and Insurability." *GeneLetter* (October) [www.geneletter.com].

"Carbon Copies Prohibited." 2001. *Public Perspective* 12, no. 3 (May/June): 44–45.

Chang, Kenneth. 2000. "Incomplete Project Is Already Paying Off." *New York Times* (June 27).

Chapman, Audrey R.; Frankel, Mark S.; and Garfinkel, Michelle S. 1999. *Stem Cell Research and Applications: Monitoring the Frontiers of Biomedical Research.* Washington, DC: American Association for the Advancement of Science and the Institute for Civil Society.

Chen, Edwin. 2001. "On Long Road to Decision, President Searched for a 'Compromise Route.'" *Lost Angeles Times* (August 10).

Chen, Edwin, and Zitner, Aaron. 2001. "Known for Quick Decisions, the President is Agonizing over the Funding of Embryo Research." *Los Angeles Times* (July 13).

Clinton, Bill. 2000. "White House Remarks on Decoding of Genome." *New York Times* (June 27).

Cohen, Jonathan R. 1999. "In God's Garden: Creation and Cloning in Jewish Thought." *Hastings Center Report* 29, no. 4 (July/August): 7–12.

Cohen, Roger. 2001. "Clash on Use of Embryos in Germany Stirs Echoes of Nazi Era." *New York Times* (May 30).

Committee on the Biological and Biomedical Applications of Stem Cell Research. 2001. *Stem Cells and the Future of Regenerative Medicine*. Washington, DC: National Academy of Sciences Press.

Commoner, Barry. 2002. "Unraveling the DNA Myth." *Harper's Magazine* 304, no. 1821 (February): 39–47.

Connolly, Ceci. 2001b. "Bush Aides Stress Curbs on Stem Cells." *Washington Post* (August 13).

Connolly, Ceci; Gillis, Justin; and Weiss, Rick. 2001. "Viability of Stem Cell Plan Doubted." *Washington Post* (August 20).

Cooper, Mary H. 2001. "Human Genome Research." In *Issues in Health Policy: Selections from the CQ Researcher*, pp. 175–193. Washington, DC: CQ Press.

"Discrimination from Gene Map Raises Concerns." 2001. *Springfield News Leader* (February 12).

Dolan DNA Learning Center. n.d. "DNA from the Beginning." Cold Spring Harbor, NY: Cold Spring Harbor Laboratory [http://vector.cshl.org/dnaftb/].

"Double-Teaming the Double Helix." 1998. *U.S. News Online* (August 17) [http://www.usnews.com/usnews/issue/980817/17dna.htm].

Duncan, David Ewing. 2001. "The Protein Hunters." *Wired* 9, no. 4 (April): 164–171.

Eilperin, Juliet. 2001. "Unborn Victims Act Wins in House." *Washington Post* (April 27).

Eiseman, Elisa. 2000. "Quick Response: Use of Fetal Tissue in Federally Funded Research." In National Bioethics Advisory Commission 2000, pp. C-1–C-7.

"Ethicist: Political Fear Holds Back U.S. Science." 2000. *The Springfield News-Leader* (January 25).

Fisher, Lawrence M. 1999. "Successful Gene Therapy on Hemophilia and Heart Cells Reported." *New York Times* (December 7).

Flannery, Ellen J., and Javitt, Gail H. 2000. "Analysis of Federal Laws Pertaining to Funding of Human Pluripotent Stem Cell Research." In National Bioethics Advisory Commission 2000, pp. D-1–D-13.

Food and Drug Administration. 1993. "Application of Current Statutory Authorities to Human Somatic Cell Therapy Products and Gene Therapy Products; Notice." *Federal Register* 58, no. 197 (October 14): 53247–53251.

———. 1997. "Proposed Approach to Regulation of Cellular and Tissue-Based Products." Washington, DC: Food and Drug Administration, U.S. Department of Health and Human Services.

Friedmann, Theodore, ed. 1999a. *The Development of Human Gene Therapy*. Cold Spring Harbor, NY: Cold Spring Harbor Laboratory Press.

———. 1999b. "The Origins, Evolution, and Directions of Human Gene Therapy." In Friedmann 1999a, pp. 1–20.

"Future of Genetic Research." 2000. *Chicago Tribute* (June 27) [http://cnews.tribune.com/news/image/0,1119,tribune-nation-67468,00.html].

Gelsinger, Paul L. 2000. Testimony before the Subcommittee on Public Health, Committee on Health, Education, Labor, and Pensions. U.S. Senate, 106th Congress, 2nd Session, February 2 [http://www.senate.gov/~labor/Hearings/feb00hrg/020200wt/frist0202/gelsing/gelsing.htm]

"Genetically Modified Monkey Created." 2001. *Springfield News-Leader* (January 12).

Goldstein, Amy. 2001. "Bush Stem Cell Policy Cools Fervor on Capital Hill." *Washington Post* (August 11).

Goldstein, Amy, and Allen, Mike. 2001. "Bush Backs Partial Stem Cell Funding." *Washington Post* (August 10).

Goode, Erica. 2001. "Building a Better Racehorse, From the Genome Up." *New York Times* (May 8).

Grady, Denise. 2000. "Son Conceived to Provide Blood Cells for Daughter." *New York Times* (October 4).

————. 2001. "Fat Is a Good Source of Stem Cells." *New York Times* (April 10).

Heath, Erin. 2001. "Zipping Up Genes Discrimination." *National Journal* 33, no. 29 (July 21): 2346–2347.

Heller, Joe. 2000. "Editorial Cartoon: Map of the Human Genome." *Springfield News-Leader* (July 8).

Henig, Robin Marantz. 2000. *The Monk in the Garden: The Lost and Found Genius of Gregor Mendel, the Father of Genetics*. Boston: Houghton Mifflin.

Herrnstein, Richard J., and Murray, Charles. 1994. *The Bell Curve: Intelligence and Class Structure in American Life*. New York: The Free Press.

Hilts, Philip J. 2000a. "Hospital in Boston Halts Gene Therapy Research." *New York Times* (February 8).

————. 2000b. "A Second Death Linked to Gene Therapy." *New York Times* (May 4).

Holtzman, Neil A., and Shapiro, David. 1998. "Genetic Testing and Public Policy." *British Medical Journal* 317, no. 7134 (March 14): 852–856.

Hook, Janet, and Brownstein, Ron. 2001. "Bush Adept at Science of Compromise." *Los Angeles Times* (August 10).

Hylton, Wil S. 2001. "Who Owns This Body?" *Esquire* 135, no. 6 (June): 102–111, 158–160.

Issues in Health Policy: Selections from the CA Researcher. 2001. Washington, DC: CQ Press.

Jeffords, James M., and Daschle, Tom. 2001. "Political Issues in the Genome Era." *Science* 291, no. 5507 (February 16): 1249–1251.

Keen, Judy. 2001. "Poll: Most Americans Back Bush on Stem-Cell Call." *USA Today* (August 14).

Khoury, Muin J.; Beskow, Laura; and Guinn, Marta. 2001. "Making the Vision of Genomic Medicine a Reality: Public Health Research Is Key." *GeneLetter* (May 1) [http://www.geneletter.com/05–01–01/features/publichealth.html].

Knowles, Lori P. 2000. "International Perspectives on Human Embryo and Fetal Tissue Research." In National Bioethics Advisory Commission 2000, pp. H-1–H-22.

Kolata, Gina. 1998. *Clone: The Road to Dolly and the Path Ahead*. New York: William Morrow and Company.

————. 2000. "In a First, Gene Therapy Saves Lives of Infants." *New York Times* (April 28).

————. 2001. "Parkinson's Research Is Set Back by Failure of Fetal Cell Implants." *New York Times* (March 8).

Kornblut, Anne E. 2001. "Congress Set to Debate Stem Cell Rule." *Boston Globe* (August 13).

Krieger, Lisa M. 2002. "Ferreting Out Flawed Embryos." *San Jose Mercury News* (March 12).

Laurence, Lisa. 1999. "Gene Therapy Breakthrough Delights Geneticists." *GeneLetter* (February) [http://www.geneletter.com/archives/genetherbreak.html].

Lemonick, Michael D. 2001. "Brave New Pharmacy." *Time* 157, no. 2 (January 15): 58–69.

Lewin, Tamar. 2001. "Commission Sues Railroad to End Genetic Testing in Work Injury Cases." *New York Times* (February 10).

Longman, Jere. 2001. "Pushing the Limits." *New York Times* (May 11).

Longman, Philip J., and Brownlee, Shannon. 2000. "The Genetic Surprise." *Wilson Quarterly* 24, no. 4 (Fall): 40–50.

MacKinnon, Leslie, 2001. "Stem Cells: The Promise and the Protest." Canadian Broadcasting Company (June 5) [www.cbc.calNational/News/Stemcells/transcript.html].

Margolis, Jonathan. 2000. "Our Special Place in History." *USA Weekend* (December 29–31): 6.

McQueen, Anjetta. 2001. "Federal Report Supports Stem Cell Research." Associated Press (July 17).

Meyer, John R. 2000. "Human Embryonic Stem Cells and Respect for Life." *Journal of Medical Ethics* 26, no. 3 (June): 166–170.

Munro, Neil, and Serafini, Marilyn Werber. 2001. "Now a Debate, in Triplicate, Over Cloning." *National Journal* 33, no. 15 (April 14): 1104–1106.

Murray, Thomas H. 2001a. "Even If It Worked, Cloning Won't Bring Her Back." *Washington Post* (April 8).

———. 2001b. "Hard Cell: The Ethics and Politics of Stem Cell Research." *American Prospect* special supplement (Fall): A7–11.

Nash, J. Madeleine. 2001. "Alzheimer's Disease: New Insights into its Cause Lead to New Drug Strategies." *Time* 157, no. 2 (January 15): 80–85.

National Academy of Sciences. n.d. "Beyond Discovery: Advances in Genetic Research That Led to Gene Testing" [http://www.nas.edu/beyond/beyond discovery.nsf/web/gene12?OpenDocument].

National Bioethics Advisory Commission. 1999. *Ethical Issues in Human Stem Cell Research*, vol. 1. Rockville, MD: National Bioethics Advisory Commission.

———. 2000. *Ethical Issues in Human Stem Cell Research*, vol. 2. Rockville, MD: National Bioethics Advisory Commission.

National Institutes of Health. 2001. *Stem Cells: Scientific Progress and Future Research Directions*. Washington, DC: National Institutes of Health.

Niebuhr, Gustav. 2001. "Religions Ponder the Stem Cell Issue." *New York Times* (August 27).

Nightingale, Stuart L. 1998. "Dear Colleagues." Letter written to Food and Drug Administration, U.S. Department of Health and Human Services (October 26) [www.fda.gov/oc/ohrt/irbs/irblet.html].

O'Connor, Eileen. 2000. "Gene Research Yields Drug That Helps Heal Chronic Ulcers, Company Announces. *CNN.com* (September 13) [http://www.cnn.com/2000/ HEALTH/09/13/genome.wounds/index.html].

Okie, Susan. 2001. "Alzheimer's Operation Is a Gene Therapy First." *Washington Post* (April 11).

Parens, Erik. 2000. "What Has the President Asked of NBAC on the Ethics and Politics of Embryonic Stem Cell Research." In National Bioethics Advisory Commission 2000, pp. I-1–I-12.

Park, Alice. 2001. "AIDS: Still No Vaccine, But Better Antiviral Drugs Are on the Way." *Time* 157, no. 2 (January 15): 70–72.

Patel, Kant, and Rushefsky, Mark E. 1999. *Health Care Politics and Policy in America.* Armonk, NY: M.E. Sharpe.

Peltonen, Leena, and McKusick, Victor A. 2001. "Dissecting Human Disease in the Postgenomic Era." *Science* 291, no. 5507 (February 16): 1224–1229 [www.sciencemag.org/genome2001/1224.html].

Pence, Gregory E. 1998. *Who's Afraid of Human Cloning?* Lanham, MD: Rowman & Littlefield.

Pennisi, Elizabeth. 1998. "After Dolly, a Pharming Frenzy." *Science* 279, no. 5351 (January 30): 646–648.

Plotz, David. 2001. "The 'Genius Babies,' and How They Grew." *Slate.com* (February 7) [http://slate.msn.com/seed/entries/01–02–07_100331.asp].

Pollack, Andrew. 2000. "The Next Chapter in the Book of Life: Structural Genetics." *New York Times* (July 4).

———. 2001. "Double Helix With a Twist." *The New York Times* (February 13).

Pope John Paul II. 1983. "Dangers of Genetic Manipulation." Address to members of the World Medical Association, October 29 [http://listserv.american.edu/catholic/church/papal/jp.ii/genmanip.asc].

Salter, Stephanie. 2001. "Low-Income Embryos Out-rank Women with Bush." *San Francisco Chronicle* (July 10).

Seelye, Katharine Q., and Bruni, Frank. 2001. "A Long Process That Led Bush to His Decision." *New York Times* (August 11).

Shadid, Anthony. 2001. "Battle Lines Drawn on Genetic Frontier." *Boston Globe* (April 25).

Shreeve, James. 2000. "Where the Genome Leads Us." *New York Times* (June 27).

Simpson, Victor L. 2001. "Pope Urges Bush Against Stem Cell Research." Associated Press (July 19).

Stolberg, Sheryl Gay. 1999. "A Death Puts Gene Therapy Under Increasing Scrutiny." *New York Times* (November 4).

———. 2002. "Breakthrough in Pig Cloning Could Aid Organ Transplants." *New York Times* (January 3).

———. 2000a. "Youth's Death Shakes New Field of Gene Experiments on Humans." *New York Times* (January 27).

———. 2000b. "Agency Failed to Monitor Patients in Gene Research." *New York Times* (February 2).

———. 2000c. "Gene Therapy Might Have Exposed 20 Children to Lethal Viruses." *New York Times* (February 11).

———. 2000d. "Despite Ferment, Gene Therapy Progresses." *New York Times* (June 6).

———. 2001a. "Stem Cell Research Advocates in Limbo." *New York Times* (January 20).

———. 2001b. "Company Using Cloning to Yield Stem Cells." *New York Times* (July 13).

———. 2001c. "U.S. Acts Quickly to Put Stem Cell Policy in Effect." *New York Times* (August 11).

———. 2001d. "Patent on Human Stem Cell Puts U.S. Officials in Bind." *New York Times* (August 17).

Stone, Deborah. 2002. *Policy Paradox: The Art of Political Decision Making*, revised ed. New York: W.W. Norton.

Swint, Sean. 2000. "Sequencing of Human Genome Is a First Step to Many Answers." CNN.com.[http://www.cnn.com/SPECIALS/2000/genome/story/medical.implications/].

Thinkquest.org. n.d. "Cloning Timelines" [http://library.thinkquest.org/24355/data/details/timeline.html?tqskip=1].

Thomas, Evan, and Clift, Eleanor. 2001. "Battle for Bush's Soul." *Newsweek* 138, no. 2 (July 9): 28–30.

Thompson, Larry. 2000. "Human Gene Therapy: Harsh Lessons, High Hopes." *FDA Consumer* 34, no. 5 (September) [http://www.fda.gov/fdac/features/2000/500_gene.html].

Thompson, Nicholas. 2001. "Gene Blues." *Washington Monthly* 33, no. 4 (April): 9–15.

Tokar, Brian (ed.). 2001. *Redesigning Life: The Worldwide Challenge to Genetic Engineering.* New York: Zed Books.

Toner, Robin. 2001. "Conservatives Pressure Bush in Cell Debate." *New York Times* (July 11).

"U.S. Stem Cell Decision Will Likely Have 'Big Impact' in Europe, Wall Street Journal Europe Reports." 2001. Kaisernetwork.org (August 10).

Wachbroit, Robert. 1997. "Genetic Encores: The Ethics of Human Cloning." *Philosophy and Public Affairs* 17, no. 4 (Fall): 1–7.

Wade, Nicholas. 1999a. "Government Says Ban on Human Embryo Research Does Not Apply to Cells." *New York Times* (January 20).

———. 1999b. "Patient Dies While Undergoing Gene Therapy." *New York Times* (September 29).

———. 2000a. "Skin Cells Bring Cloning a Step Nearer to Efficiency." *New York Times* (January 5).

———. 2000b. "Genetic Code of Human Life Is Cracked by Scientists." *New York Times* (June 27).

———. 2000c. "Now, the Hard Part: Putting the Genome to Work." *New York Times* (June 27).

———. 2001a. "Stem Cells Yield Promising Benefits." *New York Times* (March 31).

———. 2001b. "A New Source for Stem Cells Is Reported." *New York Times* (April 12).

———. 2001c. "Age-Old Question Is New Again." *New York Times* (August 15).

———. 2001d. "Officials Say Bush's New Stem Cell Policy May Streamline the Research Process." *New York Times* (August 18).

Watson, James D. 1997, 1968 [original]. *The Double Helix: A Personal Account of the Discovery of the Structure of DNA.* London: Weidenfeld & Nicolson.

Weiss, Rick. 2000a. "Ignorance Undercuts Gene Tests' Potential." *Washington Post* (December 2).

———. 2000b. "Gene Research Rule Proposed." *Washington Post* (December 13).

———. 2001a. "New Rule for Gene Therapy Tests Proposed." *Washington Post* (January 18).

———. 2001b. "New Potential for Stem Cells Suggested." *Washington Post* (April 27).

———. 2001c. "Legal Barriers to Human Cloning May Not Hold Up." *Washington Post* (May 23).

———. 2001d. "Changing Conceptions." *Washington Post* (July 15).

Wertz, Dorothy C. 1998. "Possible Uses of Human Cloning: Some Case Scenarios." *Gene Letter* 3, no. 1 (August) [www.geneletter.org.0898/humancloning.html.].

Wilmut, Ian. 1998. "Cloning for Medicine." *Scientific American* 279, no. 6 (December) [http://www.sciam.com/1998/1298issue/1298wilmut.html].

Zitner, Aaron. 2000. "Cloned Goat Would Revive Extinct Line." *Los Angeles Times* (December 24).

———. 2001. "Embryos Created for Stem Cell Research" *Los Angeles Times* (July 11).

Zoon, Kathryn C. 2001a. Letter written to Food and Drug Administration, U.S. Department of Health and Human Services. March 28 [http://www.fda.gov/cber/ltr/aaclone.pdf].

———. 2001b. Statement by Kathryn M. Zoon, Ph.D., Director, Center for Biologics Evaluation and Research, Food and Drug Administration, Department of Health and Human Services before the Subcommittee on Oversight and Investigations, Committee on Energy and Commerce, U.S. House of Representatives, 107th Congress, First Session, March 28.

References to Chapter 5

"Aides Report: Bush Medical Privacy Act is Part of Wider Strategy." 2001. *Wall Street Journal* (April 13).

Allen, Anita L. 1997. "Genetic Privacy: Emerging Concepts and Values." In Rothstein 1997a, pp. 31–559.

Allen, Arthur. 1998a. "Exposed." *Washington Post* (February 8).

———. 1998b. "Medical Privacy? Forget It." *Medical Economics* 75, no. 9 (May 11): 150–157 [http://www.findarticles.com/m3229/n9_v75/20853024/p1/article.jhtml].

American Hospital Association. 2001a. Letter to Tommy G. Thompson, Secretary of the Department of Health and Human Services commenting on the regulations on Standards for Privacy of Individually Identifiable Health Information. March 30 [http://www.aha.org/ar/Comment/letters.asp?lookupLetterID=229].

———. 2001b. "American Hospital Association Detailed Comments: 'Standards for Privacy of Individually Identifiable Health Information, 66 *Federal Register* 12738, March 30 [http://www.aha.org/ar/Comment/PrivacyDetailB0330.asp].

"Automating Health Care." 1994. *Economist* 330, no. 7855 (March 19): 5–7.

Banisar, David, and Davies, Simon. 1999. "Global Trends in Privacy Protection." *John Marshall Journal of Computer and Information Law* 18 (Fall). Lexis-Nexis.

Bazelon Center for Mental Health Law. 1998. *Legislative Update: Privacy of Medical Records.* Washington, DC: Bazelon Center for Mental Health Law [www.bazelon.org/bazelon/medrecs.html].

Bergman, Rhonda. 1993. "The Long March Toward Progress: In Pursuit of the Computer-Based Patient Record." *Hospitals & Health Networks* 67, no. 18 (September 20): 42–48.

Biesecker, Barbara Bowles. 1997. "Privacy in Genetic Counseling." In Rothstein 1997a, pp. 108–125.

Blevins, Sue, and Kaigh, Robin. 2001. *The Final Federal Medical Privacy Rule: Myths and Facts.* Washington, DC: Institute for Health Freedom [http://www.forhealthfreedom.org/Publications/Privacy/MedPrivFacts.html].

Burris, Scott, and Gostin, Lawrence O. 1997. "Genetic Screening from a Public Health Perspective: Some Lessons from the HIV Experience." In Rothstein 1997a, pp. 137–158.

Cate, Fred H. 1997. *Privacy in the Information Age.* Washington, DC: Brookings Institution Press.

Claybrook, Joan. 2002. "Statement of Joan Claybrook, President, Public Citizen, On the Office of Management and Budget 2001 Report to Congress on the Costs and Benefits of Regulations and Unfunded Mandates on States, Local and Tribal Entities." United States House of Representatives, Committee on Government Reform, Subcommittee on Energy Policy, Natural Resources and Regulatory Affairs (March 12). Testimony may be found at Public Citizen's Web site: www.citizen.org.

Clayton, Paul, and Sheehan, Jerry. 1997. "Commentary: Beware Risk to Privacy in Putting Medical Records on Internet." *Detroit News* (May 11).

Council of Europe, n.d. *Convention for the Protection of Human Rights and Fundamental Freedoms* [http://conventions.coe.int/Treaty/EN/CadreListeTraites.htm].

Cushman, F. Reid, and Detmer, Don E. 1997. "Information Policy for the U.S. Health Sector: Engineering, Political Economy, and Ethics" Report for the Milbank Memorial Fund. [http://www.med.harvard.edu/publications/Milbank/MILBNK.doc].

Demorsky, Susan. 1990. "Automation of Medical Records Can Boost Cash Flow." *Healthcare Financial Management* 44, no. 10 (October 1): 21–28.

Department of Health and Human Services. 1998a. "HHS Proposes Administrative Simplification Standards for Health Care Transactions." Washington, DC: U.S. Department of Health and Human Services, May 7 press release.

———. 1998b. "Shalala Proposes National Standard Employer Identifier." Washington, DC: U.S. Department of Health and Human Services, May 16 press release.

———. 1998c. "HHS Proposes Security Standards For Electronic Health Data." Washington, DC: U.S. Department of Health and Human Services, August 11 press release.

———. 1999a. "HHS Proposes First-Ever National Standards To Protect Patients' Personal Medical Records." Washington, DC: U.S. Department of Health and Human Services, October 29 press release.

———. 1999b. "Standards for Privacy of Individually Identifiable Health Information; Proposed Rule." *Federal Register* 64, no. 212 (November 3): 55917–60065.

———. 2000a. "HHS Announces Electronic Standards To Simplify Health Care Transactions." Washington, DC: Department of Health and Human Services, August 11 press release.

———. 2000b. "HHS Announces Final Regulation Establishing First-Ever National Standards To Protect Patients' Personal Medical Records." Washington, DC: Department of Health and Human Services, December 20 press release.

———. 2000c. "Protecting the Privacy of Patients' Health Information: A Summary of the Final Regulation." Washington, DC: Department of Health and Human Services, December 20 Fact Sheet.

———. 2001a. "Statement By HHS Secretary Tommy G. Thompson." Washington, DC: Department of Health and Human Services, February 23.

———. 2001b. "Statement by HHS Secretary Tommy G. Thompson Regarding the Patient Privacy Rule." Washington, DC: Department of Health and Human Services, April 12.

Etzioni, Amitai. 1999. *The Limits of Privacy.* New York: Basic Books.

Flaherty, David H. 1995. "Privacy and Data Protection in Health and Medical Information.' Notes for presentation by David H. Flaherty, information and privacy commissioner, to the 8th world congress on medical informatics, Vancouver, July 27 [www.maap.mb.ca/Focus/flaherty.html].

Gallup Organization. 2000. "Public Attitudes Toward Medical Privacy." September, submitted to Institute for Health Information Freedom [http://forhealthfreedom.org/Gallupsurvey/IHF-Gallup.pdf].

Gardner, Elizabeth. 1989. "Computer Dilemma: Clinical Access vs. Confidentiality." *Modern Healthcare* 19, no. 44 (November 3): 32–42.

Gillespie, Ed, and Bob Schellas, eds. 1994. *The Contract with America: The Bold Plan by Rep. Newt Gingrich, Rep. Dick Armey, and the House Republicans to Change the Nation.* New York: Times Books.

Goldman, Janlori. 1995. "Statement of Janlori Goldman, deputy director, Center for Democracy and Technology, before the Senate Committee on Labor and Human Resources on S.1360 The Medical Record Confidentiality Act of 1995" [www.cdt.org/policy/healthpriv/jlg_111495_test.html].

———. 1998. "Protecting Privacy to Improve Health Care." *Health Affairs* 17, no. 6 (November/December): 47–60.

———. 2001. "Testimony before the Senate Committee on Health, Education, Labor and Pensions, 'Making Patient Privacy a Reality: Does the Final HHS Regulation Get the Job Done?'" U.S. Senate, 107th Congress, 1st Session, February 8 [http://www.healthprivacy.org/usr_doc/48751.pdf].

Goldman, Janlori, and Hudson, Zoe. 2000. "Virtually Exposed: Privacy and E-Health." *Health Affairs* 19, no. 6 (November/December): 140–148.

Goldman, Janlori; Schwartz, Paul; and Tang, Paul. 2000. "Roundtable: Medical Privacy." *Issues in Science and Technology* 16, no. 4 (Summer) [http://www.nap.edu/issues/16.4/goldman.htm].

Goldman, Michael A. 2001. "Beleaguered: Efforts at Banning Genetic Discrimination." *GeneLetter* (May 1) [http://www.geneletter.com/05-01-01/features/discrimination.html].

Goldsmith, Jeff. 2000. "The Internet and Managed Care: A New Wave of Innovation." *Health Affairs* 19, no. 6 (November/December): 42–56.

Gostin, Lawrence O.; Lazzarini, Zita; and Flaherty, Kathleen M. 1997. "Legislative Survey of State Confidentiality Laws, with Special Emphasis on HIV and Immunization. Washington, DC: Electronic Privacy Information Center [http://www.epic.org/privacy/medical/cdc_survey.html].

Hasson, Judi. 1993. "Access to Medical Files Reform Issue." *USA Today* (July 27).

Health Privacy Project. 2001. "Medical Privacy Stories." Washington, DC: Health Privacy Project, Institute for Heath Care Research and Policy, Georgetown University [http://www.healthprivacy.org/usr_doc/privacystories2%2Epdf].

Health Privacy Working Group. 1999. *Best Principles for Health Privacy.* Washington, DC: Health Privacy Project, Institute for Heath Care Research and Policy, Georgetown University.

Heath, Erin. 2001. "Zipping Up Genes Discrimination." *National Journal* 33, no. 29 (July 21): 2346–2347).

Heinlein, Gary. 1996. "Easier Access to Medical Files Raises Privacy Fears." *Detroit News* (May 14).

Hodge, James G.; Gostin, Lawrence O.; and Jacobson, Peter D. 1999. "Legal Issues Concerning Electronic Health Information: Privacy, Quality, and Liability." *Journal of the American Medical Association* 282, no. 15 (October 20): 1466–1471.

Hollowell, Edward E., and Ethridge, James E. 1989. "Drug and Alcohol Abuse: Medical Record Confidentiality." *Journal of Practical Nursing* 39, no. 1 (March): 46–49.

Human Rights Campaign. 1998. "Medical Records Privacy" [www.hrc.org/issues/aids/aidspriv.html].

Ignagni, Karen, and Stewart, Kristin. 2001. "A Renewed Opportunity for Medical Privacy." *GeneLetter* (April 1) [http://www.geneletter.com/04–01–01/features/privacy2.html].

James, Frank. 2000. "Consent Issue Clouds New Medical Privacy Rules." *Washington Post* (September 5).

Janda, Kenneth; Berry, Jeffrey M.; and Goldman, Jerry. 1995. *The Challenge of Democracy: Government in America*, 4th ed. Boston: Houghton Mifflin.

Kaminer, Maggie Ilene. 2001. "How Broad Is the Fundamental Right to Privacy and Personal Autonomy." *American University Journal of Gender, Social Policy & the Law* 9: 395–422.

Kass, Nancy E. 1997. "The Implications of Genetics Testing for Health and Life Insurance." In Rothstein 1997a, pp. 299–316.

Kleinke, J.D. 1998. "Release 0.0: Clinical Information Technology in the Real World." *Health Affairs* 17, no. 6 (November/December): 23–38.

———. 2000. "Vaporware.com: The Failed Promise of the Health Care Internet." *Health Affairs* 19, no. 6 (November/December): 57–71.

Krebs, Brian. 2000. "Medical Privacy Concerns Heightened by Genome Mapping" (July 17) [www.computeruser.com/clickit/printout/news/297700920002602880.html].

Le Bris, Sonia, and Knoppers, Bartha Maria. 1997. "International and Comparative Concepts of Privacy." In Rothstein 1997a, pp. 418–448.

Lumsdon, Kevin. 1993. "Computerized Patient Records Gain Converts." *Hospitals* 67, no. 7 (April 5): 44.

Lyons, Barry R. 2001. "Evolving Privacy Issue Shows Some States Leading, Others Lagging; Federal Government Taking a Middle Course." *CPN Stateline* [www.cnponline.org/Issue%20Briefs/Statelines/statelin0601.htm].

"Medical Privacy Rules Raise Questions." 2001. UPI (April 18) [http://www.healthy.net/asp/templates/news.asp?Id=2118].

Moran, Donald W. 1998. "Health Information Policy: On Preparing for the Next War." *Health Affairs* 17, no. 6 (November/December): 9–22.

Nagel, Denise. 1995. "Medical Privacy? Technology Is Eroding Confidentiality." *Newsday* (October 27).

National Conference of State Legislatures. 2001. "State Genetic Privacy Laws" [www.ncsl.org/programs/health/Genetics].

National Organization for Rare Disorders, Inc. 1998. "Medical Records Privacy and Prescriptions." (July 29). New Fairfield, CT: National Organization for Rare Disorders, Inc. [www.rarediseases.org/odu/records.htm].

Office for Civil Rights. 2001. "Standards for Privacy of Individually Identifiable Health Information." Washington, DC: U.S. Department of Health and Human Services. 45 CFR Parts 160 and 164 [http://www.hhs.gov/ocr/hipaa/finalmaster.html].

———. 2002. "National Standards to Protect the Personal Health Information." Washington, DC: U.S. Department of Health and Human Services [www.hhs.gov/ocr/hipaa/bkgrnd.html].

Office of Information and Regulatory Affairs. 2001. *Making Sense of Regulation: 2001 Report to Congress on the Costs and Benefits of Regulations and Unfunded Mandates on States, Local and Tribal Entities.* Washington, DC: U.S. Office of Management and Budget.

O'Harrow, Robert O. Jr. 1998. "Prescription Sales, Privacy Fears." *Washington Post* (February 15).

————. 2001a. "Protecting Patient Data." *Washington Post* (March 23).

————. 2001b. "Privacy Notices Criticized." *Washington Post* (June 22).

Orentlicher, David. 1997. "Genetic Privacy in the Patient Physician Relationship." In Rothstein 1997a, pp. 77–91.

Orwell, George. 1949. *1984.* New York: New American Library.

Patel, Kant, and Rushefsky, Mark E. 1999. *Health Care Politics and Policy in America,* 2nd. ed. Armonk, NY: M.E. Sharpe.

Pear, Robert. 2002. "Bush Acts to Drop Core Privacy Rule on Medical Data." *New York Times* (March 22).

————. 2001. "White House Plans to Revise New Medical Privacy Rules." *New York Times* (April 8).

Pergament, Eugene. 1997. "A Clinical Geneticist Perspective of the Patient-Physician Relationship." In Rothstein 1997a, pp. 92–107.

Perry, John L. 2001. "Medical 'Privacy' Rules Target You for Marketing." Newsmax.com (April 21) [http://www.newsmax.com/archives/articles/2001/4/20/132917.shtml].

Pritts, Joy; Goldman, Janlori; Hudson, Zoe; Berenson, Aimee; and Hadley, Elizabeth. 1999. *The State of Health Privacy: An Uneven Terrain.* Washington, DC: Health Privacy Project, Institute for Heath Care Research and Policy, Georgetown University.

Raspberry, William. 2001. "Is Labeling Sex Offenders Over the Line?" *Washington Post* (June 4).

Richman, Sheldon. 2001. "Should Community Rights Override Individual Rights to Privacy? A Book Review." Washington, DC: Institute for Health Freedom (January 22) [www.forhealthfreedom.org/Publications/Privacy/CommunityRule.html].

Rosen, Jeffrey. 2000. "Why Privacy Matters." *Wilson Quarterly* 24, no. 4 (Autumn): 32–38.

Rothstein, Mark A., ed. 1997a. *Genetic Secrets: Protecting Privacy and Confidentiality in the Genetic Era.* New Haven, CT: Yale University Press.

————. 1997b. "The Law of Medical and Genetic Privacy in the Workplace." In Rothstein 1997a, pp. 281–298.

Rushefsky, Mark E., and Patel, Kant. 1998. *Politics, Power and Policy Making: The Case of Health Reform in the 1990s.* Armonk, NY: M.E. Sharpe.

Safire, William. 2001. "Scalia on Privacy." *New York Times* (June 21).

Samet, Jonathan M., and Bailey, Linda A. 1997. "Environmental Population Screening." In Rothstein 1997a, pp. 197–211.

Schwartz, Paul M. 1997. "European Data Protection Law and Medical Privacy." In Rothstein 1997a, pp. 392–417.

Simon, Stephanie. 2001. "Privacy at Stake in New Abortion Strategy." *Los Angeles Times* (July 6).

Standler, Ronald B. 1997. "Privacy Law in the USA" [http://www.rbs2.com/privacy.htm#anchor222222].

Starr, Paul. 1982. *The Social Transformation of American Medicine.* New York: Basic Books.

Stolberg, Sheryl Gay. 1998. "Privacy of Medical ID Code Doubted." *New York Times* (July 20).

Stone, Deborah. 1993. "The Struggle for the Soul of Health Insurance." *Journal of Health Politics, Policy and Law* 18, no. 2 (Summer): 287–317.

————. 2002. *Policy Paradox: The Art of Political Decision Making*, revised ed. New York: W.W. Norton.

Sykes, Charles J. 1999. *The End of Privacy.* New York: St. Martin's Press.

Tapellini, Donna. 2001. "Medical Privacy's Tangled Web." Wired.com (January 15) [http://www.wired.com/news/technology/0,1282,40989,00.html].

Tiefer, Charles. 1994. *The Semi-Sovereign Presidency: The Bush Administration's Strategy for Governing Without Congress.* Boulder, CO: Westview Press.

Universal Declaration of Human Rights. 1998. Eleanor and Franklin Roosevelt Web site [http://www.udhr50.org/index.htm].

Walsh, Edward. 2001. "High-Tech Devices Require a Warrant." *Washington Post* (June 12).

Warren, Samuel D., and Brandeis, Louis D. 1890. "The Right to Privacy." *Harvard Law Review* IV, no. 5 (December 15): 193–220 [http://www.lawrence.edu/fac/boardmaw/Privacy_brand_warr2.html].

Westin, Alan F. 1967. *Privacy and Freedom.* New York: Atheneum Press.

Wheeler, David L. 1999. "Is the Loss of Personal Privacy the Price of Medical Research?" *Chronicle of Higher Education* 46, no. 4 (September 17) [www.chronicle.com/weekly/v46/io4/04a02101.htm].

Wood, Charles Cresson. 1991. "Burning Computer Security, Privacy, and Freedom Issues." *Computers & Security* 10, no. 6 (October 1): 524–532.

Zweig, Franklin M.; Walsh, Joseph T.; and Freeman, Daniel M. 1997. "Courts and the Challenges of Adjudicating Genetic Testing's Secrets." In Rothstein 1997a, pp. 332–351.

References to Chapter 6

Baker, Laurence C., and Wheeler, Susan K. 1998. "Managed Care and Technology Diffusion: The Case of MRI." *Health Affairs* 17, no. 5 (September/October): 195–207.

Baker, Laurence C.; Cantor, Joel C.; Long, Stephen H.; and Marquis, M. Susan. 2000. "HMO Market Penetration and Costs of Employer-Sponsored Health Plans." *Health Affairs* 19, no. 5 (September/October): 121–128.

Belkin, Gary S. 1997. "The Technocratic Wish: Making Sense and Finding Power in the 'Managed Care' Medical Marketplace." *Journal of Health Politics, Policy and Law* 22, no. 2 (April): 509–532.

Birkett, Donald J.; Mitchell, Andrew S.; and McManus, Peter. 2001. "A Cost-Effectiveness Approach to Drug Subsidy and Pricing in Australia." *Health Affairs* 20, no. 3 (May/June): 104–114.

Blank, Robert H. 1997. *The Price of Life: The Future of American Health Care.* New York: Columbia University Press.

————. 1988. *Rationing Medicine.* New York: Columbia University Press.

Bloche, M. Gregg. 2000. "U.S. Health Care After *Pegram:* Betrayal at the Bedside?" *Health Affairs* 19, no. 5 (September/October): 224–227.

Bloche, M. Gregg, and Jacobson, Peter D. 2000. "The Supreme Court and Bedside Rationing." *JAMA, the Journal of the American Medical Association* 284, no. 21 (December 6): 2776–2779.

Bridgewater, Benjamin. 1998. "Is Rationing Down Under Upside Down?" *British Medical Journal* 316, no. 7139 (April 18): 1251–1252.

British Medical Association. 2001. *Healthcare Funding Review.* London, England [www.bma.org.uk].

Brown, Lawrence D. 1991. "The National Politics of Oregon's Rationing Plan." *Health Affairs* 10, no. 2 (Summer): 28–51.

Buchanan, Allen. 1998. "Managed Care: Rationing without Justice, But Not Unjustly." *Journal of Health Politics, Policy and Law* 23, no. 4 (August): 617–634.

Bureau of the Census. 2000. *Statistical Abstract of the United States 2000.* Washington, DC: U.S. Department of Commerce.

Callahan, Daniel. 1998. *False Hopes: Why America's Quest for Perfect Health is a Recipe for Failure.* New York: Simon & Schuster.

Carey, Benedict; Ornstein, Charles; and Rosenblatt, Robert A. 2001. "Open Questions." *Los Angeles Times* (September 24).

Chernomas, Robert, and Sepehri, Ardeshir. 1995. "The Canadian Health Care System as a Managed Care Model for the United States." *Health Care Management* 2, no. 1 (October): 183–190.

Children's Defense Fund. n.d. "What's CHIP? An Introduction to the Children's Health Insurance Program." Washington, DC: Children's Defense Fund [http:// www.childrensdefense.org/health-chip.htm].

Chinitz, David, and Shalev, Carmel. 1998. "Israel's Basket of Health Services: The Importance of Being Explicitly Implicit." *British Medical Journal* 317, no. 7164 (October 10): 1005–1007.

Cookson, Richard, and Dolan, Paul. 2000. "Principles of Justice in Health Care Rationing." *Journal of Medical Ethics* 26, no. 5 (October): 323–329.

Cutler, David M., and McClellan, Mark. 2001. "Is Technological Change in Medicine Worth It?" *Health Affairs* 20, no. 5 (September/October): 11–29.

Daniels, Norman. 1991. "Is the Oregon Plan Fair?" *Journal of the American Medical Association* 265, no. 17 (May 1): 2232–2235.

———. 1994. "Four Unsolved Rationing Problems: A Challenge." *Hastings Center Report* 24, no. 4 (July–August): 27–29.

Danish Council of Ethics. 1997. *Priority Setting in the Health Service.* Copenhagen, Denmark: Danish Council of Ethics.

Dean, Malcolm. 1999. "Drug Rationing Comes Out into the Open in the UK." *Lancet* 354, no. 9179 (August 21): 657.

Dorozynski, Alexander. 1997. "French Doctors Break with National Health Insurance." *British Medical Journal* 314, no. 7073 (January 4): 8.

Durand De Bousingen, Denis. 1999. "Doctors Protest Against German Health Care Reforms." *Lancet* 354, no. 9184 (September 25): 1103.

Eddy, David M. 2001. "The Use of Evidence and Cost Effectiveness by the Courts: How Can It Help Improve Health Care?" *Journal of Health Politics, Policy and Law* 26, no. 2 (April): 387–408.

Emanuel, Ezekiel J. 2000. "Justice and Managed Care: Four Principles for the Just Allocation of Health Care Resources." *Hastings Center Report* 30, no. 8 (May–June): 8–16.

Employment Benefits Research Institute. 2001. "Issue Brief: Employment-Based Health Benefits: Trends and Outlook." (May) [www.ebri.org].

Evans, Robert G. 1992. "Canada: the Real Issues." *Journal of Health Politics, Policy and Law* 17, no. 4 (Winter): 739–762.

Feder, Judith; Komisar, Harriet L.; and Niefeld, Marlene. 2000. "Long-Term Care in the United States: An Overview." *Health Affairs* 19, no. 3 (May/June): 40–56.

Feek, Colin M. 1999. "Experience with Rationing Health Care in New Zealand." *British Medical Journal* 318, no. 7194 (May 15): 1346–1348.

Frank, Richard G. 2001. "Prescription Drug Prices: Why Do Some Pay More Than Others Do?" *Health Affairs* 20, no. 2 (March/April): 115–128.

Frankel, Stephen; Ebrahim, Shah; and Smith, George Davey. 2000. "The Limits to Demand for Health Care." *British Medical Journal* 321, no. 7252 (July 1): 40–44.

Fuchs, Victor R. 1998. "Ethics and Economics: Antagonists or Allies in Making Health Policy?" *Western Journal of Medicine* 168, no. 3 (March): 213–216.

Furrow, Barry R. 1997. "Managed Care Organizations and Patient Injury: Rethinking Liability." *Georgia Law Review* 31: 419–508.

Gabel, Jon R. 1999. "Job-Based Health Insurance, 1977–1988: The Accidental System Under Scrutiny." *Health Affairs* 18, no. 6 (November/December): 62–74.

Garber, Alan M. 2001. "Evidence-Based Coverage Policy." *Health Affairs* 20, no. 5 (September/October): 62–85.

General Accounting Office. 2000. *Prescription Drugs: Increasing Medicare Beneficiary Access and Related Implications.* Washington, DC: U.S. General Accounting Office.

Gold, Marsha. 2001. "Medicare+Choice: An Interim Report Care." *Health Affairs* 20, no. 4 (July/August): 120–138.

Graig, Laurene A. 1999. *Health of Nations: An International Perspective on U.S. Health Care Reform.* Washington, DC: CQ Press.

Gribbin, August. 2001. "HMOs Are Sick, and There's No Cure in Sight." *Washington Times* (July 30).

Hacker, Jacob S. 2001. "Policy Feedback in the Private Sector: Workplace Benefits and the American Welfare State." Paper prepared for delivery at the 2001 annual meeting of the American Political Science Convention, August 30–September 2, 2001, San Francisco.

———. 2002. *The Divided Welfare State: The Battle over Public and Private Social Benefits in the United States.* New York: Columbia University Press.

Hacker, Jacob S., and Theodore R. Marmor. 1999. "The Misleading Language of Managed Care." *Journal of Health Politics, Policy and Law* 24, no. 5 (October): 1033–1043.

Hadorn, D.C. 1991. "The Oregon Priority-Setting Exercise: Quality of Life and Public Policy." *Hastings Center Report* 21, no. 3 (May/June): supplement 11–16.

Hall, Mark A.; Kidd, Kristin E.; and Dugan, Elizabeth. 2000. "Disclosure of Physician Incentives: Do Practices Satisfy Purposes?" *Health Affairs* 19, no. 4 (July/August): 156–164.

Ham, Chris. 1998. "Retracing the Oregon Trail: The Experience of Rationing and the Oregon Health Plan." *British Medical Journal* 316, no. 7149 (June 27): 1965–1969.

Hammer, Peter J. 2001. "*Pegram v. Herdrich*: On Peritonitis, Preemption, and the Elusive Goal of Managed Care Accountability." *Journal of Health Politics, Policy and Law* 26, no. 4 (August): 767–787.

Health Care Financing Administration (HCFA). 2000. *Medicare 2000: 35 Years of Improving Americans' Health and Security.* Washington, DC: Health Care Financing Administration.

———. 2001. "State Children's Health Insurance Program, Aggregate Enrollment Statistics for the Fifty States and the District of Columbia for Federal Fiscal Year (FFY) 2000." Washington, DC: Health Care Financing Administration [http://www.hcfa.gov/init/fy2000.pdf].

Heffler, Stephen; Levit, Katharine; Smith, Sheila; Smith, Cynthia; Cowan, Cathy;

Lazanby, Helen; and Freeland, Mark. 2001. "Health Spending Growth Up in 1999; Faster Growth Expected in Future." *Health Affairs* 20, no. 2 (March/April): 193–203.

Holahan, John. 2001. "Restructuring Medicaid Financing: Implications of the NGA Proposal." Menlo Park, CA: Kaiser Commission on Medicaid and the Uninsured.

Holm, Soren. 1998. "Goodbye to the Simple Solutions: The Second Phase of Priority Setting in Health Care." *British Medical Journal* 317, no. 7164 (October 10): 1000–1002.

Hope, Tony. 2001. "Rationing and Life-Saving Treatments: Should Identifiable Patients Have Higher Priority." *Journal of Medical Ethics* 27, no. 3 (June): 179–185.

Hunter, David J. 1995. "Rationing: The Case for 'Muddling Through Elegantly.'" *British Medical Journal* 311, no. 7008 (September 23); 811.

Jacobs, Lawrence; Marmor, Theodore; and Oberlander, Jonathan. 1999. "The Oregon Health Plan and the Political Paradox of Rationing: What Advocates and Critics Have Claimed and What Oregon Did." *Journal of Health Politics, Policy and Law* 24, no. 1 (February): 161–180.

Jecker, Nancy S., and Meslin, Eric M. 1994. "United States and Canadian Approaches to Justice in Health Care: A Comparative Analysis of Health Care Systems and Value." *Theoretical Medicine* 15, no. 2 (June 1): 181–200.

Klein, Rudolph. 1998. "Puzzling Out Priorities: Why We Must Acknowledge That Rationing Is a Political Process." *British Medical Journal* 317, no. 7164 (October 10): 959–960.

Kleinert, Sabine. 1998. "Rationing of Health Care: How Should It Be Done?" *Lancet* (October 17): 1244.

Kleinke, J.D. 2001. "The Price of Progress: Prescription Drugs in the Health Care Market." *Health Affairs* 20, no. 5 (September/October): 43–60.

Kopelman, Loretta M., and Palumbo, Michael G. 1997. "The U.S. Health Care System: Inefficient and Unfair to Children (Managed Care Phase Two-Structural Changes and Equity Issues)." *American Journal of Law & Medicine* 23, nos. 2–3 (Summer/Fall): 319–337.

Kriz, Margaret. 2001. "Future Shock." *National Journal* 33, no. 21 (May 26): 1556–1560.

Lamm, Richard D. 1998. "Marginal Medicine." *JAMA, the Journal of the American Medical Association* 280, no. 10 (September 9): 931–933.

Leichter, Howard M. 1999. "Oregon's Bold Experiment: Whatever Happened to Rationing?" *Journal of Health Politics, Policy and Law* 24, no. 1 (February): 147–160.

Light, Donald W. 1997. "The Real Ethics of Rationing." *British Medical Journal* 314, no. 7100 (July 12): 112–115.

Lindblom, Charles E. 1959. "The Science of Muddling Through." *Public Administration Review* 14, no. 2 (Spring): 79–88.

Lindblom, Charles E., and Woodhouse, Edward J. 1993. *The Policy-Making Process*, 3d ed. Englewood Cliffs, NJ: Prentice-Hall.

Luce, Bryan R., and Brown, Ruth E. 1994. "The Impact of Technology Assessment on Decisions by Health Care Providers and Payers." In Annetine C. Gelijns and Holly V. Dawkins, *Adopting New Medical Technology*, pp. 49–58. Washington, DC, National Academy Press.

Marmor, Theodore R. 2000. *The Politics of Medicare*, 2nd ed. New York: Aldine de Gruyter.

McClellan, Mark; Spatz, Ian D.; and Carney, Stacie. 2000. "Designing a Medicare Prescription Drug Benefit: Issues, Obstacles, and Opportunities." *Health Affairs* 19, no. 2 (March/April): 26–41.

Mechanic, David. 1997. "Muddling Through Elegantly: Finding the Proper Balance in Rationing." *Health Affairs* 16, no. 5 (September/October): 83–92.

Mello, Michelle M.; and Brennan, Troyen A. 2001. "The Controversy Over High-Dose Chemotherapy with Autologous Bone Marrow Transplant for Breast Cancer." *Health Affairs* 20, no. 5 (September/October): 101–117.

Merlis, Mark. 2000. "Caring for the Frail Elderly: An International Review." *Health Affairs* 19, no. 3 (May/June): 141–149.

Moon, Marilyn. 1996. *Medicare Now and in the Future*, 2nd ed. Washington, DC: Urban Institute Press.

Morgan, M. Granger. 1995. "Death by Congressional Ignorance: How the Congressional Office of Technology Assessment—Small and Excellent—Was Killed in the Frenzy of Government Downsizing." *Pittsburgh Post-Gazette* (August 2).

Mulrow, Cynthia D., and Lohr, Kathleen N. 2001. "Proof and Policy from Medical Research Evidence." *Journal of Health Politics, Policy and Law* 26, no. 2 (April): 247–266.

National Center for Health Statistics. 2001. *Health, United States, 2001*. Washington, DC: U.S. Department of Health and Human Services.

National Information Center on Health Services Research and Health Care Technology. n.d. "Ten Basic Steps of HCTA." National Library of Medicine [http://www.nlm.nih.gov/nichsr/ta101/ta10105.htm].

Neus, Elizabeth. 2001. "Big Employers Face HMO Hikes." *Arizona Republican* (July 26).

Newdick, Christopher. 1997. "Resource Allocation in the National Health Service." *American Journal of Law & Medicine* 23, no. 2–3 (Summer–Fall): 291–318.

Nissenson, Allen R., and Rettig, Richard G. 1999." Medicare's End-Stage Renal Disease Program: Current Status and Future Prospects." *Health Affairs* 18, no. 1 (January/February): 161–179.

Noble, Alice A., and Troyen, A. Brennan. 1999. "Managed Care Regulation: Developing Better Rules." *Journal of Health Politics, Policy and Law* 24, no. 6 (December): 1275–1305.

Norheim, Ole Frithjof. 1999. "Healthcare Rationing: Are Additional Criteria Needed for Assessing Evidence Based Clinical Practice Guidelines?" *British Medical Journal* 319, no. 1722 (November 27): 1426–1429.

Oberlander, Jonathan B. 1998. "Medicare: The End of Consensus." Paper delivered at the annual meeting of the American Political Science Association, Boston, MA, September 3–6.

———. 2000. "Is Premium Support the Right Medicine for Medicare?" *Health Affairs* 19, no. 5 (September/October 2000): 84–99.

Oberlander, Jonathan B.; Marmor, Theodore; and Jacobs, Lawrence. 2001. "Rationing Medical Care: Rhetoric and Reality in the Oregon Health Plan." *Canadian Medical Association Journal* 164, no. 11 (May 29): 1583–1587.

Office of Management and Budget. 2001. *Budget of the United States Government, Fiscal Year 2002; Historical Tables*. Washington, DC: Office of Management and Budget, Executive Office of the President.

Okie, Susan. 2001. "More HMOs Quit Medicare Plan." *Washington Post* (September 22).

Organization for Economic Cooperation and Development. 2001. "OECD in Figures 2001." Paris, France: Organization for Economic Cooperation and Development [http://www.oecd.org/publications/figures/].

Palazzolo, Daniel J. 1999. *Done Deal? The Politics of the 1997 Budget Agreement.* New York: Chatham House.

Park, Edwin, and Ku, Leighton. 2001. *Administration Medicaid and CHIP Waiver Policy Encourages States to Scale Back Benefits Significantly and Increase Cost-Sharing for Low-Income Beneficiaries.* Washington, DC: Center for Budget and Public Priorities.

Patel, Kant, and Rushefsky, Mark E. 1998. "The Health Policy Community and Health-Care Reform in the US." *Health: An Interdisciplinary Journal for the Social Study of Health, Illness and Medicine* 2, no. 4 (October): 459–484.

———. 1999. *Health Care Politics and Policy in America,* 2nd ed. Armonk, NY: M.E. Sharpe.

———. 2001. "Canadian Health Care System" In Khi V. Thai, Edward T. Wimberley, and Sharon M. McManus, eds., *Handbook of International Health Care Systems,* pp. 79–98. New York: Marcel Dekker.

Pear, Robert 2000. "Medicare Spending for Care at Home Plunges by 45%." *New York Times* (April 18).

———. 2001a. "Bush Drug Plan Calls for Using Discount Cards." *New York Times* (July 10).

———. 2001b. "H.M.O.'s Plan to Drop Medicare, Calling Fees Too Low." *New York Times* (September 21).

———. 2001c. "Number of Uninsured Drops for 2nd Year." *New York Times* (September 27).

Poisal, John A., and Murray, Lauren. 2001. "Growing Differences Between Medicare Beneficiaries With and Without Drug Coverage." *Health Affairs* 20, no. 2 (March/April): 74–85.

Reagan, Michael D. 1999. *The Accidental System: Health Care Policy in America.* Boulder, CO: Westview Press.

"Report Urges More Honest Approach to Rationing." 2001. *British Medical Journal* 322, no. 7282 (February 10): 316.

Rivlin, Michael. 1999. "Should Age Based Rationing of Health Care Be Illegal?" *British Medical Journal* 319, no. 7221 (November 20): 1379.

Robinson, James C. 2002. "Renewed Emphasis on Consumer Cost Sharing in Health Insurance Benefit Design." *Health Affairs.* Web exclusive: www.healthaffairs.org. (pp. W139–W154).

Rodwin, Marc A. 2001. "The Politics of Evidence-Based Medicine." *Journal of Health Politics, Policy and Law* 26, no. 2 (April): 438–446.

Roos, Noralou P.; Brownell, Marni; Shapiro, Evelyn; and Roos, Leslie L. 1998. "International Update: Good News About Difficult Decisions: The Canadian Approach to Hospital Cost Control." *Health Affairs* 17, no. 5 (September/October): 239–246.

Rottenberg, Simon, and Theroux, David J. n.d. "Rationing Health Care: Price Controls are Hazardous to our Health." Oakland, CA: The Independent Institute [http://www.independent.org/tii/Research/RottenbergBackgrounder.html].

Rushefsky, Mark E., and Patel, Kant. 1998. *Politics, Power & Policy Making: The Case of Health Care Reform in the 1990s.* Armonk, NY: M.E. Sharpe.

Russell, Louise B.; Gold, Marthe R.; Seigel, Joanna E.; Daniels, Norman; and Weinstein, Milton C. 1996. "The Role of Cost-Effectiveness Analysis in Health and Medicine." *Journal of the American Medical Association* 276, no. 14 (October 9): 1172–1177.

Sabin, James E. 1998. "Fairness as a Problem of Love and the Heart: A Clinician's Perspective on Priority Setting." *British Medical Journal* 317, no. 7164 (October 10): 1002–1004.

Serafini, Marilyn Werber. 1997. "Brave New World." *National Journal* 29, no. 33 (August 16): 1636–1639.

Slawson, David C., and Shaughnessy, Allen F. 2001. "Using 'Medical Poetry' to Remove the Inequities in Health Care Delivery." *Journal of Family Practice* 50, no. 1 (January): 51–65.

Starr, Paul. 1982. *The Social Transformation of American Medicine.* New York: Basic Books, 1982.

Stone, Deborah. 2002. *Policy Paradox: The Art of Political Decision Making,* revised ed. New York: W.W. Norton.

Sullivan, Kip. 2000. "On the 'Efficiency' of Managed Care Plans." *Health Affairs* 19, no. 4 (July/August): 139–148.

Technological Change in Health Care Research Network. 2001. "Technological Change Around the World: Evidence from Heart Attack Care." *Health Affairs* 20, no. 3 (May/June): 25–42.

The Century Foundation. 2000. "An Outpatient Prescription Drug Benefit for Medicare." Idea Brief No. 10 (June). Washington, DC: The Century Foundation.

Ubel, Peter A. 2000. *Pricing Life: Why It's Time for Health Care Rationing.* Cambridge, MA: MIT Press.

Walker, Michael, and Goodman, John C. 1993. "Health Care Rationing: Canada's Lesson." *Consumers' Research Magazine* 76, no. 11 (November): 26–29.

Weisbrod, Burton A., 1994. "The Nature of Technological Change: Incentives Matter!" In Annetine C. Gelijns and Holly V. Dawkins, *Adopting New Medical Technology,* pp. 8–48. Washington, DC: National Academy Press.

White, Joseph. 1995. *Competing Solutions: American Health Care Proposals and International Experience.* Washington, DC: Brookings Institution.

———. 1999. "Uses and Abuses of Long-Term Medicare Cost Estimates." *Health Affairs* 18, no. 1 (January/February): 63–79.

———. 2001. *False Alarm: Why the Greatest Threat to Social Security and Medicare Is the Campaign to 'Save' Them.* Baltimore: Johns Hopkins University Press.

References to Chapter 7

Abraham, Kenneth S., and Weiler, Paul C. 1994a. "Enterprise Medical Liability and the Choice of the Responsible Enterprise." *American Journal of Law & Medicine* 20: 29–36.

———. 1994b. "Enterprise Medical Liability and the Evolution of the American Health Care System." *Harvard Law Review* 108: 381–436.

Alter, Jonathan. 2001. "Fighting the HMO Meanies." *Newsweek* 138, no. 6 (August 6): 33.

American Association of Health Plans. 2001. Press Release: "Statement of AAHP President Karen Ignagni on Approval of Patients' Rights Legislation by US House" (August 2) [ww.aahp.org].

Anders, George. 1996. *Health Against Wealth: HMOs and the Breakdown of Medical Trust.* Boston: Houghton Mifflin.

Angell, Marcia. 2001. "A Wrong Turn on Patients' Rights." *New York Times* (June 23).

Balz, Dan, and Harris, John F. 2001. "For Bush, Losing the Initiative on Patients' Rights." *Washington Post* (July 23).

Baumgartner, Frank R., and Jones, Bryan R. 1993. *Agendas and Instability in American Politics.* Chicago: University of Chicago Press.

Beatty, Jack, ed. 2001. *Corporations: How the Corporation Changed America.* New York: Broadway Books.

Bellah, Robert N.; Madsen, Richard; Sullivan, William M.; Swidler, Ann; and Tipton, Steven M. 1991. *The Good Society.* New York: Vintage Books.

Bloche, M. Gregg. 2000. "U.S. Health Care after *Pegram*: Betrayal at the Bedside?" *Health Affairs* 19, no. 5 (September/October): 224–227.

———. 2001. "Look Out! That's the Wrong Way to Patients Rights." *Washington Post* (July 22).

Bodenheimer, Thomas. 2000. "Selective Chaos." *Health Affairs* 19, no. 4 (July/August): 200–205.

Bodenheimer, Thomas, and Sullivan, Kip. 1998. "How Large Employers Are Shaping the Health Care Marketplace" (first of two parts). *New England Journal of Medicine* 338, no. 14 (April 2): 1003–1007.

Brahams, Diana. 2000. "UK: Impact of European Human Rights Law." *Lancet* 356, no. 9239 (October 21): 1433–1434.

Broder, David S. 2001. "Battle of Anecdotes." *Washington Post* (June 26).

Brodie, Mollyann; Brady, Lee Ann; and Altman, Drew E. 1998. "Media Coverage of Managed Care: Is There a Negative Bias?" *Health Affairs* 17, no. 1 (January/February): 9–25.

Browne, Anthony. 2001. "Milburn Eats Up Patients' Rights." *New Statesman* 130, no. 4525 (February 19): 25–26.

Butler, Patricia. 2001. "Key Characteristics of State Managed Care Organization Liability Laws: Current Status and Experience." Menlo Park, CA: Kaiser Family Foundation.

———. 2000. "ERISA and State Health Care Initiatives: Opportunities and Obstacles." New York: The Commonwealth Fund.

———. 1997. "Managed Care Plan Liability: An Analysis of Texas and Missouri Legislation." Menlo Park, CA: Kaiser Family Foundation.

California Health Policy Roundtable. 1999. "Health Plan Liability." Berkeley: Center for Health and Public Policy Studies, University of California.

Cerminara, Kathy L. 1998. "The Class Action Suit as a Method of Patient Empowerment in the Managed Care Setting." *American Journal of Law & Medicine* 23: 7–58.

Coan, L. Frank Jr. 1996. "You Can't Get There From Here: Questioning the Erosion of ERISA Preemption in Medical Malpractice Actions Against HMOs." *Georgia Law Review* 30: 1023–1059.

Congressional Budget Office. 1997. *Trends in Spending by the Private Sector.* Washington, DC: Congressional Budget Office.

Court, Jamie, and Smith, Francis. 1999. *Making a Killing: HMOs and the Threat to Your Health.* Monroe, ME: Common Courage Press.

Crook, Clive. 2001. "Counting Up the Bill for the Patients' Bill of Rights." *National Journal* 33, no. 26 (June 30): 2074–2075.

Dalleck, Geraldine, and Pollitz, Karen. 2000. "External Review of Health Plan Decisions: An Update." Menlo Park, CA: Kaiser Family Foundation.

Daniels, Norman, and Sabin, James. 1998. "The Ethics of Accountability in Managed Care Reform." *Health Affairs* 17, no. 5 (September/October): 50–64.
Danish Council of Ethics. 1997. *Priority Setting in the Health Service.* Copenhagen, Denmark: Danish Council of Ethics.
Department of Health and Human Services. 1998. "Progress Report in Implementing the Patients' Bill of Rights at the Department of Health & Human Services." Washington, DC: U.S. Department of Health and Human Services [aspe.os.dhhs.gov/health/vpreport.htm].
Dolan, Maura. 2001. "Medicare Patients Can Sue HMOs." *Los Angeles Times* (May 4).
Doroshow, Joanne. 2001. "Deja Vu All Over Again: Bush and Tort Reform." Tompaine.com (January 9).
Dudley, R. Adams, and Luft, Harold S. 2001. "Managed Care in Transition." *New England Journal of Medicine* 344, no. 14 (April 5): 1087–1092.
Enthoven, Alain C. 1978 "Consumer Choice Health Plans (first of two parts)." *New England Journal of Medicine* 298 (March 23): 650–658.
Enthoven, Alain C., and Kronick, Richard. 1989. "A Consumer-Choice Health Plan for the 1990s: Universal Health Insurance in a System Designed to Promote Quality and Economy" (first of two parts). *New England Journal of Medicine* 320, no. 1 (January 5): 29–37.
Etheredge, Lynn. 1997. "Promarket Regulation: An SEC-FASB Model." *Health Affairs* 16, no. 6 (November/December): 22–25.
Fallows, James. 1995. "A Triumph of Misinformation," *Atlantic Monthly* 275, no. 1 (January): 26–37.
FamiliesUSA. 1997. "Leading Health Plans and National Consumer Groups Announce Unprecedented Agreement for Consumer Protection Standards in Managed Care." Washington, DC: FamiliesUSA [http://www.familiesusa.orghmoagre.htm].
———. 1998. "Hit and Miss: State Managed Care Laws." Washington, DC: FamiliesUSA.
———. 2001a. "Medicaid Managed Care Consumer Protection Regulations: No Patients' Rights for the Poor?" Washington, DC: FamiliesUSA.
———. 2001b. "House Action on Patients' Rights." (August 3) [www.familiesusa.org].
Foundation for Taxpayer and Consumer Rights. 2001. "Press Release: Norwood-Bush Amendment to Patients' Rights Erases More Generous CA Law." (August 2) [http://consumerwatchdog.org/healthcare/pr/pr001812.php3].
Freudenheim, Milt. 2001a. "A Changing World is Forcing Changes on Managed Care." *New York Times* (July 2).
———. 2001b. "In a Shift, an H.M.O. Rewards Doctors for Quality Care." *New York Times* (July 11).
Furrow, Barry R. 1997. "Managed Care Organizations and Patient Injury: Rethinking Liability." *Georgia Law Review* 31: 419–508.
Gabel, Jon R. 1999. "Job-Based Health Insurance, 1977–1988: The Accidental System Under Scrutiny." *Health Affairs* 18, no. 6 (November/December): 62–74.
Gabel, Jon R.; Ginsburg, Paul B.; Whitmore, Heidi H.; and Pickreign, Jeremy D. 2000. "Withering on the Vine: The Decline of Indemnity Health Insurance." *Health Affairs* 19, no. 5 (September/October): 152–157.
Gallagher, Thomas H.; St. Peter, Robert S.; Chesney, Margaret; and Lo, Bernard. 2001. "Patients' Attitudes Toward Cost Control Bonuses for Managed Care Physicians." *Health Affairs* 20, no. 2 (March/April): 186–192.

Gaynor, Martin; Haas-Wilson, Deborah; and Vogt, William B. 2000. "Are Invisible Hands Good Hands? Moral Hazard, Competition, and Second-Best in Health Care Markets." *Journal of Political Economy* 108, no. 5 (October): 992–1005.

Gold, Marsha. 2001. "Medicare+Choice: An Interim Report Card." *Health Affairs* 20, no. 4 (July/August): 120–138.

Goldstein, Amy. 2001a. "Senate's Health Care Bill Lags behind Some HMOs." *Washington Post* (July 1).

———. 2001b. "Medicaid Rights Will be Deferred." *Washington Post* (August 15).

Goldstein, Army, and Eilperin, Juliet. 2001. "House Passes Patients' Rights." *Washington Post* (August 3).

Gonzalez, Jose L. 1998. "A Managed Care Organization's Medical Malpractice Liability for Denial of Care: The Lost World." *Houston Law Review* 35 (Fall): 715–799.

Hacker, Jacob S. 1997. *The Road to Nowhere: The Genesis of Clinton's Plan for Health Security.* Princeton, NJ: Princeton University Press.

Hacker, Jacob S., and Marmor, Theodore R. 1999. "The Misleading Language of Managed Care." *Journal of Health Politics, Policy and Law* 24, no. 5 (October): 1033–1043.

Havighurst, Clark C. 1997a. "Perspective: 'Putting Patients First': Promise or Smoke Screen?" *Health Affairs* 16, no. 6 (November/December): 123–125.

———. 1997b. "Making Health Plans Accountable for the Quality of Care." *Georgia Law Review* 31: 587–647.

———. 2000a. "American Health Care and the Law—We Need to Talk!" *Health Affairs* 19, no. 4 (July/August): 84–106.

———. 2000b. "Vicarious Liability: Relocating Responsibility for the Quality of Medical Care." *American Journal of Law & Medicine* 26: 7–28.

———. 2001. "Consumers versus Managed Care: The New Class Actions." *Health Affairs* 20, no. 4 (July/August): 8–27.

Health Care Financing Administration. 2000. *Medicare 2000: 35 Years of Improving Americans' Health and Security.* Washington, DC: Health Care Financing Administration.

Health Insurance Association of America. 2001. Press Release: "Patients' Rights Bill Still Hurts Patients, Increases Number of Uninsured" (August 2) [www.HIAA.org].

Heffler, Stephen; Levit, Katharine; Smith, Sheila; Smith, Cynthia; Cowan, Cathy; Lazenby, Helen; and Freeland, Mark. 2001. "Health Spending Growth Up in 1999; Faster Growth Expected in Future." *Health Affairs* 20, no. 2 (March/April): 193–203.

Henry, James F. 1996/1997. "Liability of Managed Care Organizations after *Dukes v. U.S. Healthcare:* An Elemental Analysis." *Cumberland Law Review* 27: 681–716.

Hibbard, Judith H.; Jewett, Jacquelyn J.; Legnini, Mark W.; and Tusler, Martin. 1997 "Choosing a Health Plan: Do Large Employers Use the Data?" *Health Affairs* 16, no. 6 (November/December): 172–180.

Holahan, John; Zuckerman, Stephen; Evans, Alison; and Rangarajan, Suresh. 1998. "Medicaid Managed Care in Thirteen States." *Health Affairs* 17, no. 3 (May/June): 43–63.

Hoff, John S. 2000. "The Patients' Bill of Rights: A Prescription for Massive Federal Regulation." *The Heritage Foundation Backgrounder*, no. 1350 (February 29).

Hunt, Sandra; Saari, John; and Traw, Kelly. 1998. "Litigation and Appeal Experience of CalPERS, Other Large Public Employers, and a Large California Health Plan."

Menlo Park, CA: Kaiser Family Foundation [http://www.kff.org/content/archive/1415/erisa.html].

Ignagni, Karen. 1998. "Covering a Breaking Revolution: The Media and Managed Care." *Health Affairs* 17, no. 1 (January/February): 26–34.

Johnson, Haynes, and Broder, David S. 1996. *The System: The American Way of Politics at the Breaking Point*. Boston: Little, Brown.

Jones, David A. 1997. "'Putting Patients First': A Philosophy in Practice." *Health Affairs* 16, no. 6 (November/December): 115–120.

"Justices to Decide Legality of HMO 2nd Opinion Statutes." 2001. Associated Press (June 30).

Kaiser Commission on Medicaid and the Uninsured. 2001. "Pieces of the Puzzle." Menlo Park, CA: Kaiser Commission on Medicaid and the Uninsured.

Kaiser Family Foundation. 2001. "Recent Findings on Public Attitudes towards Patients' Rights and Managed Care." Menlo Park, CA: Henry J. Kaiser Family Foundation.

Kelso, J. Clark. 1999. "Alternative Approaches to Liability: Models for Health Plan Liability." Menlo Park, CA: Kaiser Family Foundation.

King, Michele R. 1998. "Restricting the Corporate Practice of Medicine: Subverting ERISA to Hold Managed Care Organizations Accountable for Health Care Treatment Decisions—the Texas Initiative." *Delaware Journal of Corporate Law* 23: 1203–1236.

Kingdon, John W. 1984. *Agendas, Alternatives, and Public Policies*. Boston: Little, Brown.

Kinsley, Michael. 2001. "Liberalism a la Mode." Slate.com (June 21).

Kronick, Richard. 1999. "Waiting for Godot: Wishes and Worries in Managed Care." *Journal of Health Policy, Politics and Law* 24, no. 5 (October): 1099–1106.

Kumar, Sanjay. 1995. "Indian Supreme Court Upholds Patients' Rights." *Lancet* 346, no. 8987 (November 25): 1418.

Lewis, Stephanie. 2001. "A Guide to the Federal Patients' Bill of Rights Debate." Menlo Park, CA: Kaiser Family Foundation.

Leyerle, Betty. 1994. *The Private Regulation of American Health Care*. Armonk, NY: M.E. Sharpe.

Lind, JoEllen. 1998. "Liberty, Community, and Framers' Intent." *The Responsive Community: Rights and Responsibilities* 8, no. 4 (Fall): 13–23.

Mariner, Wendy K. 1999. "Going Hollywood with Patient Rights in Managed Care." *JAMA, the Journal of the American Medical Association* 281, no. 9 (March 3): 861.

Marmor, Theodore R. 2000. *The Politics of Medicare*, 2nd ed. Hawthorne, NY: Aldine de Gruyter.

Marquis, M. Susan, and Long, Stephen H. 1999. "Trends in Managed Care and Managed Competition, 1993–1997." *Health Affairs* 18, no. 6 (November/December): 75–88.

Marsteller, Jill A., and Bovbjerg, Randall R. 1999. "Federalism and Patient Protection: Changing Roles for State and Federal Government." Washington, DC: Urban Institute.

Marwick, Charles. 1998. "'Bill of Rights' for Patients Sent to Clinton." *Journal of the American Medical Association* 279, no. 1 (January 7): 7–8.

Maxwell, James; Temin, Peter; and Watts, Corey. 2001. "Corporate Health Care Purchasing Among Fortune 500 Firms." *Health Affairs* 20, no. 3 (May/June): 181–188.

Mayes, Rick. 2001. "From Medicare's Rescue to the Managed Care Revolution: How Congress Inadvertently Transformed American Medicine." Paper presented at the 2001 Annual Meeting of the American Political Science Association, San Francisco, August–September.

McConnell, Grant. 1966. *Private Power & American Democracy*. New York: Vintage Books.

McDonough, John E. 2001. "Using and Misusing Anecdote in Policy Making." *Health Affairs* 20, no. 1 (January/February): 207–212.

McEldowney, Rene, and Murray, William L. 2000. "Not Just for Bureaucrats Anymore: Bureaucrat Bashing, Overhead Democracy, and Managed Care." *Administration & Society* 32, no. 1 (March): 93–110.

Mechanic, David. 1996. "Changing Medical Organization and the Erosion of Trust." *Milbank Memorial Fund Quarterly/Health and Society* 74, no. 2 (Spring): 178–189.

———. 1998. "The Functions and Limitations of Trust in the Provision of Medical Care." *Journal of Health Politics, Policy and Law* 23, No. 4 (August 1998): 661–686.

———. 2000. "Managed Care and the Imperative for a New Professional Ethic." *Health Affairs* 19, no. 5 (September/October): 100–111.

Miller, Robert H., and Luft, Harold S. 1997. "Does Managed Care Lead to Better or Worse Quality of Care?" *Health Affairs* 16, no. 5 (September/October): 7–25.

Milligan, Susan. 2001. "Bush Signals Compromise on Patients Rights Bill." *Boston Globe* (July 27).

Minow, Nell. 1996. "Whom Should Corporations Serve?" *The Responsive Community: Rights and Responsibilities* 6, no. 2 (Spring): 39–49.

Mintz, Morton. 2000. "#18 Mort Wants to Know: Corporate Crime Series (Part 3): How About Equal Treatment for Corporations and Humans?" [www.tompaine.com].

Mitchell, Alison, and Pear, Robert. 2001. "Senate Considers Patients' Rights in Test with Bush." *New York Times* (June 18).

Moffit, Robert E. 2001a. "A Dozen Better Ideas for a Patients' Bill of Rights." Washington, DC: The Heritage Foundation (June 20).

———. 2001b. "Importing HCFA-Style Regulation into the Private Sector Through the Patient's Bill of Rights." Washington, DC: The Heritage Foundation. (June 27).

Moore, David W. 2001a. "Public Supports Patient's Bill of Rights." Gallup Poll News Service [www.gallup.org] (July 9).

———. 2001b. "Overwhelming Public Support for Concept of Patient's Bill of Rights." Gallup Poll News Service [www.gallup.org] (July 30).

———, and Carroll, Joseph. 2001. "Patient's Bill of Rights Important to Americans." Gallup Poll News Service [www.gallup.org] (June 20).

Moran, Donald W. 1997. "Federal Regulation of Managed Care: An Impulse in Search of a Theory." *Health Affairs* 16, no. 6 (November/December): 7–21.

Mullan, Fitzhugh. 2001. "A Founder of Quality Assessment Encounters a Troubled System Firsthand." *Health Affairs* 20, no. 1 (January/February): 137–141.

Neus, Elizabeth. 2001. "Big Employers Face HMO Hikes." *The Arizona Republic* (July 26).

Noble, Alice A., and Brennan, Troyen A. 1999. "Managed Care Regulation: Developing Better Rules." *Journal of Health Politics, Policy and Law* 24, no. 6 (December): 1275–1305.

Office of the Press Secretary. 1998. "President Clinton Issues Directive Aimed at Ensuring that Federal Health Plans Come into Compliance with the Patients' Bill of Rights." Washington, DC: Executive Office of the President [www.healthlaw.org/whitehousepress980220.html].

Palazzolo, Daniel J. 1999. *Done Deal? The Politics of the 1997 Budget Agreement.* NY: Chatham House.

Patel, Kant, and Rushefsky, Mark E. 1999. *Health Care Politics and Policy in America,* 2nd ed. Armonk, NY: M.E. Sharpe.

"Patients' Bill of Rights." 2001. Interview with Gregg Bloch. Tompaine.com (July 24).

"Patients' Rights." 1991. *Lancet* 338, no. 8776 (November 9): 1199.

Pauley, Mark V. 1971. *Medical Care at Public Expense: A Study in Applied Welfare Economics.* New York: Praeger.

Pear, Robert. 1996. "Managed Care Officials Agree to Mastectomy Hospital Stays." *New York Times* (November 15).

———. 1998. "White House Adds Broad Protections in Medicare Rules." *New York Times* (June 23).

———. 2001. "States Dismayed by Federal Bills on Patient Rights." *New York Times* (August 12).

Phillips, Kathryn; Fernyak, Susan; Potosky, Arnold L.; Schauffler, Helen Halpin; and Egorin, Melanie. 2000. "Use of Preventive Services by Managed Care Enrollees: An Updated Perspective." *Health Affairs* 19, no. 1 (January/February): 102–116.

Pollitz, Karen; Crowley, Jeffrey; Lucia, Kevin; and Bangit, Eliza. 2002. *Assessing State External Review Programs and the Effects of Pending Federal Patients' Rights Legislation.* Menlo Park, CA: Kaiser Family Foundation.

Polzer, Karl, and Butler, Patricia. 1997. "Employee Health Plan Protection Under ERISA." *Health Affairs* 16, no. 5 (September/October): 93–102.

President's Advisory Commission on Consumer Protection and Quality in the Health Care Industry. 1998 *Quality First: Better Health Care for All Americans.* Washington, DC [http://www.hcqualitycommission.gov/final/].

Pritts, Joy; Goldman, Janlori; Hudson, Zoe; Berenson, Aimee; and Hadley, Elizabeth. 1999. *The State of Health Privacy: An Uneven Terrain.* Washington, DC: Health Privacy Project, Institute for Heath Care Research and Policy, Georgetown University.

Randel, Lauren; Pearson, Steven D.; Sabin, James E.; Hyams, Tracey; and Emanuel, Ezekiel J. 2001. "How Managed Care Can Be Ethical." *Health Affairs* 20, no. 4 (July/August): 43–56.

Reagan, Michael D. 1999. *The Accidental System: Health Care Policy in America.* Boulder, CO: Westview Press.

Reinhardt, Uwe E. 1999. "The Predictable Managed Care *Kvetch* on the Rocky Road from Adolescence to Adulthood." *Journal of Health Politics, Policy and Law* 24, no. 5 (October): 897–910.

"Responsive Communitarian Platform: Rights and Responsibilities." 1991/1992. *The Responsive Community: Rights and Responsibilities* 2, no. 1 (Winter): 4–20.

Rice, Thomas. 1999. "The Microregulation of the Health Care Marketplace." *Journal of Health Politics, Policy and Law* 24, no. 5 (October): 967–972.

Richards, Tessa. 1999. "European Network for Patients' Rights Set Up." *British Medical Journal* no. 7193 (May 8): 1234.

Rochefort, David A. 1998. "The Role of Anecdotes in Regulating Managed Care." *Health Affairs* 17, no. 6 (November/December): 142–149.

Rodwin, Marc A. 1999. "Backlash as a Prelude to Managing Managed Care." *Journal of Health Politics, Policy and Law* 24, no. 9 (October): 1115–1126.

Rohrlich, Ted. 2001. "Kaiser Made It Hard to Be an MD, Critic Says." *Los Angeles Times* (September 1).

Rovner, Julie. 1999. "The Politics of Patients' Rights." *Business and Health* Supplement (July): 21–26.

Rowe, Jonathan. 2001. "Is the Corporation Obsolete?" *Washington Monthly* 33, nos. 7 & 8 (July/August): 38–42.

Rushefsky, Mark E. 2002. *Public Policy in the United States: At the Dawn of the Twenty-First Century.* Armonk, NY: M.E. Sharpe.

Rushefsky, Mark E., and Patel, Kant. 1998. *Politics, Power & Policy Making: The Case of Health Care Reform in the 1990s.* Armonk, NY: M.E. Sharpe.

Sage, William M. 2000. "UR Here: The Supreme Court's Guide for Managed Care." *Health Affairs* 19, no. 5 (September/October): 219–223.

Saltman, Richard B., and Figueras, Josep. 1998. "Analyzing the Evidence on European Health Care Reforms." *Health Affairs* 17, no. 2 (March/April): 85–108.

Senate Democratic Policy Committee. 2001. "Side-by-Side Comparison of Current Bills" [democrats.senate.gov/pbr/sidebyside.htm].

Sharf, Barbara F. 2001. "Out of the Closet and into the Legislature; Breast Cancer Stories." *Health Affairs* 20, no. 1 (January/February): 213–218.

Sharma, Dinesh C. 2000. "India Plans Stringent Measures to Improve Health-Care Quality." *Lancet* 356, no. 9238 (October 14): 1336.

Singer, Sara. 2000. "What's Not to Like about HMOs." *Health Affairs* 19, no. 4 (July/August): 206–209.

Sorian, Richard, and Feder, Judith. 1999. "Why We Need a Patients' Bill of Rights." *Journal of Health Policy, Politics and Law* 24, no. 5 (October): 1137–1144.

Spragens, Thomas A. Jr. 1991/1992. "The Limitations of Libertarianism; Part I." *The Responsive Community: Rights and Responsibilities* 2, no. 1 (Winter): 27–37.

Starr, Paul. 1982. *The Social Transformation of American Medicine.* New York: Basic Books.

Stone, Deborah. 2002. *Policy Paradox: The Art of Political Decision Making,* revised edition. New York: W.W. Norton.

Sullivan, Kip. 2000. "On the 'Efficiency' of Managed Care Plans." *Health Affairs* 19, no. 4 (July/August): 139–148.

Tapper, Jake. 2001. "The Healthcare Disaster That Wasn't." Salon.com (July 17).

Taylor, Stuart Jr. 2001. "What a Cure! Higher Medical Costs and More Uninsured." *National Journal* 33, no. 26 (June 30): 2071–2072.

Thorpe, Kenneth E. 1997. "The Health Care System in Transition: Care, Cost, and Coverage." *Journal of Health Policy, Politics and Law* 22, no. 2 (April): 339–361.

Ubel, Peter A. 2000. *Pricing Life: Why It's Time for Health Care Rationing.* Cambridge, MA: MIT Press.

U.S. Bureau of the Census. 1995. *Statistical Abstract of the United States, 1995.* Washington, DC: U.S. Government Printing Office.

Weber, Wim. 2000. *Lancet* 356, no. 9241 (November 4): 1584.

Weinstein, Michael M. 2001. "Will Patients' Rights Fix the Wrongs?" *New York Times* (June 24.)

White, Joseph. 1995. *Competing Solutions: American Health Care Proposals and International Experience.* Washington, DC: The Brookings Institution.

————. 1999. "Choice, Trust, and Two Models of Quality." *Journal of Health Politics, Policy and Law* 24, no. 5 (October): 993–999.

Wise, Jacqui. 1997. "Patient's Charter Will Emphasise Patients' Responsibilities." *British Medical Journal* 315, no. 7114 (October 18): 962–972.

World Health Organization/Europe. 1994. *A Declaration on the Promotion of Patients' Rights in Europe.* Copenhagen, Denmark: World Health Organization/Europe.

————. 2002. "43 European Countries Have Yet to Enact Laws on Patients' Rights." Press release. Copenhagen, Denmark: World Health Organization/Europe (May 24).

References to Chapter 8

AAMC General Physician Task Force. 1993. "AAMC Policy on the Generalist Physician." *American Medicine* 68: 1–6.

Abbott, A.V. 1998. "Approaching Death: Improving Care at the End of Life." *Education for Health: Change in Training and Practice* 11, no. 3 (November): 405–407.

"Abraham Flexner: Unrestrained in Medicine, He Revolutionized the Way Doctors Are Taught." 1990. *Life* 13, no. 12 (Fall): 99.

Association of American Medical Colleges (AAMC). 1996. *Medical School Admission Requirements, 1997–1998,* 47th edition. Washington, DC: Association of American Medical Colleges.

Astin, J.A. 1998. "Why Patients Use Alternative Medicine." *Journal of American Medical Association* 279, no. 19 (May 20): 1548–1553.

Bailey, Ronald. 1999. "Warning: Bioethics May Be Hazardous to Your Health." *Reason* 31, no. 4 (August-September): 24–31.

Barzansky, Barbara. 2000. "Commentary: Research Specialty Choice: The Challenge Is in the Details." *Education for Health: Change in Training and Practice* 13, no. 2 (July): 197–201.

Berman, Brian M. 2001. "Complementary Medicine and Medical Education: Teaching Complementary Medicine Offers a Way of Making Teaching More Holistic." *British Medical Journal* 322, no. 7279 (January 20): 121–122.

Berman, Woen D.; Lewith, D.K; and Stephens, C.B. 2001. "Can Doctors Respond to Patients' Increasing Interest in Complementary and Alternative Medicine?" *British Medical Journal* 322, no. 7279 (January 20): 154–157.

Bettelheim, Adriel. 2000. "Computers and Medicine," in *Issues in Health Care,* Selections from CQ Researcher, 213–230. Washington, DC: Congressional Quarterly Press.

Biddiss, Michael. 1997. "Tomorrow's Doctors and the Study of the Past." *Lancet* 349, no. 9055 (March 22): 874–876.

Bonner, Thomas N. 1995. *Becoming a Physician: Medical Education in Britain, France, Germany, and the United States, 1750–1945.* New York: Oxford University Press.

Brink, Susan. 1998. "The Challenge of Diverse Cultures: Training Doctors for a Changing World." *U.S. News & World Report* 124, no. 8 (March 2): 86.

Callahan, Daniel. 1997. "Restoring the Proper Goals of the Healing Arts." *Chronicle of Higher Education* 43, no. 33 (April 25): A52.

Calman, Kenneth, and Downie, Robin. 1996. "Why Arts Courses for Medical Curricula." *Lancet* 347, no. 9014 (June 1): 1499–1500.

Carlisle, David M., and Gardner, Jill E. 1998. "The Entry of Underrepresented Minority Students into Medical Schools: An Evaluation of Recent Trends." *American Journal of Public Health* 88, no. 9 (September): 1314–1318.

Carnegie Commission on Higher Education. 1970. *Higher Education and the Nation's Health: Policies for Medical and Dental Education: A Special Report and Recommendations.* New York: McGraw-Hill.

Carnegie Council on Policy Studies in Higher Education. 1976. *Progress and Problems in Medical and Dental Education: Federal Support Versus Federal Control: A Report of the Carnegie Council on Policy Studies in Higher Education.* San Francisco: Jossey-Bass.

Cassell, Eric J. 1999. "Historical Perspective of Medical Residency Training: 50 Years of Changes." *Journal of the American Medical Association* 281, no. 13, (April 7): 123.

Christakis, Nicholas A. 1995. "The Similarity and Frequency of Proposals to Reform US Medical Education." *Journal of American Medical Association* 274, no. 9 (September 6): 706–711.

Clancy, David S.; Marci, Carl D.; McDonough, C. Geoffrey; Peppercorn, Jeffrey M.; Roberts, Thomas G.; Smith, Allison L.; and Winickoff, Jonathan. 1995. "A Call for Health Policy Education in the Medical School Curriculum." *Journal of American Medical Association* 274, no. 13 (October 4): 1084–1085.

Cohen, Jordan. 1998. "Time to Shatter the Glass Ceiling for Minority Faculty." *Journal of American Medical Association* 280, no. 9 (September 2): 821–822.

———. 1995. "Generalism in Medical Education: The Next Steps." *American Medicine* 70, no. 1 (January): S7–S9.

Cohn, Felicia; Harrold, Joan; and Lynn, Joanne. 1997. "Medical Education Must Deal with End-of-Life Care." *Chronicle of Higher Education* 43, no. 38 (May 30): A56.

Comarow, Avery. 2000. "Your Medical School May Be Suffering from Ill Health." *U.S. News & World Report* 128, no. 14 (April 10): 78–79.

Cruess, Sulvia R., and Cruess, Richard L. 2000. "Professionalism: A Contract Between Medicine and Society." *Canadian Medical Association Journal* 162, no. 5 (March 7): 668–669.

Dan, Bruce. 1997. "The Rise and Rise of U.S. Medical Education." *Lancet* 349, no. 9044 (January 4): 65.

Davis, Howard C. 1994. "The Report to Congress on the Appropriate Federal Role in Assuring Access by Medical Students, Residents, and Practice Physicians to Adequate Training in Nutrition." *Public Health Reports* 109, no. 6 (November–December): 824–826.

Detmer, Don E. 1996. "Information and Communications." In *2020 Vision: Health Care in the 21st Century*, ed. Institute of Medicine, 24–36. Washington, DC: National Academy Press.

DeVille, Kenneth. 1999. "Defending Diversity: Affirmative Action and Medical Education." *American Journal of Public Health* 89, no. 8 (August): 1256–1261.

"Doctors Lack Training in Easing Suffering." 1998. *USA Today* 126, no. 2633 (February): 12–13.

Doyal, Len, and Gillon, Raanan. 1998. "Medical Ethics and Law as a Core Subject in Medical Education." *British Medical Journal* 316, no. 7145 (May 30): 1623–1624.

Editorial. 1994. "Community-Bespoke Doctoring: Incorporating Community Medicine into Medical School Curricula." *Lancet* 343, no. 8898 (March 12): 613–614.

Eichold, Samuel. 1999. "Bachelor of Arts Versus Bachelor of Science." *Southern Methodist Journal* 92, no. 10 (October): 1029–1030.

Elam, Carol L.; Wilson, David; Wilson Emery A.; and Schwartz, Richard. 1995. "Physicians for the 21st Century: Implications for Medical Practice, Undergraduate Preparation and Medical Education." *KMA Journal* 93 (June): 247–252.

Ellis, David. 2000. *Technology and the Future of Health Care: Preparing for the Next 30 Years.* San Francisco: Jossey-Bass.

Enarson, Cam, and Burg, Frederic D. 1992. "An Overview of Reform Initiatives in Medical Education: 1906 Through 1992." *Journal of American Medical Association* 268, no. 9 (September 2): 1141–1143.

Evelyn, Jamilah. 1998. "Medical Association Wants More Minorities in Medical Schools." *Black Issues in Higher Education* 15, no. 11 (July 23): 8.

Field, Marilyn J., and Cassel, Christine K. 1997. *Approaching Death: Improving Care at the End of Life.* Washington, DC: National Academy Press.

Flexner, Abraham. 1910. *Medical Education in the United States and Canada.* New York: Carnegie Foundation for the Advancement of Teaching. Reprinted. New York: Arno Press, 1972.

———. 1908. *The American College: A Criticism.* New York: Century Company.

Flores, Glenn. 2000. "The Teaching of Cultural Issues in U.S. and Canadian Medical Schools." *Journal of American Medical Association* 284, no. 3 (July 19): 284.

Fox, Ellen. 1997. "Predominance of the Curative Model of Medical Care: A Residual Problem." *Journal of American Medical Association* 278, no. 9 (September 3): 761–763.

Fox, Renee C. 1999. "Teaching the Nonbiomedical Aspects of Medicine: The Perennial Pattern." *Daedalus* 128, no. 4 (Fall): 1, 25.

Fredericks, Marcel A., and Mundy, Paul. 1976. *The Making of a Physician: A Ten-Year Longitudinal Study of Social Class, Academic Achievement, and Changing Professional Attitudes of a Medical School Class.* Chicago: Loyola University Press.

Fye, Bruce W. 1991. "The Origin of the Full-Time Faculty System: Implications for Clinical Research." *Journal of American Medical Association* 265, no. 12 (March 27): 1555–1562.

Geiger, H. Jack. 1998. "Comment: Ethnic Cleansing in the Groves of Academe." *American Journal of Public Health* 88, no. 9 (September): 1299–1300.

Gillon, Raanan. 2000. "Welcome to Medical Humanities and Why." *Journal of Medical Ethics* 26, no. 3 (June): 155–156.

Goodenough, Ursula, and Park, Robert L. 1996. "Magic Versus Medicine: What Future Doctors Need to Know About Alternative Treatments." *Chronicle of Higher Education* 43, no. 13 (November 22): B6.

Greenberg, Larrie W. 1994. "Improving the Way We Educate Medical Students: A Priority for the 1990s." *Southern Methodist Journal* 87, no. 5 (May): 564–566.

Gunn, Albert E. 1999. "The Healing Profession Needs Healers: The Crisis in Medical Education." *Issues in Law & Medicine* 15, no. 2 (Fall): 125–140.

Guze, Phyllis A. 1995. "Cultivating Curricular Reform." *Academic Medicine* 70, no. 11 (November): 971–973.

Hanson, Mark J., and Callahan, Daniel, eds. 1999. *The Goals of Medicine: Setting New Priorities.* Washington, DC: Georgetown University Press.

Hawkins, Denise B. 1997. "Hostile Environment." *Black Issues in Higher Education* 14, no. 20 (November 27): 18–19.

Hunt, Carl E.; Kallenberg, Gene A.; and Whitcomb, Michael E. 1999. "Trends in

Clinical Education of Medical Students." *Archives of Pediatric & Adolescent Medicine* 153, no. 3 (March): 297.

Institute for the Future. 2000. *Health & Health Care 2010: The Forecast, the Challenge.* San Francisco: Jossey-Bass.

Jonas, Harry S.; Etzel, Sylvia I.; and Barzansky, Barbara. 1990. "Undergraduate Medical Education." *Journal of American Medical Association* 264, no. 7 (August 15): 801–809.

Jonas, Steven. 1978. *Medical Mystery: The Training of Doctors in the United States.* New York: W.W. Norton.

Kassirer, Jerome P. 1976. "Redesigning Graduate Medical Education—Location and Content." *New England Journal of Medicine* 335, no. 7 (August 15): 507–509.

Kaufman, Martin. 1976. *American Medical Education: The Formative Years, 1765–1910.* Westport, CT: Greenwood Press.

Lamarine, Roland J. 2001. "Alternative Medicine: More Than a Harmless Option." *Journal of School Health* 71, no. 3 (March): 114–116.

Langone, John. 1994. "The Making of a Good Doctor." *America* 170, no. 3 (January 29): 4–7.

Lee, Philip R. 1995. "Health System Reform and the Generalist Physician." *American Medicine* 70, no. 1 (January): S10–S13.

Lewin, Marion E., and Rice, Barbara. 1994. *Balancing the Scales of Opportunity: Enduring Racial and Ethnic Diversity in the Health Professions.* Washington, DC: National Academy Press.

Li, Benfu. 2000. "Ethics Teaching in Medical Schools." *Hastings Center Report* 30, no. 4 (July–August): S30–S32.

Loudon, Rhian F.; Anderson, Pauline M.; Gill, Paramjit S.; and Greenfield, Sheila M. 1999. "Educating Medical Students for Work in Culturally Diverse Societies." *Journal of American Medical Association* 282, no. 9 (September 1): 875.

Ludmerer, Kenneth M. 1991. "Washington University and the Creation of the Teaching Hospital." *Journal of American Medical Association* 266, no, 14 (October 9): 1981–1983.

———. 1985. *Learning to Heal: The Development of American Medical Education.* New York: Basic Books.

Madoff, Morton A. 1993. "Reflections on a Century of Excellence." *Journal of American Medical Association* 269, no. 14 (April 14): 1846–1847.

Magnus, Stephen A., and Mick, Stephen S. 2000. "Medical Schools, Affirmative Action, and the Neglected Role of Social Class." *American Journal of Public Health* 90, no. 8 (August): 1197–1201.

Mahaney, Francis X., Jr. 1994. "Minorities Remain Underrepresented in Science and Medicine." *Journal of the National Cancer Institute* 86, no. 2 (January 19): 83.

Mangan, Katherine S. 1997. "Blurring the Boundaries Between Religion and Science." *Chronicle of Higher Education* 43, no. 26 (March 7): A14.

———. 1996. "A Medical School Changes Its Curriculum to Increase the Emphasis on Care and Compassion." *Chronicle of Higher Education* 43, no. 12 (November 15): A12–A13.

Markel, Howard. 2000. "The University of Michigan Medical School, 1850–2000: An Example Worthy of Imitation." *Journal of American Medical Association* 283, no. 7 (February 16): 915.

Marston, Robert Q. 1992. "The Robert Wood Johnson Foundation Commission on Medical Education: The Sciences of Medical Practice, Summary Report." *Journal of American Medical Association* 268, no. 9 (September 2): 1144–1145.

Martensen, Robert L. 1995. "Sundown Medical Education: Top-Down Reform and its Social Displacements." *Journal of American Medical Association* 273, no. 4 (January 25): 271.

May, David. 2001. "February Survey Results: Alternative Medicine." *Modern Healthcare* 31, no. 12 (March 19): 58.

"Medical Education in Need of Reform, Foundation Report Concludes." 1992. *Health Care Financing Review* 14, no. 2 (Winter): 210–211.

Micozzi, Marc S. 1996. "The Need to Teach Alternative Medicine." *Chronicle of Higher Education* 42, no. 49 (August 16): A48.

"Minorities Lead Drop on Applications to U.S. Medical Schools." 1998. *Family Practice Management* 5, no. 3 (March): 33.

National Research Council. 1985. *Nutrition Education in U.S. Medical Schools.* Washington, DC: National Academy Press.

Nesbitt, John. 1984. *Megatrends: Ten New Directions Transforming Our Lives.* New York: Warner Books.

Nickens, Herbert. 1996. "Affirmative Action Is Indispensable if We want Doctors for the 21st Century." *Black Issues in Higher Education* 13, no. 12 (August 8): 1.

Noonan, David. 2000. "An Ailing Profession." *Newsweek* 136, no. 13 (September 25): 32–34.

Noren, Jay. 1997. "A National Physician Workforce Policy." *Public Health Reports* 112, no. 3 (May/June): 219–221.

Norwood, William F. 1971. *Medical Education in the United States Before the Civil War.* Reprint Edition. New York: Arno Press & New York Times (1944).

Nuland, Sherwin B. 1999. "The Uncertain Art." *American Scholar* 68, no. 2 (Spring): 125–127.

Okasha, Ahmed. 1997. "The Future of Medical Education and Teaching: A Psychiatric Perspective." *American Journal of Psychiatry* 154, no. 6 (June): S77–S85.

Patel, Kant. 1999. "Physicians for the 21st Century: Challenges Confronting Medical Education in the United States." *Evaluation & the Health Professions* 22, no. 3 (September): 379–399.

Pauli, Hannes G.; White, Kerr L.; and McWhinney, Ian R. 2000. "Medical Education, Research, and Scientific Thinking in the 21st Century." *Education for Health: Change in Training & Practice* 13, no. 2 (July): 173–186.

Primary Care and the Education of the Generalist Physician: Coming of Age. 1995. *Academic Medicine* 70, no. 1 (January): S1–S116.

Puchalski, Christina M. 1998. "Spirituality and Medicine." *World & I* 13, no. 6 (June 13): 180–185.

Rabinowitz, Howard K.; Hojat, Mohammadreza; Veloski, J. Jon; Rattner, Susan L.; Robeson, Mary R.; Xu, Gang; Appel, Marilyn H.; Cochran, Carol; Jones, Robert L.; and Kanter, Steven L. 1999. "Who Is a Generalist?" *Evaluation & the Health Profession* 22, no. 4 (December): 497–502.

Reed, Alfred Z. 1921. *Training for the Public Profession of the Law: Historical Development and Principal Contemporary Problems of Legal Education in the United States: With Some Account of Conditions in England and Canada.* New York: Carnegie Foundation for the Advancement of Teaching.

Reiling, Jennifer. 1999. "Early Methods of Medical Education." *Journal of American Medical Association* 282, no. 9 (September 1): 814.

"Report: Nation Must Diversify Its Medical Workforce." 1999. *Black Issues in Higher Education* 15, no. 23 (January 7): 9.

Rogers, David. 1978. *American Medicine: Challenges for the 1980s.* Cambridge: MA: Ballinger.

Rothman, David J. 1997. "Let's Make a Doctor, or Let's Make a Deal." *New York Times.* (September 17): A23, A31.

Sheehan, Myles N. 1996. "The Changing Face of American Medical Education." *America* 174, no. 4 (February 10): 14–19.

Shorr, Andrew F. 2000. "Regulatory and Educational Initiatives Fail to Promote Discussion Regarding End-of-Life Care." *Journal of American Medical Association* 283, no. 22 (June 14): 2909.

Skelton, J.R.; Macleod, J.A.A.; and Thomas, C.P. 2000. "Teaching Literature and Medicine to Medical Students, Part II: Why Literature and Medicine?" *Lancet* 356, 9246 (December 9): 2001–2002.

Skolnick, Andrew A. 1997. "End-of-Life Care Movement Growing." *Journal of American Medical Association* 278, no. 12 (September 24): 967–969.

Stephenson, Anne; Higgs, Roger; and Sugarman, Jeremy. 2001. "Teaching Professional Development in Medical Schools." *Lancet* 357, no. 9259 (March 17): 867–870.

Steyer, Terrence E. 2001. "Complementary and Alternative Medicine: A Primer." *Family Practice Management* 8, no. 3 (March): 37–42.

Sullivan, William M. 2000. "Medicine Under Threat: Professionalism and Professional Identity." *Canadian Medical Association Journal* 162, no. 5 (March 7): 673–675.

Sulmasy, Daniel, and Lynn, Joanne. 1997. "End-of-Life Care." *Journal of American Medical Association* 277, no. 23 (June 18): 1854–1855.

Toner, Joseph M. 1874. *Annals of Medical Progress and Medical Education in the United States Before and During the War of Independence.* Washington, DC: Government Printing Office.

"Teaching Medical Ethics and Law Within Medical Education: A Model for the UK Core." *Journal of Medical Ethics* 24, no. 3 (June): 188–192.

Trevalon, Melanie, and Murray-Garcia, Jann. 1998. "Cultural Humility Versus Cultural Competence: A Critical Distinction in Defining Physician Training Outcomes in Multicultural Education." *Journal of Health Care for the Poor and the Underserved* 9, no. 2 (May): 117–126.

Verby, John E.; Newell, Paul J.; Andersen, Susan A.; and Swentko, Walter M. 1991. "Changing the Medical School Curriculum to Improve Patient Access to Primary Care." *Journal of American Medical Association* 266, no. 1 (July 3): 110–113.

Weinstock, Matthew. 1998a. "Diploma Mill Docs." *AHA News* 34, no. 11 (March 23): 7.

———. 1998b. "Panel Recommends Big Changes in the Way Doctors Are Trained." *AHA News* 34, no. 22 (June 8): 22–25.

———. 1997. "Minority Enrollment at Med Schools Falls as Affirmative Action Wanes." *AHA News* 33, no. 44 (November 10): 5.

Weisbrod, Burton A. 1994. "The Nature of Technological Change: Incentives Matter." In *Adopting New Medical Technology*, eds. Annetine C. Gelijns and Holly V. Dawkins, 8–48. Washington DC: National Academy Press.

Wetzel, Miriam S.; Eisenberg, David M.; and Kaptchuk, Ted J. 1998. "Courses Involving Complementary and Alternative Medicine at US Medical Schools." *Journal of American Medical Association* 280, no. 9 (September 2): 784–787.

Wolf, Stewart. 1998. "Medicine at the Rubicon." *Integrative Physiological and Behavioral Science* 33, no. 4 (October–December): 312–314.

———. 1997. *Educating Doctors: Crisis in Medical Education: Research and Practice.* New Brunswick, NJ: Transaction Publishers.

Worley, Paul; March, Robyn; and Worley, Elizabeth. 2000. "Scanning the Horizon of Training for General Practice." *Medical Teacher* 22, no. 5 (September): 452–455.

Zhang, Daqing, and Cheng, Zhifan. 2000. " Medicine is a Humane Art: The Basic Principle of Professional Ethics in Chinese Medicine." *Hastings Center Report* 30, no. 4 (July–August): S8–S12.

References to Chapter 9

Bates, David W., and Gawande, Atul A. 2000. "The Impact of the Internet on Quality Measurement." *Health Affairs* 19, no. 6 (November–December): 104–114.

Boulding, Mark E. 2000. "Self-Regulation: Who Needs It?" *Health Affairs* 19, no. 6 (November–December): 132–139.

Donaldson, Molla S., and Sox, Harold C., eds. 1992. *Setting Priorities for Health Technology Assessment: A Model Process.* Washington, DC: National Academy Press.

"Drug Company Influence on Medical Education in USA." Lancet 356, no. 9232 (September 2): 781.

Ellis, David. 2000. *Technology and the Future of Health Care: Preparing for the Next 30 Years.* San Francisco: Jossey-Bass.

Fried, Bruce M.; Weinreich, Gadi; Cavalier, Gina M.; and Lester, Katheleen J. 2000. "E-Health: Technologic Revolution Meets Regulatory Constraint." *Health Affairs* 19, no. 6 (November–December): 124–131.

Goldman, Janlori, and Hudson, Zoe. 2000. "Virtually Exposed: Privacy and E-Health." *Health Affairs* 19, no. 6 (November–December): 140–148.

Goldsmith, Jeff. 2000. "The Internet and Managed Care: A New Wave of Innovation." *Health Affairs* 19, no. 6 (November–December): 42–56.

Hanson, Mark J., and Callahan, Daniel. 1999. "The Goals of Medicine: Setting New Priorities." In *The Goals of Medicine: The Forgotten Issue in Health Care Reform,* ed. Mark J. Hanson, and Daniel Callahan, 1–54. Washington, DC: Georgetown University Press.

Harris, Janice. 2001. "Shaping the System and Culture of Health Care." *Dermatology Nursing* 13, no. 2 (April): 86.

Kassirer, Jerome P. 2000. "Patients, Physicians, and the Internet." *Health Affairs* 19, no. 6 (November–December): 115–123.

Kleinke, J. D. 2000. "Vaporware.com: The Failed Promise of the Health Care Internet: Why Internet Will Be the Next Thing Not to Fix the U.S. Health Care System." *Health Affairs* 19, no. 6 (November–December): 57–71.

Lara, Maria E., and Goodman, Clifford, eds. 1990. *National Priorities for the Assessment of Clinical Conditions and Medical Technologies.* Washington, DC: National Academy Press.

Luce, Bryan R., and Brown, Ruth E. 1994. "The Impact of Technology Assessment on Decisions by Health Care Providers and Payers." In *Adopting New Medical Technologies*, ed. Annetine C. Gelijns and Holly V. Dawkins, 49–58. Washington, DC: National Academy Press.

Lumpkin, John R. 2000. "E-Health, HIPAA, and Beyond." *Health Affairs* 19, no. 6 (November–December): 149–151.

McCarthy, Michael. 2000. "Medical-Education Companies Come Under Fire in USA." *Lancet* 356, no. 9228 (August 5): 494.

Mechanic, David. 1993. "America's Health Care System and Its Future: The View of a Despairing Optimist: Fifty years of Looking Ahead." *Medical Care Research & Review* 50, no. 1 (Spring): 7–42.

Mosteller, Frederick, and Falotico-Taylor, Jennifer, eds. 1989. *Quality of Life and Technology Assessment*. Washington, DC: National Academy Press.

Neumann, Peter J., and Weinstein, Milton C. 1991. "The Diffusion of New Technology: Costs and Benefits to Health Care." In *The Changing Economics of Medical Technology*, ed. Annetine C. Gelijns and Ethan A. Halm, 21–34. Washington, DC: National Academy Press.

Parente, Stephen T. 2000. "Beyond the Hype: A Taxonomy of E-Health Business Models." *Health Affairs* 19, no. 6 (November–December): 89–102.

Parker, Che. 2001. "IOM Sees 'Chasm' in U.S. Health Care; Offers Bridge to 21st Century System." *AHA News* 37, no. 9 (March): 1–2.

Patel, Kant, and Rushefsky, Mark. 1999. *Health Care Politics and Policy in America*. 2nd edition. Armonk, NY: M.E. Sharpe.

Perry, Seymour, and Pillar, Barbara. 1990. "A National Policy for Health Care Technology Assessment." *Medical Care Research & Review* 47, no. 4 (Winter): 401–417.

Relman, Arnold S. 2000. "Why Johnny Can't Operate." *New Republic* 223, no. 14 (October 2): 37–43.

Robinson, James C. 2000. "Financing the Health Care Internet." *Health Affairs* 19, no. 6 (November–December): 72–88.

Schneider, Eric C., and Eisenberg, John M. 1998. "Strategies and Methods for Aligning Current and Best Medical Practices: The Role of Information Technologies." *Western Journal of Medicine* 168, no. 5 (May): 311–318.

Silverman, Ross. 2000. "Regulating Medical Practice in the Cyber Age: Issues and Challenges for the State Medical Boards." *American Journal of Law and Medicine* 26, nos. 2 & 3 (Summer–Fall): 255–276.

Thomas, Lewis. 1975. *The Lives of a Cell*. New York: Bantam Books.

Wagner, Norman. 2000. "Commentary on Medical Education and Training in the Information Age." *Clinical & Investigative Medicine* 23, no. 4 (August): 248–255.

Wildes, Kevin W. 1994. "Health Reform and the Seduction of Technology." *America* 170, no. 12 (April 9): 30.

Wolf, Stewart. 1998. "Medicine at the Rubicon." *Integrative Physiological and Behavioral Science* 33, no. 4 (October–December): 312–314.

Index

About the Authors

Kant Patel (Ph.D., University of Houston, 1976) is Professor of Political Science at Southwest Missouri State University. He teaches courses in the areas of health policy and politics, policy analysis, and approaches to political analysis. He has published articles in journals such as *Evaluation and Health Profession, Health Policy and Education, Political Methodology, Journal of Political Science, Health,* and *Health and Social Policy,* among others. He is coauthor (with Mark Rushefsky) of *Health Care Politics and Policy in America,* second edition (M.E. Sharpe 1999) and *Politics, Power and Policy Making: Health Care Reform in the 1990s* (M.E. Sharpe 1998).

Mark Rushefsky (Ph.D., State University of New York at Binghamton, 1977) is professor of political science at Southwest Missouri State University. He teaches and writes on public policy and public administration. He is the author of *Making Cancer Policy* and *Public Policy in the United States: Toward the 21st Century,* third edition (M.E. Sharpe 2002). He is coauthor (with Kant Patel) of *Health Care Politics and Policy in America,* second edition (M.E. Sharpe 1999) and *Politics, Power and Policy Making: Health Care Reform in the 1990s* (M.E. Sharpe 1998).

DATE	DUE
SEP 1 5 2013	